Leasehold disputes

a guide to Leasehold Valuation Tribunals

SECOND EDITION

Francis Davey and Justin Bates

Legal Action Group
2008

This edition published in Great Britain 2008
by LAG Education and Service Trust Limited
242 Pentonville Road, London N1 9UN
www.lag.org.uk

© Francis Davey and Justin Bates

First edition 2004

British Library Cataloguing in Publication Data
a CIP catalogue record for this book is available from the British Library.

This book has been produced using Forest Stewardship Council (FSC) certified paper. The wood used to produce FSC certified products with a 'Mixed Sources' label comes from FSC certified well-managed forests, controlled sources and/or recycled material.

ISBN 978 1 903307 62 5

Typeset by Regent Typesetting, London
Printed in Great Britain by Hobbs the Printer, Totton, Hampshire

Leasehold disputes

a guide to Leasehold Valuation Tribunals

Francis Davey is a barrister at 169 Temple Chambers, practising in all aspects of property and housing law. He regularly appears in the LVT and advises on leasehold disputes.

Justin Bates is a barrister at Arden Chambers, London, specialising in all aspects of housing and property law. He regularly appears in the LVT and Lands Tribunal and has appeared in a number of the most significant decisions concerning the powers of the LVT, including *Continental Properties v White*. He is also the editor of the *LVT Bulletin* and has also written various articles on housing, community care and property law for *Journal of Housing Law*, *Solicitors Journal* and *Legal Action*.

The purpose of the Legal Action Group is to promote equal access to justice for all members of society who are socially, economically or otherwise disadvantaged. To this end, it seeks to improve law and practice, the administration of justice and legal services.

Preface

When we first began to give advice on Leasehold Valuation Tribunals (LVTs) it very quickly became clear that there was a considerable amount of relevant law, from a variety of sources, that had never been collected together. It is as a result of that experience that we have written this book.

Since the first edition of this book in 2004, the have been a number of significant decisions of both the Lands Tribunal and Court of Appeal. In addition, most (but not all) of the matters which were formerly marked as 'not in force' are now in force. For the most part, our predictions about these future developments were proved accurate.

This book is aimed at anyone likely to find themselves before (or considering applying to) an LVT. We hope that it is comprehensive enough to satisfy the needs of lawyers and advisers, while being accessible enough for users to represent themselves at tribunal hearings. We have taken on board a number of comments from users and reviewers since the first edition.

We do not deal with the subject of leasehold enfranchisement or the compulsory purchase of the freehold. These subjects are comprehensively covered elsewhere and, in any event, anyone thinking of purchasing property would almost certainly want to involve a solicitor. In addition, we have only mentioned Estate Management Schemes in passing, because they are rarely encountered in practice. We hope to have covered all the remaining areas of the LVT's jurisdiction.

In a change from the first edition, the position in Wales is also considered in the book and changes from the position in England are noted.

It is normal in the context of residential landlord and tenant law for the terms 'leaseholder' and 'tenant' to be used in opposition. The former referring to a tenant under a long lease, while the latter is used to refer to someone with a shorter interest. This distinction is v not one made in the legislation, nor is it a useful one in the context of most of the LVT's jurisdiction. For this reason the term 'tenant' has been used throughout this book inclusively.

The term landlord is usually, but not exclusively, used to refer to the lessor and anyone with a right to collect service charges. Unless the context suggests otherwise, we have chosen to use the latter definition throughout.

The law is as stated on 3 April 2008, although, where possible, reference has been made to recent case law at the proof stage. We are grateful for the patience and assistance of Esther Pilger and the staff at LAG, who have ensured that the book was delivered more-or-less on schedule.

Any comments, corrections, suggestions or correspondence can be directed to either of us at the addresses below.

Francis Davey
169 Temple Chambers
3–7 Temple Avenue
London EC4Y 0DA

Justin Bates
Arden Chambers
2 John Street
London WC1N 2ES

Contents

Preface   v
Table of cases   xi
Table of statutes   xvii
Table of statutory instruments   xxiii
Abbreviations   xxxi

1   Introduction   1
History   2
Organisation   3
Hearings   4
Precedent   5
Outline of this book   5

2   Service charges   7
Introduction   9
Advice for tenants   10
What is a service charge?   10
Challenging the payability of service charges   11
Statutory preconditions for recovery   20
Equitable principles   25
Reasonableness   27
Holding service charges   29

3   Tenants' rights to information   33
Introduction   35
Advice to tenants   36
General information and rights   37
Summary of rights and obligations   38
Summaries of costs   40
Statements of account   44
Management audit   45
Recognised Tenants' Associations   47

4   Consultation on service charges   51
Introduction   54

Advice for tenants   54
Old consultation requirements   55
New consultation requirements   58
Qualifying long-term agreements   64
Dispensation   65
Transitional provisions   66

5   Insurance   85
Introduction   86
Advice for tenants   87
Common areas of difficulty   87
Challenging insurance cover   88
Failure to pay out insurance monies   91
Arranging your own insurance   92
Rights to information in relation to insurance   93
Right to notify insurer of a claim   94

6   Administration charges   95
Introduction   96
Advice to tenants   97
Why were administration charges introduced?   97
What is an administration charge?   98
Administration charges in practice   99
Types of administration charges   100
Challenging non-variable administration charges   102
Challenging variable administration charges   103
Estate management schemes   105

7   Variation of leases   107
Introduction   108
Advice for tenants   109
Application to vary an individual lease   109
Grounds for varying a lease   110
Application to vary other leases   112
Application by a majority   112
Orders varying a lease   113
Procedural considerations   115
Insurance of dwellings houses   115

8   Appointment of a manager   117
Introduction   119
Advice for tenants   120
The role of a manager   121
Pre-application procedure   121
Grounds for the appointment of a manager   123

Entitlement to apply for the appointment of a manager   124
Grounds for the appointment of a manager   126
The extent of the property to be managed   130
The management functions to be conferred   131
Persons likely to be appointed as a manager   132
Directions   132
Variation or discharge   133
RTM company   133
Miscellaneous   134
Consultation about managing agents   134

9   Right to manage   137
Introduction   139
Advice to tenants   140
Properties to which the RTM applies   141
Excluded properties   145
The RTM company   146
Notice inviting participation   148
Notice of claim   151
Rights of inspection   153
Counter notice   153
Withdrawal of a claim notice   155
Costs of the RTM process   156
Acquiring the right to manage   156
Duty to pay uncommitted service charges   157
Approvals   157

10 Forfeiture   159
Introduction   160
Advice for tenants   160
An introduction to forfeiture   161
Breach of covenant to pay rent   163
Breach of other covenants   165
Breach of covenant to pay service or administration charges   166
Jurisdiction of the LVT   167

11 Right to buy leases   169
Introduction   170
Advice for tenants   171
Service charges   171
Administration charges   171
Consultation provisions   172
Loans   172
Directions issued by the Secretary of State   173

12 Funding 175
Introduction 176
Advice for tenants 176
Legal aid 177
Legal expenses insurance 178
Pro bono services 179

13 Procedure in the LVT 181
Introduction 184
Advice for tenants 184
Starting a case 185
Track allocation 195
Interim matters 197
Procedure at the final hearing 201
Precedent in the LVT 205
Costs 205
Enforcement 208
Appeals 208

14 Worked examples 213
Appointment of a manager 214
Service charge dispute 220

APPENDICES

A Legislation and Directions 227

B Residential Property Tribunal Service application forms 289

C RPTS guidance on tenants' associations 321

D Useful addresses 327

Index 331

Table of cases

References in the right-hand column are to paragraph numbers.

3, 12, 23 and 29 St Andrew's Square, Re LON/00AW/
    LSL/2003/0027 (LVT)   2.62
9 Grange Bungalows, London Road, South Mertsham,
    Surrey L82/99/SY (LVT), Re   2.39
18, 56 & 66 Fenlake Road and 25 & 64 Christie Road,
    Bedford Stapleton and others, Re v Bedford Pilgrims
    Housing Association CAM/96/UT/SC/011 (LVT)   2.38
23–45 The Woodfines, Hornchurch, Essex, RM11 3HR, LVT/
    INS/030/003/99   5.26
26 and 28 Birdhurst Rise, South Croydon LON/00AH/
    NAM/2003/006 (LVT)   8.6
A2 Airways Housing Group v Taylor and others
    LRX/36/2006 (Lands Tribunal)   2.79
Anderton and Milner's Contract, Re (1890) 45 Ch D 476   10.6
Anger v London Borough of Camden, LRX81/2007, Lands
    Tribunal   4.67
Arrowdell Limited v Coniston Court (North) Hove Limited
    LRA/72/2005, [2007] RVR 39 (Lands Tribunal)   13.85, 13.110
Aylesbond Estates Ltd v Macmillan and others (2000) 32
    HLR 1, [1999] L&TR 127   13.9
Bandar Properties v JS Darwen [1968] 2 All ER 305, 19 P&CR
    785   5.20
Beacon Carpets v Kirby [1985] QB 755, [1984] 3 WLR 489   5.34
Berrycroft Management v Sinclair Gardens Investments
    (1997) 29 HLR 444, (1998) 75 P&CR   5.24, 5.25
Billson v Tristrem [2000] L&TR 220   2.79
Blocks C, E and G, Cherry Blossom Close, Chequers Way,
    London, N13 LVT/INS/027/003/00 (LVT)   5.19, 5.25
Bluestorm Ltd v Portvale Holdings Ltd [2004] HLR 49, [2004]
    3 EGLR 38   2.76
Botterill v Hampstead Garden Suburbs Trust Limited
    LRX/135/2007 (Lands Tribunal)   6.21, 6.23,
    6.24
Broomleigh Housing Association v Hughes (1999) EGCS 143   2.79

Burlesden Court, East Cliff Road, Dawlish, Devon EX7 OBP
    LVT/HA/00/10, Re   2.39
CIN Properties Limited v Barclays Bank [1986] 1 EGLR 59   2.50
Canary Riverside Pte Ltd v Schilling and others sub nom
    Schilling v Canary Riverside Development Ltd
    LRX/65/2005 & LRX/26/2005, (Lands Tribunal)   2.21, 2.27,
                                                                       13.93, 13.94
Capital and Counties Freehold Equity Trust Ltd v BL plc
    [1987] 2 EGLR 49   2.55
Cawsand Fort Management Company Ltd v Stafford and
    others [2007] EWCA Civ 1187, [2007] 48 EG 145   8.9, 8.21,
                                                                       8.51, 8.52
Central London Property Trust Ltd v High Trees Ltd [1947]
    KB 130   10.9
Chelsea Properties v Earl Cadogan and Cadogan Estates
    LRA/69/2006 (Lands Tribunal)   13.110
Collin v Duke of Westminster [1985] 1 QB 581, [1985] 1 All
    ER 463   2.66
Colney Hatch Court Ltd v Sen LON/00AC/LSC/2003/0006   2.79
Continental Property Ventures v White and White [20060 1
    EGLR 85, [2007] L&TR 4, LRX/60/2005 (Lands Tribunal)   2.68, 2.79
Cornillie v Saha (1996) 72 P&CR 147   10.7
Coventry City Council v Cole [1994] 1 WLR 398, (1993) 25
    HLR 555   2.11, 6.8,
                                                                       6.16
Daejan Properties Limited v London Leasehold Valuation
    Tribunal [2001] EWCA Civ 1095, [2002] HLR 23, [2001] 3
    EGLR 28   13.99
De Campomar v The Trustees of the Pettiward Estate
    LRA/29&30/2004 (Lands Tribunal)   13.57
Denning v Beamsafe Ltd and others BIR/00CS/
    LVM/2006/001 (LVT)   8.64
Drewett v Bold LRX/90/2005 (Lands Tribunal)   6.38
Earl Cadogan v 27/29 Sloane Gardens Ltd LRA/9/2005,
    [2006] 24 EG 178   2.28
Earl Cadogan and others v Sportelli and others [2007] EWCA
    Civ 1042, [2007] RVR 314   1.24, 13.88
Eltham Properties Limited v Kenny LRX/161/2006 (Lands
    Tribunal)   4.68
Embassy Court Residents' Association v Lipman (1984) 271
    EG 545   2.28, 2.48,
                                                                       2.49
Expert Clothing Service and Sales Ltd v Hillgate House Ltd
    [1986] 1 Ch 340, [1985] 3 WLR 359   10.10
Finchbourne Limited v Rodrigues [1976] 3 All ER 581   2.50, 2.67,
                                                                       2.78
Forcelux Ltd, Re LRX/33/2003 (Lands Tribunal)   6.11, 6.33
Forcelux v Sweetman [2001] 2 EGLR 173   2.79
Francis v Cowcliffe (1977) 33 P&CR 368   2.75

Gaingold Ltd and another v WHRA RTM Ltd LRX/19/2005,
   [2006] 1 EGLR 81, [2006] EG 122 (Lands Tribunal)   9.34
Gianfrancesco v Haughton, LRX/10/2007 (Lands Tribunal)   7.21
Gibson Investments Ltd v Chesterton Plc [2003] EWHC 1255,
   (2002) L&TR 32   2.40
Gilje v Charlegrove Securities Ltd [2002] 1 EGLR 41   2.28
Gilje v Charlesgrove Investments Ltd [2003] EWHC 1284,
   [2003] 36 EG 110, July 2003 *Legal Action* 27   2.56
Granby Village (Manchester) Management Co Ltd v
   Unchained Growth plc [2000] 1 WLR 739, August 1999
   Legal Action 23   2.45
Hackney LBC v Thompson [2001] L&TR 7   2.37
Havenridge Ltd v Boston Dyers Ltd [1994] 2 EGLR 73   2.67, 2.78,
    5.20
Heron Maple Court v Central Estates [2002] 1 EGLR 35   2.9, 2.24
Hillingdon LBC v ARC Ltd [1998] 3 WLR 754, [1998] 39 EG
   202   2.59
Hodgett v Knox, 12 November 1999, Central London CC   4.66
Holding & Management Ltd v Property Holding &
   Investment Trust Plc [1989] 1 WLR 1313, [1990] 1 All ER
   938   2.32, 13.94
Holding and Management (Solitaire) Ltd v 1–16 Finland St
   RTM Ltd [2007] 45 EG 162, LRX/138/2006 (Lands
   Tribunal)   9.20
Hyams and Anderson v Wilfred East Housing Co-operative
   Ltd [2007] 3 EG 126, LRX/102/2005 (Lands Tribunal)   2.55
Hyde Housing v George Williams LRX/53/1999 (Lands
   Tribunal)   2.79
Iperion Investments v Broadwalk House Residents Ltd [1995]
   2 EGLR 47, (1994) 27 HLR 196   13.94
Isbicki v Goulding [1989] 1 EGLR 236   2.32
Islington LBC v Abdel-Malek LRX/90/2006 (Lands Tribunal)   2.56
Jollybird v Fairzone [1990] 2 EGLR 55   2.30
Khar v Delmounty Ltd (1998) 75 P&CR 232, [1996] EGCS
   183   10.33
Kleinwort Benson Ltd v Lincoln City Council [1999] 2 AC 153   2.62
Loder Dyer v Cadogan Estates Ltd [2001] EGLR 149   13.94
London and Winchester Properties Ltd's Appeal, Re (1983)
   45 P&CR 429 (Lands Tribunal)   13.106
London Borough of Haringey v Ball, unreported, 6
   December 2004, Central London CC   4.17, 4.18
London Borough of Islington v Abdel-Malek LRX/90/2006
   (Lands Tribunal)   4.15
Longmint Ltd v Marcus [2004] 3 EGLR 171, LRX/25/2003
   (Lands Tribunal)   2.11
McDougall v Easington (1989) 58 PC&R 201, (1989) 21 HLR
   310   2.43
Marcenco v Jacramel (1964) 191 EG 433   2.75
Martin v Maryland Estates, unreported, 26 April 1999, CA   4.64, 4.65

Mathews v Smallwood [1910] 1 Ch 777   10.7
Maunder Taylor v Blaquiere [2002] EWCA Civ 1633, [2003] 1
   WLR 379   8.7, 8.8, 8.52
Maunder Taylor v Joshi LRX/107/2005 (Lands Tribunal)   8.10, 8.58,
                                                                      8.59

Mean Fiddler Holdings Ltd v London Borough of Islington
   ACQ/29/2001 (Lands Tribunal)   13.57
Minja Properties Ltd v Cussins Property Group [1998] 2
   EGLR 52   2.43, 2.44
Morgan v Stainer (1993) 25 HLR 467, [1993] 33 EG 87   13.92
Mohammadi v Anston Investments Ltd [2003] EWCA Civ
   981, [2004] HLR 8   2.56
Moorcroft Estates v Doxford (1979) 254 EG 871   2.35
Morshead Mansions, Re LRX/49/2002 (Lands Tribunal)   8.57, 8.62,
                                                                      8.64

Mullaney v Maybourne Grange (Croydon) Management
   Group Co Ltd [1986] 1 EGLR 70   2.32, 2.44
Mumford Hotels v Wheeler and another [1964] 1 Ch 117   5.32
Newham LBC v Zeb [2004] EWCA Civ 55, [2005] QB 37,
   [2004] 3 WLR 417   2.45
Oakfern Properties Ltd v Ruddy [2006] EWCA Civ 1389,
   [2007] 3 WLR 524   2.9, 2.24
Oakwood Court (Holland Park) Ltd v Daejan Properties Ltd
   [2007] 1 EGLR 121, Central London CC   9.23, 9.24,
                                                                      9.25

Orchard Court Residents Association v St Anthony Homes
   Ltd [2003] EWCA Civ 1049, [2003] 2 EGLR 28   8.67, 13.111
Parsons v Trustees of Henry Smith's Charity [1974] 1 WLR
   435   9.18
Peile v Executors of WAC Maidman LVT/SC/010/98   2.83
Penman v Upavon Enterprises Ltd [2002] L&TR 10, [2001] 25
   EG 158   13.99
Petrou v Metroplitan Properties Company Ltd LVT/
   AOM/014/013/98 (LVT)   8.39
Pole Properties v Feinberg (1982) 43 PC&R 121, (1981) 259
   EG 417   2.39
R v London Leasehold Valuation Tribunal ex p Daejan
   Properties Ltd [2001] EWCA Civ 1095, [2002] HLR 2   1.10, 2.60,
                                                                      2.65

R v Marylebone Magistrates' Court ex p Westminster
   Council [1999] JHL D51, QBD   3.48, 3.49
R v Paddington Rent Tribunal ex p Bell London Properties
   Ltd [1949] 1 KB 666, [1949] 1 All ER 720   13.79
R (on the application of Public Transport (UK)) v Humber
   Bridge Board [2003] EWCA Civ 842, [2004] 2 WLR 98   4.54
R (on the application of Sinclair Investments (Kensington)
   Limited) v The Lands Tribunal and others [2005] EWCA
   Civ 1305, [2006] 3 All ER 650, [2006] HLR 11   13.111, 13.112
Rapid Results College v Angell (1986) 277 EG 856   2.29

Richmond Housing Partnership v Smith LRX/10/2005
    (Lands Tribunal)   4.14
Rigby v Wheatley LRX/84/2004 (Lands Tribunal)   2.50
St Mary's Mansions v Limegate Investment [2002] EWCA Civ
    1491, [2003] HLR 24   2.32, 13.92
Saunders v Vantier (1841) 1 Beav 115   2.90
Scott & G&O Properties Ltd LON/00AH/LSL/2004/0078
    (LVT)   5.17
Scottish Mutual Assurance Plc v Jardine Public Relations
    [1999] EGCS 43   2.79
Sella House v Mears [1989] 1 EGLR 65, (1989) 21 HLR 147   13.92
Sheales and others v Parry LON/00AN/LAM/2007/0011 (LVT)   8.61
Sinclair Gardens Investments (Kensington) Ltd v Poets
    Chase Freehold Company Ltd [2007] EWHC 1776 (Ch),
    [2007] 49 EG 104   9.71
Sinclair Gardens Investments (Kensington) Ltd v Wang and
    others LRX/89/2005 (Lands Tribunal)   2.13
Sinclair Gardens (Investments) Ltd v Oak Investments RTM
    Company Limited LRX/52/2004, [2005] RVR 426   9.59, 9.70
Staghold v Takeda and another (2005) 47 EG 146, 8 August
    2005, Central London CC   13.93
Steel & Morris v United Kingdom App No 68416/01, (2005)
    41 EHRR 403, ECtHR   12.13
Stylli v Hamberton Properties Ltd [2002] EWHC 394 (Ch D)   8.71
Sutton (Hastoe) Housing Association v Williams (1988) 20
    HLR 321, [1988] 1 EGLR 56   2.36
Swanston Grant (Luton) Management Limited v Eileen
    Langley-Essen LRX/12/2007 (Lands Tribunal)   10.40
Taber v Macdonald (1999) 31 HLR 73   3.9, 3.48
Tenants of Langford Court v Doren LRX/37/2000, [2002] 5
    JHL D8 (Lands Tribunal)   13.94
Tickmead Ltd v Interasia World Wide Ltd and others LON/
    OOBK/LVL/2004/0002/01 (LVT)   7.33
Trafalgar Court RTM Company Ltd v Wells and others CAM/
    33UF/LOA/2005/0001 (LVT)   13.57
Tredegar v Harwood [1929] AC 72   5.20
Veena SA v Cheong [2003] 1 EGLR 175   2.79
Villatte v 38 Cleveland Square Management Ltd [2002]
    EWCA Civ 1549   13.55
Volosinovici v Corvan Properties Ltd LRX/67/2006 (Lands
    Tribunal)   13.54, 13.55,
                                                             13.56, 13.94
Vural v Securities (1990) 60 P&CR 258   5.35
Wellcome Trust v Romines [1999] 3 EGLR 229 (Lands
    Tribunal)   13.106
West Midland Baptist (Trust) Association (Inc) v
    Birmingham Corporation [1968] 2 QB 188   1.24, 13.88
Westminster City Council v Hammond, 26 October 1995,
    Central London CC, December 1995 *Legal Action* 19   2.54

Williams v Southwark LBC (2001) 33 HLR 22   2.83, 5.11
Wilson v Stone [1998] 26 EG 153   4.66
Yorkbrooke Investments Ltd v Batten [1985] 2 EGLR 100,
     (1986) 18 HLR 25   2.25, 2.75,
                                                           2.76, 2.79,
                                                           13.56

Table of statutes

References in the right-hand column are to paragraph numbers.

Access to Justice Act 1999
 s6(8)   12.12
 Sch 2 para 2   12.7
Charities Act 1993
 s96   8.29
Commonhold and Leasehold Reform
  Act 2002   1.11, 1.12,
 1.26, 2.1, 2.7, 2.52, 2.58, 2.60,
 2.69, 2.92, 2.93, 2.94, 3.2,
 3.50, 3.52, 3.58, 4.4, 4.7, 4.59,
 6.2, 6.4, 6.5, 6.6, 6.12, 6.14,
 6.19, 6.22, 8.49, 10.18, 10.30,
 12.11
 Pt 2 Ch 1   9.1
 s27A   2.60, 6.37
 s27A(3)   6.37
 s72(1)(a)   9.16
 s72(1)(b)   9.16
 s72(1)(c)   9.16
 s72(2)   9.18
 s72(3)(a)   9.19
 s72(3)(b)   9.19
 s72(4)   9.19
 s72(5)   9.19
 s73(2)(a)   9.41
 s73(2)(b)   9.41
 s73(4)   9.42
 s73(5)   9.43
 s74(1)(a)   9.47
 s74(1)(b)   9.47
 s74(5)   9.46
 s75(3)   9.28
 s75(4)   9.28
 s75(5)   9.29
 s75(6)   9.29

Commonhold and Leasehold Reform
  Act 2002 continued
 s75(7)   9.29
 s76   5.36, 9.28
 s77   5.36
 s78(1)   9.52
 s78(2)   9.53
 ss78(4)–(5)   9.56
 s78(7)   9.57
 s79(2)   9.62
 s79(4)   9.63
 s79(5)   9.63
 s79(6)   9.66
 s79(6)(a)   9.64
 s79(6)(b)   9.64
 s79(6)(c)   9.64
 s79(8)   9.64
 s79(9)   9.64
 s80   9.66, 9.71
 s80(2)–(7)   9.66
 s81(1)   9.69
 s81(2)   9.69
 ss81(3)–(4)   9.71
 s82(1)   9.49
 s82(2)(a)   9.50
 s82(2)(b)   9.50
 s82(3)   9.51
 s82(7)   9.79
 s83   9.72
 s84   9.66
 s84(1)   9.73
 s84(2)   9.74, 9.75
 s84(3)   9.77, 13.12
 s84(4)   9.78
 s84(5)   9.78

Commonhold and Leasehold Reform
Act 2002 *continued*

s85	9.65, 9.91
s85(2)	13.12
s86	9.80
s87(1)(a)	9.81
s87(1)(b)	9.82
s87(4)	9.83
s88(1)	9.84
s88(2)	9.85
s88(3)	9.86
s88(4)	9.87, 13.12
s89	9.88
s90(2)	9.89
s90(4)	9.90
s90(6)	9.91
s94(1)	9.92
s94(2)	9.94
s94(3)	9.95, 13.12
s94(4)	9.93
s98(2)	9.96
s98(4)	9.97
s99(1)	9.98, 13.12
s99(5)	9.99
s103	13.12
s107	9.51
s109	9.29
s112	9.17
s118	9.16
s152	3.50
s157	3.58
s159(1)	6.43, 6.44
s159(3)	6.45, 13.12
s159(6)	13.12
s164	5.36
s164(2)	5.37
s164(2)(a)	5.37
s164(2)(b)	5.37
s164(2)(c)	5.37
s164(3)	5.38
s164(4)	5.38
s164(8)	5.39
s164(9)	5.39
s166	10.18, 10.19
s166(6)	10.23
s166(7)	10.22
s167	10.18, 10.24
s167(3)	10.26
s168	10.30, 10.38

Commonhold and Leasehold Reform
Act 2002 *continued*

s168(4)	10.31, 13.12
s175(1)	13.99
s175(2)	13.100
s175(4)	13.110
Sch 6 para 1(1)	9.32
Sch 6 para 1(2)	9.32
Sch 6 para 1(3)	9.33
Sch 6 para 2	9.35
Sch 6 para 3	9.36
Sch 6 paras 3(2)–(5)	9.37
Sch 6 para 4	9.38
Sch 6 para 5(1)(a)	9.39
Sch 6 para 5(1)(b)	9.39
Sch 6 para 5(2)	9.39
Sch 6 para 5(3)	9.39, 13.12
Sch 7	9.54
Sch 7 para 8	8.36, 8.68
Sch 7 para 16	6.26
Sch 10 para 11	13.96
Sch 10 para 14	8.49
Sch 10 para 16(1)	3.58
Sch 10 para 16(3)	3.58
Sch 11	6.3, 6.9, 6.36
Sch 11 para 1	8.43
Sch 11 para 1(3)	6.10
Sch 11 para 2	6.32
Sch 11 para 3	13.12
Sch 11 para 3(1)	6.26
Sch 11 para 3(3)	6.29
Sch 11 para 3(4)	6.29
Sch 11 para 3(6)	6.30
Sch 11 para 4	3.21
Sch 11 para 4(2)	13.12
Sch 11 para 4(3)	3.26, 13.12
Sch 11 para 4(4)	3.26
Sch 11 para 5	13.12
Sch 11 para 5(1)	6.34
Sch 11 para 5(2)	13.12
Sch 11 para 5(3)	13.12
Sch 11 para 5(4)	6.35
Sch 11 para 5(6)	6.36
Sch 11 para 8(3)	13.12
Sch 11 para 10	13.12
Sch 11 para 16	13.12
Sch 12 para 2	13.6

Commonhold and Leasehold Reform
  Act 2002 *continued*
  Sch 12 para 3   13.6
  Sch 12
    para 3(1)()a   13.6
  Sch 12
    para 3(1)(b)   13.6
  Sch 12 para 4   13.60
  Sch 12 para 4(1)   13.62
  Sch 12 paras
    4(3)–4(4)   13.62
  Sch 12 para 7   13.51
  Sch 12 para 10(2)   13.90
  Sch 12
    para 10(3)(a)   13.91
Companies Act 1989
  s25   3.44
Financial Services and Markets Act
  2002
  s19   5.37
Fire Prevention (Metropolis) Act
  1774
  s83   5.32
Housing Act 1980   1.3
  s523   2.53
Housing Act 1985
  Pt 5   9.28, 11.1
  s1   9.38
  ss45–48   11.2
  s125   11.6, 11.7,
        11.8
  s125A(2)   11.7
  s125B   11.7
  s125C   11.7
  s450A(2)   11.11
  s450A(4)(a)   11.11
  s450A(4)(b)   11.11
  Sch 6 para 6   11.9
  Sch 6 para 16B   11.8
  Sch 6 para 16C   11.8
Housing Act 1988
  ss27–28   10.13
Housing Act 1996
  s16   11.1
  s17   9.28
  s81   10.34, 10.35
  s81(2)   10.36
  s84   3.66
  s84(3)   3.67

Housing Act 1996 *continued*
  s84(4)   3.68
  s84(5)   3.67
  s219   11.14
  s219(1)(a)–(b)   11.14
  s219(4)   11.14
  Sch 4   3.66
Housing Grants, Construction and
  Regeneration Act 1996
  Pt 1   2.53
Insolvency Act 1986
  Pt 1   9.83
Landlord and Tenant Act 1927
  s19   6.8
Landlord and Tenant Act 1954
  Pt 2   8.28, 8.32,
        9.28
Landlord and Tenant Act 1985
        1.5, 2.58, 3.1,
        4.3
  s1   3.10
  s1(1)   3.10, 3.11
  s1(2)   3.9
  s2(1)   3.12
  s2(2)   3.13
  s2(3)   3.13
  s2(4)   3.9
  s3(1)   3.14, 3.15
  s3(3)   3.9
  s3(3A)   3.16
  s3A(3)   3.9
  s11   2.23
  s13   2.23
  s18   2.22, 5.9, 6.7
  s18(1)   2.7
  s18(2)   2.10
  s18(3)   2.10
  s19   2.78, 5.23,
        8.42, 13.94
  s20   4.7, 4.18,
        4.65, 4.70
  s20(1)   4.24
  s20(3)   4.9
  s20(3)(B)   4.10
  s20(4)   4.11, 4.25
  s20(4)(a)   4.16
  s20(4)(e)   4.13
  s20(5)   4.12, 4.24
  s20(9)   4.63, 4.66

Landlord and Tenant Act 1985 *continued*		Landlord and Tenant Act 1985 *continued*	
s20A(1)	2.53	s28(4)(c)	3.44
s20A(2)	2.53	s28(4)(d)	3.44
s20B	2.54	s28(4)(e)	3.44
s20B(1)	2.54	s28(6)	3.45
s20B(2)	2.54	s29(1)	3.63
s20C	13.9, 13.12,	s29(2)	3.64
	13.27, 13.74,	s29(3)	3.64
	13.93, 13.94	s29(5)	3.65
s20ZA	13.12	s30	2.8, 2.9,
s20ZA(1)	4.67		13.12
s20ZA(2)	4.60, 4.70	s30B	3.69, 8.73
s21	3.31, 3.57	s30B(1)	3.70, 8.74
s21(1)	3.31, 3.34	s30B(2)	3.72, 8.76
s21(1)(a)	3.31	s30B(3)	3.71, 8.75
s21(1)(b)	3.32	s30B(4)(a)	3.73, 8.77
s21(2)	3.42	s30B(4)(b)	3.73, 8.78
s21(3)	3.42	s30B(5)	3.74, 8.79
s21(4)	3.43	s30B(6)	3.75, 8.80
s21(5)	3.34, 3.35	s30B(8)	9.54
s21(5A)	3.36	s34	3.9
s21(6)	3.41	Sch 1 para 2	5.41
s21A	13.12	Sch 1 para 3	5.429.54
s21B	3.21	Sch 1 para 6	5.43, 5.46
s21B(3)	3.26	Sch 1 para 7	5.44
s21B(4)	3.26	Sch 1 para 7(2)	5.44
s22(2)	3.46	Sch 1 para 8	5.13, 5.25,
s22(4)	3.47		5.31, 13.12
s22(5)(a)	3.47	Sch 1 para 8(2)	5.14
s22(5)(b)	3.47	Sch 1 para 8(3)	5.15
s22(6)	3.47	Sch 1 para 8(4)	5.30
s24(9)	8.63	Sch 1 para 8(6)	5.31
s24(9A)	8.65	Sch 1 para 9	5.43, 5.46
s24(10)	8.66	Landlord and Tenant Act 1987	
s25	3.48, 3.49		1.6, 2.58,
s26	2.22		9.80, 14.6,
s27	8.42		14.8
s27A	2.68, 2.72,	Pt 2	9.2, 9.64,
	13.12		9.92
s27A(1)	2.12	s21	3.50, 3.51
s27(1)(a)–(e)	2.14	s21(1)	3.46, 8.31
s27A(2)	2.12	s21(2)	8.24
s27A(3)	2.15	s21(3)(a)	8.26, 8.27
s27A(3)(a)–(e)	2.16	s21(3)(b)	8.29
s27A(4)	2.19	s21(3A)	8.28
s27A(5)	2.12, 2.19	s21(4)(a)	8.31
s28(2)	3.44	s21(4)(b)	8.31
s28(4)(b)	3.44	s21(5)	8.31

Landlord and Tenant Act 1987
continued

s21(6)	8.71
s21(7)	8.32
s21(11)	8.53
s22	8.22, 8.36, 8.36
s22(1)	8.11
s22(2)	8.13
s22(2)(e)	8.14
s22(3)	8.18, 8.19, 8.20, 13.12
s22(4)	8.12
s23	8.16, 8.22
s24	8.39, 14.26
s24(1)	8.72, 13.12
s24(2)(a)	8.33
s24(2)(a)(i)	8.37
s24(2)(ab)	8.33, 8.40
s24(2)(aba)	8.33, 8.43
s24(2)(abb)	8.49
s24(2)(ac)	8.33
s24(2)(b)	8.34
s24(2A)	8.41
s24(2ZA)	8.35
s24(4)	8.54
s24(5)	8.55
s24(5)(c)	8.57
s24(6)	8.70
s24(7)	8.17
s24(8)	8.69
s24(9)	13.12
s24(11)	8.38
s35	13.12
s35(1)	7.7
s35(2)	7.7, 7.9
s35(2)(a)	7.10
s35(2)(b)	7.12
s35(2)(c)	7.14
s35(2)(d)	7.17
s35(2)(e)	7.18, 7.19
s35(2)(g)	7.20
s35(3)	7.15, 7.17
s35(3A)	7.18
s35(4)	7.19
s35(5)	7.39
s36	7.22, 13.12
s36(2)	7.22
s36(3)	7.24

Landlord and Tenant Act 1987
continued

s37	7.25, 13.12
s37(2)	7.26
s37(3)	7.29
s37(5)	7.28
s37(6)	7.27
s38	7.30
s38(4)	7.30
s38(5)	7.31
s38(6)(a)	7.35
s38(6)(b)	7.36
s38(7)	7.13
s38(8)	7.31
s38(10)	7.34
s39	13.23
s39(1)	7.37
s39(2)	7.37
s39(3)	7.38
s39(3)(b)	13.12
s39(4)	7.38
s39(5)	7.38
s40(1)	7.40, 13.12
s40(4A)	7.41
s40(4B)	7.41
s42	2.62, 2.84, 2.90
s42(2)	2.84, 2.86
s42(3)	2.86
s42(4)	2.89
s42(5)	2.88
s42(6)	2.89
s42(7)	2.89
s42(8)	2.89
s42(9)	2.86
ss42–42A	8.49
s42A	2.94
s42A(1)	2.94
s42A(2)	2.94
s42A(3)	2.95
s42A(9)	2.95
s47	2.51, 6.42
s47(1)(a)	3.17
s47(1)(b)	3.17
s47(2)	3.18
s47(3)	2.51
s48(1)	3.19
s48(2)	3.19
s48(3)	3.20

Landlord and Tenant Act 1987
continued

s52(2)	2.91
s54	8.12
s56	8.30
s58(1)	2.87, 8.26
s58(2)	8.28
ss58(1)(a)–58(3)	8.28
s59(3)	7.8
s60	8.25, 8.29

Law of Property Act 1925

s146	6.8, 6.11, 6.14, 10.27, 10.28, 10.29, 10.30, 10.32, 10.34, 10.35
s146(3)	6.8
s149(6)	9.28

Leasehold Reform Act 1967

Pt 1	5.36
s19	6.43

Leasehold Reform, Housing and
      Urban Development Act 1993

	9.1, 9.23
Pt 1 Ch 4	6.43
s70	13.16
s72	13.16
s76(2)(a)	3.54
s76(2)(b)	3.54
ss76–84	3.53
s77(1)	3.55
s77(3)	3.55
s77(4)(a)	3.55
s77(4)(b)	3.55
s78(1)	3.53
s78(4)	3.56

Leasehold Reform, Housing and
      Urban Development Act 1993
continued

s78(5)	3.56
s78(6)	3.56
s79(2)	3.57
s80(2)	3.59
s80(3)	3.59
s80(5)	3.60
s81(1)	3.61
s81(1)(c)	3.61
s81(6)	3.62
s81(7)	3.62
s87	8.45
s94	6.43

Limitation Act 1980	2.57, 2.58, 2.59, 2.60, 2.61, 2.62, 2.63
s5	2.62
s8	2.62
s9	2.62, 2.67
s19	2.62
s21(1)	2.62
s32(1)	2.62

Local Government Act 2000

s2	4.61

Local Government and Housing Act
      1989   2.53

Protection from Eviction Act 1977

s1	10.13
s2	10.13

State Pensions Credit Act 2002

	13.32

Unfair Contract Terms Act 1977

	2.45

Table of statutory instruments

References in the right-hand column are to paragraph numbers.

Administration Charges (Summary of Rights and Obligations)(England) Regulations 2007 SI No 1258	3.23, 6.42
reg 2	3.29
reg 4	3.28
Administration Charges (Summary of Rights and Obligations)(Wales) Regulations 2007 SI No 3162	3.23, 6.42
reg 2	3.29
reg 4	3.28
Approval of Code of Management Practice (Private Retirement Housing)(England) Order 2005 SI No 3307	8.45
Approval of Code of Practice (Private Retirement Housing)(Wales) Order 2007 SI No 578	8.45
Approval of Codes of Management Practice (Residential Property)(England) Order 2004 SI No 1802	8.45
Approval of Codes of Management Practice (Residential Property) Order 1996 SI No 2839	8.45
Approval of Codes of Management Practice (Residential Property)(Wales) Order 2006 SI No 178	8.45
Civil Procedure Rules 1998 SI No 3132	13.1
Pt 56 PD15	13.7
r70.4	13.97
r70.5	13.98
r70.6	13.98
Pt 70 PD 4.1-4.2	13.98
Pt 70 PD 4.3	13.98
Commonhold and Leasehold Reform Act 2002 (Commencement No 2 and Savings)(England) Order 2003 SI No 1986	2.13, 3.22
Sch 2 para 8	6.41
Commonhold and Leasehold Reform Act 2002 (Commencement No 2 and Savings and Transitional Provisions) Order 2004 SI No 3056	5.36

Commonhold and Leasehold Reform Act 2002
  (Commencement No 2 and Savings)(Wales) Order
  2003 SI No 669   2.13, 3.22
    Sch 2 para 8   6.41
Commonhold and Leasehold Reform Act 2002
  (Commencement No 2 and Savings and Transitional
  Provisions)(Wales) Order 2004 SI No 1353   5.36
Commonhold and Leasehold Reform Act 2002
  (Commencement No 4) (Wales) Order 2007
  SI No 3161   3.22
Commonhold and Leasehold Reform Act 2002
  (Commencement No 6) (England) Order 2007
  SI No 1256   3.22
Housing (Right to Acquire) Regulations 1997 SI No 619   11.1
Housing (Right to Buy)(Service Charges) Order 1986
  SI No 2195   11.8
Housing (Service Charge Loans) Regulations 1992
  SI No 1708
    reg 3   11.12
    reg 5   11.13
    reg 6   11.13
    Sch 1   11.13
Landlord and Tenant (Notice of Rent)(England) Regulations
  2004 SI No 3096   10.19, 10.20
Landlord and Tenant (Notice of Rent)(Wales) Regulations
  2005 SI No 1355   10.19, 10.20
    reg 3(2)   10.20
Lands Tribunal Rules 1996 SI No 1022   13.3
    r5C(1)   13.103
    r5C(2)   13.103
    r5C(5)   13.104
    r5F(1)   13.105
    r6   13.102
    r35   13.103
    PD paras 5.2-5.5   13.102
    PD para 5.6   13.105
    PD para 5.7   13.100
    PD para 5.8   13.107
    PD para 5.9   13.108
Leasehold Houses (Notice of Insurance Cover) (England)
  Regulations 2004 SI No 3097   5.38
Leasehold Houses (Notice of Insurance Cover) (Wales)
  Regulations 2005 SI No 1354   5.38
Leasehold Valuation Tribunals (Fees) (England) Regulations
  2003 SI No 2089   13.25
    reg 3   13.28
    reg 3(1)   13.13
    reg 3(1)(e)   13.10

Leasehold Valuation Tribunals (Fees) (England) Regulations 2003 *continued*

reg 3(8)	13.21
reg 4	13.8, 13.23
reg 5	13.30
reg 5(1)	13.22
reg 5(2)	13.22
reg 5(3)	13.22
reg 5(4)	13.22
regs 5(5)–(6)	13.24
reg 6	13.26
reg 6(3)	13.26
reg 7	13.31
reg 7(1)	13.26
reg 7(2)	13.26
reg 7(3)	13.31
reg 8	13.32
reg 8(4)	13.33
reg 9(1)	13.95
reg 9(2)	13.95
reg 11	13.11
reg 14(2)	13.30
Sch 2 para 2	13.15
Sch 2 para 3	13.16
Sch 2 para 4	13.17
Sch 2 para 5	13.18
Sch 2 para 6	13.19
Sch 2 para 7	13.20

Leasehold Valuation Tribunals (Fees) (Wales) Regulations
2004 SI No 683 (W71) — 13.25

reg 4	13.8

Leasehold Valuation Tribunals (Procedure) (England)
Regulations 2003 SI No 2099 — 7.39, 13.1

reg 6	13.42
reg 6(2)(a)	13.43
reg 6(2)(b)	13.42
reg 6(4)	13.43
reg 8(1)	13.46
reg 8(2)	13.47
reg 8(4)	13.48
reg 9	13.49
reg 9(3)	13.49
reg 10	13.49
reg 10(3)	13.49
reg 11	2.65, 13.54
reg 11(1)(a)	13.51
reg 11(1)(b)	13.51
reg 11(3)	13.52
reg 11(4)(a)	13.53
reg 11(4)(b)	13.53

Leasehold Valuation Tribunals (Procedure) (England) Regulations 2003
  continued

reg 12(1)	13.58
reg 12(2)	13.58
reg 12(3)	13.60
reg 12(3)(a)	13.44
reg 13(1)(a)	13.36
reg 13(1)(b)	13.36
reg 13(2)	13.37
reg 13(3)	13.36
reg 13(4)	13.36
reg 13(5)	13.37
reg 14(3)	13.67
reg 14(6)	13.65
reg 14(8)	13.67
reg 15(1)	13.86
reg 15(2)	13.87
reg 15(3)	13.87
reg 16(2)	13.83, 13.84
reg 17(1)(a)	13.77
reg 17(1)(b)	13.77
reg 17(2)	13.77
reg 17(3)	13.78
reg 17(8)	13.79
reg 18(2)	13.75
reg 18(3)	13.75
reg 18(7)	13.76
reg 19	13.96
reg 20(a)	13.101
reg 20(b)	13.101
reg 24	13.101

Leasehold Valuation Tribunals (Procedure)(Wales)
  Regulations 2004 SI No 681 — 7.39, 13.1, 13.2

National Assembly for Wales (Transfer of Functions) Order
  1999 SI No 672 — 8.14

Public Contracts Regulations 2006 — 4.43

Right to Manage Companies (Memorandum and Articles of
  Association)(England) Regulations 2003 SI No 2120 — 9.46
  Sch 1 Pt 1 — 9.46

Right to Manage Companies (Memorandum and Articles of
  Association)(Wales) Regulations 2004 SI No 675 — 9.46
  Sch 1 Pt 1 — 9.46

Right to Manage (Prescribed Particulars and
  Forms)(England) Regulations 2003 SI No 1988
  reg 3(2) — 9.54
  reg 4 — 9.67
  reg 5 — 9.75
  Sch 1 — 9.54

Right to Manage (Prescribed Particulars and Forms)(England) Regulations
2003 *continued*
  Sch 2 — 9.67
  Sch 3 — 9.75, 9.76
Right to Manage (Prescribed Particulars and Forms) (Wales)
Regulations 2004 SI No 678 — 9.55, 9.68
Rights of Re-entry and Forfeiture (Prescribed Sum and
Period) (England) Regulations 2004 SI No 3086 — 10.25
Rights of Re-entry and Forfeiture (Prescribed Sum and
Period) (Wales) Regulations 2005 SI No 1352 — 10.25
Service Charge Contributions (Authorised Investments)
Order 1988 SI No 1284 — 2.88
Service Charge (Estimates and Consultation Order) 1988
SI No 1285 — 4.10
Service Charges (Consultation Requirements) (Amendment)
Regulations 2004 SI No 2665 — 4.32
Service Charges (Consultation Requirements) (England)
Regulations 2003 SI No 1987 — 4.29
  reg 2 — 4.33
  reg 2(1) — 4.39
  reg 3 — 4.61, 4.70
  reg 4 — 4.25
  reg 4 para 3A — 4.29
  reg 5 — 11.10
  reg 6 — 4.24
  reg 7 — 4.70, 11.10
  Sch 1 — 4.72
  Sch 1 para 1(1) — 4.72
  Sch 1 para 1(1)(a) — 4.72
  Sch 1 para 1(1)(b) — 4.72
  Sch 1 para 1(2)(a) — 4.72
  Sch 1 para 1(2)(b) — 4.72
  Sch 1 para 1(2)(c) — 4.72
  Sch 1 para 1(2)(d) — 4.72
  Sch 1 para 1(2)(e) — 4.72
  Sch 1 para 4(4) — 4.53
  Sch 1 para 5 — 4.41
  Sch 1 para 5(1) — 4.72
  Sch 1 para 5(2) — 4.72
  Sch 1 para 5(6) — 4.38
  Sch 1 para 6(1) — 4.72
  Schs 1-4 para 2(1) — 4.34, 4.35
  Schs 1-4 para 2(2) — 4.35
  Sch 2 — 4.42, 4.72
  Sch 2 para 1(1) — 4.72
  Sch 2 para 1(1)(a) — 4.72
  Sch 2 para 1(1)(b) — 4.72
  Sch 2 para 1(2)(a) — 4.72
  Sch 2 para 1(2)(b) — 4.72

Service Charges (Consultation Requirements) (England) Regulations 2003
  continued

Sch 2 para 1(2)(c)	4.72
Sch 2 para 1(2)(d)	4.72
Sch 2 para 1(2)(e)	4.72
Sch 2 para 1(2)(f)	4.72
Sch 2 para 4	4.41
Sch 2 para 4(3)	4.38
Sch 2 para 7	4.72
Sch 4 Pt 1	4.42
Sch 4 Pt 1 para 1(1)	4.72
Sch 4 Pt 1 para 1(1)(a)	4.72
Sch 4 Pt 1 para 1(1)(b)	4.72
Sch 4 Pt 1 para 1(2)(a)	4.72
Sch 4 Pt 1 para 1(2)(b)	4.72
Sch 4 Pt 1 para 1(2)(c)	4.72
Sch 4 Pt 1 para 1(2)(d)	4.72
Sch 4 Pt 1 para 1(2)(e)	4.72
Sch 4 Pt 1 para 3	4.72
Sch 4 Pt 1 para 4	4.41
Sch 4 Pt 1 para 4(3)	4.38
Sch 4 Pt 1 para 6	4.72
Sch 4 Pt 2	4.72
Sch 4 Pt 2 para 1(1)	4.72
Sch 4 Pt 2 para 1(1)(a)	4.72
Sch 4 Pt 2 para 1(1)(b)	4.72
Sch 4 Pt 2 para 1(2)(a)	4.72
Sch 4 Pt 2 para 1(2)(b)	4.72
Sch 4 Pt 2 para 1(2)(d)	4.72
Sch 4 Pt 2 para 1(2)(e)	4.72
Sch 4 Pt 2 para 3	4.72
Sch 4 Pt 2 para 4(5)(b)	4.72
Sch 4 Pt 2 para 4(5)(c)	4.72
Sch 4 Pt 2 para 4(7)	4.38
Sch 4 Pt 2 para 4(8)	4.72
Sch 4 Pt 2 para 4(10)	4.72
Sch 4 Pt 2 para 5	4.72
Sch 4 Pt 2 para 6(1)	4.72
Sch 4 Pt 2 para 6(3)	4.72
Service Charges (Consultation Requirements)(Wales) Regulations 2004 SI No 684	4.29
reg 2	4.33
reg 2(1)	4.39
reg 3	4.61, 4.70
reg 4	4.25
reg 4 para 3A	4.29
reg 5	11.10
reg 6	4.24
reg 7	4.70, 11.10

Service Charges (Consultation Requirements)(Wales) Regulations 2004
continued

Sch 1 para 4(4)	4.53
Sch 1 para 5	4.41
Sch 1 para 5(6)	4.38
Schs 1-4 para 2(1)	4.34, 4.35
Schs 1-4 para 2(2)	4.35
Sch 2 para 4	4.41
Sch 2 para 4(3)	4.38
Sch 2 para 4(7)	4.42
Sch 4 Pt 1 para 4	4.41
Sch 4 Pt 1 para 4(3)	4.38
Sch 4 pt 1 para 4(7)	4.42
Sch 4 Pt 2 para 4(7)	4.38

Service Charges (Summary of Rights and Obligations and
Transitional Provision)(England) Regulations 2007

SI No 1257	3.23
reg 2	3.29
reg 4	3.28

Service Charges (Summary of Rights and Obligations and
Transitional Provision)(Wales) Regulations 2007 SI

No 3160	3.23
reg 2	3.29
reg 4	3.28

Social Landlords Discretionary Reduction of Service Charges
(England) Directions 1997   11.15
Social Landlords Mandatory Reduction of Service Charges
(England) Directions 1997   11.15, 11.16
Unfair Terms in Consumer Contracts Regulations 1999 SI

No 083	2.45
reg 7(2)	2.47
reg 8(1)	2.46

Abbreviations

CLRA 2002	Commonhold and Leasehold Reform Act 2002
Consultation Regs 2003	Service Charges (Consultation Requirements) (England) Regulations 2003
Fees Regs 2003	Leasehold Valuation Tribunals (Fees) (England) Regulations 2003
HA 1996	Housing Act 1996
LA 1980	Limitation Act 1980
LRHUDA 1993	Leasehold Reform, Housing and Urban Development Act 1993
LTA 1985	Landlord and Tenant Act 1985
LTA 1987	Landlord and Tenant Act 1987
LVT	Leasehold Valuation Tribunal
LVT Fees Regs 2003	Leasehold Valuation Tribunal (Fees) (England) Regulations 2003
LVT Procedure Regs	Leasehold Valuation Tribunals (Procedure) (England) Regulations 2003
PTR	Pre-trial review
QLTA	Qualifying Long-Term Agreement
RAC	Rent Assessment Committee
RPTS	Residential Property Tribunal Service
RTA	Recognised Tenants' Association
RTB	Right to Buy tenancy
RTM	Right to Manage
SC(CR)(E) Regs 2003	Service Charges (Consultation Requirements) (England) Regulations 2003
SC(CR)(W) Regs 2004	Service Charges (Consultation Requirements) (Wales) Regulations 2004
UTCCR 1999	Unfair Terms in Consumer Contracts Regulations 1999

CHAPTER 1

Introduction

1.2   History

1.15   Organisation

1.18   Hearings

1.24   Precedent

1.26   Outline of this book

1.1   This book is intended to give advice to residential tenants in a dispute with their landlords which might bring them before a Leasehold Valuation Tribunal.

History

1.2   Leasehold Valuation Tribunals are another name for Rent Assessment Committees. Rent Assessment Committees (RACs) were set up to adjudicate disputes concerning the registration of rents under the Rent Acts. RACs consist of three people: a legally qualified 'chair' assisted by two 'wing members' who will not normally be lawyers but are appointed because of their expertise in housing.

1.3   The Housing Act 1980 transferred jurisdiction over leasehold enfranchisement to RACs. While exercising this jurisdiction an RAC is called a Leasehold Valuation Tribunal (LVT).

1.4   An LVT is therefore an RAC which is exercising certain powers given to it. When sitting as an LVT an RAC is governed by different procedural rules, and at least one member must 'be experienced in the valuation of land'.

1.5   The Landlord and Tenant Act (LTA) 1985, gave LVTs the power to determine whether any service charge paid by the tenant of a flat (later a dwelling) was reasonable. This proved to be a fertile source of applications to the LVT, so that it has eclipsed much of its other work.

1.6   The LTA 1987 gave the LVT power to appoint a manager to manage residential leasehold property, where the existing management has been defective for some reason. The LVT could supervise the appointed manager, vary the manager's remit or dismiss them. Tenants were also given the right to challenge their landlord's choice of insurer before the LVT.

1.7   However, over the years it became clear that there were a number of problems with the LVT's jurisdiction.

1.8   Tenants had experienced considerable frustration with the narrowness of the LVT's power to decide questions concerning service charges. All the LVT was supposed to do was to rule on whether a charge was reasonable; it was given no power to decide whether the charge was properly payable on construction of the lease; or whether statutory consultation requirements had been complied with. Tenants were forced to frame many applications so that they appeared to be reasonableness challenges, hiding a challenge that was really being brought on some other ground.

1.9   The LVT did not have jurisdiction over 'improvements', which were not part of the statutory definition of a service charge. Much time was spent in arguing whether work done by a landlord was an 'improvement' or a 'repair', a distinction which was hard to make in any principled way in practice.

1.10   In 2001 the problems faced by tenants were further compounded by the decision of the Court of Appeal in *R v London Leasehold Valuation Tribunal ex p Daejan Properties Ltd* which held that, where a tenant had already paid a service charge, they would not normally be able to challenge the charge before an LVT, drastically reducing the scope of the LVT's power.

1.11   The Commonhold and Leasehold Reform Act (CLRA) 2002 addressed many of these problems and extended the LVT's power to consider any question concerning the payability of a service charge; the definition of service charges was enlarged to include 'improvements'; and it was expressly provided that a challenge could still be made even where a tenant had already paid the charge.

1.12   CLRA 2002, also created a new 'Right To Manage' (RTM). Prior to the Act, the LVT could appoint a new manager only if some defect were shown in the existing management arrangements. RTM allows tenants to set up a company, known as an RTM company, and if a majority of tenants join the company and go through the correct procedure, the landlord can be forced to accept the RTM company as a new manager, regardless of whether there is any fault in the existing management.

1.13   Service charge litigation has revealed that there were a number of charges being levied by landlords that did not fall into the statutory definition of a service charge, but which might still be unreasonable and constitute a burden on the tenant. The most common such charges are now known as 'administration charges', and the LVT was given a very similar jurisdiction over them as it has for service charges.

1.14   An existing power, possessed by the court, to vary inadequate leases has been extended to the LVT, and the power to create a new set of procedural rules for the LVT was introduced.

Organisation

1.15   LVTs are administered in England by the Residential Property Tribunal Service (RPTS). In Wales the LVT is part of the responsibility of the Welsh Assembly. While there is a significant degree of similarity between the English and Welsh LVTs, both are dealt with in this book and the differences noted where appropriate.

1.16   In England, each LVT Chair is appointed by the Lord Chancellor, other members being appointed by the Department for Communities and Local Government. In Wales, appointment is a matter for the Welsh Assembly.

1.17   Almost all panel members work part-time, the principal exception being the Senior President, who is also the president of the London Panel and is assisted by three full-time Vice Presidents.

Hearings

1.18   Hearings can take place anywhere, and are often held in public buildings, such as civic centres or church halls, hired for the purpose. It is even possible for an LVT to meet in the property itself, such as in the case of a disabled tenant who would find it otherwise very difficult to attend the tribunal elsewhere.

1.19   Some of the panels, in particular the London Panel, have dedicated hearing rooms, and where they are available, hearings will often take place there.

1.20   The intention is that hearings should avoid the formality of a courtroom so that they are not intimidating for lay applicants. All participants remain seated throughout a hearing and no court dress is used. An LVT is free to decide on the procedure it adopts at a hearing, which gives a great deal of flexibility which should be used to put lay applicants further at their ease.

1.21   Despite these measures, many disputes in front of an LVT can become factually or legally complex. Applicants often find it difficult to organise their cases clearly and to appreciate points of law raised against them. This can only become more of a problem as the LVT gains a more complex set of jurisdictions.

1.22   Applicants are free to represent themselves or to appoint any other representative (who need not be legally qualified) to speak for them. There are valuers and surveyors who make a practice of appearing before LVTs (mostly on behalf of landlords).

1.23   In general no public funding is available for representation at an LVT and it can be difficult and expensive for tenants to obtain representation. The Leasehold Advisory Service (LEASE) provides a telephone advice line and helpful introductory publications concerning the LVT. In London, the College of Law offers a free advice and representation service, which is staffed by student lawyers.

Precedent

1.24 The LVT is not a court and LVTs' decisions are not capable of binding each other,[1] although, in practice, the LVT is keen to promote consistency. Despite the fact that the Lands Tribunal is not a 'court of record', the LVT will generally follow the decisions of the Lands Tribunal. It is entirely proper for the Lands Tribunal to give guidance to LVTs.[2] The LVT (and Lands Tribunal) are bound by decisions of the High Court, Court of Appeal and House of Lords. Appeals from a decision of the LVT may be made, with permission of either Tribunal, to the Lands Tribunal, and from there to the Court of Appeal.

1.25 Past decisions of the LVT, dating back to 1998, can be found at the LEASE website (www.lease-advise.org). A similar service is now also provided by the RPTS itself and their website (www.rpts.gov.uk) contains a comprehensive list of LVT decisions in England. There is no online record of LVT decisions in Wales.

Outline of this book

1.26 Chapter 2 deals with what is currently the most important area of the LVT's jurisdiction, service charges. It discusses the existing case law on their payability and discusses changes made by the CLRA 2002. In considering whether and how to challenge a service charge demand, it is important for a tenant to have as much information as possible. Chapter 3 explains what rights a tenant has to demand information from or have information supplied by their landlord.

1.27 When landlords undertake large works, or enter into contracts lasting longer than a year, to which their tenants will have to contribute in their service charges, they are required to go through a relatively elaborate consultation process concerning their work. Should they fail to consult properly the amount they are allowed to recover from their tenants is capped. The law on consultation is covered in chapter 4.

1.28 Sometimes a tenant is required to pay insurance to an insurer that has been chosen by a landlord. Such payments are not service

1 *West Midland Baptist (Trust) Association (Inc) v Birmingham Corporation* [1968] 2 QB 188.
2 *Earl Cadogan and others v Sportelli and others* [2007] EWCA Civ 1042; [2007] RVR 314.

charges, so that a tenant would not be able to challenge them in the normal way. An LVT has a jurisdiction to hear a challenge by a tenant to such insurance arrangements; this is the subject of chapter 5.

1.29   Chapter 6 deals with certain miscellaneous charges, called administration charges, that might be recovered by a landlord from a tenant and that are not covered by the definition of service charges. The power of the LVT over administration charges is similar to, but not quite the same as, that it exercises of service charges.

1.30   Sometimes the root of a dispute between landlord and tenant is a poorly drafted lease. Any party to a lease can apply to an LVT to have the lease altered (varied) on various grounds. Chapter 7 explores the situations when such a variation can be ordered, and the process by which variation takes place.

1.31   Chapter 8 describes the power of an LVT to appoint a manager where there has been some failure of management of a property; and also the ways in which the LVT supervises the manager once appointed.

1.32   Chapter 9 discusses the alternative route by which tenants may force the appointment of their own management company, a so-called RTM company, regardless of any preceding fault.

1.33   Chapter 10 gives a brief sketch of the power that a landlord has to take back the property they have leased if the tenant is at fault in paying the rent or complying with a covenant in their lease. This is a process known as forfeiture and would be quite severe but for residential leases the law has curbed the power of landlords to forfeit in various ways. This chapter also explains how the LVT becomes involved in a forfeiture situation.

1.34   Chapter 11 deals with the specific considerations applicable to properties purchased under the 'right to buy' scheme and chapter 12 provides an overview of the various ways in which a tenant might attempt to secure and fund legal representation before the LVT.

1.35   Chapter 13 deals with procedure in the LVT, from issuing an application through to the decision and any subsequent appeal.

1.36   Tenants involved in the purchase of their freehold, or an extension or renewal of their lease should expect to have legal advice (since they are involved in a process of conveyancing). This book does not attempt to deal with the LVT's jurisdiction over leasehold enfranchisement, or the other statutory rights of tenants to purchase the freehold of their property. These matters will be largely ignored hereafter.

CHAPTER 2

Service charges

2.1   **Introduction**

2.3   **Advice for tenants**

2.7   **What is a service charge?**

2.12   **Challenging the payability of service charges**

2.22   Which tenancies are affected?

2.24   Who may apply to an LVT?

2.25   Burden and standard of proof

2.28   Payable under the lease

2.31   Sweeping up clauses

2.33   Apportionment

2.40   Repairs and improvements

2.45   Unfair terms

2.48   Management fees

2.50   Contractual preconditions for recovery

2.51   **Statutory preconditions for recovery**

2.51   Demands for service charges

2.53   Grant aided works

2.54   Stale service charges

2.57   Limitation of service charges
            Does the Limitation Act 1980 apply? • *What is the limitation
            period?* • *An alternative view*

continued

2.68   Equitable principles

2.69   Set-off
         Payment of service charges and compliance by the landlord with his covenants

2.77   Other equitable principles?

2.78   Reasonableness

2.80   Insurance

2.84   Holding service charges

2.88   Investment of trust funds

2.89   Termination of the lease
         Commonhold and Leasehold Reform Act 2002 reforms

Key points

- A service charge is any variable sum of money paid by the tenant which is payable, directly or indirectly, for services, repairs, maintenance, improvements, insurance or management of the property. It may or may not be included in the tenants' rent.
- A landlord may not recover for something that is not clearly set out in the lease. Courts interpret alleged service charge clauses restrictively.
- Service charges relate to services actually provided. They are not a source of profit for landlords.
- As a general rule, the fact that a tenant is behind with service charge payments does not allow a landlord to stop providing services.
- The LVT may decide whether a service charge is payable. A charge is payable only to the extent that it is reasonable.
- An LVT may also decide the person to whom service charges are payable; who is liable to pay the charge; the amount which is payable; and the date and the manner of payment.
- The fact that a tenant has paid a service charge does not prevent an application to the LVT.
- Anyone may apply to an LVT for a determination of the payability of a service charge. Most applications are made by either tenants, landlords or managing agents.
- All service charges must be demanded within 18 months of being incurred.
- Landlords who arrange insurance for a property and recover the cost as a service charge must reduce the charge by the amount of any commission they receive to their tenants.
- Landlords hold service charge contributions on trust.
- There is probably no limitation period for a tenant to bring a service charge dispute before the LVT.

Introduction

2.1   Service charges are sums of money paid by tenants to landlords for services and works provided or done by the landlords under the lease. The Leasehold Valuation Tribunal (LVT) has long been able to adjudicate on whether or not service charges are reasonable. The introduction of the Commonhold and Leasehold Reform Act (CLRA) 2002 has effected a major extension of the LVT's jurisdiction. The LVT may now decide any question of payability of service charges, including whether or not they are reasonable.

2.2   When considering the question of payability of a service charge, there are four main issues which may arise:

(a) payability under the lease;
(b) statutory controls over service charges;
(c) equitable principles which may apply; and
(d) reasonableness.

Advice for tenants

2.3   Most leases of flats place the landlord under an obligation to do works and provide services for the benefit of the tenants, with a corresponding obligation on the tenants to pay for those works or services. These service charges are a source of contention between the landlord and tenant. Tenants often feel that they have a greater stake in the property than the freeholder and resent being presented with bills in respect of works which they either did not support or would have wished to have done differently.

2.4   Sometimes, particularly where the landlord is a tenant-owned company, these disputes will break out between individual tenants. Works may need to be done urgently, but one or two recalcitrant tenants will be unwilling to contribute to the costs of the necessary works.

2.5   The LVT can now deal with almost all such disputes. Some disputes before the LVT will be purely question of law, some will be entirely questions of fact and many will be a mixture of the two.

2.6   It is vital for any tenant who wishes to challenge the reasonableness of a service charge to obtain comparable evidence to bolster their case. This is also true for any case involving an allegation of breach of covenant by the landlord. The vast majority of service charge cases that fail, do so for lack of evidence and failure to appreciate the principles of reasonableness (see below para 2.78).

What is a service charge?

2.7   A service charge means an amount payable by a tenant of a dwelling as part of, or in addition to, the rent which is payable directly, or indirectly, for services, repairs, maintenance, improvements[1] or insurance or the landlord's costs of management and the whole or part of which varies or may vary according to the relevant costs.[2] Thus, not all charges payable under the lease are service charges. For examples of other kinds of charge see chapter 6 on administration charges.

2.8   A 'landlord' includes anyone with a right to enforce the payment of service charges.[3] For example, some modern leases are 'tripartite'. The parties to the lease being the freeholder, tenant and a property manager and the lease gives the property manager the power to recover service charges for the work they carry out. Such a manager would not ordinarily have any interest in the property but would still be a 'landlord' for the purposes of this chapter.

2.9   The concept of 'a tenant' for these purposes is a broad one. It may include a party who has sublet his flat as well as the sub-tenant. It is also possible to be a tenant of more than one flat or of additional (non-residential) parts of the building.[4] Statutory tenants and subtenants are included.[5]

2.10   'Relevant costs' are costs or estimated costs which are incurred or to be incurred by or on behalf of the landlord (or a superior landlord) in connection with matters for which the service charge is payable[6] and include overheads.[7]

2.11   Any sum which is wholly fixed under the lease is not a service charge[8] although a sum which has a fixed and variable element will be.[9]

Challenging the payability of service charges

2.12   An application may be made to the LVT to determine whether a service charge is payable.[10] An application may be made whether or not

---

1   Improvements were added by CLRA 2002.
2   Landlord and Tenant Act (LTA) 1985 s18(1).
3   LTA 1985 s30.
4   *Oakfern Properties Ltd v Ruddy* [2006] EWCA Civ 1389; [2007] 3 WLR 524 approving *Heron Maple Court v Central Estates* [2002] 1 EGLR 35.
5   LTA 1985 s30.
6   LTA 1985 s18(2).
7   LTA 1985 s18(3).
8   *Coventry City Council v Cole* [1994] 1 WLR 398; (1993) 25 HLR 555.
9   *Longmint Ltd v Marcus* [2004] 3 EGLR 171; LRX/25/2003 (Lands Tribunal).
10   LTA 1985 s27A(1).

the service charge has been paid[11] and the fact that a tenant has paid does not amount to an admission on their behalf.[12]

2.13   This jurisdiction is not dependent on when the service charges in question were incurred, paid or demanded but on when the application to the LVT was made. So long as it was made after 30 September 2003[13] the LVT may consider issues of payability.[14]

2.14   If any such application is made, the LVT may also determine:[15]

(a) the person by whom it is payable;
(b) the person to whom it is payable;
(c) the amount which is payable;
(d) the date at, or by, which it is payable; and
(e) the manner in which it is payable.

2.15   In addition, an application may be made for a determination as to whether, if costs were incurred for services, repairs, maintenance, improvements, insurance or management of any specified description, a service charge would be payable in respect of those costs.[16]

2.16   If any such application is made, the LVT may also determine:[17]

(a) the person by whom it would be payable;
(b) the person to whom it would be payable;
(c) the amount which would be payable;
(d) the date at, or by, which it would be payable, and
(e) the manner in which it would be payable.

2.17   This jurisdiction clearly permits an application to be made in advance of costs being incurred. In practice, it is more likely to be useful where any dispute between the landlord and tenant can be resolved in its entirety before any work is done, for example where the dispute is one of construction of the lease.

2.18   While in principle it is possible to apply to an LVT for a determination of the reasonable costs for carrying out building work in

---

11 LTA 1985 s27A(2).
12 LTA 1985 s27A(5).
13 In respect of applications to the LVT in England and 30 March 2004 for applications to the LVT in Wales; Commonhold and Leasehold Reform Act 2002 (Commencement No 2 and Savings) (England) Order 2003 SI No 1986; Commonhold and Leasehold Reform Act 2002 (Commencement No 2 and Savings) (Wales) Order 2004 SI No 669.
14 *Sinclair Gardens Investments(Kensington) Ltd v Wang and others* LRX/89/2005 (Lands Tribunal).
15 LTA 1985 ss27A(1)(a)–(e).
16 LTA 1985 s27A(3).
17 LTA 1985 ss27A(3)(a)–(e).

advance of the work being done if the costs subsequently prove to be considerably more (or less) than this figure, there is nothing to stop either party from applying back to the LVT for a determination of the payability and reasonableness of the new sums.[18]

2.19   The LVT may not hear any application concerning a service charge which:[19]

(a) has been agreed or admitted by the tenant;

(b) has been, or is to be, referred to arbitration pursuant to a post-dispute arbitration agreement to which the tenant is a party;

(c) has been the subject of determination by a court; or

(d) has been the subject of determination by an arbitral tribunal pursuant to a post-dispute arbitration agreement.

2.20   Recall that the mere act of payment of a service charge does not amount to an admission and therefore does not preclude the LVT's jurisdiction.[20]

2.21   The Lands Tribunal[21] has suggested that the LVT may not be the appropriate forum for resolving all disputes[22] arising under the lease. If there are already court proceedings ongoing, the LVT may, pursuant to its inherent jurisdiction, adjourn those matters, to be determined by the court.

Which tenancies are affected?

2.22   The right to apply for a determination of the payability of service charges, described in this chapter, applies only to residential tenancies.[23] Tenancies of local authorities, a National Park Authority or a new town corporation are not affected unless the tenancies are long leases.[24] There is no reason why housing association tenancies, even if they are secure, should not be covered.

2.23   In practice, tenancies under short leases – those of less than seven years[25] – are unlikely to be paying service charges because in

---

18 *Compton Court, Victoria Crescent, London, SE19* LVTP/SC/008/091 and 092/01 (LVT).

19 LTA 1985 s27A(4).

20 LTA 1985 s27A(5).

21 *Canary Riverside Pte Ltd v Schilling and others* LRX/65/2005 (Lands Tribunal).

22 The examples given in the Lands Tribunal were those relating to mistake and voidable leases, misrepresentation or forgery.

23 LTA 1985 s18.

24 LTA 1985 s26.

25 LTA 1985 s13.

such leases the landlord is given the responsibility for the majority of repair and maintenance.[26]

Who may apply to an LVT?

2.24   There is no restriction on who may apply to an LVT for the determination of service charges. In practice most, if not all applications will be made by tenants, landlords and managing agents. There may be situations where some other party has an interest in a determination such as a guarantor of the service charges of a tenant. Where an applicant has no financial interest in the outcome of a determination, they are likely to have their application dismissed[27] by the LVT as being frivolous.[28]

Burden and standard of proof

2.25   A particular difficulty with the LVT is the question of burdens and standards of proof.[29] In many cases, having heard the evidence, it will not matter as the LVT will be able to form a view based on what it has seen and heard. However, it will not always be that simple.

2.26   There are a few general rules, such as the principle that 'he who asserts must prove': that is, that a party who wishes to rely on a proposition must prove it. But the incidence of the burden of proof will vary from case to case.

2.27   The common situation is where a tenant challenges service charges. In such a case the burden will be on the tenant adduce some evidence to suggest that there might be a question mark over any service charges demanded. If he or she fails to do so, then the application must fail. If he produces sufficient evidence then the respondent must provide sufficient evidence to establish that the service charges are payable. If the landlord produces no evidence, then its case should fail.[30]

---

26 LTA 1985 s11.
27 See para 13.51.
28 *Oakfern Properties Ltd v Ruddy* [2006] EWCA Civ 1389; [2007] 3 WLR 524 approving *Heron Maple Court v Central Estates* [2002] 1 EGLR 35.
29 See, generally, Timothy Fancourt QC, 'Property law update', *New Law Journal*, 14 July 2006, p1132.
30 *Yorkbrook Investments Ltd v Batten* [1985] 2 EGLR 100; (1986) 18 HLR 25; *Schilling v Canary Riverside Development Ltd* LRX/26/2005 & LRX/65/2005 (Lands Tribunal).

Payable under the lease

2.28 Any service charge claimed by the landlord must be clearly provided for under the lease and must have been apparent to a reasonable tenant. In deciding whether the words used achieve this end, they must be given their natural meaning and must be seen in their context. If, having applied this approach, the meaning of the clause is ambiguous, then any ambiguity must be resolved against the interests of the landlord and in favour of the tenant.[31]

2.29 Even under a lease which contains a detailed service charge clause, there may be items which fall outside the wording of the clause. These cannot be charged to the tenant. There is no presumption that landlords should recoup all their expenditure.[32]

2.30 In the absence of clear wording to the contrary, a lease will not be read so as to enable the landlord to make a profit.[33]

Sweeping up clauses

2.31 Landlords sometime attempt to rely on general clauses within a lease which appear to allow them to recover all expenditure not covered by another clause. These clauses are known as 'sweeping up' clauses.

2.32 When such clauses have been considered by the courts they have generally been construed restrictively, as the following examples illustrate.

Example 1

A lease contained a provision which allowed recovery of repairs and a proviso that the landlord might, at his reasonable discretion, hold, add to, extend, vary or make any alteration in the rendering of the services at any time in his absolute discretion, provided that it would make for more efficient management and conduct of the building. It was held that this did not cover repairs to external walls where this was not already expressly included. The wide words were to be read as only relating to works for which he could already charge, not as a discretionary powers to add more works to that list.[34]

---

31 *Embassy Court Residents' Association v Lipman* (1984) 271 EG 545; *Gilje v Charlegrove Securities Ltd* [2002] 1 EGLR 41; *Earl Cadogan v 27/29 Sloane Gardens Ltd* LRA/9/2005; [2006] 24 EG 178.

32 *Rapid Results College v Angell* (1986) 277 EG 856.

33 *Jollybird v Fairzone* [1990] 2 EGLR 55.

34 *Jacob Isbicki v Goulding* [1989] 1 EGLR 236.

Example 2

A provision entitling a landlord to recover the cost of providing and maintaining additional services or amenities did not permit the landlord to recover the cost of installing double-glazed windows.[35]

Example 3

A clause allowed the maintenance trustee to recover costs associated with works necessary to maintain the building as a high class block of flats. This would go beyond repair but did not extend to the maintenance of the structure of the building. It covered things such as high speed lifts and air conditioning which would be unique to a high class block of flats.[36]

Example 4

A clause permitting the recovery of 'the cost of all other services which the lessor may, at its absolute discretion, provide or install ...' did not cover legal fees relating to an action against the tenants.[37]

Apportionment

2.33   In blocks of flats, most service charge clauses apportion the total expenditure of the landlord amongst the tenants. Service charges are only recoverable to the extent permitted under the lease, hence the apportionment between tenants is to be governed by the terms specified in the lease.

2.34   Typically a lease will apportion service charges in one of four ways:

(a) by floor area;
(b) by rateable value;
(c) by fixed proportions; or
(d) by a duty to pay a 'fair proportion' or words to that effect.

2.35   Apportionment by floor area or fixed proportions is unlikely to pose any significant difficulties. If the service charges are apportioned by

---

35 *Mullaney v Maybourne* [1986] 1 EGLR 70.
36 *Holding & Management Ltd v Property Holding & Investment Trust plc* [1989] 1 WLR 1313; [1990] 1 All ER 938.
37 *St Mary's Mansions v Limegate Investment* [2002] EWCA Civ 1491; [2003] HLR 24.

rateable value this means the rateable value from time to time, so that the tenant's proportion will vary according to any fluctuations in the relevant rateable value.[38] The rateable value is that at the date when the expense is incurred or paid.[39]

2.36   Where a lease obliges the tenant to pay a 'reasonable part' or a 'fair proportion' of the costs of works to a block of flats this may include a sum up to the total individual cost in respect of work in each tenant's property. For example, where a lease obliged a tenant to pay a reasonable part of the costs of works to a block of flats, and the landlord replaced all the windows, it was reasonable for the tenant to pay the whole cost of the landlord replacing the windows in the tenant's flat.[40]

2.37   The phrase 'due proportion' is usually taken to mean a reasonable or fair proportion of the relevant charges.[41]

2.38   It appears to be possible to argue that the method of apportioning service charges between tenants may make those charges unreasonable. For example where the charges were apportioned by surface area of each unit but the amount of work done on each unit varied widely; 'the inequity of the cost apportionment under the terms of the leases (was) an additional factor contributing to the unreasonableness of the (landlord's) course of action.' [42]

2.39   Where there has been an unexpected change in circumstances, the courts (and, one presumes, the LVT[43]) will make considerable efforts to ensure that a fair proportion is paid. For example, where a lease provided that the cost of heating was to be apportioned according to floor area, and the circumstances changed as a result of the installation of a new heating system which served a greater floor area, the Court of Appeal decided that a 'fair and reasonable' proportion should be paid with reference to the tenants use of the system and not according to floor area.[44]

---

38 *Moorcroft Estates v Doxford* (1979) 254 EG 871.

39 *Moorcroft Estates v Doxford* (1979) 254 EG 871.

40 *Sutton (Hastoe) Housing Association v Williams* (1988) 20 HLR 321; [1988] 1 EGLR 56.

41 *Hackney LBC v Thompson* [2001] L&TR 7.

42 *Re 18,56 & 66 Fenlake Road and 25 & 64 Christie Road, Bedford Stapleton and others v Bedford Pilgrims Housing Association* CAM/96/UT/SC/011 (LVT).

43 *Re Burlesden Court, East Cliff Road, Dawlish, Devon EX7 0BP* LVT/HA/00/10 (LVT) although see *Re 9 Grange Bunglows, London Road , South Mertsham, Surrey L82/99/SY* (LVT) for a case where the LVT declined to take this approach.

44 *Pole Properties v Feinberg* (1982) 43 P&CR 121; (1981) 259 EG 417.

Repairs and improvements[45]

2.40   Many leases permit a landlord to recover as a service charge the cost of any repairs done to the property, most private leases did not allow a landlord to recover for work done to improve the property that went beyond a mere repair. This distinction was always a difficult one to make as any repair will at the same time improve a property to some extent.[46]

2.41   While the distinction is no longer relevant for the purposes of the LVT's jurisdiction, it remains relevant to the construction of service charge provisions in a lease.

2.42   There is a considerable body of case law, in which the courts have emphasised that there is no single test to determine whether particular works are improvements or repairs. In practice it will be a question of fact and degree in each case. To the extent that any general principles can be gleaned from the authorities, the following would seem to be of some relevance:

2.43   In *McDougall v Easington*,[47] Mustill LJ canvassed a number of authorities and suggested three possible tests, 'which may be applied separately or concurrently as the circumstances of the individual case may demand':

> (i) whether the alterations went to the whole or substantially the whole of the structure or to only a subsidiary part;
> (ii) whether the effect of the alterations was to produce a building of a wholly different character from that which had been let;
> (iii) what was the cost of the works in relation to the previous value of the building, and what was their effect on the value and lifespan of the building?

Alternatively, one may ask 'is the repair so radical and extravagant as to amount to creating a new thing in place of what was there and not a mere replacement'.[48]

2.44   A useful example of the different outcomes that can be reached on superficially similar facts is provided by two cases on window-replacement: *Mullaney v Maybourne Grange (Croydon) Management Co Ltd*,[49] and *Minja Properties Ltd v Cussins Property Group plc*.[50] In

---

45 The authors are grateful to Ross Fentem for his assistance and comments on this point.

46 *Gibson Investments Ltd v Chesterton Plc* [2003] EWHC 1255; (2002) L&TR 32.

47 (1989) 58 P&CR 201, (1989) 21 HLR 310.

48 *Minja Properties Ltd v Cussins Property Group* [1998] 2 EGLR 52.

49 [1986] 1 EGLR 70.

50 Above, at note 48.

both cases, single-glazed windows were replaced with double-glazed ones. In *Mullaney*, the original windows were leaking water; in *Minja*, the original frames were rotten. However, the cost of installing double-glazing in *Mullaney* amounted to almost double the cost of installing windows similar to the original ones. This led Mr Jeffs QC to consider the work an improvement. By contrast, in *Minja*, Harman J reasoned that the cost of 'repairing' the rotten frames with frames that would take double-glazing was only trivially greater that installing frames to take single-glazing. So too, the subsequent installation of two panes of glass would only amount to a trivial increase in cost. Therefore, the proposed work amount to a repair.

Unfair terms

2.45 The Unfair Contract Terms Act 1977 does not apply to lease agreements.[51] However, it has been decided[52] that the Unfair Terms in Consumer Contract Regulations 1999, which implemented EU Directive 93/113/EEC, do apply to contracts in respect of interests in land. A full discussion of the regulations is beyond the scope of this work, however, it is now clear that all tenants, both of public authorities and private landlords, are entitled to the protection provided by the regulations.

2.46 The most important consequence of the regulations for our purposes, is that any term of a contract which is unfair (within the meaning of the regulations) is not binding on the consumer, in this case the tenant.[53] A tenant would therefore be able to argue that if a service charge were imposed by an unfair term of the lease, that service charge would not be payable.

2.47 The regulations also provide that where a term of a contract is capable of more than one interpretation, the interpretation most favourable to the consumer should be adopted.[54]

Management fees

2.48 In general terms the cost of employing a managing agent is not recoverable unless express provision is made for the same in the

---

51 *Granby Village (Manchester) Management Co Ltd v Unchained Growth plc* [2000] 1 WLR 739; August 1999 *Legal Action* 23.

52 *Newham LBC v Zeb* [2004] EWCA Civ 55; [2005] QB 37; [2004] 3 WLR 417.

53 Unfair Terms in Consumer Contracts Regulations (UTCCR) 1999 SI No 2083 reg 8(1).

54 UTCCR 1999 reg 7(2).

lease.[55] However, in cases where the landlord is a tenants' company, it may be possible to imply a term into the lease allowing for the recovery of such costs.[56]

2.49   There is nothing objectionable to a landlord managing a property through a connected company, but, in order to recover the costs of this management, the arrangement must be a genuine commercial agreement and not a sham.[57]

Contractual preconditions for recovery

2.50   The provision of a certificate from a surveyor or accountant is a common feature of modern residential leases. The certificate will usually give a definitive figure of the service charge expenditure and, in many cases, is a condition precedent for payment of those charges. Until the certificate is provided, the service charges are not payable.[58]

Statutory preconditions for recovery

Demands for service charges

2.51   A service charge demand must contain the name and address of the landlord and, if that address is not in England or Wales, an address in England or Wales where the tenant may serve notices on the landlord. The service charges are not payable until this information is provided.[59] This requirement does not apply to a manager appointed by the LVT.[60]

2.52   In addition, CLRA 2002 introduced additional specific requirements for service charge demands.[61]

Grant aided works

2.53   Where service charges have been incurred in respect of which a grant has been or is to be paid under the Housing Act 1985 s523, the

---

55 *Embassy Court Residents' Association v Lipman* (1984) 271 EG 545.
56 *Embassy Court Residents' Association v Lipman* (1984) 271 EG 545.
57 *Skilleter v Charles* (1991) 24 HLR 421; [1992] 1 EGLR 73.
58 *Finchbourne Limited v Rodrigues* [1976] 3 All ER 581; *CIN Properties Limited v Barclays Bank* [1986] 1 EGLR 59; *Rigby v Wheatley* LRX/84/2004 (Lands Tribunal).
59 LTA 1987 s47.
60 LTA 1987 s47(3).
61 See para 3.21.

Housing Grants, Construction and Regeneration Act 1996 Part 1 or the Regulatory Reform (Housing Assistance) (England and Wales) Order 2002 Art 3, the amount of the grant must be deducted from the costs and the amount of the service charge reduced accordingly.[62] The same applies in relation to external works under the Local Government and Housing Act 1989, where the landlord is an assisted participant in a group repair scheme.[63]

Stale service charges

2.54   Service charges must be demanded within 18 months of being incurred.[64] Alternatively, within the same 18-month period, the tenant must be notified in writing that the costs have been incurred and that he is required, under the terms of his lease, to contribute to them by the payment of a service charge.[65] Any such notice must state the nature of the works, the amount of the costs incurred and the proportion attributable to each tenant.[66] Failure to comply with these requirements means that the tenant is not liable to pay the service charges.[67]

2.55   Costs are incurred when they become payable by the landlord.[68]

2.56   These provisions have no application where:

(a) payments on account are made in respect of service charges;

(b) the actual expenditure does not exceed the payments on account and

(c) no further request for payment is made or needs to be made.[69]

They are similarly irrelevant where service charges are claimed as a charge for use an occupation (also known as 'mesne profits')[70] or where the costs have yet to be incurred.[71]

---

62 LTA 1985 s20A(1).

63 LTA 1985 s20A(2).

64 LTA 1985 s20B(1).

65 LTA 1985 s20B(2).

66 *Westminster City Council v Hammond*, 26 October 1995, Central London CC, HHJ Martin Reynolds; December 1995 *Legal Action* 19.

67 LTA 1985 s20B.

68 *Capital and Counties Freehold Equity Trust Ltd v BL plc* [1987] 2 EGLR 49; *Hyams and Anderson v Wilfred East Housing Co-operative Ltd* [2007] 3 EG 126; LRX/102/2005 (Lands Tribunal).

69 *Gilje v Charlesgrove Investments Ltd* [2003] EWHC 1284; [2003] 36 EG 110; July 2003 *Legal Action* 27.

70 *Mohammadi v Anston Investments Ltd* [2003] EWCA Civ 981; [2004] HLR 8.

71 *Islington LBC v Abdel-Malek* LRX/90/2006 (Lands Tribunal).

Limitation of service charges

2.57   The Limitation Act (LA) 1980 sets down a series of rules concerning the time within which proceedings must be issued in any given case. How these rules relate to applications to the LVT is unclear.

Does the Limitation Act 1980 apply?

2.58   There is nothing in the Limitation Act (LA) 1980 which expressly governs applications to the LVT. Nor is there any provision in the Landlord and Tenant Acts of 1985 and 1987, or CLRA 2002, which expressly restricts the period into which an LVT can enquire when determining whether service charges are payable or reasonable.

2.59   Despite this, it seems likely that LA 1980 will apply to restrict the compass of the LVT's enquiry. Applications to the Lands Tribunal have been found to be within the scope of LA 1980.[72] There is no reason why the LVT should be treated differently.

2.60   Prior to the enactment of CLRA 2002, and, in particular, prior to the extension of the LVTs jurisdiction under section 27A of that Act, the Court of Appeal had previously stated that LA 1980 was simply irrelevant to the considerations before the LVT.[73] In the light of the reforms introduced by the 2002 Act, this can no longer be regarded as good law.

What is the limitation period?

2.61   If the Limitation Act 1980 does not apply to the LVT, then there is no limitation period and parties can raise matters going back to the date that they became owners of the property.

2.62   However, on the assumption that LA 1980 does apply to applications to the LVT, there are several possible time limits which might apply. This question has recently been discussed by the LVT,[74] where the following possibilities were suggested. The application is:

(a) an application for recovery of a sum payable under an enactment.[75] This was rejected because the LVT quantifies a sum due under a lease, rather than ordering that a sum be paid under a statute;

---

72   *Hillingdon LBC v ARC Ltd* [1998] 3 WLR 754; [1998] 39 EG 202.
73   *R v London LVT ex p Daejan Properties Ltd* [2001] EWCA Civ 1095; [2002] HLR 2.
74   *Re 3, 12, 23, and 29 St Andrew's Square etc* LON/00AW/LSL/2003/0027 (LVT).
75   Limitation Act (LA) 1980 s9.

(b) an action founded on a simple contract (ie, not one made by a deed).[76] This might be applicable in respect of tenancies that were not made by deed. The LVT thought that this would not apply to applications brought by tenants (who are not seeking to recover under the lease) but only to actions for recovery of service charges by landlords;

(c) an action on a specialty (ie, a deed).[77] The LVT thought that this would not apply to a tenant, who is not trying to enforce their own covenant to pay service charges under the lease;

   (i) even if an action by a tenant were to be considered an action on a specialty, the tenant would be seeking to trigger a restitutionary remedy for money paid under a mistake. Time will only start running for such a purpose when the mistake was or could have been discovered with reasonable diligence;[78]

   (ii) by contrast an application by a landlord would be an action on a specialty, because it is the first step on the way to enforcing liabilities under the lease. Service charges which are reserved as rent may be different and are dealt with below;

(d) an action for the recovery of arrears of rent.[79] Where the landlord has brought an application under a lease for the recovery of service charges which are 'reserved' as rent, the limitation period would be six years from the date when payment first became due. This would have no application to an action begun by a tenant;

(e) an action by a beneficiary under a trust.[80] As explained below[81] service charges are normally held on trust[82] for the tenants. The LVT thought that this section of the Act would only apply where a landlord had misappropriated the service charge money for its own use. In such a case, no limitation period applies. This provision would not apply where the landlord had merely been unreasonable in their expenditure of the money, because it would be difficult to say that they had converted the service charge to their own use.

---

76 LA 1980 s5.

77 LA 1980 s8.

78 LA 1980 s32(1); *Kleinwort Benson Ltd v Lincoln City Council* [1999] 2 AC 153.

79 LA 1980 s19.

80 LA 1980 s21(1).

81 See para 2.84, below.

82 LTA 1987 s42.

2.63   After considering all these options the LVT held that an application by a tenant did not come under any provision of LA 1980. The consequence of which is that there is no statutory time limit for a tenant to bring an action. The landlord will have a limitation period of six or 12 years, depending on whether the service charges are reserved as rent.

2.64   In practice, regardless of any statutory limitation period, claims which cannot be supported by evidence are almost certain to fail. The further back in time that tenants seek to go, the harder it is likely to be to find sufficient evidence to support a challenge to service charges from those periods.

2.65   The LVT made it very clear in that it would not hesitate to use its power[83] to strike out as frivolous or vexatious or otherwise an abuse of process claims it would regard as being stale.[84]

An alternative view

2.66   It has previously been held that leasehold enfranchisement matters are 'actions on a specialty' and, hence, subject to a 12-year limitation period.[85] The point being (a) a claim based on an Act of Parliament is itself an action on a speciality and (b) the right to enfranchise is conferred by statute and has no parallel at common law.

2.67   The same logic can apply to service charge cases, It is unlikely that there is any common law requirement that service charges are required to be reasonable[86] and, in the absence of the statutory right to apply to the LVT, tenants would have no obvious remedy if faced with unreasonable service charge demands. The right both to make an application and the scope of that application arise solely out of statute is therefore apt to fall with LA 1980 s9, with a limitation period of 12 years.[87]

---

83   Leasehold Valuation Tribunals (Procedure) (England) Regulations 2003 SI No 2099 reg 11.

84   Although, in *R v London LVT ex p Daejan Properties Ltd*, above, note 73, the Court of Appeal disapproved of using procedural regulations in this manner.

85   *Collin v Duke of Westminster* [1985] 1 QB 581; [1985] 1 All ER 463.

86   See Nicholas Roberts 'Service Charges, *Daejan* and Claims in Restitution' Conv 2003, Sept/Oct 380–397; *Finchbourne Ltd v Rodrigues* [1976] 3 All ER 581, *Havenridge Ltd v Boston Dyers Ltd* [1994] 2 EGLR 73.

87   See Justin Bates and Francis Davey, 'Service charges and limitation periods – a timeless question', [2005] 8 JHL 3.

Equitable principles

2.68 Prior to the 2002 Act, the LVT's jurisdiction was limited to considering whether or not service charges were reasonably incurred and whether or not works were of a reasonable standard and so questions of equity could not arise. The Lands Tribunal has held that the effect of section 27A of the Landlord and Tenant Act (LTA) 1985 is that this is no longer the case.[88]

Set-off

2.69 Sometimes tenants wish to raise the fact that their landlord had breached a covenant under the lease, and, as a result of damages suffered by the tenants, their service charge liability ought to be reduced.

2.70 This could occur where the breach of covenant by the landlord is a breach of covenant to repair which has lead to an increased service charge bill or where the breach of covenant has caused other kinds of damage.

2.71 A set-off[89] is a situation where A has a liability to B and B has a closely connected liability to A, such that B can reduce his liability to A by the amount that A owes to B. A set-off is pleaded as a part of a defence in a civil claim.

2.72 For example, if a section of fence blows down and the landlord does not repair it immediately, considerable damage might then be caused by vandals breaking in and causing damage. If the landlord were to sue the tenant in a county court for failure to pay service charges, the tenant could set off the cost of the damage caused by the vandals against any service charges owed.

2.73 The Lands Tribunal has held that the effect of the 2002 reforms and the introduction of section 27A and the jurisdiction to consider the 'payability' of service charges has empowered the LVT to determine questions of set-off. Allegations of breach of covenant on the part of the landlord may be considered when determining the 'payability' of the service charges. Where the breaches of covenant give rise to a claim for damages, the LVT may determine these matters by way of an equitable set-off.[90]

---

88 *Continental Property Ventures v White and White* [2006] 1 EGLR 85; [2007] L&TR 4; LRX/60/2005 (Lands Tribunal). See also Justin Bates, 'Landlords beware of delays to repair', [2006] 168 PLJ 14.

89 Strictly speaking an equitable set-off.

90 See above, note 88.

Payment of service charges and compliance by the landlord with his covenants

2.74   A landlord faced with a set-off claim, such as that discussed above, may argue that any non-compliance with his covenants was due to the failure of the tenant to pay service charges. In addition, many leases contain terms which appear to make the provision of services and works conditional upon the payment of service charges.

2.75   It had previously been thought that there was no relationship between the two matters. Merely because a tenant was not paying service charges did not entitle a freeholder to stop providing services or doing necessary works.[91] This view reached a high point with the decision in *Yorkbrook Investments v Batten*[92] when the Court of Appeal held that, in all the circumstances of the case, it was not the intention of the parties that the lessee pay his full charges before the landlord complete his obligations.

2.76   However, the Court of Appeal has recently stepped back from this position. In *Bluestorm Ltd v Portvale Holdings Ltd*[93] it was tentatively suggested that *Yorkbrook* did not create any rule of law that a landlord must always complete his covenants, even if the tenant is in breach. There were two points to consider in each case:

(a) the contractual intentions of the parties when each lease was drawn up; and

(b) the 'pure principle of benefit and burden' which enabled the lease to define the scope of the benefits and burdens each party was subject to.

Other equitable principles?

2.77   Other equitable principles, such as waiver, estoppel and variation, are likely to be justiciable in the LVT on the same reasoning. Advisers should remind themselves of the Lands Tribunal's warning concerning the appropriateness of the LVT as a forum.[94]

---

91   *Marenco v Jacramel* (1964) 191 EG 433; *Francis v Cowcliffe* (1977) 33 P&CR 368.

92   (1986) 18 HLR 25; [1985] 2 EGLR 100.

93   [2004] HLR 49; [2004] 3 EGLR 38.

94   See para 2.21.

Reasonableness

2.78 Whether or not service charges are required to be reasonable at common law is unclear.[95] For most residential leases, the common law position is irrelevant. By LTA 1985 s19, service charges are only payable to the extent that they are reasonably incurred and, where they are incurred in respect of services or works, only if the services or works are of a reasonable standard.

2.79 No definition of 'reasonable standard' or 'reasonably incurred' is found in the legislation and there is no presumption either for or against reasonableness.[96] However, the following general principles have emerged:

- The fact that something is contemplated in the lease does not automatically make it reasonable to incur costs in respect of that item.[97]
- The fact that it is 'reasonable' to have a service provided does not automatically mean that the costs associated will be 'reasonably incurred'.[98]
- The requirement that costs be 'reasonably incurred' does not mean that the relevant expenditure must be the cheapest available. On the other hand, the landlord may not charge a figure that is grossly out of line with the market norm.[99]
- When examining the method of repair (or provision of services) chosen by the landlord, the level to be reimbursed by the tenant will be assessed with reference to whether the landlord would have chosen this method of repair (or provision of services), if he were to bear the costs himself.[100]
- It follows from this that the correct perspective when examining the question of reasonableness is that of the landlord.[101]

---

95 See Nicholas Roberts 'Service Charges, *Daejan* and Claims in Restitution' Conv 2003, Sept/Oct 380–397; *Finchbourne Ltd v Rodrigues* [1976] 3 All ER 581; *Havenridge Ltd v Boston Dyers Ltd* [1994] 2 EGLR 73.

96 *Yorkbrook Investments v Batten* (1986) 18 HLR 25; [1985] 2 EGLR 100.

97 *Veena SA v Cheong* [2003] 1 EGLR 175. The fact that a porter for a block of flats was contemplated in a lease did not mean that a full time porter, as opposed to a part time porter, was reasonable.

98 *Veena SA v Cheong* [2003] 1 EGLR 175. While it may be reasonable to have a cleaner provided for a block of flats, that will not necessarily mean that the particular cleaner in question represents costs 'reasonably incurred'.

99 *Forcelux v Sweetman* [2001] 2 EGLR 173.

100 *Hyde Housing v George Williams* LRX/53/1999 (Lands Tribunal).

101 *Forcelux v Sweetman*, above, note 99.

- The fact that tenants may suggest that they could, acting individually, provide services cheaper than those provided by the landlord, is irrelevant. Landlords are entitled to use qualified personnel and any comparisons by the tenant must be on a 'like for like' basis.[102]
- The fact that the landlord has adopted an appropriate procedure for incurring the costs does not mean that the costs will be reasonably incurred if they are in excess of an appropriate market rate.[103]
- The fact that tenants have a time limited interest in the property is a material factor when considering 'reasonableness'.[104]
- Where services are not provided to a reasonable standard, then a deduction on account of the deficiency may be made and it need not be the case that the whole of a relevant item be disallowed.[105]
- The nature and location of the property is a relevant consideration as to what level of services is reasonable, with a luxury block in Mayfair having different demands to a converted house on the Old Kent Road.[106]
- Actions taken pursuant to legal advice are likely to be reasonable. Conversely, failing to take relevant legal advice is evidence of unreasonableness.[107]
- Where it is possible for works to be done at no charge to the tenant (eg, under a guarantee) to carry out works at a cost to the tenant will render the whole of those costs unreasonable unless there is some good reason to do so.[108]
- It is irrelevant whether or not the tenant will benefit from the works, so long as he is obliged to pay for them under his lease.[109]

---

102 *Colney Hatch Court Ltd v Sen* LON/00AC/LSC/2003/0006; *A2 Airways Housing Group v Taylor and others* LRX/36/2006 (Lands Tribunal).

103 *Forcelux v Sweetman*, above, note 99.

104 A tenant with a three-year lease could not be required to pay for roof replacement works which would fulfil the landlord's repairing obligations over 20 years or more when such works were not necessary to fulfil the obligations over the shorter period of the tenant's lease: *Scottish Mutual Assurance Plc v Jardine Public Relations* [1999] EGCS 43.

105 *Yorkbrook Investments v Batten*, above, note 96.

106 *Veena SA v Cheong*, above, note 97.

107 *Fernandez v Shanterton Second Management Company Ltd* LRX/153/2006 (Lands Tribunal).

108 *Continental Property Ventures v White*, above, note 90.

109 *Broomleigh Housing Association v Hughes* (1999) EGCS 143, *Billson v Tristrem* [2000] L&TR 220.

Insurance

2.80 The following situations are a common cause of confusion:

(a) the landlord is required under the terms of the lease to insure the property and is permitted to recover the cost of insurance from the tenant; and

(b) the tenants are required to insure but only with an insurer selected by the landlord.

2.81 In the first case, the insurance premiums form part of the service charge and may be challenged as set out above. In the second case, the premium payments are not service charges and the tenants' only recourse is to challenge the landlord's choice of insurer.[110]

2.82 The two situations can be difficult to distinguish in practice, but the lease should make it clear whether the obligation to insure is on the landlord or the tenant.

2.83 Landlords are often paid large commissions for selecting particular insurers, who then recover the cost of the commission via higher premium payments which will ultimately be borne by the tenants. A distinction should be drawn between commissions which are, in effect, payments to the landlord for providing a service on behalf of the insurance company, and simple profit-making.[111] The former can be kept by the landlord but the latter should be credited to the leaseholders. The landlord should not recover more than the net amount of the insurance premium.[112]

Holding service charges

2.84 A landlord holds monies paid for service charges on trust for the tenants.[113] This includes interest and any investments representing those monies paid in respect of service charges.[114] A common example will be a sinking or reserve fund, although these provisions apply to all service charges.

2.85 There are two particularly significant implications of this:

(a) the money is safe from creditors in the event that the landlord become bankrupt or otherwise insolvent;

---

110 See chapter 5.
111 *Williams v Southwark LBC* (2001) 33 HLR 22.
112 *Peile v Executors of WAC Maidman* LVT/SC/010/98 (LVT).
113 LTA 1987 s42.
114 LTA 1987 s42(2).

(b) the landlord and their agent are subject to the ordinary duties of trustees in relation to the monies held and will be liable for breach of trust if the money is misappropriated or not adequately safeguarded or invested.

2.86   The landlord may hold the monies in one or more funds.[115] The money is held on trust to defray service charges in respect of which they were demanded and then for the current tenants.[116] Any terms which are inconsistent with these provisions are of no effect.[117]

2.87   These provisions do not apply to any exempt landlord. An exempt landlord is:[118]

(a) a district, county, county borough or London borough council;
(b) the Common Council of the City of London;
(c) the London Fire and Emergency Planning Authority;
(d) the Council of the Isles of Scilly;
(e) a police authority;
(f) a joint authority;
(g) the Commission for New Towns;
(h) a development corporation;
(i) an urban development corporation;
(j) a housing action trust;
(k) the Broads Authority;
(l) a National Park Authority;
(m) the Housing Corporation;
(n) a housing trust which is a charity;
(o) a registered social landlord;
(p) a fully mutual housing association;
(q) a joint waste authority.

Investment of trust funds

2.88   If the landlord wishes to invest the service charge monies, he may do so only:[119]

(a) with the Bank of England;
(b) with a UK-based deposit-taking business in an account which will yield interest;

115 LTA 1987 s42(2).
116 LTA 1987 s42(3).
117 LTA 1987 s42(9).
118 LTA 1987 s58(1).
119 LTA 1987 s42(5); Service Charge Contributions (Authorised Investments) Order 1988 SI No 1284.

(c) with a building society account which will yield interest; or

(d) in building society shares.

Termination of the lease

2.89   Unless the lease provides to the contrary,[120] tenants are deemed to be entitled to a share of the service charge fund which is proportionate to their liabilities to pay service charges.[121] However, the termination of a lease does not entitle a tenant to receive any part of the trust fund[122] unless there are no remaining tenants, in which case the fund shall be retained by the landlord.[123]

2.90   While LTA 1987 s42 makes detailed provision for the distribution of the funds in the event that the leasehold interests all come to an end, there is no provision made at all in respect of what should happen if the freehold is transferred. In particular, there is no obligation on a landlord to transfer the trust fund to the purchaser upon a sale of the revision.[124]

2.91   Disputes in relation to these provisions are dealt with by the county court, rather than the LVT.[125]

Commonhold and Leasehold Reform Act 2002 reforms

2.92   The Commonhold and Leasehold Reform Act 2002 makes some radical changes to the regime outlined above. At the time of writing, these provisions are only in force for the purposes of allowing subordinate regulations to be made.

2.93   It appears unlikely that the government will ever bring them into force in their current form. The consultation paper '*Commonhold and Leasehold Reform Act 2002 – a consultation paper on regular statements of account and designated client accounts*' [126] stated that the government was considering further amendment to the 2002 reforms before bringing them into force.

---

120 LTA 1987 s42(8).

121 LTA 1987 s42(4).

122 LTA 1987 s42(6).

123 LTA 1987 s42(7).

124 Presumably the tenants could apply under the rule in *Saunders v Vantier* (1841) 1 Beav 115, put an end to the trust and distribute the assets between them.

125 LTA 1987 s52(2).

126 Department of Communities and Local Government, June 2007, available at www.communities.gov.uk/documents/corporate/pdf/regular-statements

2.94   As things currently stand, the 2002 Act would introduce section 42A into LTA 1987. Service charges would continue to be held on trust, but would now be held in an 'authorised account'.[127] This would be an account held with a specific financial services provider. The landlord must have informed the financial service provider that the payments are being held on trust for the purposes of paying service charges and must hold no other monies in the account.[128]

2.95   Tenants would have the right to withhold payments where they had reasonable grounds for believing that the landlord was not holding the monies in an authorised account.[129] A new power to inspect relevant documents related to the trust account would also be introduced.[130]

127 LTA 1987 s42A(1).
128 LTA 1987 s42A(2).
129 LTA 1987 s42A(9).
130 LTA 1987 s42A(3).

CHAPTER 3

Tenants' rights to information

3.1	**Introduction**
3.5	**Advice to tenants**
3.9	**General information and rights**
3.10	Disclosure of landlord's identity
3.14	Change of landlord
3.17	Demands for service charges
3.19	Address for service
3.21	**Summary of rights and obligations**
3.30	**Summaries of costs**
3.31	Accounting periods
3.35	What a summary must contain
3.41	Certification of the summary
3.42	Request for a summary of costs by a Recognised Tenants' Association
3.44	Qualified accountants
3.46	Supporting accounts
3.48	Penalties for failure to provide summaries of cost, etc
3.50	**Statements of account**
3.53	**Management audit**
3.66	**Recognised Tenants' Associations**

continued

3.66   Appointment of a surveyor

3.69   Consultation on managing agents

Key points

- Tenants have rights to information about their service charges.
- At the moment tenants can demand a summary of relevant costs from their landlord.
- A summary must be broken down into 12-month 'accounting periods'. This must contain information about the cost of works done or to be done, how this is to be paid for and the balance of the tenants' service charge accounts. In some cases it must be certified by an accountant.
- Tenants may already request a 'management audit' whereby an auditor is empowered to inspect the landlord's financial accounts relating to the property.
- Recognised Tenants' Associations have additional powers of consultation, especially in relation to managing agents and can appoint a surveyor whose powers are similar to those of an auditor under a management audit.
- The landlord must provide the following information when asked: the name and address of the landlord; if the landlord is a corporation, the names and addresses of the directors and company secretary.
- If the landlord changes, the new landlord must inform the tenants of this fact.

Introduction

3.1   The Landlord and Tenant Act (LTA) 1985 gives tenants certain rights to obtain information from and about their landlord. The most important of these empower tenants to obtain information about the basis of their service charge bills and to inspect documents on which those bills are based.

3.2   The intention was that the reforms contained in the Commonhold and Leasehold Reform Act (CLRA) 2002 would strengthen these rights, but pressure from a number of groups, in particular housing associations, has led the government to consider altering the proposed reforms. This will be discussed more fully at the end of this chapter.

3.3   Except where otherwise noted, the rights described in this chapter may be exercised by any tenant who is required to pay service charges and would be able to challenge those service charges in an LVT.[1]

3.4   The principal defects of the existing system are that:

(a) it requires the tenant to be aware of the right and to be proactive about seeking the information;

(b) the landlord may delay giving the information for some time after the end of the relevant accounting period which means that a tenant may have already paid for a service charge before they have sufficient information to know whether it might be reasonable; and

(c) enforcement requires a criminal prosecution, something that will be beyond the capacity of most tenants. Though a local authority can bring such a prosecution they have no duty to do so and are likely to be unwilling to spend time and money on a private dispute. If the landlord is a local authority, there is not even the sanction of a criminal prosecution to enforce compliance.

Advice to tenants

3.5   Information is the key to all leasehold disputes, whether because of a desire to challenge the service charges or simply in order to make an informed decision about whether to attempt to exercise the right to manage.

3.6   The vast majority of leases will confer very few, if any, rights to information about the landlord's activities. The statutory rights are particularly important.

3.7   While failure by a landlord to comply with a number of the obligations dealt with in this chapter is often a criminal offence, a private prosecution is not usually a realistic option. It is exceptionally unlikely that the police will intervene in such disputes. Far more use is the right to withhold service charges until certain information is received.

3.8   Alternatively, serious consideration should be given to forming a Recognised Tenants' Association (RTA) and exercising the right to a management audit or the appointment of a surveyor. The involvement of an external professional is often an effective way of persuading a recalcitrant landlord to provide information.

---

1   See para 2.22.

General information and rights

3.9 There is a certain minimum amount of information which must be made available to all tenants. Failure to comply with these provisions without a reasonable excuse is a summary offence punishable by a fine.[2] While tenants are entitled to bring private prosecutions[3] it is more common for the local housing authority to do so.[4]

Disclosure of landlord's identity

3.10 All tenants have right to know their landlord's identity.[5] A tenant may make a written request asking for the landlord's name and address, which may be made to anyone who demands, or the last person who received, any rent payable, or to anyone acting as agent for the landlord.[6]

3.11 That person must then supply a written statement of the landlord's name and address within 21 days from receipt of the request.[7]

3.12 If, after a successful request for the landlord's name and address, a tenant discovers that the landlord is a corporation, he or she may make a request in writing for the name and address of every director and the secretary (if any) of the corporation.[8]

3.13 Such a request may be made to any person who demands rent (but not anyone who has merely received it) or is acting as agent of the landlord.[9] Within 21 days of receiving the request that person must respond with the relevant names or addresses.[10]

Change of landlord

3.14 If the landlord sells their interest in the property to a new landlord, the new landlord has a duty to give notice of this in writing to the tenant within two months or on the next day that rent is payable, whichever is the later.[11]

---

2 Landlord and Tenant Act (LTA) 1985 ss 1(2), 2(4), 3(3) and 3A(3).
3 See for example *Taber v Macdonald* (1999) 31 HLR 73.
4 LTA 1985 s34.
5 LTA 1985 s1.
6 LTA 1985 s1(1).
7 LTA 1985 s1(1).
8 LTA 1985 s2(1).
9 LTA 1985 s2(3).
10 LTA 1985 s2(2).
11 LTA 1985 s3(1).

3.15   Such a notice should indicate the new landlord's name and address.[12]

3.16   A former landlord will still be liable under any covenants in the lease until they have given the tenant notice in writing of the new landlord's name and last-known address; or the new landlord has informed the tenant of its name and current address.[13]

Demands for service charges

3.17   Any written demand for rent or service charges must contain the name and address of the landlord.[14] If the landlord's address is outside England and Wales, the demand must also contain an address that is within England and Wales where notices – such as notices in proceedings – may be served.[15]

3.18   If such a demand does not contain the landlord's address and (where required) an address for service, the services charges demanded are not due until that information is supplied.[16]

Address for service

3.19   A landlord must also provide the tenant with an address in England and Wales at which notices may be served on him by the tenant.[17] Failure to do so entitles the tenant to withhold payment of service charges, rent or administration charges.[18]

3.20   This provision does not apply if a manager or receiver has been appointed for the property by any court or tribunal.[19]

Summary of rights and obligations

3.21   A demand for payment of service or administration charges must be accompanied by a summary of the rights and obligations of tenants of dwellings in relation to them.[20]

12 LTA 1985 s3(1).
13 LTA 1985 s3(3A).
14 LTA 1987 s47(1)(a).
15 LTA 1987 s47(1)(b).
16 LTA 1987 s47(2).
17 LTA 1987 s48(1).
18 LTA 1987 s48(2).
19 LTA 1987 s48(3).
20 LTA 1985 s21B (service charges), CLRA 2002 Sch 11 para 4 (administration charges).

3.22   This requirement applies to any demand for service charges served on or after 1 October 2007 (in England) or 30 November 2007 (in Wales) and to any administration charges payable on or after 30 September 2003 (in England) and 31 March 2004 (in Wales).[21]

3.23   The form of summary is prescribed for both forms of charge.[22] The summary must be printed or typewritten in a font no smaller than 10 point.[23]

3.24   A combined demand for service and administration charges must be accompanied by both summaries.

3.25   The forms prescribed in Wales are identical in content to those prescribed in England but must be provided in English and Welsh.

3.26   A tenant who has received a demand which does not contain such a summary may withhold payment.[24] Any provisions of the lease relating to non-payment or late payment have no effect during the period that the tenant withholds service charges.[25]

3.27   There is no provision for a landlord to ask an LVT to dispense with this requirement, if a tenant is validly withholding service charges the only recourse for the landlord is to serve another demand this time with an accompanying summary.

3.28   Where a demand for service charges is served before the relevant date, but a subsequent demand is served after that date, the subsequent demand will only have to be accompanied by a summary of rights and obligations if it refers to service charges due on or after the relevant date.[26]

---

21 Commonhold and Leasehold Reform Act 2002 (Commencement No 2 and Savings) (England) Order 2003 SI No 1986; Commonhold and Leasehold Reform Act 2002 (Commencement No 2 and Savings) (Wales) Order 2004 SI No 669; Commonhold and Leasehold Reform Act 2002 (Commencement No 6) (England) Order 2007 SI No 1256; Commonhold and Leasehold Reform Act 2002 (Commencement No 4) (Wales) Order 2007 SI No 3161.

22 By the Service Charges (Summary of Rights and Obligations, and Transitional Provision) (England) Regulations 2007 SI No 1257, Service Charges (Summary of Rights and Obligations, and Transitional Provisions)(Wales) Regulations 2007 SI No 3160, Administration Charges (Summary of Rights and Obligations) (England) Regulations 2007 SI No 1258, and Administration Charges (Summary of Rights and Obligations) (Wales) Regulations 2007 SI No 3162 respectively.

23 Ibid, reg 3 in all cases.

24 LTA 1985 s21B(3) (service charges), CLRA 2002 Sch 11 para 4(3) (administration charges).

25 LTA 1985 s21B(4) (service charges), CLRA 2002 Sch 11 para 4(4) (administration charges).

26 Above, note 22, reg 4 in all cases.

3.29   Local authorities, National Park Authorities, new town corporations and all leases which are not long leases are not included in the scope of these provisions.[27]

Summaries of costs

3.30   It is often difficult to know, when faced with a service charge bill, on what basis it has been calculated. In particular it is rarely clear what sums have been invoiced to the landlord and what sums have been paid out. Without this information a tenant is in a poor position to challenge the service charges before an LVT.[28]

Accounting periods

3.31   A tenant may request in writing that their landlord supply them with a 'summary of relevant costs' for the previous 'accounting period'.[29] An accounting period is 12 months long.[30] If the service charge accounts are made up in 12-month periods then the previous accounting period will be the one that last ended before the request was made.[31]

3.32   If the service charge accounts are made up in periods not of 12 months then the relevant accounts will be for the 12-month period ending on the date of the request.[32]

3.33   For example, if the landlord makes up service charge accounts in two six-month periods being January to June and July to December and a tenant makes a request for a summary of costs on 20 September 2004 the accounting period for the purposes of the act will run from 21 September 2003 until 20 September 2004. The landlord would therefore have to adapt their own accounts to give a summary of this period.

3.34   The summary of costs will summarise the costs that were incurred and were then payable by or demanded from the tenant.[33]

27 Above, note 22, reg 2 in all cases.
28 See Akah-Douglas, 'Service charges: applicant's failure to comply with LVT's directions – power to dismiss' (2007) 11 L & T Rev 189 for a discussion of the problem.
29 LTA 1985 s21.
30 LTA 1985 s21(1).
31 LTA 1985 s21(1)(a).
32 LTA 1985 s21(1)(b).
33 LTA 1985 s21(1).

Any cost, part or all of which has been, or will be, passed on to the tenant as part of their service charge bill, must be included in the summary.[34] The focus is on cost to the landlord rather than amount payable by the tenant.

What a summary must contain

3.35   The summary must include:[35]

(a) a statement of any works in respect of which various grants of public money have been or are to be paid;

(b) details of how the costs have been or will be reflected in demands for service charges;

(c) a summary of whether any demands for payment have been made in respect of any of the costs (for example, as invoices from contractors) and if so whether any money has been paid;

(d) the total amount of money received by the landlord up to the end of the accounting period in respect of 'relevant dwellings' that is still standing to the credit of those tenants (ie, surplus money that has not yet been spent on relevant costs).

3.36   Item (d) is obscure. 'Relevant dwellings' are defined as the dwelling belonging to the person asking for the summary and the dwelling belonging to 'a person whose obligations under the terms of his or her lease as regards contributing to relevant costs relate to the same costs'.[36] Here it is unclear whether 'relate to the same costs', means identical costs, or that the tenants of the dwellings contribute to some of the same costs.

3.37   This ambiguity is illustrated by the following example. Consider a small development consisting of two blocks, A and B, each of two flats. The leases of the flats require that the tenants contribute to the costs of their block and to the costs of a shared garden. Block A is larger and has higher upkeep costs than block B. The landlord will be required to keep three separate trust funds, one for block A, one for block B and one for the garden. If a tenant in block B asks for a summary of relevant costs, are all the flats 'relevant dwellings', or are only the flats in block B?

3.38   In the first interpretation the tenant would be supplied with a single figure showing the aggregate of all the money standing to the

---

34   LTA 1985 s21(5).

35   LTA 1985 s21(5).

36   LTA 1985 s21(5A).

credit of tenants in both blocks. This could be quite misleading as
the block A fund has nothing to do with their service charges.

3.39   The second interpretation is no more helpful because it omits any
payments made by tenants of block A in respect of the garden.

3.40   Neither interpretation seems to be useful and both conflict with
the manner in which service charges are held on trust. This is unfortunate as an obligation to state the amount standing to the credit
of each trust fund would be much more useful.

Certification of the summary

3.41   If there are more than four relevant dwellings, in order for the summary to be valid a qualified accountant[37] must have certified that the
summary is a fair summary complying with the requirements set
out above and being sufficiently supported by accounts, receipts and
other documents produced to them.[38]

Request for a summary of costs by a Recognised Tenants' Association

3.42   A request for a summary of costs may be made by the secretary of
a Recognised Tenants' Association that represents the tenant. The
summary should then be supplied to the secretary of the tenant's
association.[39] The request may also be served on an agent of the landlord or a person who receives rent on behalf of the landlord, who
must then forward it as soon as possible to the landlord.[40]

3.43   The landlord must comply with the request within six months of
the end of the relevant accounting period or within one month of the
request whichever is the later.[41]

Qualified accountants

3.44   For the purposes of certifying summaries of cost a qualified accountant is someone who is eligible for appointment as a company auditor
under the Companies Act 1989 s25.[42] They must *not* be:

---

37 See para 3.44 below.
38 LTA 1985 s21(6).
39 LTA 1985 s21(2).
40 LTA 1985 s21(3).
41 LTA 1985 s21(4).
42 LTA 1985 s28(2).

(a) an officer, employee or partner of the landlord or, where the landlord is a company, of an associated company;[43]

(b) a partner or employee of any such officer or employee;[44]

(c) a managing agent of the landlord for any premises to which any of the costs covered by the summary in question relate or the statement of account relates;[45] or

(d) an employee or partner of any such agent.[46]

3.45 Where the landlord is one of the following public authorities:

(a) a local authority;

(b) a new town corporation;

(c) a National Park Authority; or

(d) an emanation of the Crown;

then the qualified accountant may be an officer or employee of the landlord and may be a member of the Chartered Institute of Public finance and Accountancy.[47]

Supporting accounts

3.46 Once a summary of relevant costs has been received (even if it has not been demanded under LTA 1987 s21(1)) by a tenant or secretary of a recognised tenants' association, the recipient may, within six months of receiving the summary, make a request in writing to the landlord to afford them facilities to inspect the accounts, receipts and other supporting documents and to take copies or extracts from them.[48]

3.47 The facilities for inspection must be made available within one month of the request being made and must be made available for at least two months.[49] No charge may be made for the inspection of documents[50] though a reasonable charge may be made for the taking of copies or extracts.[51] There is nothing to stop the landlord recovering the cost of making documents available for inspection as part of the service charge bill provided that the lease would allow them to do so.[52]

---

43 LTA 1985 s28(4)(b).
44 LTA 1985 s28(4)(c).
45 LTA 1985 s28(4)(d).
46 LTA 1985 s28(4)(e).
47 LTA 1985 s28(6).
48 LTA 1985 s22(2).
49 LTA 1985 s22(4).
50 LTA 1985 s22(5)(a).
51 LTA 1985 s22(5)(b).
52 LTA 1985 s22(6).

Penalties for failure to provide summaries of cost, etc

3.48   Failure to provide a summary of relevant costs, or access to supporting accounts is a summary offence, punishable by a fine on level 4 of the standard scale.[53] It is not an abuse of process to prosecute a landlord who fails to provide some of the information in a summary of costs, although a trivial failure may lead the court to impose no penalty[54] but it is not an offence for a landlord to fail to provide a document they do not have.[55]

3.49   A landlord has a defence of reasonable excuse.[56] For example, if there were a binding arbitration clause, it might be reasonable for a landlord to fail to fully comply with a request for supporting accounts where it would be open to the tenant to take any dispute with the landlord to arbitration.[57]

Statements of account

3.50   CLRA 2002 proposed a number of reforms. Section 21 was to be repealed and re-enacted so as to introduce the concept of a 'statement of account'.[58]

3.51   The key points of the new section 21 would be:

(a) To place the onus on the landlord to provide a statement of account, which would be in much the same form as the existing summary of information, whether or not it is requested by the tenant.

(b) The statement of account would have to be provided within six months of the end of the accounting period to which it related.

(c) If a landlord were to fail to comply with their accounting obligations, a tenant would be able to withhold paying a relevant part of their service charges until the landlord did comply.

3.52   The government announced in 2005[59] that they would not be implementing the provisions as set out in CLRA 2002. A consultation paper

---

53   LTA 1985 s25.

54   *R v Marylebone Magistrates' Court ex p Westminster Council* [1999] JHL D51, QBD.

55   *Taber v Macdonald* (1999) 31 HLR 73.

56   LTA 1985 s25.

57   *R v Marylebone Magistrates' Court ex p Westminster Council* [1999] JHL D51, QBD.

58   CLRA 2002 s152.

59   *Accounting for Service Charge Monies: the Way Forward*, ODPM news release 005/0156, 29 July 2005. Available at Government News Network (www.gnn.gov.uk) reference: 118995P.

was published in July 2007[60] proposing a revised set of accounting provisions. The result of that consultation has not yet been published.

Management audit

3.53   In certain circumstances,[61] tenants may appoint an auditor to conduct what is called a 'management audit'. The purpose of any audit is to ascertain whether the landlord's obligations to the tenants, including his management obligations, are being discharged effectively and efficiently.[62]

3.54   A management audit must be requested by a minimum number of 'qualifying tenants' – the number depending on the number of dwellings in the 'qualifying premises'. Where there are only two dwellings either or both tenants may request a management audit.[63] If there are more than two dwellings at least two thirds of the tenants must make a request.[64]

3.55   A 'qualifying tenant' is a tenant of a dwelling under a long lease that is not a business lease.[65] Each dwelling may have at most one qualifying tenant.[66] If a dwelling is sub-let on a long lease the superior tenant is not a qualifying tenant.[67] If a dwelling is leased to more than one person jointly they are treated as being jointly the qualifying tenant.[68]

3.56   The auditor, who must not be a tenant, must either be a qualified accountant[69] or a qualified surveyor.[70] A qualified surveyor is a fellow or professional associate of either the Royal Institution of Chartered Surveyors or the Incorporated Society of Valuers and Auctioneers.[71]

60 *Commonhold and Leasehold Reform Act 2002 – A Consultation Paper on Regular Statements of Account and Designated Client Accounts* (07 HC 04774). Available at www.communities.gov.uk
61 Leasehold Reform, Housing and Urban Development Act (LRHUDA)1993 ss76–84.
62 LRHUDA 1993 s78(1).
63 LRHUDA 1993 s76(2)(a).
64 LRHUDA 1993 s76(2)(b).
65 LRHUDA 1993 s77(1).
66 LRHUDA 1993 s77(3).
67 LRHUDA 1993 s77(4)(a).
68 LRHUDA 1993 s77(4)(b).
69 See para 3.44 above.
70 LRHUDA 1993 s78(4).
71 LRHUDA 1993 s78(5).

An auditor may appoint any person to assist them with carrying out the audit.[72]

3.57   The auditor is entitled to the following information and assistance:[73]

(a) a summary of costs;[74]
(b) reasonable facilities for inspecting, copying or taking extracts from the accounts, receipts and other documents supporting the summary; and
(c) reasonable facilities for inspecting copying or taking extracts from any other document which is reasonably required by him.

He is also entitled to inspect the premises.[75]

3.58   If the relevant provisions of CLRA 2002[76] relating to statements of account[77] are brought into force, the auditors powers will be extended accordingly

3.59   In order to exercise the right to have a management audit, the auditor must give a notice to the landlord, which must be signed by all those tenants who are requesting the audit.[78] The notice must:[79]

(a) state the name and address of each tenant;
(b) state the name and address of the auditor;
(c) identify the documents which the auditor requires to inspect, or copies of which the auditor requires; and
(d) if the auditor is proposing to carry out an inspection of the common parts, state a date, which must be between one and two months from the date of giving notice, on which the auditor will be making the inspection.

3.60   Such a notice is duly given to a landlord if it is given to a person who receives rent on behalf of the landlord. Such a person must forward the notice immediately to the landlord.[80]

3.61   The landlord may respond by sending copies of requested documents, or affording facilities for their inspection or copying (as the case may be) or the landlord may give a notice objecting to the supply

---

72 LRHUDA 1993 s78(6).
73 LRHUDA 1993 s79(2).
74 As provided for by LTA 1985 s21, see para 3.30 above.
75 LRHUDA 1993 s79(4).
76 CLRA 2002 s157; Sch 10 paras 16(1),(3), on a date to be appointed.
77 See para 3.50 above.
78 LRHUDA 1993 s80(2).
79 LRHUDA 1993 s80(3).
80 LRHUDA 1993 s80(5).

of documents, giving reasons for the objection.[81] The landlord may also either approve the date for the proposed inspection by the auditor, or propose an alternative date, which must not be later than two months from the date of the notice.[82]

3.62   Where within two months of a notice, the landlord or any other person has failed to comply with any of its requirements,[83] an application may be made to a court for an order requiring compliance. Such an application must be made within four months of the date of the notice.[84]

Recognised Tenants' Associations

3.63   A Recognised Tenants' Association (RTA) may act on its own behalf in requesting information from a landlord and has (at present) a number of additional rights in respect of consultation.

3.64   A tenants' association only becomes recognised if:[85]

(a) a written notice to this effect is given by the landlord to the secretary of the association; or

(b) a certificate to this effect is given by the local Rent Assessment Committee.

A landlord may rescind a notice of recognition giving a minimum of six months' notice.[86] Any member of the Rent Assessment Committee panel may cancel a certificate.[87]

3.65   Though the Secretary of State has a power to regulate the granting of certificates recognising an RTA no such regulations have been made.[88] In practice the panels seem to be willing to recognise any properly constituted association. Appendix C sets out the process for the creation of an RTA.

Appointment of a surveyor

3.66   The Housing Act 1996 s84 empowers a RTA to appoint a surveyor, who must be a qualified surveyor in the same sense as for a management

81 LRHUDA 1993 s81(1).
82 LRHUDA 1993 s81(1)(c).
83 LRHUDA 1993 s81(6).
84 LRHUDA 1993 s81(7).
85 LTA 1985 s29(1).
86 LTA 1985 s29(2).
87 LTA 1985 s29(3).
88 LTA 1985 s29(5).

audit.[89] The rights and powers of a surveyor are similar to that of an auditor appointed under the right to a management audit and are set out in Housing Act 1996 Sch 4.

3.67   The appointment of a surveyor is straightforward and may be done by giving the landlord (or any person who receives rent on his behalf[90]) notice in writing.[91]

3.68   The surveyor ceases to be appointed if either the RTA gives the landlord notice to that effect or the RTA ceases to exist (which presumably encompasses an RTA that ceases to be recognised even if the association continues).[92]

Consultation on managing agents

3.69   Recognised Tenants' Associations have the right to be consulted about managing agents.[93]

3.70   The association may, at any time, serve a notice on the landlord requesting him to consult the association in relation to the appointment or employment of a managing agent.[94]

3.71   If such an agent is employed, the landlord must, within a month of service of the notice, reply by service of a further notice on the association specifying the obligations which the manager discharges on his behalf and allowing a reasonable period for the association to comment on the manner in which the managing agent has been discharging the obligations and the desirability of this continuing.[95]

3.72   If no such agent is employed when the notice is served, the landlord must – before employing any managing agent at any future stage – serve a notice setting out the name of the proposed managing agent, the obligations he proposes to have the agent discharge and allowing a period of at least one month for the association to make observations on the appointment.[96]

3.73   In either case, once the initial notice has been served, the landlord must – at least once every five years – serve on the association a notice specifying any changes which have occurred since the date of the last notice served on him by the association and allow the asso-

---

89 See para 3.56 above.
90 Housing Act (HA) 1996 s84(5).
91 HA1996 s84(3).
92 HA 1996 s84(4).
93 LTA 1985 s30B.
94 LTA 1985 s30B(1).
95 LTA 1985 s30B(3)
96 LTA 1985 s30B(2).

ciation a reasonable period to comment on the manner in which the managing agent has discharged his obligations and the desirability of him continuing to do so.[97] He must also serve on the association the name and proposed duties of any new managing agent and allow a period of not less than one month for comments.[98]

3.74   The residents association may release the landlord from these obligations at any stage by serving a notice on him to this effect.[99]

3.75   Any consultation obligations cease if the property becomes vested in a new landlord, although they may be reasserted in the manner set out above.[100]

---

97 LTA 1985 s30B(4)(a).
98 LTA 1985 s30B(4)(b).
99 LTA 1985 s30B(5).
100 LTA 1985 s30B(6).

CHAPTER 4

Consultation on service charges

4.1	**Introduction**
4.6	**Advice for tenants**
4.7	**Old consultation requirements**
4.7	Applicability
4.9	Costs threshold
4.11	Consultation procedure under the old rules
	Urgent work exception • *What is an estimate?*
4.19	**New consultation requirements**
4.24	Cost thresholds
4.26	Accounting periods
4.33	Relevant periods
4.34	Inspection of information
4.36	Connection to the landlord
4.40	Estimation of costs
4.43	Public notice
4.44	Observations
4.46	Estimates
4.59	**Qualifying long-term agreements**
4.60	What is a QLTA?
4.61	Agreements which are not QLTAs
4.62	**Dispensation**

continued

4.63   Old consultation provisions

New consultation provisions

4.70   Transitional provisions

Accounting periods: key

Key points

- The Commonhold and Leasehold Reform Act (CLRA) 2002 reformed the nature of a landlord's duties to consult. The old rules are still relevant for any work carried out between 1 April 1986 and 30 October 2003.
- A landlord must consult where work is done which would require a tenant to contribute more than £250 in any 12-month 'accounting period'.
- A Qualifying Long Term Agreement (QLTA) is an agreement made on behalf of the landlord for a period of over 12 months.
- If a tenant would have to contribute to the cost of a QLTA more than £100 in any accounting period the landlord must also consult before entering into the QLTA.
- It is possible to ask the LVT to dispense with consultation requirements.
- For agreements that are not QLTAs, the landlord must supply detailed information relating to the proposed project, including its estimated cost.
- He must obtain at least one estimate from a party wholly unconnected with him. Any connection to a party must be disclosed.
- Certain public works must comply with the public tendering process requirements.
- QLTAs must be preceded by a notice of intention to enter the agreement. Among other requirements, the landlord must invite representations from the tenants and must have regard to these representations.
- The landlord must then put at least two proposals (essentially 'quotes') to the tenants. One such proposal must be from a person wholly unconnected with the landlord. Again, tenants may comment on the proposals.
- A failure by the landlord to comply with his duties to consult tenants will not necessarily prevent the landlord recovering the costs incurred as service charges. At best, it will allow the LVT to 'cap' the amount which can be recovered.

Introduction

4.1   A tenant is at a great disadvantage when challenging the reasonableness of a service charge. If the work has been done badly, a decision by a Leasehold Valuation Tribunal (LVT) that no service charge is payable in respect of it may be of little comfort.

4.2   It will also be difficult to show that the cost incurred by the landlord was unreasonable because the tenant will rarely be in a position to obtain quotations from alternative contractors who are unlikely to go to the trouble of quoting for work that has already been done by someone else.

4.3   In order to put tenants on a more equal footing, landlords have been required since the Landlord and Tenant Act (LTA) 1985 came into force to carry out a consultation on any 'major works' to the premises the cost of which will be recovered from the tenant through the service charge bill. 'Major works' were defined relative to a 'costs threshold' per tenant – if the works exceeded the threshold consultation was required on penalty of the landlord's service charges being capped at that threshold.

4.4   There were some significant reforms to the consultation provisions made by the Commonhold and Leasehold Reform Act (CLRA) 2002.

4.5   Tenants' advisers should always check that a landlord has carried out the proper consultation process. It is important to understand that a failure to properly consult will not prevent any service charges being recovered: instead the tenants will be liable only for a capped sum. Under some circumstances (for example, where the work needed to be done urgently) the LVT may allow a landlord to recover service charges even where they have not properly consulted. A failure to consult is not decisive.

Advice for tenants

4.6   The consultation provisions are very complicated, but, in essence, are aimed at allowing tenants the opportunity to comment on the proposals of their landlord before contracts for works or services are carried out. While failure to consult can lead to the landlord being capped as to the maximum amounts recoverable by way of service charges, this is not an automatic result. The LVT has the power to dispense with the consultation requirements where it is reasonable to do so and a failure to comply with the requirements should not necessarily lead to a landlord being punished.

Old consultation requirements

Applicability

4.7   Before its amendment by CLRA 2002,[1] LTA 1985 s20 set out rules ('the old consultation rules') for consultation by the landlord in respect of works. The old consultation rules applied to any work done from 1 April 1986 to 30 October 2003 (in England) or 31 March 2004 (in Wales) and to certain works done after that date[1] whose cost exceeds a cost threshold.

4.8   The old consultation rules are still of importance because applications will continue to be made to LVTs in respect of work done before the new rules came into force.

Costs threshold

4.9   The cost threshold under the old consultation rules for works done on or after 1 April 1986 but before 1 September 1988 is the greater of £500 or £25 multiplied by the number of dwellings let to the tenants concerned.[2]

4.10   For work done on or after 1 September 1988 the cost threshold is the greater of £1,000 or £50 multiplied by the number of tenants liable to pay the relevant service charge.[3]

Consultation procedure under the old rules

4.11   If there is no Recognised Tenant's Association, the landlord must:[4]

(a) obtain at least two estimates for the works, one of which must be from a person wholly unconnected with the landlord;

(b) provide a copy of the estimates to each tenant or display them in one or more places likely to come to the notice of all tenants;

(c) provide a notice describing the works to be carried out and inviting observations on them and the estimates. The notice must also give the name and address of the person to whom observations must be sent and the closing date for observations (which must

---

1   See para 4.19 below.
2   LTA 1985 s20(3) as unamended.
3   LTA 1985 s20(3)(b) as amended by the Service Charge (Estimates and Consultation Order) 1988 SI No 1285.
4   LTA 1985 s20(4) as unamended.

not be earlier than one month after the date on which the notice was given or displayed);

(d) have regard to any observations received.

4.12   Where there is a Recognised Tenant's Association[5] the landlord must:[6]

(a) give the secretary of the association a notice containing a detailed specification of the works and specifying a reasonable period within which the association may propose to the landlord the name of one or more persons from whom estimates should be obtained;

(b) obtain at least two estimates for the works, one of which must be from a person wholly unconnected with the landlord;

(c) provide a copy of the estimates to the secretary of the association;

(d) give a notice to each tenant which must describe the works to be carried out; summarise the estimates; tell the tenant of the right to inspect and take copies of the estimates and the detailed specification of the works; invite observations on the works and estimates and give the name and address of the person to whom observations must be sent and the closing date for observations (which must not be earlier than one month after the date on which the notice was given or displayed);

(e) have regard to any observations received.

Urgent work exception

4.13   In either case where the work is urgent, the work be commenced before the expiry of the date given in the notice to tenants.[7]

What is an estimate?

4.14   The requirement to supply estimates under the old consultation regulations is a requirement to supply the estimates given to the landlord. A summary of the estimates or a note of the estimated figure is inadequate.[8]

4.15   The extent of a landlord's duties under the old consultation rules was considered in *London Borough of Islington v Abdel-Malek*.[9] Isling-

---

5   See para 3.63.
6   LTA 1985 s20(5) as unamended.
7   LTA 1985 s20(4)(e) as unamended.
8   *Richmond Housing Partnership v Smith* LRX/10/2005 (Lands Tribunal).
9   LRX/90/2006 (Lands Tribunal).

ton had obtained estimates for work to a number of blocks, including those of the respondent tenant. The council had supplied a summary of the successful contractor's tender to the tenants, which was found to be quite inadequate.

4.16   The Lands Tribunal accepted that 'the works' in section 20(4)(a) of the LTA 1985 referred to the works on the tenant's building. In practical terms this meant the council were obliged to supply all estimates (not merely the lowest) that related to works on the tenant's building and that it should be possible for the tenant to compare the various estimates for that work as it related to the tenant's building.

4.17   Many landlords attempt to rely on the judgment of HHJ Cooke in *London Borough of Haringey v Ball*[10] made in Central London County Court on 6 December 2004 as authority for the following propositions:

(a) there is no statutory form of notice;[11]
(b) an estimate need have no detail – and indeed might be 'on half of the back of an envelope' – and need not be linked to any specification;[12]
(c) a tender is a form of estimate;[13]
(d) the rules should be interpreted purposively (and thus, a landlord should not be punished for any technical defects). Where the substance of the rules has been complied with, the court should lean more to a purposive approach than a literal one.[14]

4.18   Point (d) is clearly wrong. LTA 1985 s20 sets out strict rules with which a landlord must comply. There is no indication in the Act that complying with their substance is sufficient, and the two Lands Tribunal authorities discussed above show that what might appear to be a technical failure to comply is still such a failure. In the *Haringey* case itself, the judge accepted that section 20 was mandatory, rather than merely directory. While compliance with the substance of the rules may be a relevant factor in any application for dispensation[15] it is not relevant to the issue of compliance in the first instance.

---

10 Unreported, Central London County Court, 6 December 2004, on file with the authors.
11 Ibid, at para 34.
12 Ibid, at para 36(b).
13 Ibid.
14 Ibid, at para 37.
15 See para 4.62.

New consultation requirements

4.19   Under the new regime, the obligation to consult arises in a much wider range of circumstances.

4.20   Most agreements made by a landlord for more than a year will now be called Qualifying Long-Term Agreements (QLTAs) (see para 4.59 onwards). Before the landlord enters such an agreement, various consultation processes are prescribed. Should the landlord fail to consult, the amount of cost under the agreement that they can recover from a tenant will be capped.

4.21   In addition, a landlord will still have to consult with tenants before undertaking any work on the building or premises, which is called 'qualifying work'. Failure to consult on qualifying work will result in the amount of the costs of work which can be recovered in a tenant's service charges being capped.

4.22   There are five different procedures, where the landlord proposes to:

(a) enter a QLTA, where public notice is required;
(b) enter a QLTA, where public notice is not required;
(c) carry out work under an existing QLTA;
(d) carry out work (not under a QLTA) where public notice is required; or
(e) carry out work (not under a QLTA) where public notice is not required.

4.23   This part of the chapter introduces a number of concepts common to all consultation requirements. The detailed consultation requirements are set out in tables 1–5 at the end of this chapter which should be read in conjunction with this part of the chapter.

Cost thresholds

4.24   With respect to qualifying works, the consultation provisions apply where the costs result in the relevant contribution of any tenant being more than £250.[16] If the consultation requirements are not complied with or a dispensation given by the LVT then the relevant contribution of every tenant will be capped at £250.[17]

---

16 LTA 1985 s20(5); Service Charges (Consultation Requirements) (England) Regulations (SC(CR)(E)R) 2003 SI No 1987; Service Charges (Consultation Requirements) (Wales) Regulations (SC(CR)(W)R) 2004 SI No 684 reg 6 in each case.
17 LTA 1985 s20(1).

4.25   The cost threshold for QLTAs is £100 in any accounting period.[18]

Accounting periods

4.26   'Accounting periods' are all 12 months long. The first accounting period begins on the 'relevant date'. The original consultation regulations set a different 'relevant date' depending on whether the service charge accounts were made up for 12-month periods or not. Where the accounts are made up for 12-month periods, the first period is the one that starts immediately after the one that contains the date on which the regulations came into force. Where accounts are not made up for 12-month periods, the first period would begin on the date the regulations come into force.

4.27   Unfortunately this, relatively logical, scheme does not cover a situation where a landlord chooses to make up service charge accounts in 12-month periods but does not do so until after the regulations came into force – as would be the case with the majority of new leasehold properties.

4.28   In an attempt to correct this, further regulations were passed. These provide for the situation where the landlord intends to enter a QLTA on or after 12 November 2004 (in England) or 31 May 2005 (in Wales); and the landlord has not between 31 October 2003 and that date made up service charge accounts referable to a QLTA, payable in respect of the dwellings to which the intended QLTA relate.

4.29   Currently, the relevant date (the date on which the first accounting period starts) is then the beginning of the first period for which service charges referable to the intended agreement relate.[19] This overrides the earlier provisions where the two conflict.[20]

4.30   One oddity about the rules, which has not been altered by the new regulations, is that there may be a period starting on 30 October 2003 and ending at some point before 30 October 2004 which is not part of any accounting period. This period of time would appear to be disregarded by the regulations so that regardless of what a tenant's contribution is within that period the consultation requirements will not be engaged.

4.31   A second oddity is that the amending regulations take effect where a landlord has not made up service charge accounts between 31 October 2003 and the date when the amending regulations come

18 LTA 1985 s20(4); SC(CR)(E) Regs 2003; SC(CR)(W) Regs 2004; reg 4 in each case.
19 SC(CR)(E) Regs 2003; SC(CR)(W) Regs 2004.
20 SC(CR)(E) Regs 2003; SC(CR)(W) Regs 2004; reg 4 para 3A in each case.

into force. The regulations do not affect a case where a QLTA was entered into in that period but service charge accounts are not drawn up that relate to it until after that period.

4.32   It is a testament to the shoddy and confused way in which the government has approached these rules that the first attempt to amend the regulations by the Service Charges (Consultation Requirements) (Amendment) (England) Regulations 2004[21] failed because the regulations as passed by Parliament were still in draft form: where two dates should have appeared the word '*date*' appeared instead. In order to assist advisers, a key for determining the relevant date is to be found at para 4.71 below.

Relevant periods

4.33   In most cases, where a landlord must give a notice, the notice must state a 'relevant period' within which any responses from tenants must be received. The relevant period is defined to be '30 days beginning with the date of the notice.'[22] In this context 'date of the notice' must be the date on which the notice is given, rather than any other date, or the definition of 'relevant period' would not be sufficiently certain. There is no provision for deeming service of a notice.

Inspection of information

4.34   Many of the notices required as part of the consultation process require the landlord to supply detailed information, for example concerning estimates and details of work that needs to be done. The landlord has the option, rather than sending the information with the notice, to indicate a place where the information can be inspected and hours when inspection may take place.[23]

4.35   Both the place and the hours for inspection must be reasonable.[24] No charge may be made for the inspection.[25] The landlord must enable copies to be taken or supply to the tenant on request, and for no charge, a copy.[26]

---

21 SI No 2665.
22 SC(CR)(E) Regs 2003; SC(CR)(W) Regs 2004; reg 2 in each case.
23 SC(CR)(E) Regs 2003; SC(CR)(W) Regs 2004; Schs 1–4 para 2(1) in each case.
24 Ibid.
25 Ibid.
26 SC(CR)(E) Regs 2003; SC(CR)(W) Regs 2004; Schs 1–4 para 2(2) in each case.

Connection to the landlord

4.36   Another feature common to the consultation procedures is the idea of a person connected to the landlord. In some cases a landlord will need to obtain at least one estimate from a person wholly unconnected with them and in other cases they will have to indicate if there is a connection (and what that connection is) between them and a party to an agreement.

4.37   There is no exhaustive definition of what 'connection' means and a common-sense approach is likely to be taken by the LVT. The purpose of having such a concept is to increase the transparency of the consultation and tendering process.

4.38   Some relationships are deemed to be a connection and they are:[27]

(a) a company is connected to its directors and managers and their close relatives;
(b) a company is connected to any other company if any of its directors or managers is, or is to be a director or manager of the other company; or
(c) a company is connected to a partner in a partnership if any partner in the partnership is a director or manager of the company or is a close relative of such a director or manager.

This list is in no way exhaustive and there are certain to be many other situations where a connection will be found.

4.39   For the purposes of the regulations a person's 'close relative' is a person's spouse, cohabitee, parent, parent-in-law, son, son-in-law, daughter, daughter-in-law, brother, brother-in-law, sister, sister-in-law, step-parent, step-son or step-daughter. A person's cohabitee is either a person of the opposite sex who is living with that person as a husband or wife or a person of the same sex living with that person in a relationship which has the characteristics of the relationship between husband and wife.[28]

Estimation of costs

4.40   In order for the consultation process to be realistic the landlord will have to give an estimate of the cost of the work.

---

27 SC(CR)(E) Regs 2003; SC(CR)(W) Regs 2004; Sch 1 para 5(6), Sch 2 para 4(3), Sch 4 Pt 1 para 4(3), Sch 4 Pt 2 para 4(7) in each case.
28 SC(CR)(E) Regs 2003; SC(CR)(W) Regs 2004; reg 2(1) in each case.

4.41   Where it is practical for the landlord to estimate the relevant contribution of each tenant's unit of occupation then that estimate should be given. Where it is not practical to do that but it is practical to estimate the total amount of expenditure on the building or other premises to which either the agreement relates, or on which the work is being done, then that estimate should be given. Failing that, if it is practical to give the current unit cost or hourly or daily rate that would apply to any works to be done then that rate should be given.[29]

4.42   Where it is not practical for the landlord to give any of this information they must explain why they are unable to comply and give a date by when they expect to be able to supply the estimated amount, cost, or rate as the case may be.[30]

Public notice

4.43   Certain works or agreements are required to be advertised by means of a notice published in the Official Journal of the European Union pursuant to the Public Contracts Regulations 2006. In such circumstances, the consultation provisions are considerably truncated, as it is the 2006 Regulations which govern the award of the contract, rather than any provisions of landlord and tenant law.

Observations

4.44   There are many stages in the consultations procedures where the landlord is required to 'have regard to' any observations made in the relevant period. Similar language was used in the old section 20 consultation requirement. (see paras 4.11–4.12).

4.45   Although it will be difficult to show that a landlord has not had 'regard to' any particular observation, the fact that work was started or action taken before the receipt of an observation (and thus within the relevant period) would be conclusive evidence that no regard was given to it. In most cases the landlord will have to explain their response to any observations, the failure to do that is better evidence that no regard was had.

---

29 SC(CR)(E) Regs 2003; SC(CR)(W) Regs 2004 Sch 1 para 5, Sch 2 para 4, Sch 4 Pt 1 para 4 in each case.

30 This saving provision is only available in Schs 2 and 4 Pt 1, SC(CR)(E) Regs 2003; SC(CR)(W) Regs 2004; Sch 2 para 4(7) and Sch 4 Pt 1 para 4(7) in each case.

Estimates

4.46   For those agreements which do not require public notice, the notice of intention will have invited tenants and tenants' associations to nominate a person from whom an estimate in respect of the relevant matters or works should be sought.

4.47   The intention of the regulations seems to be that the landlord should be required to obtain quotations from at least one person nominated by a tenant and at least one nominated by a tenants' association. As will be explained, the regulations are so poorly drafted that it is unclear whether this effect has been achieved.

4.48   Where a single nomination is made by one tenant then the landlord should obtain an estimate from the person so nominated.

4.49   Where several tenants each make a single nomination, a simple principle of majority selection is applied: the landlord must obtain a nomination from the person who received the most votes.

4.50   Where more than one person receives the most votes (ie, there is a tie for first place) the landlord may choose to obtain an estimate from any one of the persons who came top.

4.51   Oddly this principle of majoritarianism is abandoned if any tenant nominates more than one person.

4.52   It would seem that the regulations intend the landlord to be able to select any person nominated by a tenant under these circumstances.

4.53   In fact this limb of the regulations only comes into play where a tenants' association has also made more than one nomination, the circumstance of one tenant making many nominations and a tenants' association making none is not envisaged.[31]

4.54   The court and, by extension, one presumes an LVT, has the power to interpret badly drafted statutory instruments so as to fill in any lacunae.[32] The problem is that it is not entirely clear what was intended.

4.55   The regulations also make the implicit assumption that there is only one Recognised Tenants' Association in any block. This need not be the case.

4.56   Even if an LVT were to assume the regulations were intended to require that a landlord obtained an estimate from at least one person nominated by a Recognised Tenants' Association a landlord could

---

31   Sch 1 para 4(4).

32   *R on the application of Public Transport (UK) v Humber Bridge Board* [2003] EWCA Civ 842; [2004] 2 WLR 98.

subvert the process by recognising their own association (which they have the power to do) which might contain only one tenant.

4.57   This association could then nominate any person of the landlord's choosing.

4.58   There does not appear to be any way to prevent an unscrupulous landlord taking advantage of these loopholes.

Qualifying long-term agreements

4.59   CLRA 2002 introduced the concept of a qualifying long-term agreement (QLTA). By entering into a QLTA a landlord can avoid detailed consultation over works done under the agreement. However, a landlord will be required to have consulted on the QLTA in the first place.

What is a QLTA?

4.60   A QLTA is any agreement made by or on behalf of a landlord or superior landlord for a period of more than 12 months.[33]

Agreements which are not QLTAs

4.61   The following agreements are not QLTAs:[34]

(a) a contract of employment;

(b) a management agreement made by a local housing authority and a tenant management organisation or any body established under the Local Government Act 2000 s2;

(c) if the parties to the agreement are a holding company and one or more of its subsidiaries or two or more subsidiaries in the same holding company;

(d) if, at the time the contract is entered into, there are no tenants of the building to which the agreement relates and the agreement is for not more than five years;

(e) an agreement entered into before 31 October 2003 (England) or 31 March 2004 (Wales) which had a duration of more than 12 months; or

(f) an agreement for a term of more than 12 months for which public notice had been given before 31 October 2003 (England) or 31 March 2004 (Wales).

33 LTA 1985 s20ZA(2).
34 SC(CR)(E) Regs 2003; SC(CR)(W)Regs 2004; reg 3 in each case.

Dispensation

4.62　Where a landlord has not complied with the relevant consultation provisions, the amount they will be able to recover from a tenant will be capped at the relevant cost threshold. This can have harsh consequences in certain circumstances. In order to alleviate any potential problems there is a power to dispense with the consultation requirements. For cases covered by the old consultation rules, this power was vested in the court and, for the new consultation rules, the LVT has jurisdiction.

Old consultation provisions

4.63　The court may, if it is satisfied that the landlord acted reasonably, dispense with all or any of the consultation requirements.[35]

4.64　This does not create a general dispensing power in the court. It is a two-stage process under which the court has a discretion to dispense with any or all of the consultation requirements only if the court has first been satisfied that the landlord has acted reasonably.[36]

4.65　The concept of 'acting reasonably' is assessed by considering whether or not the landlord acted reasonably in all the circumstances where section 20 was not complied with.[37]

4.66　Both the county court[38] and the LVT[39] had taken the view that LTA 1985 s20(9) was enacted to deal with emergencies or where the tenant was unavailable for consultation.

New consultation provisions

4.67　Under the new consultation rules, the LVT may dispense with any or all of the requirements where it considers it reasonable to do so.[40] Dispensation may be given before a QLTA is entered into or works are done, but the LVT should not grant vague and open-ended dispensations.[41]

35　LTA 1985 s20(9) as unamended.
36　*Martin v Maryland Estates*, unreported, 26 April 1999, CA, per Robert Walker LJ.
37　Ibid.
38　*Hodgett v Knox*, Central London CC, 12 November 1999.
39　*Wilson v Stone* [1998] 26 EG 153.
40　LTA 1985 s20ZA(1).
41　*Anger v London Borough of Camden*, LRX81/2007, Lands Tribunal.

4.68   This is a one-stage test and does not require any proof that the landlord has acted reasonably. When considering whether or not to dispense with the requirements, the most important consideration will usually be the degree of prejudice there is to tenants for a failure to comply with the procedure. It will usually be reasonable to give dispensation from the new consultation requirements where there has been a minor breach of procedure that has not prejudiced the tenants.[42]

4.69   Examples might be where it is simply impractical to carry out a full consultation; where a particularly good price is available for goods and services but only for a short period of time; where an emergency required works to be completed urgently or where the tenants themselves support the application. In all circumstances, landlords should attempt to comply with as much of the formal consultation requirements as possible or, at the very least, have some form of informal consultation.

Transitional provisions

4.70   There are a number of transitional provisions that affect whether work is governed by the old or new regulations, and, if so, which Schedule of the Consultation Regulations 2003 (England) and 2004 (Wales) governs the work. The following table should provide a useful summary. In order to determine which consultation provisions apply start at the top of the table and work down.

Work begun before 31 October 2003 (England)[43] or 31 March 2004 (Wales)[44]	Old
A section 20 notice has been given or displayed before 31 October 2003 (England)[45] or 31 March 2004 (Wales)[46]	Old
A public notice was issued before 31 October 2003 (England)[47] or 31 March 2004 (Wales);[48] the agreement under which the work is done was made on or after that date; and was for 12 months or less	Old

42   *Eltham Properties Limited v Kenny* LRX/161/2006 (Lands Tribunal).
43   SC(CR)(W) Regs 2004 reg 3.
44   SC(CR)(E) Regs 2003; SC(CR)(W) Regs 2004 reg 7 in each case.
45   SC(CR)(E) Regs 2003; SC(CR)(W) Regs 2004 reg 7 in each case.
46   SC(CR)(E) Regs 2003 reg 3.
47   SC(CR)(W) Regs 2004 reg 3.
48   SC(CR)(E) Regs 2003 reg 3.

Work carried out at any time between 31 October 2003 and 31 December 2003 (England)[49] or 31 March 2004 and 31 May 2004 (Wales)[50]	Old
Work done on or after 31 December 2003 (England)[51] or 31 May 2004 (Wales),[52] pursuant to an agreement made before 31 October 2003 (England) or 31 March 2004 (Wales)	Schedule 3
Public notice was issued before 31 October 2003 (England)[53] or 31 March 2004 (Wales)[54] and the work was done on or after 31 October 2003 (England) or 31 March 2004 (Wales) under an agreement for more than 12 months	Schedule 3
Work done under an agreement for 12 months or less[55]	Schedule 4
Work done under an agreement made before 31 October 2003 (England)[56] or 31 March 2004 (Wales)[57] and for more than 12 months	Schedule 4
Work done under an agreement of more than 12 months duration, where public notice was given before 31 October 2003 (England)[58] or 31 March 2004 (Wales)[59]	Schedule 4
Work done under any other agreement that is a QLTA[60]	Schedule 3
Work done in any situation not covered above[61]	Schedule 4

Key

Old   Covered by the former LTA 1985 s20
Schedules 3 and 4   Consultation Regulations

49   SC(CR)(W) Regs 2004 reg 3.
50   SC(CR)(E) Regs 2003 reg 3.
51   SC(CR)(W) Regs 2004 reg 3.
52   SC(CR)(E) Regs 2003 reg 3.
53   SC(CR)(W) Regs 2004 reg 3.
54   SC(CR)(E) Regs 2003 reg 7
55   SC(CR)(W) Regs 2004 reg 7.
56   SC(CR)(E) Regs 2003 reg 7.
57   SC(CR)(W) Regs 2004 reg 7.
58   LTA 1985 s20ZA(2); SC(CR)(E) Regs 2003; SC(CR)(W) Regs 2004 reg 7 in each case.
59   SC(CR)(E) Regs 2003 reg 3
60   SC(CR)(W) Regs 2004 reg 3.
61   SC(CR)(E) Regs reg 3.

Accounting periods: key

4.71   **England**
1. Does the landlord intend to enter into a QLTA on or after 12 November 2004?
Yes: go to question 2.
No: go to question 4.

2. Has the landlord made up service charge accounts in the period beginning on 31 October 2003 and ending on 12 November 2004?
Yes: go to question 3.
No: the first accounting period begins on the same day as the first period for which service charges referable to the QLTA are payable.

3. Do those service charge accounts relate to a QLTA?
Yes: go to question 4.
No: the first accounting period begins on the same day as the first period for which service charges referable to the QLTA are payable.

4. Are the service charges accounts made up by the landlord for periods of 12 months?
Yes: go to question 5.
No: the first accounting period begins on 31 October 2003.

5. Were service charges made up for a period containing 31 October 2003?
Yes: the first accounting period starts on the day after the service charge period containing 31 October 2003 ends.
No: there is no first accounting period.

4.72   **Wales**
1. Does the landlord intend to enter into a QLTA on or after 31 May 2005?
Yes: go to question 2.
No: go to question 4.

2. Has the landlord made up service charge accounts in the period beginning on 31 October 2003 and ending on 31 May 2005?
Yes: go to question 3.
No: the first accounting period begins on the same day as the first period for which service charges referable to the QLTA are payable.

3. Do those service charge accounts relate to a QLTA?
Yes: go to question 4.
No: the first accounting period begins on the same day as the first period for which service charges referable to the QLTA are payable.

4. Are the service charges accounts made up by the landlord for periods of 12 months?

Yes: go to question 5.

No: the first accounting period begins on 31 March 2004.

5. Were service charges made up for a period containing 31 March 2004?

Yes: the first accounting period starts on the day after the service charge period containing 31 March 2004 ends.

No: there is no first accounting period.

Note

An example of a 'no first accounting period' would be a landlord who first made up annual service charge accounts (because of the grant of a new lease) on 1 November 2003 and entered into a QLTA on the same day. Until there is an intention of the landlord to enter into a new QLTA, there can be no accounting period. In Wales the situation is worse, a landlord whose first annual service charge accounts were drawn up on 1 April 2004 and included costs for a QLTA on 1 April 2005 can never have a first accounting period.

Table 1 Qualifying long-term agreements: no public notice required[62]

Notice of intention	

The landlord must give notice in writing of their intention to enter into the agreement[63] to:
 a) each tenant;[64] and
 b) to any Recognised Tenants' Association.[65]
	The notice must:
	 a) describe, in general terms, the 'relevant matters' (that is the subject matter of the agreement) or specify a place where a description of them can be inspected (see para 4.34);[66]
	 b) state the landlord's reasons for considering it necessary to enter into the agreement;[67]
	 c) if the relevant matters include qualifying works, state the landlord's reasons for considering it necessary to carry out those works;[68]
	 d) invite the making in writing of observations in relation to the proposed agreement[69] specifying:
	   (i) the address to which observations may be sent;
	   (ii) that they must be within the relevant period; and
	   (iii) the date on which the relevant period ends;[70]
	 e) invite each tenant and the association (if any) to propose, within the relevant period, the name of a person from whom the landlord should try to obtain an estimate in respect of the relevant matters.

The landlord must 'have regard to' any observations made in response to the notice of intention during the relevant period.	

62 SC(CR)(E) Regs 2003; SC(CR)(W) Regs 2004 Sch 1.
63 Sch 1 para 1(1).
64 Sch 1 para 1(1)(a).
65 Sch 1 para 1(1)(b).
66 Sch 1 para 1(2)(a).
67 Sch 1 para 1(2)(b).
68 Sch 1 para 1(2)(c).
69 Sch 1 para 1(2)(d).
70 Sch 1 para 1(2)(e).

Notice of intention *continued*	
The landlord must obtain estimates from 'nominated persons'.	See para 4.46 for a discussion of the landlord's duties concerning collection of estimates.
The landlord must prepare proposals, such that: a) there are at least two proposals;[71] b) one proposal must be that the agreement is made with someone wholly unconnected with the landlord;[72] c) where any estimates have been received from a 'nominated person' in response to the notice of intention during the relevant period there must be a proposal based on each such estimate. Each of these conditions may be independent – for example if two nominations were made of persons connected with the landlord, the landlord would still be required to produce a third proposal based on a person wholly unconnected with them.	The proposal must contain the following: a) the name and address of all parties (other than the landlord) to the proposed agreement and of any connection (see para 4.36) they have between the party and the landlord. b) An estimate of the relevant costs or rate must be given as explained in para 4.40. c) If the landlord proposes to appoint an agent to undertake some of the landlord's duties then the proposal must state whether the proposed agent is or is not a member of a professional body or trade association and whether they subscribe to any code of practice or voluntary accreditation scheme relevant to their function. d) Where observations have been made before the relevant date (to which the landlord will have to have had regard) the landlord must summarise the observations and set out their response to them.

---

71 Sch 1 para 5(1).
72 Sch 1 para 5(2).

Notice of proposals	

The landlord must give notice in writing of their proposals to:[73]
a) each tenant; and
b) to any Recognised Tenants' Association
	The notice must:
	a) either be accompanied by a copy of each proposal or specify the place and hours at which the proposals may be inspected;
	b) invite the making, in writing, of observations in relation to the proposals; and specify –
	  (i) the address to which such observations may be sent;
	  (ii) that they must be delivered within the relevant period; and
	  (iii) the date on which the relevant period ends.

Landlord enters into the QLTA	
Notice of entering into agreement	
Within 21 days of entering into the QLTA, the landlord must give notice in writing to the tenants and any Recognised Tenants' Association.	This does not apply where the agreement is with either: a) the person who submitted the lowest estimate; or b) a nominated person. The notice must: a) state the landlord's reasons for making that agreement or specify the place and hours at which a statement of those reasons may be inspected; and b) where he has received observations to which (in accordance with paragraph 7) he is required to have regard, summarise the observations and respond to them or specify the place and hours at which that summary and response may be inspected.

73 Sch 1 para 6(1).

Table 2 Qualifying long-term agreements: public notice required[74]

Notice of intention	

The landlord must give notice in writing of their intention to enter into the agreement[75] to:
a) each tenant;[76] and
b) to any Recognised Tenants' Association.[77]
	The notice must:
	a) describe, in general terms, the 'relevant matters' (that is the subject matter of the agreement) or specify a place where a description of them can be inspected (see para 4.34);[78]
	b) state the landlord's reasons for considering it necessary to enter into the agreement;[79]
	c) if the relevant matters include qualifying works, state the landlord's reasons for considering it necessary to carry out those works;[80]
	d) the reason why the landlord is not inviting recipients to nominate persons from whom they should try to obtain an estimate is that public notice of the relevant matters is to be given;[81]
	e) invite the making in writing of observations in relation to the proposed agreement[82] specifying:
	  (i) the address to which observations may be sent;
	  (ii) that they must be within the relevant period; and
	  (iii) the date on which the relevant period ends.[83]

74 Sch 2.
75 Sch 2 para 1(1).
76 Sch 2 para 1(1)(a).
77 Sch 2 para 1(1)(b).
78 Sch 2 para 1(2)(a).
79 Sch 2 para 1(2)(b).
80 Sch 2 para 1(2)(c).
81 Sch 2 para 1(2)(d).
82 Sch 2 para 1(2)(e).
83 Sch 2 para 1(2)(f).

Notice of intention *continued*	
The landlord must 'have regard to' any observations made in response to the notice of intention during the relevant period.	
Preparation of a proposal	
The landlord must prepare a proposal.	The proposal must contain: a) the name and address of all parties (other than the landlord) to the proposed agreement and of any connection (see para 4.36) they have between the party and the landlord; b) an estimate of the relevant costs or rate must be given as explained in para 4.40; c) if the landlord proposes to appoint an agent to undertake some of the landlord's duties then the proposal must state whether the proposed agent is or is not a member of a professional body or trade association and whether they subscribe to any code of practice or voluntary accreditation scheme relevant to their function; d) where observations have been made before the relevant date (to which the landlord will have to have had regard) the landlord must summarise the observations and set out their response to them.
Notice of proposal	
The landlord must give notice of their proposal to: a) each tenant; and b) to any Recognised Tenants' Association	The notice must: a) either be accompanied by a copy of the proposal or specify the place and hours at which the proposal may be inspected; b) invite the making, in writing, of observations in relation to the proposal; and specify – (i) the address to which such observations may be sent; (ii) that they must be delivered within the relevant period; and (iii) the date on which the relevant period ends.

Response to observations	
Where the landlord has received any observations on the notice of proposal, they must within 21 days of their receipt, by notice in writing to the person by whom the observations were made, state their response to the observations.[84]	
Where the landlord has stated that it was not reasonably practicable for the landlord to ascertain the current unit cost or hourly or daily rate applicable to the relevant matters, when the landlord has received sufficient information to enable them to estimate the amount, cost or rate they must within 21 days give notice in writing of the estimated amount, cost or rate to: a) each tenant; and b) to any Recognised Tenants' Association.	

84 Sch 2 para 7.

Table 3 Works: no public notice required[85]

Notice of intention	

The landlord must give notice in writing of their intention to carry out qualifying works[86] to:
a) each tenant;[87] and
b) to any Recognised Tenants' Association.[88]
	The notice must:
	a) describe, in general terms, the works proposed to be carried out or specify a place where a description of them can be inspected (see para 4.34);[89]
	b) state the landlord's reasons for considering it necessary to carry out the proposed works;[90]
	c) invite the making in writing of observations in relation to the proposed agreement[91] specifying:
	  (i) the address to which observations may be sent;
	  (ii) that they must be within the relevant period; and
	  (iii) the date on which the relevant period ends.[92]
	d) invite each tenant and the association (if any) to propose, within the relevant period, the name of a person from whom the landlord should try to obtain an estimate for the carrying out of the proposed works.

The landlord must 'have regard to' any observations made in response to the notice of intention during the relevant period.[93]	

85 Sch 4 Part 2.
86 Sch 1 para 1(1).
87 Sch 1 para 1(1)(a).
88 Sch 1 para 1(1)(b).
89 Sch 4 Part 2 para 1(2)(a).
90 Sch 4 Part 2 para 1(2)(b).
91 Sch 4 Part 2 para 1(2)(d).
92 Sch 4 Part 2 para 1(2)(e).
93 Sch 4 Part 2 para 3.

Notice of intention *continued*	
The landlord must then obtain estimates for carrying out the proposed works.	At least one of the estimates must be that of a person wholly unconnected with the landlord. One or more of the estimates may have to be obtained from someone nominated in response to the notice of intention, see para 4.46 for a discussion.
The landlord must make all estimates available for inspection.[94]	
Paragraph (b) statement	
The landlord must prepare a statement (called a 'paragraph (b) statement') and supply it free of charge to: a) each tenant; and b) to the secretary of any Recognised Tenants' Association.	The paragraph (b) statement must contain: i) as regards at least two of the estimates[95] – and including any estimate received from a nominated person,[96] the amount specified in the estimate as the estimated cost of the proposed works; ii) where the landlord has received observations in response to the notice of intention to which he was required to have regard, a summary of the observations and his response to them.
Notice under para 4(10)	

The landlord must, but notice in writing, to:
a) each tenant; and
b) to any Recognised Tenants' Association.
	The notice must:
	a) specify the place and hours at which the estimates may be inspected;
	b) invite the making, in writing, of observations in relation to those estimates and specify –
	  (i) the address to which such observations may be sent;
	  (ii) that they must be delivered within the relevant period; and
	  (iii) the date on which the relevant period ends.

94 Sch 4 Part 2 para 4(5)(c).
95 Sch 4 Part 2 para 4(5)(b).
96 Sch 4 Part 2 para 4(8).

Notice under para 4(10) *continued*	
The landlord must have regard to any observations made in the relevant period.[97]	
Notice of entering into contract	
Within 21 days of entering into the contract for the works, give notice in writing to the tenants and any Recognised Tenants' Association[98]	This does not apply where the contract is with either: a) the person who submitted the lowest estimate; b) a nominated person.[99] The notice must: a) state his reasons for making awarding the contract or specify the place and hours at which a statement of those reasons may be inspected; and b) where the landlord has received observations in relation to the estimates to which they are required to have regard, summarise the observations and respond to them or specify the place and hours at which that summary and response may be inspected.

97 Sch 4 Part 2 para 5.
98 Sch 4 Part 2 para 6(1).
99 Sch 4 Part 2 para 6(3).

Table 4 Works: public notice required

Notice of intention	

The landlord must give notice in writing of their intention to carry out qualifying works[100] to:
a) each tenant;[101] and
b) to any Recognised Tenants' Association.[102]
	The notice must:
	a) describe, in general terms, the works proposed to be carried out or specify a place where a description of them can be inspected (see para 4.34);[103]
	b) state the landlord's reasons for considering it necessary to carry out the proposed works;[104]
	c) invite the making in writing of observations in relation to the proposed agreement[105] specifying:
	  (i) the address to which observations may be sent;
	  (ii) that they must be within the relevant period; and
	  (iii) the date on which the relevant period ends;[106]
	d) state that the reason why the landlord is not inviting recipients of the notice to nominate persons from whom he should try to obtain an estimate for carrying out the works is that public notice of the works is to be given.[107]

The landlord must 'have regard to' any observations made in response to the notice of intention during the relevant period.[108]	

100 Sch 4 Part 1 para 1(1).
101 Sch 4 Part 1 para 1(1)(a).
102 Sch 4 Part 1 para 1(1)(b).
103 Sch 4 Part 1 para 1(2)(a).
104 Sch 4 Part 1 para 1(2)(b).
105 Sch 4 Part 1 para 1(2)(d).
106 Sch 4 Part 1 para 1(2)(e).
107 Sch 4 Part 1 para 1(2)(c).
108 Sch 4 Part 1 para 3.

Paragraph 4 statement	
The landlord must prepare a statement (called a 'paragraph 4 statement') and supply it free of charge to: a) each tenant; and b) to the secretary of any Recognised Tenants' Association.	The paragraph 4 statement must contain: a) the name and address of the person with whom the landlord proposes to contract; and b) particulars of any connection between them (apart from the proposed contract); c) an estimate of costs if that is reasonably practicable (see para 4.40); and d) where the landlord has received observations in response to their notice of intention to which they are required to have regard, the statement shall summarise the observations and set out the landlord's response to them.
Notification of proposed contract	
The landlord must, but notice in writing, to: a) each tenant; and b) to any Recognised Tenants' Association.	The notice must contain: a) the paragraph 4 statement b) invite the making, in writing, of observations in relation to those estimates and specify – (i) the address to which such observations may be sent; (ii) that they must be delivered within the relevant period; and (iii) the date on which the relevant period ends.
The landlord must have regard to any observations made in response to the notification of proposed contract during the relevant period.[109]	

Supplementary information	
Where the landlord has stated that it was not reasonably practicable for the landlord to ascertain the current unit cost or hourly or daily rate applicable to the relevant matters, when the landlord has received sufficient information to enable them to estimate the amount, cost or rate they must within 21 days give notice in writing of the estimated amount, cost or rate to: a) each tenant; and b) where a Recognised Tenants' Association represents some or all of the tenants, to the association.	

Table 5 Works done under a qualifying long-term agreement

Notice of intention	
The landlord must give notice in writing of their intention to enter into the agreement[110] to: a) each tenant;[111] and b) to any Recognised Tenants' Association.[112]	The notice must: a) describe, in general terms, the 'relevant matters' (that is the subject matter of the agreement) or specify a place where a description of them can be inspected (see para 4.34);[113] b) state the landlord's reasons for considering it necessary to enter into the agreement;[114] c) if the relevant matters include qualifying works, state the landlord's reasons for considering it necessary to carry out those works;[115] d) invite the making in writing of observations in relation to the proposed agreement[116] specifying: (i) the address to which observations may be sent; (ii) that they must be within the relevant period; and (iii) the date on which the relevant period ends;[117] and e) invite each tenant and the association (if any) to propose, within the relevant period, the name of a person from whom the landlord should try to obtain an estimate in respect of the relevant matters.

110 Sch 4 Part 1 para 1(1).
111 Sch 4 Part 1 para 1(1)(a).
112 Sch 4 Part 1 para 1(1)(b).
113 Sch 4 Part 1 para 1(2)(a).
114 Sch 4 Part 1 para 1(2)(b).
115 Sch 4 Part 1 para 1(2)(c).
116 Sch 4 Part 1 para 1(2)(d).
117 Sch 4 Part 1 para 1(2)(e).

Notice of intention *continued*	
The landlord must 'have regard to' any observations made in response to the notice of intention during the relevant period.	

CHAPTER 5

Insurance

5.1	**Introduction**
5.4	**Advice for tenants**
5.6	**Common areas of difficulty**
5.7	No or inadequate insurance provision
5.9	Insurance premiums as service charges
5.12	Tenant required to insure
5.13	**Challenging insurance cover**
5.16	Unsatisfactory in any respect
	Level of cover is inadequate or excessive • *The cover is defective in some other respect* • *The cover is not provided by a reputable company*
5.21	Excessive premium payments
	Excessive from the tenant's point of view • *How much is excessive?*
5.30	Remedies
5.32	**Failure to pay out insurance monies**
5.36	**Arranging your own insurance**
5.40	**Rights to information in relation to insurance**
5.44	**Right to notify insurer of a claim**

Key points

- Disputes arise on one of three grounds.
  - If the lease contains no, or inadequate provision for insuring the property, consider varying the lease (see chapter 7).
  - If the landlord organises the insurance themselves and recovers the cost of premiums from the tenant, the tenant will be paying for the insurance through their service charges (see chapter 2 for information on challenging service charges).
  - If the tenant organises the insurance but must use an insurer nominated or otherwise selected by their landlord, the tenant may challenge that choice of insurer, such a challenge is the subject of this chapter.
- Tenants may argue that the insurance cover is unsatisfactory in any respect or the premiums are excessive.
- 'Unsatisfactory' insurance includes situations where the level of cover is inadequate or excessive, there is a material misdescription which might lead the insurers to declining liability or the cover is not provided by a reputable company.
- The phrase 'excessive premium' is not defined.
- Landlords often receive commissions from insurers. These are hard to challenge in themselves but can be used as evidence that the landlord is not negotiating at arms length in an open market.

Introduction

5.1   A common area of dispute between tenants and landlords is the provision of insurance cover. This may flow from entirely legitimate differences of view, often from the fact that tenants, having time-limited interests in the property, take a different view of some risks when compared with freeholders.

5.2   There are a number of potential insurance problems which might arise from time to time. If the lease contains no or inadequate provision for insuring the property, it should be varied. If the landlord is recovering an excessive amount by way of service charges, then a challenge to those charges should be considered.

5.3   This chapter deals mainly with the situation where a tenant is obliged under the terms of their lease to insure with a company nominated or selected by the landlord. The tenant may challenge that choice of insurer if the cover is unsatisfactory or the premiums excessive.

Advice for tenants

5.4 As with most leasehold disputes, access to relevant information is key. Tenants of flats have a number of rights to obtain information which they should make full use of in order to determine what sort of insurance problem they are dealing with. Not all insurance disputes will be resolved in the same manner. A variation of the terms of the lease may be more effective than trying to challenge the landlord's chosen insurance company.

5.5 In the event of any challenge to the quality of the insurance cover, it is vital to obtain 'like-for-like' quotes.

Common areas of difficulty

5.6 There are three ways in which a dispute about insurance can arise, all of which have different remedies.

No or inadequate insurance provision

5.7 Some leases make no provision for insurance or do not properly specify who is to insure particular parts of the building. In these circumstances tenants run the risk of having to pay for serious damage without any insurance protection.

5.8 Tenants are free to negotiate their own cover but there is a more satisfactory solution: that of applying for a variation of the lease, which is discussed in chapter 7.

Insurance premiums as service charges

5.9 A common situation is for a lease to put the duty to insure on the landlord, who is then permitted to recover the cost of the insurance premiums from the tenants. In such a situation the costs recovered from the tenants are service charges.[1]

5.10 Such payments are subject to the same kinds of challenge as other service charges, a full discussion of which may be found in chapter 2.

---

1 Landlord and Tenant Act (LTA) 1985 s18.

5.11   A problem that arises in the particular instance of service charges for insurance is that landlords are often paid large commissions for selecting particular insurers.[2] The insurance company then recovers the cost of the commission via higher premium payments which will ultimately be born by the tenants. A full discussion of this particular problem is also found in para 2.80.

Tenant required to insure

5.12   A further possibility is that the tenant is responsible for the insurance. This is particularly common for owners of leasehold houses. In such situations the lease almost always requires the tenant to use a particular insurer or one nominated by the landlord.

Challenging insurance cover

5.13   Where the lease requires the tenant to insure the property with an insurer nominated or approved by the landlord then the tenant or the landlord may apply to an LVT for a determination of:[3]

(a) whether the insurance which is provided is unsatisfactory in any respect; or

(b) whether the premium payments are excessive.

5.14   There is nothing to prevent an applicant asking the LVT to rule on both questions in a single application. Similarly, there is no reason why a landlord could not bring an application and ask for a determination that the insurance is satisfactory and/or not excessively expensive.[4] This may forestall any future disagreements between landlord and tenant.

5.15   No application may be made in respect of any matter which has been agreed or admitted by the tenant; has been referred to arbitration pursuant to an arbitration agreement to which the tenant is a party or has already been determined by a previous arbitration or tribunal.[5]

---

2   See for example *Williams v Southwark LBC* (2001) 33 HLR 224.
3   LTA 1985 Sch para 8.
4   LTA 1985 Sch para8(2).
5   LTA 1985 Sch para 8(3).

Unsatisfactory in any respect

5.16 'Unsatisfactory in any respect' is not defined in the legislation, but is clearly a widely drafted provision. The following are examples of the most usual complaints.

Level of cover is inadequate or excessive

5.17 This would include situations where the policy fails to deal with a likely risk, or is simply far too cautious. A failure to insure against flood damage if the property were near a river prone to flooding would clearly be an example of inadequate cover. Similarly, while terrorism insurance might be appropriate for properties in larger cities, it may well be seen as excessive in respect of a cottage in an isolated, rural area.[6]

5.18 Tenants should also ensure that the insurance policy provides for the property to be insured up to its re-build value. Though such a failure has never been raised before an LVT, it would seem to fall within 'unsatisfactory in any respect'. Were an LVT not to so accept, an application to vary the lease to this effect should be considered.

The cover is defective in some other respect

5.19 Examples include a material misdescription of the property in the insurance policy or other error which might lead to the insurers declining liability.[7]

The cover is not provided by a reputable company

5.20 There is a long line of case law to the effect that when a landlord has a covenant to insure the property, they must do so with an insurer of repute and good standing.[8] In practice, it should be considered adequate to insure with a firm of national repute.

Excessive premium payments

5.21 As has already been made clear there is considerable confusion in the case law and literature between challenging a landlord-nominated

---

6 *Scott & G&O Properties Ltd* LON/00AH/LSL/2004/0078 (LVT).
7 *Re Blocks C, E and G, Cherry Blossom Close, Chequers Way, London, N13* LVT/INS/027/003/00 (LVT).
8 *Tredegar v Harwood* [1929] AC 72; *Bandar Properties v JS Darwen* [1968] 2 All ER 305; 19 P&CR 785; *Havenridge Ltd v Boston Dyers Ltd* [1994] 2 EGLR 73; [1994] 49 EG 111.

insurer on the grounds of excessive premium payments and challenging the reasonableness of premium payments recovered as service charges. The two situations are quite distinct and will depend on a construction of the lease as to whether insurance is effected by the landlord or the tenant.

5.22   In particular, there has been a tendency to assume that case law that concerns the recovery of service charges applies equally to a challenge made to a landlord-nominated insurer.

Excessive from the tenant's point of view

5.23   Landlord and Tenant Act (LTA) 1985 s19, which governs the reasonableness of service charges, has been interpreted in a manner which focuses on the reasonableness of the landlord.[9] By contrast challenges to the landlord's nominated insurer on the grounds that a premium payment is excessive, focuses on the payment from the point of view of the tenant.[10]

5.24   It is common for landlords to cite the case of *Berrycroft Management*[11] as authority that if they have negotiated the insurance at arms length in an open market, any premium payment will not be excessive.

5.25   *Berrycroft* is a service charge case and has no direct application to the challenge to a landlord-nominated insurer. To treat arms length negotiation as determinative of the question of whether premium payments are excessive, would be 'to emasculate the protection afforded to leaseholders by . . . paragraph 8 [of LTA 1985 Sch 1]'.[12] At best, arms length negotiations for an insurer is evidence which an LVT might take into account in deciding whether premium payments are excessive.

How much is excessive?

5.26   Premium payments are not excessive simply because they are not the cheapest. There is clearly a range of reasonable premiums available to any landlord and they cannot be faulted because they have not selected the cheapest available.[13]

9 See para 2.78 above.
10 *Harker v Forcelux Ltd* M/INS/3 (LVT).
11 *Berrycroft Management v Sinclair Gardens Investments* (1997) 29 HLR 444; (1998) 75 P&CR 210.
12 *Re Blocks C, E and G, Cherry Blossom Close, Chequers Way, London, N13* LVT/INS/027/003/00 (LVT).
13 *23–45 The Woodfines, Hornchurch, Essex, RM11 3HR*, LVT/INS/030/003/99 (LVT).

5.27   As a rule of thumb, LVTs do not seem impressed by evidence from tenants that they could obtain a number of quotations at 20–30 per cent less than the premium imposed by the landlord's insurer. Conversely where the landlord's insurer is charging premiums over twice the size of quotations obtained by tenants, the LVT has almost always found those to be excessive.

5.28   When seeking to challenge the premiums, LVTs are entitled to use their local knowledge of the insurance market. Much more important is for tenants to obtain evidence of alternative like-for-like quotes.

5.29   In cases where the insurer passes on to the landlord a proportion of the insurance premiums as a 'commission' or other payment, it could be argued that the premiums are thereby excessive since they enable the landlord to make a profit. Surprisingly, there are no reported cases on this point.[14]

Remedies

5.30   If an LVT finds the insurance arrangements to be unsatisfactory, it may make an order requiring the landlord to nominate an insurer specified in the order or requiring the landlord to nominate another insurer who will be capable of meeting the requirements listed in the order.[15] Tenants are advised to bring evidence of the insurers they wish to see nominated and their reasons for so wishing.

5.31   Any agreement by the tenant (other than an arbitration agreement) which purports to provide for an alternative method of resolution or determination of insurance issues is void in so far as it would trespass on the rights of either party to make an application under paragraph 8.[16]

Failure to pay out insurance monies

5.32   There have been reports of situations where a landlord refuses to apply money obtained as a result of a claim under an insurance policy. Such situations are comparatively rare, since a lease with an insurance provision should also contain a covenant to apply the

---

14 See the discussion for a similar situation where the insurance is paid for through the service charge bill at para 2.80.

15 LTA 1985 Sch para 8(4).

16 LTA 1985 Sch para 8(6).

sums received by way of insurance to the rebuilding or repairing of the property. Insurance legislation often exists to overcome this problem, for example, section 83 of the Fire Prevention (Metropolis) Act 1774 provides that certain tenants may claim on their landlord's policy in respect of a fire.[17]

5.33   If a lease does not contain a covenant in the terms suggested above then it should be varied. This should be done by agreement with the landlord but failing that an application to the LVT to vary the lease may be necessary.[18]

5.34   If the policy of insurance is taken out in the names of both the tenant and landlord they will be entitled to share any insurance payments in the same proportion as their respective interests in the premises. This may provide an alternative means to ensuring tenants are able to put insurance money back into the property.[19]

5.35   A third possible remedy in this situation is to sue the landlord for breach of covenant. Where a tenant pays a proportion of the premium of an insurance policy in favour of the landlord, the latter is obliged to exercise the rights conferred by the policy to protect the tenant's interest.[20]

Arranging your own insurance

5.36   Since 28 February 2005 (in England)[21] and 31 May 2005 (in Wales)[22] where a tenant has a long lease[23] of a house[24] and is required by the lease to insure the house with an insurer nominated or approved by the landlord, the tenant is not required to effect the insurance with the landlord's insurer if the tenant instead ensures that the house is insured under a policy of insurance with an authorised insurer.[25]

---

17 See also *Mumford Hotels v Wheeler and another* [1964] 1 Ch 117.
18 See chapter 7.
19 *Beacon Carpets v Kirby* [1985] QB 755; [1984] 3 WLR 489.
20 *Vural v Securities* (1990) 60 P&CR 258.
21 Commonhold and Leasehold Reform Act 2002 (Commencement No 5 and Savings and Transitional Provisions) Order 2004 SI No 3056.
22 Commonhold and Leasehold Reform Act 2002 (Commencement No 2 and Savings) (Wales) Order SI No 1353.
23 CLRA 2002 ss76 and 77.
24 As defined in Part 1 of the Leasehold Reform Act 1967.
25 CLRA 2002 s164.

5.37   If a tenant chooses to take such a step, there are a number of guarantees which must be contained in the policy of insurance:[26]

(a) the policy must protect both the interests of the landlord and the tenant;[27]

(b) the policy must cover all the risks which the lease requires to be covered;[28]

(c) the amount of cover must not be less than that which the lease requires to be provided by insurance.[29]

In addition, there is a strict procedure to be followed by any tenant thinking of taking this route.

5.38   The tenant must give the landlord a notice of cover in prescribed form.[30] The notice of cover must be served on the landlord within 14 days of the date on which it took effect or was renewed.[31] In the case of a new landlord, the tenant may be requested to provide a copy of the notice of cover within one month and 14 days of the new landlord acquiring the interest of the previous landlord.[32]

5.39   If the notice of cover is to be posted to the landlord, it must be sent to the address specified by the landlord, either as the address for service of notices or, if that is unknown, the address used for demands for rent. Alternatively, the landlord may nominate an entirely different address in England or Wales.[33] It is strongly recommended that any such notice of cover be sent by recorded delivery.

Rights to information in relation to insurance

5.40   If a tenant or Recognised Tenants' Association is faced with a service charge demand in respect of insurance, the tenant possesses certain additional rights to information.

---

26 CLRA 2002 s164(2).

27 CLRA 2002 s164(2)(a); see also Financial Services and Markets Act 2002 s19.

28 CLRA 2002 s164(2)(b).

29 CLRA 2002 s164(2)(c).

30 Leasehold Houses (Notice of Insurance Cover) (England) Regulations 2004 SI No 3097 or Leasehold Houses (Notice of Insurance Cover) Wales Regulations 2005 SI No 1354.

31 CLRA 2002 s164(3).

32 CLRA 2002 s164(4).

33 CLRA 2002 ss164(8) and (9).

5.41   The landlord can be required to provide a written summary of the insurance in respect of the property, setting out: [34]

(a) the amount insured under any relevant policy;
(b) the name of the insurer;
(c) the risks insured against.

5.42   Within six months of receiving such information, the tenant may require the landlord to allow him access to the original policy itself and any related accounts. Copies of such documents may be taken.[35]

5.43   Failure on the part of the landlord to comply (subject to a defence of reasonable excuse) with these duties is a criminal offence punishable by a fine.[36] This does not apply to tenants whose landlords are a local authority, a National Park Authority or a new town corporation.[37]

Right to notify insurer of a claim

5.44   Any tenant who pays a service charge in respect of insurance provision is also entitled to report any damage which may be subject of a claim under the insurance policy to the insurers.[38] However, this right is only exercisable if the insurance policy requires a person insured to give notice of any claim within a specified period.[39] If this is the case, the tenant has the right, within that period, to contact the insurer in writing and specify the nature of the damage.

5.45   This does not confer on a tenant the right to make a claim under the policy, or to compel a landlord to do so or to spend any insurance monies received on reinstatement of the property.

5.46   Failure on the part of the landlord to comply (subject to a defence of reasonable excuse) with these duties is a criminal offence punishable by a fine.[40] This does not apply to tenants whose landlords are a local authority, a National Park Authority or a new town corporation.[41]

---

34 LTA 1985 Sch para 2.
35 LTA 1985 Sch para 3.
36 LTA 1985 Sch para 6.
37 LTA 1985 Sch para 9.
38 LTA 1985 Sch para 7.
39 LTA 1985 Sch para 7(2).
40 LTA 1985 Sch para 6.
41 LTA 1985 Sch para 9.

CHAPTER 6

Administration charges

6.1   Introduction

6.4   Advice to tenants

6.6   Why were administration charges introduced?

6.10   What is an administration charge?
6.11   Problems with this definition

6.14   Administration charges in practice

6.19   Types of administration charges

6.25   Challenging non-variable administration charges

6.32   Challenging variable administration charges

6.43   Estate management schemes

Key points

- Prior to CLRA 2002, leases could provide for the payments which were neither rent nor service charges. Some of these are now classified as 'administration charges'.
- An administration charge is one charged by a landlord in association with the cost of:
  - granting approvals
  - considering applications
  - providing information
  - failures by tenants to make a payment
  - breaches of covenant.
- Some administration charges are classified as 'variable'.
- If a sum is specified in the lease or calculated by reference to a formula then it is not 'variable'.
- The LVT has the power to vary leases where 'fixed' charges are unreasonable. The variation is binding for the future on all parties and any successors to the lease. This remedy cannot be used to challenge sums which have already become payable.
- A tenant may apply to the LVT for a determination of the payability of an administration that was payable after 30 September 2003.
- 'Variable' administration charges are payable only to the extent the amount is reasonable.
- A tenant has the right to withhold any administration charges until the landlord provides a summary of the rights and obligations of the tenant in relation to those charges.

Introduction

6.1   Administration charges are charges other than service charges demanded by a landlord. They do not have to be specified under the lease. Obvious examples include charges for giving consent to alteration, late payment fees and charges for giving information.

6.2   Since the passage of the Commonhold and Leasehold Reform Act (CLRA) 2002, these charges have been regulated through two distinct mechanisms. First, variable administration charges are only payable to the extent that they are reasonable. Second, the LVT is empowered to vary any clause of the lease which deals with non-variable administration charges.

6.3   While this division might appear logical and straightforward, in practice, the distinction between these two types of charge is difficult to draw. In addition, the jurisdiction of the LVT has been severely curtailed as a result of what appears to be an oversight in the drafting of CLRA 2002 Sch 11.

Advice to tenants

6.4   A landlord will frequently charge (or attempt to charge) for items of expenditure which are not service charges in that they are either:

(a) not specified in the lease;
(b) if they are specified in the lease are for fixed amounts; or
(c) do not vary with the relevant costs of the landlord.

Until the CLRA 2002, these charges were unregulated.

6.5   CLRA 2002 attempted to regulate these charges but, through a combination of poor drafting and confused (and confusing) Lands Tribunal decisions, the protections which parliament intended to create will in some cases have limited value.

Why were administration charges introduced?

6.6   One cannot understand the current confusion in this area of law without understanding what mischief parliament was attempting to remedy when it legislated to regulate administration charges in CLRA 2002.

6.7   For a charge to be a 'service charge' it must:[1]

(a) be payable under the lease; and
(b) vary with the relevant costs of the landlord.

6.8   This means that there will be circumstances where a landlord is entitled to charge a tenant where that charge is not a service charge and where, absent any other protection, the tenant would lose the protections described in other parts of this work. For example:

(a) Where a lease forbids alteration of the property, a tenant would have to seek the consent of the landlord to any alteration. The

---

1   Landlord and Tenant Act (LTA) 1985 s18.

landlord has no obligation to give consent[2] and may charge the tenant any fee they wish for doing so.

(b) Where a landlord serves a section 146 notice[3] they have a statutory right to recover any reasonable costs and expenses where relief from forfeiture is given by the court or the breach is waived by the landlord at the request of the tenant.[4] Such a charge (not arising under the lease) would not be a service charge.

(c) The lease might contain provision for a fixed charge by the land-lord. This is relatively common in the case of consents or some-times the supply of information by the landlord. Such a fee would not vary with the relevant costs and would also not be a service charge.[5]

6.9 Schedule 11 of CLRA 2002, introduced a new concept, the 'adminis-tration charge', which covers some of these circumstances. Tenants were given rights in relation to administration charges which are similar (but not identical) to those relating to service charges.

What is an administration charge?

6.10 An administration charge is an amount payable by a tenant of a dwelling as part of or in addition to the rent which is payable, directly or indirectly for one of the following:[6]

(a) costs associated with the granting of approvals under the lease, or considering applications for such approvals, such as consent to alterations;

(b) for or in connection with the provision of information or docu-ments by or on behalf of the landlord or a person who is a party to the lease other than as a landlord or tenant, such as would arise in connection with the sale of the leasehold;

(c) charges arising out of a failure by the tenant to make a payment due under the lease;

(d) charges arising from a breach or alleged breach of covenant.

---

2 Unless the lease stipulates that the alteration may not be made without consent, in which case the landlord may not unreasonably withhold consent (LTA 1927 s19).

3 A notice required before forfeiting the lease for breach of most covenants other than those to pay rent – see chapter 10.

4 Law of Property Act 1925 s146(3).

5 *Coventry CC v Cole* [1994] 1 WLR 398; [1994] 1 All ER 997.

6 CLRA 2002 Sch 11 para 1(3).

Problems with this definition

6.11 A puzzling aspect of this list is that some of the charges appear to overlap with amounts that are already covered by the definition of service charges. For example, the following provision (or wording to the same effect) is very commonly found as a tenant covenant in long leases:

> The tenant will pay the landlord's costs of preparing and serving a notice under section 146 of the Law of Property Act 1925 whether or not relief is given by the court.

A charge made under such a provision is a service charge[7] but would also seem to be an administration charge under clause (d) above.

6.12 The explanatory notes to CLRA 2002 stated that the aims of the act included:

> introduc[ing] the right to challenge the reasonableness of one-off charges not recovered as service charges ('administration charges');

which suggests that the drafters of the Act believed that administration charges (as defined) were distinct from service charges. It is unclear whether this assumption is correct. The reader of the Act is left wondering whether a charge that falls into the overlap (such as the one just described) is a service charge, an administration charge or both.

6.13 The question has practical implications: the regimes for control of service and administration charges are, as will be seen below, different in some important respects, for example there is no requirement to consult[8] on administration charges whereas there may be for sums that will be recovered via the service charge bill.

Administration charges in practice

6.14 The authors' view is that CLRA 2002 cannot have meant to remove existing protection from tenants – so the charge for service of a section 146 notice will be a service charge (whether or not it is also an administration charge).

6.15 In practice, there are two broad categories of situation where there is no doubt at all that a charge cannot be a service charge and therefore can only be an administration charge.

---

7   *Re Forcelux Ltd* LRX/33/2003 (Lands Tribunal).

8   See chapter 4.

6.16   First, where the lease specifies a charge that does not vary with the relevant cost (and so is not a 'service charge').[9] For example, where fixed sums are charged for late payment of rent or service charges, or for permission to assign, or where a percentage fee (or interest charge) is specified in the lease as a penalty for late payment of rent or service charges. Examples such as these are widespread and it is quite clear they fall only into the 'administration charge' category.

6.17   Second, the definition of administration charge applies to *any* charge whether it is specified in the lease or not. A common situation facing many tenants is that they require permission from their landlord – for example for assigning the property – but no sum charged or method of charging is specified in the lease. Such a sum cannot be a service charge (which would only apply to a sum payable under the lease).[10] Again it is clear that these charges are administration charges not service charges.

6.18   These two broad categories encompass the vast majority of cases that will be seen by advisers.

Types of administration charges

6.19   CLRA 2002 divides administration charges into two classes:

(a) Those which are:
   (i) specified in the lease; or
   (ii) calculated according to a formula specified in the lease.
(b) Any other administration charge, which is known as a 'variable administration charge'.

6.20   Most commentators[11] understood 'formula' in this context to be intended to be read narrowly. It was assumed that (a)(i) above applied to express sums specified in the lease – for example a fee of £100 for approval of an assignment – and that (a)(ii) applied to methods of calculation that did not vary with relevant costs, for example where an express sum was specified to increase with inflation. This view was encouraged by the fact that charges falling under (b) are described as 'variable'. The opposite of variable is 'fixed' and there has been

---

9 *Coventry CC v Cole* [1994] 1 WLR 398; [1994] 1 All ER 997.
10 But see remarks on the case of *Bold* following, in which the Lands Tribunal may have seriously weakened the usefulness of the law covering this class of examples.
11 See for example Tanfield Chambers, *Service Charges and Management: Law and Practice* (Sweet and Maxwell, 2005) at p112.

a strong temptation to described charges under (a) (which are not given any name by the Act) as 'fixed administration charges'. Variable charges were then seen as being analogous to service charges which also vary with the relevant cost.

6.21   The Lands Tribunal appears to take a different view in *Botterill v Hampstead Garden Suburbs Trust Limited*:[12]a case on the identical distinction made for 'estate charges.'[13] The charge in question was described as

> a sum equal to a proportionate part of the expenses of the Trust in operating the scheme in an economical, efficient and consistent manner during that financial year ..., the proportion to be calculated by dividing the said expenses by the number of enfranchised properties on the 6th April in the financial year and rounding up to the nearest 10p ...

6.22   The tribunal decided that the scheme of dividing the costs between the charge payers was a 'formula' within the meaning of CLRA 2002 and therefore that the charge was not a variable charge. Further, 'specified in the lease' could be understood to apply to any term in a lease that provided for the recovery of the charge from the tenant (whether fixed or not). Taking this view to its logical conclusion would mean that variable administration charges would be exclusively those that are not payable under the lease, that is, those charges described in para 6.17 above.

6.23   In our view, *Botterill* cannot be right. The charge payers in *Botterill* had no way of challenging the underlying reasonableness of the costs incurred by the estate manager (the equivalent of the landlord for estate charges). There is no requirement that non-variable administration or estate charges be reasonable, all a tenant or charge payer is able to do is apply for the variation of the terms of the lease or estate management agreement to make those terms reasonable, but a proportional apportionment clause need not be objectionable even where the underlying costs are.

6.24   In a statement made in passing by the judge in *Botterill* he observed that the charge payers could always challenge the reasonableness of the charges. In this he was mistaken, which suggests that *Botterill* may be open to challenge on the basis that the judge was mistaken as to the relevant law to be applied.

---

12 LRX/135/2007 (Lands Tribunal).

13 As to which, see para 6.43, below.

Challenging non-variable administration charges

6.25   The only way to challenge an administration charge that is not variable is by an application to vary the lease. There is a specific procedure for varying the terms of the lease that determine the amount of an administration charge which is quite distinct from that discussed in chapter 7 which allows a far more general variation of leases.

6.26   A party to the lease may apply to the LVT for an order varying the lease on the following grounds:[14]

(a) the administration charge specified in the lease is unreasonable, or

(b) any formula specified in the lease is unreasonable.

A 'right to manage' company[15] is treated as being a party to the lease for these purposes.[16]

6.27   There does not seem to be any reason why a landlord should not apply for the increase of a non-variable administration charge provision in the lease that was unreasonably small. A court appointed manager would not be able to make an application of this kind because he or she would not be a party to the lease. He or she might be able to apply to an LVT to vary the terms of his or her appointment so that he or she is allowed to charge a suitable fee.[17]

6.28   As yet there is no guidance on how 'unreasonable' will be construed. It seems likely that the LVT will take a similar approach to that employed when dealing with service charges, and, as such, the test will be whether or not the charge is unreasonable from the landlord's perspective.[18]

6.29   The tribunal may accept or reject the variation proposed in the application but it also has the express power to make any other variation as it thinks fit.[19] Alternatively, the LVT may direct that the parties to the lease make arrangements to have it varied in a manner as directed.[20]

6.30   Any variation will be binding for the duration of the lease on the parties to the lease and any successors in title. Interestingly, predecessors in title are also bound by the variations.[21] The Act does not

---

14 CLRA 2002 Sch 11 para 3(1).
15 See chapter 9.
16 CLRA 2002 Sch 7 para 16.
17 See para 8.56 below.
18 See para 2.78 above.
19 CLRA 2002 Sch 11 para 3(3).
20 CLRA 2002 Sch 11 para 3(4).
21 CLRA 2002 Sch 11 para 3(6).

say expressly that any variation of the lease will only take effect from a particular date and have no retrospective effect, but it would seem surprising if the phrase 'duration of the lease' was meant to cover periods of time before the application and, in the authors' view, variation of leases is meant to be purely prospective.

6.31 This would appear to mean that if a non-variable administration charge becomes payable, there is no remedy from an LVT for a tenant who wishes to dispute it, even if it is clearly unreasonable. He or she may have grounds for varying the lease but this will only affect future payments.

Challenging variable administration charges

6.32 The provisions that control variable administration charges are similar to those already discussed for service charges.[22] One key difference is that a service charge is only payable to the extent that it has been reasonably incurred and any works paid for by the charge are to a reasonable standard, whereas a variable administration charge is only payable to the extent that it is reasonable.[23]

6.33 It has been suggested[24] that this difference means that in the case of service charges the focus is on the reasonableness of the way in which the landlord incurred the charges, but for an administration charge, the LVT need only focus on the sum actually charged.

6.34 As with service charges, an application may be made to an LVT to determine:[25]

(a) the person by whom the charge is payable;
(b) the person to whom it is payable;
(c) the amount which is payable;
(d) the date at which it is payable; and
(e) the manner in which it is payable.

6.35 As with service charges, the application may be made whether or not payment has been made, but not if the matter has been agreed or admitted by the tenant, has been referred to an arbitration process, or has been determined by a court or arbitration process.[26]

---

22 See chapter 2.
23 CLRA 2002 Sch 11 para 2.
24 In *Forcelux*, note 7, above.
25 CLRA 2002 Sch 11 para 5(1)
26 CLRA 2002 Sch 11 para 5(4).

6.36   Any agreement by the tenant (other than an arbitration agreement) which purports to provide for an alternative method of resolution or determination of administration charges is void in so far as
it would trespass on the rights of either party to make an application
under Schedule 11.[27]

6.37   A second key difference between the procedure for determining
the payability of administration charges and the similar procedure
for service charges is that there is no analogy of the two limbs of LTA
1985 s27A, in particular there is no equivalent of section 27A(3): an
application to determine, if costs were incurred, whether a service
charge would be payable. This leads to the question, if the costs of an
administration charge have not yet been incurred, can those potential costs be the subject of a decision by the LVT.

6.38   In *Drewett v Bold*[28] the Lands Tribunal decided that the answer
was 'no'.

6.39   The case involved an application by the tenants for a retrospective
grant of a licence to alter their property. The tenants challenged the
reasonableness of a sum of £7,747.52 plus additional fees of £2,000
plus VAT demanded by the landlords for the retrospective licence.
The Lands Tribunal held that the LVT could only determine the reasonableness of the administration charge in respect of work that had
already been done by the landlord.

6.40   This creates a difficult situation for leaseholders such as Miss
Bold. Where permission to alter is sought, most of the work to be
done by the landlord, for example in instructing a surveyor to consider any plans for the proposed work and a solicitor to alter any relevant plans in the lease, will be done after the permission is give.
Such permission will only be given in consideration of a sum agreed,
which would exclude the jurisdiction of the LVT because the tenant
will have agreed the sum. Miss Bold was left in the position of having a right that was, to her, essentially useless.

6.41   The right to challenge administration charges only applies to administration charges which became payable on or after 30 September 2003 (in England)[29] or 31 March 2004 (in Wales).[30]

6.42   As with service charges, an administration charge is only due

---

27 CLRA 2002 Sch 11 para 5(6).
28 LRX/90/2005 (Lands Tribunal).
29 Commonhold and Leasehold Reform Act 2002 (Commencement No 2 and
    Savings) (England) Order 2003 SI No 1986 Sch 2 para 8.
30 Commonhold and Leasehold Reform Act 2002 (Commencement No 2 and
    Savings) (Wales) Order 2004 SI No 669 Sch 2 para 8.

once the landlord has provided their name and address[31] and information regarding the tenants rights and obligations have been supplied with any demand.[32] These matters are discussed in chapter 3.

Estate management schemes

6.43   Where a group of tenants have bought the freehold, some land may remain in their former landlord's hands (for example, communal gardens or roads). It may be that this land needs money to be spent on it and the landlord will wish to recover the cost of maintaining the 'estate' from the former tenants. There are three statutory situations where the landlord may retain a right to impose charges on the tenant.[33] In this chapter such a system of freehold management is called will be referred to as an 'estate management scheme' (EMS); the charges under such a scheme being known as 'estate charges.'[34]

6.44   Unlike the situation with service and administration charges, where only charges for certain specified classes of cost are service or administration charges, any cost that an occupier or someone with an interest in land is obliged to pay under an EMS is an estate charge.[35]

6.45   LVTs exercise similar control over estate charges as they do over administration charges. The only important difference in the treatment of estate charges is that there is no concept of a 'party to a lease' for an EMS. Anyone who has an obligation to pay any estate charge may apply for the variation of an EMS in respect of non-variable estate charges.[36]

6.46   The creation of EMSs, or their variation for reasons unconnected with estate charges, is properly considered as part of the process of enfranchisement and thus beyond the scope of this work. Estate management schemes are comparatively rare and it is hoped that any readers of this work will not be affected by them.

---

31 LTA 1987 s47.

32 Administration Charges (Summary of Rights and Obligations) (England) Regulations 2007 SI No 1258; Administration Charges (Summary of Rights and Obligations) (Wales) Regulations 2007 SI No 3162.

33 Leasehold Reform Act 1967 s19; Leasehold Reform, Housing and Urban Development Act 1993, Part 1, Chapter 4 and s94.

34 CLRA 2002 s159(1).

35 CLRA 2002 s159(1).

36 CLRA 2002 s159(3).

CHAPTER 7

Variation of leases

7.1	**Introduction**
7.5	**Advice for tenants**
7.7	**Application to vary an individual lease**
7.9	**Grounds for varying a lease**
7.10	Repair or maintenance
7.12	Insurance
7.14	Repair or maintenance of any installations
7.17	Provision or maintenance of services
7.18	The recovery of expenditure for the benefit of another party
7.19	The computation of service charges
7.20	Other grounds
7.22	**Application to vary other leases**
7.25	**Application by a majority**
7.30	**Orders varying a lease**
7.39	**Procedural considerations**
7.40	**Insurance of dwellings houses**

Key points

- Any party to a lease may apply to vary a lease. Right to manage companies are treated as a party, but managing agents are not.
- An application may be made if the lease of a flat fails to make satisfactory provision for:
  - repair or maintenance of the building
  - repair or maintenance of the installations
  - insurance
  - provision or maintenance of services
  - recovery of expenditure
  - computation of service charges.
- The lease of a house may only be varied if it fails to make satisfactory provision for the insurance of the house.
- It is possible to apply to have a number of leases, such as all those relating to a block of flats, to be varied at once. A qualified majority of tenants would be needed in these situations.
- A Leasehold Valuation Tribunal may order compensation to be paid to any person suffering loss or disadvantage as a result of the variation. It must refuse to vary a lease where this would result in substantial prejudice to any person.
- The varied lease is binding on third parties and any successors in title.
- It is the duty of the applicant to inform the respondent and anyone else they know or have reason to believe may be affected by the variation. Failure to do so may result in the variation being set aside or the payment of damages to those affected.
- Proposed variations should be drafted by a legally qualified person in order to reduce the prospect of delay, re-drafting and amendment. The LVT will not want to accept a variation that will cause problems in the future.

Introduction

7.1   Many leases are, by any objective view, defective. For example the lease may not specify who is to pay for work that needs to be done or it may allocate service charges in a way that does not add up to 100 per cent of the total cost. These kinds of situation may arise because the lease was poorly drafted or because it was drafted before the development of modern property management. This chapter explains one remedy open to the parties to a lease: an application to an LVT for the variation of a lease.

7.2   There is also a procedure whereby a group of tenants can apply to vary all the leases in respect of a property.

7.3   There is an alternative procedure for the variation of the insurance provision of a leasehold house and this is the only power the LVT has to vary such a lease.

7.4   Unlike all other applications to an LVT it is the duty of the applicant to notify respondents and others who might be affected by the application. Any person who should have been notified of an application to vary a lease, but was not, may apply to have the variation cancelled or modified, or sue the applicant(s) for damages.

Advice for tenants

7.5   Often, the most effective way of resolving seemingly intractable disputes is to vary the lease. While the landlord and tenant are always entitled to come to a commercial agreement to this effect, the LVT has a power to impose variations on individual leases where the lease makes unsatisfactory provision for a number of specified matters and corresponding powers to ensure uniformity across the leases in a property.

7.6   When considering any variation, professional advice will almost always be necessary, if only to produce a draft of the proposed variation. The LVT will not accept a variation which it fears will simply cause further difficulties in later years. In addition, the Land Registry will often have specific requirements for the form of any order varying the lease.

Application to vary an individual lease

7.7   Any party to the lease may apply for its variation[1] if the lease fails to make satisfactory provision with respect to one or more specified matters.[2] In general terms they are: repair or maintenance of the building, insurance, repair or maintenance of installations; provision or maintenance of services, recovery of expenditure and the computation of service charges.

1   Landlord and Tenant Act (LTA) 1987 s35(1).
2   LTA 1987 s35(2).

7.8   The lease to be varied must have been granted for more than 21 years; be perpetually renewable or a right to buy lease.[3]

Grounds for varying a lease

7.9   The LVT may only vary a lease if it fails to make satisfactory provision with respect to one or more of the following matters.[4]

Repair or maintenance

7.10   'Repair or maintenance' applies not only to the repair or maintenance of the flat itself and the building in which it is contained but of any other land or building which is let to the tenant or over which the tenant also has rights under the lease.[5]

7.11   Thus if the lease fails to provide for repair or maintenance to external garages, recreation areas or laundries an application to vary the lease could be made so as to make the landlord responsible for their upkeep, subject to the recovery of costs through the service charge bill.

Insurance

7.12   In the same way, 'insurance' means insurance cover in respect of the flat itself and the building in which it is contained but of any other land or building which is let to the tenant or over which the tenant also has rights under the lease.[6]

7.13   The power of the LVT to vary provisions of a lease concerning insurance is restricted in three ways. The LVT cannot vary a term of the lease which gives the landlord the right to nominate an insurer; nor may the LVT insert a term that requires the landlord to nominate a list of insurers from which the tenant would be entitled to select; nor may the lease be varied so that it requires insurance with a particular insurer.[7]

---

3   LTA 1987 s59(3).
4   LTA 1987 s35(2).
5   LTA 1987 s35(2)(a).
6   LTA 1987 s35(2)(b).
7   LTA 1987 s38(7).

Repair or maintenance of any installations

7.14 'Repair or maintenance of any installations' applies to those which are reasonably necessary to ensure that occupiers of the flat enjoy a reasonable standard of accommodation.[8]

7.15 This includes factors relating to the common parts of the building containing the flat as well as the safety and security of the flat, its occupiers and the common parts of that building and so ought certainly to apply to door entry systems, for example.[9]

7.16 It is less clear how far 'necessary' extends. Lighting of the common parts and lifts giving access to upper floors in high-rise flats would seem uncontroversial while provision of cable television is almost certainly not required for the enjoyment of a reasonable standard of accommodation.

Provision or maintenance of services

7.17 Exactly the same considerations as above apply to provision or maintenance of services, so that cleaning of the common parts would certainly be included while the delivery of newspapers would almost certainly not.[10]

The recovery of expenditure for the benefit of another party

7.18 A lease may make unsatisfactory provision for the recovery of expenditure by one party[11] (usually the landlord) from another party or parties (usually the tenants) if it does not specify a requirement to pay interest or other sums on arrears of service charges.[12]

The computation of service charges

7.19 A lease fails to make satisfactory provision in respect of service charges[13] if the total service charge recovery is more or less than 100

---

8 LTA 1987 s35(2)(c).
9 LTA 1987 s35(3).
10 LTA 1987 s35(2)(d) and (3).
11 LTA 1987 s35(2)(e).
12 LTA 1987 s35(3A).
13 LTA 1987 s35(2)(e).

per cent, so that the landlord either has to make up the shortfall, or recovers more than he actually paid out.[14]

Other grounds

7.20   The Secretary of State may, by regulation, add other grounds for variation as he sees fit.[15]

7.21   In all cases, the lease must fail to make satisfactory provision. It appears that this is an objective test and the fact that the applicant would wish the lease to be drafted differently is not enough.[16]

Application to vary other leases

7.22   Once an application to vary a lease (the original lease) has been made, any other party to the lease may apply to an LVT asking it to vary other leases if an order is made varying the original lease.[17] The other leases must share the same landlord as the original lease, though they need not be leases for flats in the same building.[18]

7.23   For example where a tenant applies for the variation of their lease, a respondent landlord may wish to use the opportunity to vary all their other leases in the same or a similar way. The grounds for this supplementary application must be the same as the original application. So if, for example, a respondent landlord wished to make various additional variations then a fresh application would be needed.

7.24   It must also be shown that it would be in the respondent's interest or in the interests of the other parties to the various leases to have them varied to the same effect.[19] Such applications are likely to be restricted to landlords since it is unusual that a tenant is a party to multiple leases from the same landlord.

Application by a majority

7.25   In cases where one lease is defective it will be very common for most or all the other leases of flats also to be defective. In such a case an

---

14   LTA 1987 s35(4).
15   LTA 1987 s35(2)(g).
16   *Gianfrancesco v Haughton*, LRX/10/2007 (Lands Tribunal).
17   LTA 1987 s36.
18   LTA 1987 s36(2).
19   LTA 1987 s36(3).

application for variation of some or all of the relevant leases may be made if, as defined below, a sufficient proportion of the parties to the lease agree.[20]

7.26 Such an application may be made by the landlord or any of the tenants under the lease. An application may only be made in respect of two or more leases. All the leases must be made with the same landlord though they need not all be in the same building nor need the leases be in identical terms.[21]

7.27 An application may only be made if it is supported by a minimum number of parties to the various leases involved. Where someone is a party to more than one lease he or she counts as more than one party.[22] Joint tenants of a lease count as one party.[23]

7.28 Where there are fewer than nine dwellings then all, or all but one, of the parties must agree. Where there are nine or more dwellings, at least 75 per cent of the parties must consent and no more than 10 per cent may oppose the application.[24]

7.29 Such an application may only be made if the object to be achieved by the variation cannot be satisfactorily achieved unless all the leases are varied to the same effect.[25] From this it would appear that an application of this kind is not restricted to the grounds listed above, though the restrictions on the kind of variation an LVT can make to the insurance provisions of a lease will still apply.

Orders varying a lease

7.30 If the LVT is satisfied that the grounds for an application for the variation of a lease have been made out then they may make an order varying the lease.[26] Though the LVT will normally make an order for a variation in accordance with that submitted by the applicant(s) they have the power to make any variation they think fit.[27]

7.31 The LVT only has the power to vary those leases for which the grounds for application have been made out.[28] Such an order may

20 LTA 1987 s37.
21 LTA 1987 s37(2).
22 LTA 1987 s37(6).
23 LTA 1987 s37(6).
24 LTA 1987 s37(5).
25 LTA 1987 s37(3).
26 LTA 1987 s38.
27 LTA 1987 s38(4).
28 LTA 1987 s38(5).

directly vary the lease or it may direct the parties to carry out the variation.[29]

7.32   In order to reduce the prospect of delay, re-drafting and amendment, it is suggested that any proposed variations be drafted by a legally qualified person. An LVT is likely to scrutinise the wording and terminology of the proposed variation with some care and non-lawyers may not appreciate the full effect of the proposed variation. In particular, two important checks should be carried out in respect of any proposed variation:

(a) if the proposed variation introduces a new term, that term must be adequately defined;

(b) the proposed variation must take into account any changes which will be necessitated to the rest of the lease. Although a lease contains many schedules and sections, it must be read and, after the proposed variation, must be able to continue to be read as a continuous and internally coherent document.

7.33   It may also be necessary to consult the Land Registry in order to ensure that the proposed form of variation will be capable of being registered.[30]

7.34   The LVT's power to vary a lease is moderated in three respects. First, there is a power to order that any party to the lease pay any other person (not necessarily a party to the lease) compensation for any loss or disadvantage they are likely to suffer as a result of the variation.[31]

7.35   Second, if there would be substantial prejudice to any person and where an order for payment would not be adequate compensation the LVT must not order a variation.[32]

7.36   Finally, the LVT may also refuse to make an order if for any other reason 'it would not be reasonable in the circumstances.'[33]

7.37   An order for the variation of a lease is binding on third parties and is not restricted to those who were parties to the lease at the time of the application.[34] In particular it is binding on any surety who guaranteed the performance (whether by a tenant or landlord) of any

---

29 LTA 1987 s38(8).

30 *Tickmead Ltd v Interasia World Wide Ltd and others* LON/OOBK/LVL/2004/0002/01 (LVT).

31 LTA 1987 s38(10).

32 LTA 1987 s38(6)(a).

33 LTA 1987 s38(6)(b).

34 LTA 1987 s39(1).

obligation under the lease despite the fact that the obligation may be changed by the variation.[35]

7.38 Anyone who should have been notified of the application to the LVT by the applicant, but who was not notified, may apply to the LVT for the cancellation or modification of the variation.[36] The LVT may either accede to their request or order the payment of compensation.[37] If the LVT cancels or modifies the variation it may backdate that cancellation or modification so that it takes effect on the date the original variation was ordered or it may order it to take effect on any later date that it sees fit.[38]

Procedural considerations

7.39 Unlike all other applications to the LVT, it is the duty of the applicant to notify and serve respondents and others who might be affected by the application.[39]

Insurance of dwellings houses

7.40 An application to vary the lease of a dwelling that is not a flat may also be made, but only on the ground that the lease fails to make satisfactory provision with respect to insurance, including the recovery of the costs of such insurance.[40] The power of the LVT to make an order for variation in respect of insurance provisions is restricted in the same way as for long leases of flats.

7.41 Such an application may only be made by a tenant who holds long leases in respect of two or fewer dwellings from the same landlord.[41] Where the tenant is a company this includes leases held by associated companies.[42] There is no corresponding right for a respondent

---

35 LTA 1987 s39(2).
36 LTA 1987 s39(3).
37 LTA 1987 s39(4).
38 LTA 1987 s39(5).
39 LTA 1987 s35(5) and Leasehold Valuation Tribunals (Procedure) (England) Regulations 2003 SI No 2099; Leasehold Valuation Tribunals (Procedure) (Wales) Regulations 2004 SI No 681.
40 LTA 1987 s40(1).
41 LTA 1987 s40(4A).
42 LTA 1987 s40(4B).

to apply for the variation of additional leases or for a majority of lease-holders of the same landlord to make an application for variation of a lease.

CHAPTER 8

Appointment of a manager

8.1   Introduction

8.5   Advice for tenants

8.7   The role of a manager

8.11   Pre-application procedure

8.15   Reasonable period

8.17   Errors in the notice

8.18   Dispensing with service of the notice

8.21   Grounds for the appointment of a manager

8.22   Entitlement to apply for the appointment of a manager

8.24   Properties which may have a manager appointed

        Exempt landlord • Resident landlords • Charities • Crown interest

8.31   Persons who may apply to have a manager appointed

8.33   Grounds for the appointment of a manager

8.35   Relevant person

8.37   Breach of an obligation

8.40   Demanding unreasonable service charges

8.43   Demanding unreasonable administration charges

8.45   Failure to comply with the relevant Code of Practice

8.47   Just and convenient

8.48   Other circumstances where it is just and convenient

continued

8.49   Forthcoming legislative changes

8.50   The extent of the property to be managed

8.52   The management functions to be conferred

8.56   Remuneration

8.60   Persons likely to be appointed as a manager

8.62   Directions

8.63   Variation or discharge

8.68   RTM company

8.69   Miscellaneous

8.73   Consultation about managing agents

Key points

- A common complaint of tenants is that their property has been badly managed. Many service charge disputes have poor property management as their cause. The Leasehold Valuation Tribunal (LVT) has a power to appoint a manager where problems arise.
- There are a number of limits on the right to apply to the LVT. The most important is that 'resident landlords' who live in the property and manage it themselves are usually exempt from having applications made against them.
- The LVT regards the appointment of a manager against the wishes of the landlord to be a draconian step and will usually require these preliminary stages to be completed. In exceptional circumstances, the LVT will be willing to waive compliance.
- A tenant must show that it would be just and convenient in all the circumstances for a manager to be appointed.
- The tenant must also show one of the following:
  - one of the respondents is in breach of a management obligation under the lease
  - unreasonable service charge demands have been made, are proposed or are likely to be made
  - unreasonable variable administration charge demands have been made, are proposed or are likely to be made
  - there have been breaches of the relevant codes of practice
  - other circumstances exist which make it just and convenient for the order to be made.
- There is no requirement that a professional manager be appointed but LVTs prefer this to be the case.

Introduction

8.1 Property management is a complex matter. Some landlords chose to manage their properties themselves and, in doing so, fail (whether deliberately or not) to properly perform their obligations under the lease. Some landlords choose to appoint a company or individual which holds itself out as a professional manager but this is no guarantee of quality. In situations where tenants are dissatisfied with the management of the property, either by their landlord; manager appointed by the landlord; or by a Right to Manage (RTM) company, the LVT has a power to appoint a manager and/or receiver.

8.2   The power to appoint a manager 'for cause' (that is, where there has been specific default on the part of the existing manager) is to be contrasted with the RTM provisions where the conduct of the existing management is irrelevant.[1]

8.3   The process to be followed by tenants wishing to have the LVT appoint a manager begins by giving a notice to the landlord, setting out the nature of the problem. The landlord must then be given the opportunity to remedy the problem. If he fails to do so, then an application may be made to the LVT for the appointment of a manager. Provision is also made for dispensing with service of the notice in appropriate cases.

8.4   The grounds on which an LVT may appoint a manager are set out in statute.[2] If one or more of the statutory grounds are made out, the LVT is empowered to appoint a manager on such terms as it thinks fit. The manager is not limited to carrying out the functions of the landlord under the lease and they may be given power over property which was not part of the premises being managed before the appointment.

Advice for tenants

8.5   The appointment of a manager is a very flexible power which can be used to remedy a wide variety of problems. However, an LVT appointed manager will be a neutral party. The manager will not do the bidding of either the tenants or the landlord, but will manage the property in the best interests of all parties. Tenants who wish to have a more 'hands on' role need to consider using the RTM process.

8.6   As far as possible, all tenants, not just those bringing the application, should support the appointment of a manager. LVTs regard the decision to 'strip the landlord of his right to maintain his own building' as 'draconian' and not to be invoked lightly.[3] If there are tenants who are not parties to the application, they should be asked to provide letters of support for the proposed manager suggested by the applicants.

---

1   See chapter 9.
2   See para 8.33.
3   *Re 26 and 28 Birdhurst Rise, South Croydon* LON/00AH/NAM/2003/006 (LVT).

The role of a manager

8.7 A manager appointed by the LVT is not appointed to favour the tenants, nor to carry out the functions of the landlord under the lease. The manager is appointed to oversee a scheme of management and acts independently of the parties, as a servant of the tribunal.[4] This has a number of important consequences.

8.8 First, the tenants cannot hold previous failings of the landlord against the manager and, for example, cannot raise a set-off[5] in respect of breaches of covenant by the landlord against service charge demands made by the manager.[6]

8.9 Second, because the role of the LVT is to create an effective scheme of management, rather than simply require the manager to discharge the landlord's obligations under the lease, the manager may be given power over property owned by the landlord, but which is not part of any of the flats demised to the tenants.[7]

8.10 Third, because the powers of the manager are derived from the order appointing him, the order can be worded so as to allow him to recover service charges or fees which are not included in the lease and, in effect, to remedy any defects in the drafting.[8]

Pre-application procedure

8.11 The tenant must serve a notice on the landlord and any other person who owes management obligations under the lease.[9]

8.12 The notice must be in writing and may be served by post.[10] If the landlord has a mortgage on the property, then he is obliged to pass a copy of the notice on to the mortgagee as soon as is reasonably practicable.[11]

8.13 The notice must:[12]

(a) specify the name and address of the flat and the name and address

---

4 *Maunder Taylor v Blaquiere* [2002] EWCA Civ 1633; [2003] 1 WLR 379.
5 See para 2.69.
6 *Maunder Taylor v Blaquiere*, above note 4.
7 *Cawsand Fort Management Company Ltd v Stafford and others* [2007] EWCA Civ 1187; [2007] 48 EG 145.
8 *Maunder Taylor v Joshi* LRX/107/2005 (Lands Tribunal).
9 Landlord and Tenant Act (LTA) 1987 s22(1).
10 LTA 1987 s54.
11 LTA 1987 s22(4).
12 LTA 1987 s22(2).

where notices can be served on the tenant if different from the address of the flat;

(b) include a statement that the tenant intends to make an application for an order that a manager be appointed in respect of specified premises;

(c) specify the grounds on which the tenant will ask the LVT to make the order and the matters that will be relied on by the tenant as evidence of the grounds;

(d) where the matters of which the tenant is complaining can be remedied by the landlord or other manager, include a statement requiring the landlord or manager to remedy the problems set out and giving a reasonable period for this to take place.

8.14 The Secretary of State (in Wales, the Welsh Assembly[13]) may, by regulation, specify other matters which must be included.[14] There is a similar power to specify the form of the notice.[15] No such regulations have yet been made in either case.

Reasonable period

8.15 The 'reasonable period' for remedying the problems will depend on the circumstances of each case. The more substantial the complaint, the longer will be needed to remedy it. As a general rule however, 14 days should be considered the absolute minimum 'reasonable period' that the tenant should offer.

8.16 If at the conclusion of the 'reasonable period' the tenant remains dissatisfied an application to the LVT may proceed.[16]

Errors in the notice

8.17 The LVT is entitled to proceed with the application if it thinks fit, notwithstanding that the notice which fails to comply with any of the requirements or where (in the view of the LVT) the period specified in the notice is not a reasonable period.[17]

---

13 National Assembly for Wales (Transfer of Functions) Order 1999 SI No 672.

14 LTA 1987 s22(2)(e).

15 LTA 1987 s54(3).

16 LTA 1987 s23.

17 LTA 1987 s24(7).

Dispensing with service of the notice

8.18   If it is not reasonably practicable to serve a notice on a landlord or other person, the tenant may apply to the LVT for permission to dispense with the requirement to serve a notice.[18]

8.19   If problems with properly serving the notices (for example where the landlord cannot be found) are anticipated in advance a freestanding application can be made to the LVT to make such a dispensation. On the other hand where problems with the service of notice only become apparent at a late stage the application can be considered at the hearing of the application for an order appointing a manager itself.[19]

8.20   Tenants should not rely on the LVT granting dispensation as a matter of course and will be expected to produce evidence of the impracticability of serving the notice. Evidence that the post-office were unable to deliver the documents should be sufficient. If dispensation is granted, the LVT may direct that other notices are served or other steps (such as placing an advert in a local newspaper) are taken.[20]

Grounds for the appointment of a manager

8.21   In considering whether or not to appoint a manager, the LVT must go through a four stage process:[21]

(a) it must be satisfied that the applicants are entitled to apply to have a manager appointed and that the property is one in respect of which a manager may be appointed;

(b) it must consider whether the statutory criteria for the appointment of a manager are met and whether or not to exercise its discretionary power to appoint a manager in those circumstances;

(c) it must identify the scope of the property over which the manager is to be appointed;

(d) it must determine what functions to confer upon the manager.

---

18 LTA 1987 s22(3).
19 LTA 1987 s22(3).
20 LTA 1987 s22(3).
21 *Cawsand Fort Management Company Ltd v Stafford and others* [2007] EWCA Civ 1187; [2007] 48 EG 145.

Entitlement to apply for the appointment of a manager

8.22   The power of the LVT to appoint a manager is not unfettered. A notice under section 22 must either have been served (and the period for remedial action to be taken expired) or have been dispensed with (and any additional steps specified by the LVT complied with).[22]

8.23   In addition, it must be shown both that the LVT has jurisdiction over the particular property and that the applicants are entitled to make the application.

Properties which may have a manager appointed

8.24   The LVT is empowered to appoint a manager of any premises consisting of the whole or part of a building, so long as the building contains two or more flats.[23]

8.25   A flat is, for these purposes, a separate set of premises, whether or not on the same floor, which forms part of a building; is divided horizontally from some other part of that building, and is constructed or adapted for use for the purposes of a dwelling.[24] There are, however, a number of exceptions.

Exempt landlord

8.26   No application can be made in respect of any premises where the landlord is an 'exempt landlord'.[25] An exempt landlord is:[26]

(a)   a district, county, county borough or London borough council;
(b)   the Common Council of the City of London;
(c)   the London Fire and Emergency Planning Authority;
(d)   the Council of the Isles of Scilly;
(e)   a police authority;
(f)   a joint authority;
(g)   the Commission for New Towns;
(h)   a development corporation;
(i)   an urban development corporation;

---

22   LTA 1987 s23.
23   LTA 1987 s21(2).
24   LTA 1987 s60.
25   LTA 1987 s21(3)(a).
26   LTA 1987 s58(1).

(j)   a housing action trust;
(k)   the Broads Authority;
(l)   a National Park Authority;
(m) the Housing Corporation;
(n)   a housing trust which is a charity;
(o)   a registered social landlord;
(p)   a fully mutual housing association;
(q)   a joint waste authority.

Resident landlords

8.27   No application can be made in respect of any premises where there is a resident landlord.[27]

8.28   A resident landlord is someone who occupies a flat in the premises as his only or principal residence and has done so for a period of not less than 12 months.[28] The exception does not apply if the premises are or form part of a purpose-built block of flats[29] or if at least one half of the flats in the premises are held on residential[30] long leases.[31]

Charities

8.29   No application can be made in respect of any premises included within the functional land of a charity.[32] Functional land is any land occupied by the charity or its trustees and used wholly or mainly for charitable purposes. In this context 'charity' has the restricted meaning given to it in section 96 of the Charities Act 1993[33] which (broadly speaking) excludes Church of England charities with a spiritual purpose.

Crown interest

8.30   Property subject to a Crown interest is excluded from the scope of these provisions.[34]

---

27   LTA 1987 s21(3)(a).
28   LTA 1987 s58(2).
29   LTA 1987 ss58(2)(a)–58(3).
30   ie, not business tenancies to which LTA 1954 Part 2 would apply.
31   LTA 1987 s21(3A).
32   LTA 1987 s21(3)(b).
33   LTA 1987 s60.
34   LTA 1987 s56.

Persons who may apply to have a manager appointed

8.31   Any tenant of a flat contained in premises over which the LVT has jurisdiction[35] may apply to an LVT for the appointment of a manager.[36] Where there are joint tenants, any one or more of those tenants may make the application.[37] Tenants of two or more flats may make joint applications[38] and applications may be made in respect of two or more premises.[39]

8.32   Tenants under business tenancies[40] are not entitled to apply.[41]

Grounds for the appointment of a manager

8.33   A manager may only be appointed in certain circumstances. These are that:

(a) a relevant person has breached an obligation relating to management;[42]

(b) unreasonable service charges have been or are proposed or likely to be demanded;[43]

(c) unreasonable administration charges have been or are proposed or likely to be demanded;[44]

(d) a relevant person has failed to comply with a prescribed Code of Practice.[45]

And, in all cases, that it is 'just and convenient' to appoint a manager.

8.34   In addition, there is a residual power to appoint a manager if other circumstances make it just and convenient to do so.[46]

---

35 See para 8.24 above.
36 LTA 1987 s21(1).
37 LTA 1987 s21(5).
38 LTA 1987 s21(4)(a).
39 LTA 1987 s21(4)(b).
40 Tenancies to which LTA 1954 Part 2 applies.
41 LTA 1987 s21(7).
42 LTA 1987 s24(2)(a).
43 LTA 1987 s24(2)(ab).
44 LTA 1987 s24(2)(aba).
45 LTA 1987 s24(2)(ac).
46 LTA 1987 s24(2)(b).

Relevant person

8.35   In recognition of the fact that modern property management is often carried out by persons other than the landlord, the LVT must only consider the default of a 'relevant person'.[47]

8.36   A relevant person is a landlord or any other person (including an RTM company) that owes management obligations to the tenant under the lease[48] – that is, those persons on whom a preliminary notice under section 22 of Landlord and Tenant Act (LTA) 1987[49] was served or could have been served if it had not been dispensed with.[50]

Breach of an obligation

8.37   Where the LVT is satisfied that a relevant person is in breach of an obligation owed to the tenant under the terms of his lease which relates to the management of the premises or, if the breach would only arise if the relevant person had notice of the defect, but it has not been reasonably practicable for the tenant to give the appropriate notice, then this ground is made out.[51]

8.38   The breach must be in respect of an obligation relating to the management of the premises. While there is no definition of management for these purposes, it includes matters relating to the repair, maintenance, improvement or insurance of the premises.[52]

8.39   The LVT has previously held that the question of whether or not there is a breach of an obligation must be assessed at the date of the application being issued, rather than the date of the hearing.[53] It is not obvious that this is correct. There is nothing in the wording of LTA 1987 s24 to indicate that the assessment should not be conducted by the LVT on the evidence as it currently stands. If the matter is not to be assessed as at the date of the hearing, why should it be assessed at the date of the application and not the service of the preliminary notice?

---

47 LTA 1987 s24(2ZA).
48 LTA 1987 s22; CLRA 2002 Sch 7 para 8.
49 See 8.11 above.
50 See 8.18 above.
51 LTA 1987 s24(2)(a)(i).
52 LTA 1987 s24(11).
53 *Petrou v Metropolitan Properties Company Ltd* LVT/AOM/014/013/98 (LVT).

Demanding unreasonable service charges

8.40   Where the LVT is satisfied that unreasonable service charges have been demanded, proposed or are likely to be demanded, a ground is made out.[54]

8.41   Three particular circumstances are set out in the Act in which a service charge shall be taken as unreasonable, namely:[55]

(a) if the amount is unreasonable having regard to the items for which it is payable;

(b) if the items for which it is payable are of an unnecessarily high standard; or

(c) if the items for which it is payable are of an insufficient standard with the result that additional service charges are or may be incurred.

8.42   This list is of course not exhaustive and there may be other reasons why a service charge is unreasonable. While there is a degree of overlap with the statutory limitations on service charges under LTA 1985 ss19 and 27,[56] it is not necessary to have secured a determination under these provisions before this ground can be made out (although, in practice, such a determination would provide highly compelling evidence).

Demanding unreasonable administration charges

8.43   Where the LVT is satisfied that unreasonable variable administration charges[57] have been demanded, proposed or are likely to be demanded, this ground is made out.[58]

8.44   There is no guidance as to what would constitute an unreasonable administration charge for these purposes. Presumably the LVT should adopt a similar approach to that adopted for service charges.

Failure to comply with the relevant Code of Practice

8.45   The Secretary of State (in Wales, the Welsh Assembly) has the power to approve codes of practice for property management.[59] The

54   LTA 1987 s24(2)(ab).
55   LTA 1987 s24(2A).
56   See chapter 2.
57   CLRA 2002 Sch 11 para 1. See also chapter 6.
58   LTA 1987 s24(2)(aba).
59   Leasehold Reform, Housing and Urban Development Act 1993 s87.

approved codes of practice are:

(a) the Rent Only Residential Management Code (published by the Royal Institution of Chartered Surveyors (RICS));[60]

(b) the Service Charge Residential Management Code (published by RICS);[61]

(c) the Code of Practice for Private Retirement Housing (published by the Association of Retirement Housing Managers).[62]

8.46 While in the past it was unlikely for an application for the appointment of a manager to succeed solely on the basis that there had been a breach of a code of practice, the surveyor members of LVTs appear to be taking any failure increasingly seriously. Advisers should study the relevant codes carefully and clearly set out any alleged failure.

Just and convenient

8.47 Most applications which fail do so because they fail to meet the 'just and convenient' test. Whether it is just and convenient to appoint a manager will vary from case to case and no absolute rules can exist. However, in general terms, the LVT is likely to be influenced by the following factors;

(a) the seriousness of any alleged deficiencies in the management;

(b) the effect of those deficiencies on the tenants;

(c) the duration of the deficiencies;

(d) the response of the landlord to the preliminary notice;

(e) the level of support for the application amongst the leaseholders;

(f) the conduct of the parties in the proceedings before the LVT;

(g) the respective interests of the parties (long leaseholders with many years to run are likely to have a more significant financial interest in the property than the freeholder);

(h) the suitability of the proposed manager; and

(i) the availability of other remedies.

---

60 Approval of Codes of Management Practice (Residential Property) (England) Order 2004 SI No 1802; Approval of Codes of Management Practice (Residential Property) (Wales) Order 2006 SI No 178.

61 Approval of Codes of Management Practice (Residential Property) Order 1996 SI No 2839.

62 Approval of Code of Management Practice (Private Retirement Housing) (England) Order 2005 SI No 3307; Approval of Code of Practice (Private Retirement Housing) (Wales) Order 2007 SI No 578.

Other circumstances where it is just and convenient

8.48   It is possible that the management of the property could be defective without amounting to one or more of the grounds outlined above. Alternatively, the parties may agree that the LVT should appoint a manager. In those circumstances, it may be just and convenient to appoint a manager.

Forthcoming legislative changes

8.49   The Commonhold and Leasehold Reform Act (CLRA) 2002[63] contains provisions which would allow the LVT to appoint a manager[64] where the landlord has failed to comply with the requirements to hold service charge funds in a designated trust account.[65] The provisions contained in the Act are now not likely to be brought into force in the exact form in which they were enacted. Rather, the government is currently in the process of proposing amendments to those provisions and a further date for their application.[66] Advisers should check to see if any such changes have been made.

The extent of the property to be managed

8.50   The practical purpose of the power to appoint a manager is to protect the interests of the tenants through the appointment of a manager, who will carry out the management functions which they are entitled to enjoy in relation to the premises of which their flats are part.

8.51   With this in mind, the manager may be given power over property which does not form a part of the premises that were the subject of the application. It does not matter that the tenants have no rights over the property provided that it makes sense for a manager of the property to have control of those additional parts.[67] For example, in the case of a block of flats with a garden over which the tenants had no rights (it being reserved entirely to the landlord's use), the manager could properly be appointed in respect of the block and the garden.

---

63   Sch 10 para 14.
64   LTA 1987 s24(2)(abb).
65   LTA 1987 ss42–42A.
66   See para 2.92.
67   *Cawsand Fort Management Company Ltd v Stafford and others*, above, note 7; LTA 1987 s24(3).

The management functions to be conferred

8.52   There is no limit on the management functions which can be conferred. In particular, the LVT is not limited to requiring the manager to discharge the functions of the landlord under the lease.[68]

8.53   It is clear that the concept of 'management' is to be interpreted widely, and includes repairs, maintenance, improvements and insurance of the premises.[69]

8.54   The order may make provision with respect to any matters relating to the exercise by the manager of his functions and such incidental or ancillary matters as the LVT thinks fit.[70]

8.55   In particular, an order may provide:[71]

(a) for rights and liabilities arising under contracts to which the manager is not a party to become rights and liabilities of the manager;

(b) for the manager to be entitled to prosecute claims in respect of causes of action (whether contractual or tortious) accruing before or after the date of his appointment;

(c) for remuneration to be paid to the manager by any relevant person, or by the tenants of the premises in respect of which the order is made or by all or any of those persons; and

(d) for the manager's functions to be exercisable by him either during a specified period or without limit of time.

Remuneration

8.56   If the landlord were to choose to appoint a manager, then he would be liable for the costs of management. He may, of course, be entitled to recover some or all of those costs from the tenants as a service charge, if the lease so provides.

8.57   The LVT has power[72] to provide for remuneration to be paid either by the landlord or by the tenant or to be shared. The starting point should be that the landlord will pay the costs of the manager (including disbursements and the costs of attending any LVT hearings)

---

68   *Cawsand Fort Management Company Ltd v Stafford and others*, above, note 7 ; *Maunder Taylor v Blaquiere* above, note 4.

69   LTA 1987 s21(11).

70   LTA 1987 s24(4).

71   LTA 1987 s24(5).

72   LTA 1987 s24(5)(c).

which are not recoverable from the tenants under their leases.[73]

8.58   The terms of the appointment of the manager should make clear who is to pay the manager and what his fees are to be.[74]

8.59   If the order appointing the manager merely refers to 'reasonable' fees then, in the event of a dispute, any party may apply to the LVT for a direction[75] as to what level of fees may be recovered.[76]

Persons likely to be appointed as a manager

8.60   There is no requirement that the LVT appoint a professional manager and tenants are frequently known to suggest that one of their own number be appointed. However, the LVT is often sceptical of such suggestions, fearing that this would not resolve the dispute. Tenants are strongly advised to suggest one or more possible managers and to select them from professional managers.

8.61   One of the most common grounds for rejecting a proposed manager is a perceived lack of experience – a problem which clearly should not arise in the case of professional management companies. The manager should:

(a) be familiar with the relevant legislation and codes of guidance;
(b) have relevant experience of property management; and
(c) have adequate professional indemnity insurance.[77]

Directions

8.62   If a manager is unsure or unclear about an aspect of his responsibilities, he may apply to the LVT for directions with respect to any such matters.[78] A direction should take the form of an order, requiring the manager to do (or not to do) some specific act and should not be worded as a declaration.[79] A direction cannot be used to vary the terms of the original appointment. [80]

73 *Re: Morshead Mansions* LRX/49/2002 (Lands Tribunal).
74 *Maunder Taylor v Joshi* LRX/107/2005 (Lands Tribunal).
75 See para 8.62 below.
76 *Maunder Taylor v Joshi* LRX/107/2005 (Lands Tribunal).
77 *Sheales and others v Parry* LON/00AN/LAM/2007/0011 (LVT).
78 LTA 1985 s24(4).
79 *Re: Morshead Mansions* LRX/49/200 (Lands Tribunal).
80 *Re: Morshead Mansions* LRX/49/200 (Lands Tribunal).

Variation or discharge

8.63   The LVT is empowered to vary or discharge any order which it has made and may do so conditionally or unconditionally. If the order has been registered with the land registry, the LVT is empowered to direct that the order be cancelled. [81]

8.64   The manager is entitled to apply to vary or discharge any order and may wish to do so in order to resign.[82]

8.65   If the landlord or other person on whom the preliminary notice was served applies to vary or discharge the order, the LVT may accede to the application unless it is satisfied that (a) the variation or discharge will not result in a recurrence of the circumstances which led to the order being made and it is just and convenient in all the circumstances of the case to vary or discharge the order.[83]

8.66   An order will not be discharged merely because of some subsequent development which means that the premises are no longer premises in respect of which an application for the appointment of a manager could be made because there is now a resident or exempt landlord, or the premises are now within the functional land of a charity.[84]

8.67   The power to vary includes a power to extend an existing order. There are no express criteria for extending the duration of an existing order and it is not necessary for the LVT to again make findings of fact about the default of the landlord or his managing agents.[85]

RTM company

8.68   If an RTM company[86] is exercising the right to manage, and an application is made for the appointment of a manager, the procedure outlined above applies with some variations:[87]

(a) references to the landlord are to the RTM company;
(b) the landlord is deemed to be a tenant of a flat;

---

81   LTA 1985 s24(9).
82   *Re: Morshead Mansions*, LRX/49/2002 (Lands Tribunal); *Denning v Beamsafe Ltd and others* BIR/00CS/LVM/2006/001 (LVT).
83   LTA 1985 s24(9A).
84   LTA 1985 s24(10).
85   *Orchard Court Residents Association v St Anthony Homes Ltd* [2003] EWCA Civ 1049; [2003] 2 EGLR 28.
86   See chapter 9.
87   CLRA 2002 Sch 7 para 8.

(c) the exception for exempt or resident landlords does not apply;

(d) the breach of an obligation by the RTM company is a ground for the appointment of a manager;

(e) it is just and convenient to appoint a manager if the RTM company no longer wishes to exercise the right to manage;

(f) the management order may make provision about contracts to which the RTM company is a party and the prosecution of claims in respect of causes of action, whether tortious or contractual, accruing before or after the right to manage ceases to be exercisable.

Miscellaneous

8.69   An order appointing a manager is capable of being registered at the land registry.[88]

8.70   If an order is made, the LVT may attach any conditions that it thinks fit to the order. In particular, it may suspend the operation of the order on terms.[89]

8.71   Where a tenant could apply to the LVT for the appointment of a manager, the jurisdiction of the LVT is exclusive. The tenant may not bring proceedings to appoint a manager or receiver in the High Court or county court.[90]

8.72   The LVT is empowered to appoint a manager on an interim, as well as final basis.[91] However, the procedures of the LVT are not well suited for hearing interim (particularly urgent interim) applications.

Consultation about managing agents

8.73   Recognised Tenants' Associations have the right to be consulted about managing agents.[92]

8.74   The association may, at any time, serve a notice on the landlord requesting him to consult the association in relation to the appointment or employment of a managing agent.[93]

---

88 LTA 1987 s24(8).

89 LTA 1987 s24(6).

90 *Stylli v Hamberton Properties Ltd* [2002] EWHC 394 (Ch D); LTA 1987 s21(6).

91 LTA 1987 s24(1).

92 LTA 1985 s30B.

93 LTA 1985 s30B(1).

8.75 If such an agent is employed, the landlord must, within a month of service of the notice, reply by service of a further notice on the association specifying the obligations which the manager discharges on his behalf and allowing a reasonable period for the association to comment on the manner in which the managing agent has been discharging the obligations and the desirability of this continuing.[94]

8.76 If no such agent is employed when the notice is served, the landlord must – before employing any managing agent at any future stage – serve a notice setting out the name of the proposed managing agent, the obligations he proposes to have the agent discharge and allowing a period of at least one month for the association to make observations on the appointment.[95]

8.77 In either case, once the initial notice has been served, the landlord must, at least once every five years, serve on the association a notice specifying any changes which have occurred since the date of the last notice served on him by the association and allow the association a reasonable period to comment on the manner in which the managing agent has discharged his obligations and the desirability of him continuing to do so.[96]

8.78 He must also serve on the association the name and proposed duties of any new managing agent and allow a period of not less than one month for comments.[97]

8.79 The residents association may release the landlord from these obligations at any stage by serving a notice on him to this effect.[98]

8.80 Any consultation obligations cease if the property becomes vested in a new landlord, although they may be reasserted in the manner set out above.[99]

94 LTA 1985 s30B(3).
95 LTA 1985 s30B(2).
96 LTA 1985 s30B(4)(a).
97 LTA 1985 s30B(4)(b).
98 LTA 1985 s30B(5).
99 LTA 1985 s30B(6).

CHAPTER 9

Right to manage

9.1   **Introduction**

9.8   **Advice to tenants**

9.16   **Properties to which the RTM applies**
9.18   Self-contained building or part of a building
9.28   Qualifying tenants

9.31   **Excluded properties**
9.32   Non-residential property
9.35   Buildings with self-contained parts in different ownership
9.36   Resident landlord
9.38   Local housing authority landlords
9.39   Existing or recent RTM

9.40   **The RTM company**
9.44   Setting up the RTM company
9.48   Obtaining information

9.52   **Notice inviting participation**

9.62   **Notice of claim**

9.72   **Rights of inspection**

9.73   **Counter notice**
9.77   Determination

continued

9.80   Withdrawal of a claim notice

9.84   Costs of the RTM process

9.89   Acquiring the right to manage

9.92   Duty to pay uncommitted service charges

9.96   Approvals

Key points

- CLRA 2002 created a 'no fault' right to manage. Leaseholders can now establish a Right to Manage company (RTM). This is not a simple procedure and legal professionals should be consulted.
- The first step is to establish an RTM company, which all 'qualifying tenants' are entitled to join.
- The RTM company may then obtain various information from the landlord to decide whether or not to continue the process.
- Before the right to manage can be acquired all qualifying tenants must be invited to join the company and at least half must be members. After this a notice of the company's intention to take control of the management of the property must be served on the landlord and tenants.
- At this stage anyone objecting may serve a counter, alleging for example that the RTM company was not validly formed. The LVT may then be required to adjudicate between the parties.
- If the disputes are resolved in the RTM company's favour, it will acquire the right to manage the property.
- The right to manage does not apply to all properties and cannot be established against all landlords. Most Local Authority tenancies, for example, are exempt.
- Those who establish the company are usually liable for the costs associated with the process, including the landlords costs.
- In addition, an RTM company would place tenants in the position of having to collect service charges from each other. This may mean that friendships are strained. There may be a tension between the duties of the RTM company and its directors, and the desires of friends and other tenants.

Introduction

9.1   The Commonhold and Leasehold Reform Act (CLRA) 2002[1] created a new 'no fault' right to manage. The provisions are based on those dealing with collective enfranchisement under the Leasehold Reform, Housing and Urban Development Act (LRHUDA) 1993.[2]

---

1   Chapter 1 Part 2.
2   See Radevsky and Greenish, *Hague on Leasehold Enfranchisement*, (4th edn, 2003, Sweet & Maxwell) for a comprehensive treatment of the subject.

9.2   Leaseholders can now force the landlord to transfer its management functions to a special kind of company called a Right to Manage (RTM) company. The right is available regardless of any alleged
deficiencies in the existing management. This is to be contrasted
with the 'fault based' provisions of Part 2 of the Landlord and Tenant
Act (LTA) 1987.[3]

9.3   The acquisition of the right to manage begins with the creation
of an RTM company. As soon as it is created 'qualifying tenants' are
entitled to join it. An RTM company has the right to obtain various
information from the freeholder and others in order to take the next
steps in the process.

9.4   The RTM company may then inform qualifying tenants of its intention to take over the management of the building and inviting
them to join by sending a 'notice of intention'.

9.5   Once the RTM company has sent a 'notice of intention' and more
than half of the qualifying tenants have become members of the
company it may then serve a 'notice of claim', this time on all parties
to the various leases of the flats.

9.6   Anybody objecting to the RTM company's right to acquire the
right to manage (for example because it was not validly formed) may
serve a 'counter-notice'. The LVT will resolve any disputes raised in
the counter-notice.

9.7   Once the time limit specified in a claim notice has expired and
all disputes have been resolved in favour of the RTM company, it will
take over the management functions of the building.

Advice to tenants

9.8   The establishment of an RTM company is not something to be undertaken lightly and before attempting to do so, tenants should understand what they will be taking on as well as being very clear about
what they want to achieve.

9.9   The advantage of an RTM company is that it allows long leaseholders much greater control of their property. Where a landlord has been
unwilling or incapable of managing the property or appointing an
agent to do so the right to manage has the advantage of being much
more certain than the appointment of a manager by a court or LVT.

9.10   Even where a landlord has not managed the property badly, tenants may prefer to make the management decisions themselves

3   As to which, see chapter 8.

rather than leaving them to a landlord who may have little stake in the property.

9.11   There are distinct dangers with creating an RTM company which must also carefully be considered. Depending on the size and complexity of the property, the process may be costly and most of that cost will be borne by the promoters of the company. The company will also take over many of the duties and responsibilities of the landlord.

9.12   The most difficult aspect of running an RTM company is that in order to pay for management it will have to collect service charges from tenants. This could place directors in conflict with their friends and neighbours if disputes about service charge demands arise. There will inevitably be a tension between the duties of the RTM company to ensure adequate and prompt repairs and maintenance, and the desires of the tenants to keep costs down.

9.13   There is also a difficulty with continuity of management, especially where there are a relatively small number of members of the RTM company. The moment a tenant sells their flat, they cease to be a member of the company. This means that even if the RTM starts with an enthusiastic group prepared to run it well, that group will change over the years and the RTM may run into difficulties.

9.14   Independent professional advice will almost always be necessary. It may be that the RTM company will need to employ lawyers and accountants in order to meet its legal obligations.

9.15   The RTM company represents a considerable investment in terms of time and energy on the part of the tenants and the benefits may not be entirely obvious. If the tenants objectives can be achieved without establishing an RTM company, it is almost certainly preferable to do so.

Properties to which the RTM applies

9.16   The RTM can only be exercised in respect of premises which:

(a) consist of a self-contained building or part of a building, with or without appurtenant property;[4]

(b) consist of two or more flats[5] held by qualifying tenants, and[6]

---

4   CLRA 2002 s72(1)(a).
5   CLRA 2002 s118: a separate set of premises (whether or not on the same floor) which forms part of a building; which is constructed or adapted for use for the purposes of a dwelling; and either the whole or a material part of which lies above or below some other part of the building.
6   CLRA 2002 s72(1)(b).

(c) qualifying tenants hold at least two-thirds of the number of flats in the premises.[7]

9.17   Appurtenant property means any garage, outhouse, garden, yard or appurtenances belonging to, or usually enjoyed with, the building or part or flat.[8]

Self-contained building or part of a building

9.18   A building is a self-contained building if it is structurally detached.[9] In practice, it is unlikely that there will ever be any difficulties in identifying such a building.

9.19   A self-contained part of a building is more difficult to identify. It must:

(a) constitute a vertical division of the building;[10]
(b) be capable of being redeveloped independently of the rest of the building;[11]
(c) have services which are provided by pipes, cables or other fixed installations[12] provided independently of those provided for occupiers of the rest of the building, or capable of being so provided without it being likely that there would be a significant interruption in the provision of services for occupiers of the rest of the building.[13]

9.20   The requirement that, to be a self-contained part of a building, a part of a building must constitute 'a vertical division of the building' is unqualified. One must draw a hypothetical line vertically through the building and, if the division would leave part of the building outside the line, then the property does not qualify. There is no discretion as to whether or not a building qualifies, nor is it appropriate to consider whether or not the area which falls outside of the line is material.[14]

---

7   CLRA 2002 s72(1)(c).
8   CLRA 2002 s112.
9   CLRA 2002 s72(2), see also *Parsons v Trustees of Henry Smith's Charity* [1974] 1 WLR 435.
10   CLRA 2002 s72(3)(a).
11   CLRA 2002 s72(3)(b).
12   CLRA 2002 s72(5).
13   CLRA 2002 s72(4).
14   *Holding and Management (Solitaire) Ltd v 1–16 Finland St RTM Ltd* [2007] 45 EG 162; LRX/138/2006 (Lands Tribunal).

9.21 Whether or not a part of a building is capable of being redeveloped independently of the rest of the building it likely to be a question of fact (with expert evidence likely to be necessary) in each case. Likewise, the question of whether or not services are provided independently would usually be a question of fact.

9.22 However, where services are not currently provided independently, one must consider whether nor they are capable of being so provided without it being likely that there would be a significant interruption in the provision of services for occupiers of the rest of the building.

9.23 What amounts to a 'significant interruption' for these purposes is unclear. A county court judge,[15] in a case concerning similar provisions in LRHUDA 1993, has stated that there are five steps to take:

(a) identify the services which are not independently provided to occupiers of the part of the building in respect of which the RTM is claimed;

(b) consider whether those services can be provided to the part in respect of which the RTM is claimed independently of the provision of the same service(s) to the remainder of the building;

(c) ascertain whether the works required to separate the respective parts of the services supplying the part in respect of which the RTM is claimed and the remainder of the building, so that such services would thereafter be supplied to each such parts independently of the other;

(d) assess the interruption to the latter services (ie, those not subject to the claim to exercise the RTM) which carrying out those works would entail;

(e) decide whether or not that interruption was 'significant'.

9.24 The first is a question of fact, the second, third and fourth are matters of fact requiring expert evidence and the fifth is a matter of construction of the Act, considering the fact and degree of the interruption. It is for those who are claiming the right to manage to prove that the works to separate the services could be done without resulting in a significant interruption.[16]

9.25 Significance should be judged against the fact that the RTM process is supposed to be a quick and efficient method of transferring the management of a property. The longer the duration

---

15 *Oakwood Court (Holland Park) Ltd v Daejan Properties Ltd*, [2007] 1 EGLR 121, HHJ Hazel Marshall QC, Central London County Court, 18 December 2006.

16 Ibid.

of the interruption, the more likely it is to be regarded as 'significant' although one should also have regard to the seriousness of the interruption.[17]

9.26 The interruption should be judged with reference to the availability of the service, if required. The significance does not depend on any subjective inconvenience caused to an actual occupier. For example, works to a central heating system are not to be regarded as less significant if conducted during the summer.[18]

9.27 The key goal of these legislation seems to be that the RTM company should deal only with a coherent manageable unit.

Qualifying tenants

9.28 A person is a qualifying tenant if he is the tenant of a flat granted under a long lease,[19] unless the lease is one to which LTA 1954 Part 2 (business leases) applies[20] or the lease was granted in breach of the terms of a superior lease, where that breach has not been waived. [21]

9.29 No flat has more than one qualifying tenant.[22] In the case of flats, which are held under two or more long leases, a tenant whose lease is superior to that of another tenant is not a qualifying tenant.[23] Joint tenants are regarded as jointly being the qualifying tenant.[24] Trustees who are qualifying tenants may join an RTM company unless the trust instrument expressly prohibits it.[25]

9.30 There is no requirement that the 'qualifying tenant' actually be resident in the property, nor that they own only one flat within the property.

---

17 *Oakwood Court (Holland Park) Ltd v Daejan Properties Ltd*, [2007] 1 EGLR 121, HHJ Hazel Marshall QC, Central London County Court, 18 December 2006.

18 Ibid.

19 CLRA 2002 s76: a lease (a) granted for a term exceeding 21 years; (b) granted for a term fixed by law with a covenant or obligation for perpetual renewal; (c) which took effect under Law of Property Act 1925 s149(6) (leases terminable after a death, marriage or formation of a civil partnership); (d) granted in pursuance of the right to buy under Housing Act 1985 Pt 5; (e) a shared ownership lease where the tenants share is 100 per cent; or (f) granted pursuant to the right to acquire in Housing Act 1996 s17.

20 CLRA 2002 s75(3).

21 CLRA 2002 s75(4).

22 CLRA 2002 s75(5).

23 CLRA 2002 s75(6).

24 CLRA 2002 s75(7).

25 CLRA 2002 s109.

Excluded properties

9.31   A number of properties are excluded from the scope of the RTM legislation.

Non-residential property

9.32   Any premise where the total internal floor area of the 'non-residential' parts is greater than 25 per cent.[26] A part of premises is non-residential if it is neither occupied, nor intended to be occupied, for residential purposes.[27] Common parts are treated as residential.[28]

9.33   When calculating the percentage of non-residential property, any premises or parts of the premises which are used or intended to be used in conjunction with a particular dwelling (for example, a parking space) are deemed to be residential.[29]

9.34   While it is likely to be a question of fact as to whether or not part of the premises is occupied or intended to be occupied for residential purposes, any unlawful occupation (ie, in breach of covenant) would not turn otherwise non-residential premises into residential premises.[30]

Buildings with self-contained parts in different ownership

9.35   A building which is capable of being divided into self-contained parts is not one to which the RTM applies if the self-contained parts have different freehold owners.[31]

Resident landlord

9.36   Certain premises of not more than four units, which also have a resident landlord are excluded from the scope of the RTM legislation.[32]

9.37   For this exception to apply, the premises in question must be other than a purpose-built block of flats; one of the flats must be occupied

---

26 CLRA 2002 Sch 6 para 1(1).
27 CLRA 2002 Sch 6 para 1(2).
28 CLRA 2002 Sch 6 para 1(2).
29 CLRA 2002 Sch 6 para 1(3).
30 *Gaingold Ltd and another v WHRA RTM Ltd* LRX/19/2005; [2006] 1 EGLR 81; [2006] 3 EG 122 (Lands Tribunal).
31 CLRA 2002 Sch 6 para 2.
32 CLRA 2002 Sch 6 para 3.

by the freeholder or an adult member of his family as his only or principal home for the last 12 months or, in the case of recently purchased property, there was previously a resident landlord and the new freeholder (or an adult member of his family) occupied the flat as their only or principal home within 28 days of purchasing the flat.[33]

Local housing authority landlords

9.38   Premises where any of the qualifying tenants has a local housing authority[34] as their immediate landlord are excluded from the RTM process.[35]

Existing or recent RTM

9.39   Premises in respect of which there is currently an RTM company which could exercise the right to manage are excluded from any further RTM process.[36] In addition, any premises in respect of which there has been an RTM company which could exercise the RTM in the previous four years are excluded,[37] unless the previous RTM company ceased to exercise the RTM only as a result of acquiring the freehold[38] or an LVT gives permission for a new RTM company to acquire the management.[39]

The RTM company

9.40   The first step in the acquisition of the right to manage is the creation of an RTM company in respect of the premises.

9.41   An RTM company is a company which:

(a) is limited by guarantee;[40] and

(b) has the acquisition and exercise of the right to manage certain premises as one of its objects in the memorandum of association.[41]

---

33 CLRA 2002 Sch 6 paras 3(2)–(5).
34 Housing Act 1985 s1: most commonly, a district council, unitary authority or London Borough Council.
35 CLRA 2002 Sch 6 para 4.
36 CLRA 2002 Sch 6 para 5(1)(a).
37 CLRA 2002 Sch 6 para 5(1)(b).
38 CLRA 2002 Sch 6 para 5(2).
39 CLRA 2002 Sch 6 para 5(3).
40 CLRA 2002 s73(2)(a).
41 CLRA 2002 s73(2)(b).

9.42 There can only be one RTM company in respect of any premises. If there is already an RTM company in respect of those premises or any premises containing, or contained in those premises then the second company created is not the RTM company in respect of those premises: the earlier company takes priority.[42]

9.43 If an RTM company comes to own the freehold of the premises, it ceases to be the RTM company in respect of those premises.[43] The right to manage is not seen as consistent with ownership of the property.

Setting up the RTM company

9.44 There are many firms that offer specialised RTM company creation services. Companies House also publishes a number of useful leaflets on creating and managing companies in general.

9.45 In order to create the company a number of 'promoters', who need not be qualifying tenants, must sign a memorandum of association (which sets out the company objectives) and lodge it with the company's articles of association (its constitution) at Companies House.

9.46 Standard forms for the memorandum and articles of association are prescribed by statutory instrument.[44] Any part of the RTM companies memorandum and articles which conflict with those prescribed are void.[45] One practical effect of this is that the company must have a name ending in 'RTM Company Ltd'.[46]

9.47 Once the company is created, any qualifying tenant has the right to become a member (shareholder).[47] If the RTM company acquires the right to manage then the landlord(s) of any part of whole of the premises are entitled to join on the date that the RTM is acquired.[48]

---

42 CLRA 2002 s73(4).

43 CLRA 2002 s73(5).

44 RTM Companies (Memorandum and Articles of Association) (England) Regulations 2003 SI No 2120; The RTM Companies (Memorandum and Articles of Association) (Wales) Regulations 2004 SI No 675.

45 CLRA 2002 s74(5).

46 RTM Companies (Memorandum and Articles of Association) (England) Regulations 2003 SI No 2120 Sch Part 1; The RTM Companies (Memorandum and Articles of Association) (Wales) Regulations 2004 SI No 675 Sch 1 Part 1.

47 CLRA 2002 s74(1)(a).

48 CLRA 2002 s74(1)(b).

Obtaining information

9.48   As part of the process of planning the acquisition of the right to manage, an RTM company will need information of various kinds in order, for example, to put together the notice of claim. It will also usually want to begin the process of seeking out suitable companies with which to make management contracts. Some of this information can be obtained from public sources, but the RTM company also has a right to additional information.

9.49   An RTM company may give any person a notice requiring him to provide the company with any information which is in his possession and control and which the company reasonably requires in order to prepare a claim notice[49] for claiming to acquire the right to manage the premises.[50]

9.50   In addition, where the information is recorded in a document in the person's possession or control, the RTM company may give them a notice requiring them to, at any reasonable time, permit any person authorised on behalf of the company to inspect the document (or have access to it in a readily intelligible form).[51] A copy of the document must be supplied in a readily intelligible form, although a reasonable fee may be charged.[52]

9.51   A person given either of such notices must comply with them no later than 28 days after the notice was given.[53] In default the county court is empowered to make an order requiring the person to comply with the notice.[54]

Notice inviting participation

9.52   Once established, the RTM company must give a notice to each qualifying tenant who is not yet a member (and has not yet agreed to become a member) of the RTM company.[55]

9.53   The notice (known as a 'notice of invitation to participate) must:[56]

---

49 As to which, see para 9.62 below.
50 CLRA 2002 s82(1).
51 CLRA 2002 s82(2)(a).
52 CLRA 2002 s82(2)(b).
53 CLRA 2002 s82(3).
54 CLRA 2002 s107.
55 CLRA 2002 s78(1).
56 CLRA 2002 s78(2).

(a) state that the RTM company intends to acquire the right to manage the premises;

(b) state the names of the members of the RTM company;

(c) invite the recipients of the notice to become members of the company; and

(d) contain such other particulars (if any) as may be required to be contained in notices of invitation to participate by regulations made by the Secretary of State, or Welsh Assembly (as appropriate).

9.54   In England, the Secretary of State has specified that the following additional information must be included:[57]

(a) the RTM company's registered number, the address of its registered office and the names of its directors and secretary;

(b) the names of the landlord and any third party;

(c) a statement that, subject to the exclusions mentioned in (e), if the right to manage is acquired by the RTM company, the company will be responsible for –

(i) the discharge of the landlord's duties under the lease; and

(ii) the exercise of his powers under the lease,

with respect to services, repairs, maintenance, improvements, insurance and management;

(d) a statement that, subject to the exclusion mentioned in sub-paragraph (e)(ii), if the right to manage is acquired by the RTM company, the company may enforce untransferred tenant covenants;

(e) a statement that, if the right to manage is acquired by the RTM company, the company will not be responsible for the discharge of the landlord's duties or the exercise of his powers under the lease–

(i) with respect to a matter concerning only a part of the premises consisting of a flat or other unit not subject to a lease held by a qualifying tenant; or

(ii) relating to re-entry or forfeiture;

(f) a statement that, if the right to manage is acquired by the RTM company, the company will have functions under the statutory provisions referred to in Schedule 7 to the 2002 Act;

(g) a statement that the RTM company intends or, as the case may be, does not intend, to appoint a managing agent within the meaning of section 30B(8) of the Landlord and Tenant Act 1985; and–

(i) if it does so intend, a statement

(aa) of the name and address of the proposed managing agent (if known); and

(bb) if it be the case, that the person is the landlord's managing agent; or

(ii) if it does not so intend, the qualifications or experience (if any)

57 Right to Manage (Prescribed Particulars and Forms) (England) Regulations 2003 SI No 1988 reg 3(2).

of the existing members of the RTM company in relation to the management of residential property;

(h) a statement that, where the company gives a claim notice, a person who is or has been a member of the company may be liable for costs incurred by the landlord and others in consequence of the notice;

(i) a statement that, if the recipient of the notice (of invitation to participate) does not fully understand its purpose or implications, he is advised to seek professional help; and

(j) the full text of information provided in the notes to the form set out in Schedule 1 to the Regulations.

9.55   There is no material difference in the Welsh Regulations.[58] Both Regulations contain prescribed forms which must be used.

9.56   This material must either be accompanied by a copy of the memorandum of association and articles of association of the RTM company or include a statement specifying a place in England or Wales, where the same may be inspected, the times at which they may be inspected, a place from which they may be ordered and a reasonable fee for a provision of a copy.[59]

9.57   Despite these onerous requirements, a Notice of Invitation to Participate is not invalidated by any inaccuracy in the particulars required.[60]

9.59   Additionally, it appears that there is a freestanding power in the LVT to waive any defect where it considers that there has not been any prejudice to the landlord. If there has not, the LVT should waive any default.[61]

9.60   All those qualifying leaseholders who respond to the Notice and request membership must be enrolled as members of the RTM company and their membership noted in the official records.

9.61   Although the legislation does not require the RTM company to produce any form of plan or budget, it may be wise to do so as it will both focus the minds of those involved in the RTM process and provide clear direction for the RTM company. It may also forestall any objections from leaseholders or even the landlord about the costs and standards envisaged by the RTM.

---

58   Right to Manage (Prescribed Particulars and Forms) (Wales) Regulations 2004 SI No 678.

59   CLRA 2002 ss78(4)–(5).

60   CLRA 2002 s78(7).

61   *Sinclair Gardens (Investments) Limited v Oak Investments RTM Company Limited* LRX/52/2004; [2005] RVR 426, where the Lands Tribunal held that the failure to serve a notice of invitation to participate on a qualifying tenant was immaterial where the tenant had been fully aware of the proceedings and his admission was inadvertent.

Notice of claim

9.62 Not less than 14 days after the notice of invitation to participate has been given[62] the RTM company may serve a notice of claim, stating that it wishes to acquire the RTM.

9.63 However, in order to do so, the RTM company must have the prescribed degree of support from the qualifying tenants. In premises with only two qualifying tenants, both must be members of the RTM company[63] and, in all other cases, the number of qualifying tenants who are members of the RTM company must be not less than half of the total number of flats in the premises.[64]

9.64 The claim notice must be given to anyone who is a landlord under a lease of the whole or any part of the premises;[65] any other party to a lease[66] and each qualifying tenant.[67] If a manager has been appointed under LTA 1987 Part 2, the manager must be given a copy of the claim notice[68] as must the court or LVT which appointed them.[69]

9.65 There is no need to serve a claim notice on a person who cannot be found or whose identity cannot be ascertained. In this case an application should be made to the LVT[70] who will determine what, if any further steps should be taken by the RTM company.

9.66 The notice of claim must be in writing and according to CLRA 2002 s80(2)–(7):[71]

> (2) It must specify the premises and contain a statement of the grounds on which it is claimed that they are premises to which this Chapter applies.
> (3) It must state the full name of each person who is both –
>> (a) the qualifying tenant of a flat contained in the premises, and
>> (b) a member of the RTM company,
> and the address of his flat.
> (4) And it must contain, in relation to each such person, such particulars of his lease as are sufficient to identify it, including –
>> (a) the date on which it was entered into,

---

62 CLRA 2002 s79(2).
63 CLRA 2002 s79(4).
64 CLRA 2002 s79(5).
65 CLRA 2002 s79(6)(a).
66 CLRA 2002 s79(6)(b).
67 CLRA 2002 s79(8).
68 CLRA 2002 s79(6)(c).
69 CLRA 2002 s79(9).
70 CLRA 2002 s85.
71 CLRA 2002 s80.

(b) the term for which it was granted, and

(c) the date of the commencement of the term.

(5) It must state the name and registered office of the RTM company.

(6) It must specify a date, not earlier than one month after the relevant date, by which each person who was given the notice under section 79(6) may respond to it by giving a counter-notice under section 84.

(7) It must specify a date, at least three months after that specified under subsection (6), on which the RTM company intends to acquire the right to manage the premises.

9.67   In England, the Secretary of State has specified that the following additional information must be included:[72]

(a) a statement that a person who –

(i) does not dispute the RTM's company's entitlement to acquire the right to manage; and

(ii) is the manager party under a management contract subsisting immediately before the date specified in the claim notice must give a notice in relation to the contract to the person who is the contractor party in relation to the contract and to the RTM company;

(b) a statement that, from the acquisition date, landlords under leases of the whole or any part of the premises to which the claim notice relates are entitled to be members of the RTM company;

(c) a statement that the notice is not invalidated by any inaccuracy in any of the particulars, but that a person who is of the opinion that any of the particulars contained in the claim notice are inaccurate may:

(i) identify the particulars in question to the RTM company by which the notice was given; and

(ii) indicate the respects in which they are considered to be inaccurate;

(d) a statement that a person who receives the notice but does not fully understand its purpose, is advised to seek professional help; and

(e) the information provided in the notes to the form set out in Schedule 2 to the Regulations.

9.68   There is no material difference in the Welsh Regulations.[73] Both Regulations contain prescribed forms which must be used.

9.69   A claim notice is not invalidated by any inaccuracy in any of the particulars.[74] In particular, erroneously specifying a person as being

---

72 Right to Manage (Prescribed Particulars and Forms) (England) Regulations 2003 SI No 1988 reg 4.

73 Right to Manage (Prescribed Particulars and Forms) (Wales) Regulations 2004 SI No 678.

74 CLRA 2002 s81(1).

a qualifying tenant in the claim notice did not invalidate the notice, so long as there were still a sufficient number of qualifying tenants at the relevant time.[75]

9.70   In addition, in a related context, the Lands Tribunal has stated that there is a freestanding power in the LVT to waive any defect where it considers that there has not been any prejudice to the landlord.[76]

9.71   Once a claim notice has been served, no further notice may be served so long as it continues in force unless it has been withdrawn or otherwise ceased to have effect.[77] A claim notice which fails to comply with the requirements of CLRA 2002 s80 may well be said to be a nullity. In those circumstances, there would be nothing to stop the RTM company serving a fresh notice.[78]

Rights of inspection

9.72   After a claim notice is served, those authorised by the RTM, the landlord, any other party to a lease or a manager must, upon giving ten days' written notice to any person occupying or entitled to occupy any part of the premises, be given access to that premises if it is reasonable to do so in connection with any matter arising out of the claim to the right to manage.[79]

Counter notice

9.73   Any person given a claim notice by an RTM company may give a counter-notice.[80] This must be done no later than the date specified in the claim notice.[81]

---

75 CLRA 2002 s81(2).

76 *Sinclair Gardens (Investments) Limited v Oak Investments RTM Company Limited* LRX/52/2004; [2005] RVR 426, where the Lands Tribunal held that the failure to serve a notice of invitation to participate on a qualifying tenant was immaterial where the tenant had been fully aware of the proceedings and his admission was inadvertent.

77 CLRA 2002 ss81(3)–(4).

78 See, in the context of a claim for collective enfranchisement, *Sinclair Gardens Investments (Kensington) Ltd v Poets Chase Freehold Company Ltd* [2007] EWHC 1776 (Ch); [2007] 49 EG 104.

79 CLRA 2002 s83.

80 CLRA 2002 s84(1).

81 See para 9.62 above.

9.74   The notice must contain a statement either admitting that the RTM company was on the relevant date entitled to acquire the right to manage the premises specified in the claim notice, or alleging that the RTM company was on that date not so entitled.[82]

9.75   In England, the Secretary of State has specified that the following additional information must be included:[83]

> (a) a statement that, where the RTM company has been given one or more counter-notices containing such a statement as is mentioned in paragraph (b) of subsection (2) of section 84 of the 2002 Act, the company may apply to a leasehold valuation tribunal for a determination that, on the date on which notice of the claim was given, the company was entitled to acquire the right to manage the premises specified in the claim notice;
>
> (b) a statement that, where the RTM company has been given one or more counter-notices containing such a statement as is mentioned in paragraph (b) of subsection (2) of section 84 of the 2002 Act, the company does not acquire the right to manage the premises specified in the claim notice unless –
>
>> (i) on an application to a leasehold valuation tribunal, it is finally determined that the company was entitled to acquire the right to manage the premises; or
>>
>> (ii) the person by whom the counter-notice was given agrees, or the persons by whom the counter-notices were given agree, in writing that the company was so entitled; and
>
> (c) the information provided in the notes to the form set out in Schedule 3 to these Regulations.

9.76   There is no material difference in the Welsh Regulations.[84] Both regulations contain prescribed forms which must be used.

Determination

9.77   If one or more counter-notices are received which dispute the right of the RTM company to acquire the management of the property, an application may be made by the company to the LVT for a determination of this question.[85] The onus is on the RTM company to take this step as the right to manage cannot be exercised until this matter is

---

82   CLRA 2002 s84(2).

83   Right to Manage (Prescribed Particulars and Forms) (England) Regulations 2003 SI No 1988 reg 5.

84   Right to Manage (Prescribed Particulars and Forms) (Wales) Regulations 2004 SI No 678.

85   CLRA 2002 s84(3).

determined or the person(s) who produced the counter notice give notice in writing of the withdrawal of their objections.

9.78   Any such application must be made no later than two months after the day on which the last counter-notice was given.[86] The RTM company cannot acquire the RTM unless an LVT determines that it is entitled to do so, or the person who gave the counter-notice accepts, in writing, that the RTM company is entitled to acquire the RTM.[87]

9.79   If an appeal is launched from the decision of the LVT, the RTM process is held in abeyance until the determination or abandonment of the appeal.[88]

Withdrawal of a claim notice

9.80   An RTM company may withdraw from the process at any time by service of a 'notice of withdrawal' on each person who is:[89]

(a) a landlord under a lease;
(b) a party to such a lease;
(c) a manager appointed under the 1987 Act; or
(d) a qualifying tenant.

9.81   An application is deemed to be withdrawn if, having received a counter-notice, the RTM company does not apply for a determination of the issue by the LVT within two months.[90]

9.82   If the RTM company makes the necessary application but then withdraws the application, the RTM process is deemed to have ceased.[91]

9.83   The claim notice is also deemed to be withdrawn if a winding-up order is made or a resolution for winding-up is passed; a receiver or a manager of the RTM company is appointed; if the assets of the RTM company are compromised; a voluntary arrangement (within the meaning of Part 1 of the Insolvency Act 1986) is made or the RTM company is struck off the register of companies.[92]

---

86 CLRA 2002 s84(4).
87 CLRA 2002 s84(5).
88 CLRA 2002 s82(7).
89 CLRA 2002 s86.
90 CLRA 2002 s87(1)(a).
91 CLRA 2002 s87(1)(b).
92 CLRA 2002 s87(4).

Costs of the RTM process

9.84   The RTM company is liable for the reasonable costs of the landlord, manager and other parties to the lease in respect of actions taken by them once a claim notice has been served.[93]

9.85   The costs of professional services (such as lawyers or accountants) are regarded as reasonable only to the extent that the person claiming them might reasonably have been expected to have incurred them and if he would be personally liable for those costs.[94]

9.86   The RTM company is also liable for costs incurred by any such person in proceedings before the LVT if the LVT dismisses the application for a determination that it is entitled to acquire the right to manage.[95]

9.87   In the event of a dispute about any costs claimed, the issue shall be decided by the LVT.[96]

9.88   If the RTM process is withdrawn, the general rule is that the RTM company is liable for the reasonable costs (as above) which have been incurred up to the date of withdrawal. Each person who is or has been a member of the RTM company is liable for those costs.[97]

Acquiring the right to manage

9.89   If there was no dispute as to the notice of claim, the RTM company acquires the right to manage on the date specified in the notice of claim.[98]

9.90   If there was a dispute which the LVT determined in favour of the RTM company, the acquisition date is three months after the determination becomes final.[99]

9.91   If the landlord could not be found and the RTM company made an application under section 85, the acquisition date is as set out in the order made by the LVT.[100]

---

93 CLRA 2002 s88(1).
94 CLRA 2002 s88(2).
95 CLRA 2002 s88(3).
96 CLRA 2002 s88(4).
97 CLRA 2002 s89.
98 CLRA 2002 s90(2).
99 CLRA 2002 s90(4).
100 CLRA 2002 s90(6).

Duty to pay uncommitted service charges

9.92 Where a landlord (or manager appointed under Part 2 of the Landlord and Tenant Act 1987) has collected service charges in advance, but not yet spent them all, he is under an obligation to hand the sums over to the RTM company.[101] This does not require a notice from the RTM company – the legislation places the duty firmly on the landlord, although it would be wise for the RTM company to remind the landlord of this.

9.93 The sums must be paid on the acquisition date or as soon after as is reasonably practicable.[102]

9.94 The total sum to be paid is calculated by taking any monies paid by the leaseholders as service charges plus any interest or investment income generated by such money less the landlord's outgoings on the provision of services up to the acquisition date.[103]

9.95 In the event that the landlord and RTM company cannot agree a figure, either party may apply to the LVT to determine the amount to be paid.[104]

Approvals

9.96 Many leases provide for landlords to approve certain structural or other changes to the flats before tenants can act. Once the RTM is acquired, such consent can now validly be given by the RTM company.[105]

9.97 However, in any circumstance where consent is so needed, the RTM company must give at least 14 days' notice of its proposed decision to the landlord. This 14-day period rises to 30 days in the case of assignment, under-letting, charging, parting with possession, the making of structural alternations or improvements or alterations of use.[106]

9.98 If, during the 14/30-day notice period, the landlord objects, the RTM company may only grant its approval to the proposals if:[107]

(a) the person who objected later consents in writing; or
(b) the LVT determines that such consent should be given.

101 CLRA 2002 s94(1).
102 CLRA 2002 s94(4).
103 CLRA 2002 s94(2).
104 CLRA 2002 s94(3).
105 CLRA 2002 s98(2).
106 CLRA 2002 s98(4).
107 CLRA 2002 s99(1).

9.99   An application to the LVT for a determination of this question may be made by the RTM company, the tenant, any sub-tenant or the landlord.[108]

9.100   The legislation is silent as to what criteria the LVT will use to make its decision although, given that this application can only arise if a landlord refuses to consent to the proposals, it seems likely that the test will be 'whether the landlord has acted reasonably in all the circumstances in refusing his consent'.

9.101   Presumably, in the case of structural alterations, proposals that would lower the value of the freehold will be rejected, as no reasonable landlord could be asked to consent to such activities. It also seems clear that tenants under leases with only a short time left to run will find it more difficult to show that structural alterations are reasonable than leases with a longer period to run.

108 CLRA 2002 s99(5).

CHAPTER 10

Forfeiture

10.1   **Introduction**

10.2   **Advice for tenants**

10.3   **An introduction to forfeiture**

10.3   What is forfeiture?

10.6   The right to forfeit

10.7   Waiver of forfeiture

10.12   Exercising the right to forfeit

10.14   Right to relief

10.17   **Breach of covenant to pay rent**

10.19   Notification that rent is due

10.24   No forfeiture for failure to pay small amounts

10.27   **Breach of other covenants**

10.30   Limitations on the right to forfeit: residential property

10.32   **Breach of covenant to pay service or administration charges**

10.37   **Jurisdiction of the LVT**

Key points

- Leases often contain a provision that allows the landlord to bring the lease to an end if the tenant defaults on any obligation under the lease, including a covenant to pay service charges. This is known as 'forfeiture'.
- A court order is required before a lease can be deemed forfeit.
- Where the landlord is attempting to forfeit for failure to pay service charges, the service charge in dispute must have been determined by a court, LVT or arbitral tribunal.
- Where the landlord is attempting to forfeit for breach of covenant, they must first obtain a decision of a court or the LVT that the tenant has breached the covenant.
- The landlord may not forfeit for failure to pay rent, service charges or administration charges where less than £350 has been due for less than three years.

Introduction

10.1   This chapter focuses on specific protection given to residential leaseholders against actions for forfeiture and on the ways in which the LVT can become involved in disputes concerning forfeiture. The law of forfeiture is a vast topic, and we will only develop as much of it as will be needed to put the rights of leaseholders into context. Advisers are referred to textbooks such as *Megarry and Wade: The Law of Real Property*[1] or, for a slightly more accessible book, *Forfeiture of Tenancies*.[2]

Advice for tenants

10.2   Leases often contain a provision that allows the landlord to bring the lease to an end if the tenant defaults on any obligation under the lease, including a covenant to pay service charges. This is known as 'forfeiture'. It is a very technical area of law and may involve hearings in both the LVT and the county court (or High Court). The LVT is

---

1   C Harpum (ed), rev 6th edn, 1999, Sweet & Maxwell.
2   A Kenny, 1999, Blackstone's Landlord and Tenant Series, Blackstone Press (now OUP).

(in general terms) limited to determining whether or not the tenant has acted in such a way as to permit the landlord to begin forfeiture proceedings. It is the court that will ultimately decide whether or not the lease should be forfeited and, if not, on what terms the tenant should be permitted to remain.

An introduction to forfeiture

What is forfeiture?

10.3   Many leases have a provision which allows the landlord to bring the lease to an end if the tenant defaults on any of their covenants in the lease – including covenants to pay rent and service charges. This process is known as 'forfeiture'.

10.4   For many landlords forfeiture represents a convenient way to enforce a tenant's obligations but it is a power that is capable of creating a serious injustice. The tenant stands to lose their investment in their leasehold property, which may be out of all proportion to any damage suffered by the landlord.

10.5   The common law makes a distinction between forfeiture for breach of covenant to pay rent and forfeiture for breach of any other covenant. The distinction arose because the damage to a landlord from a failure to pay rent can be calculated exactly whereas the effect of breaches of other covenants can be harder to quantify.

The right to forfeit

10.6   There is no common law right to forfeit so that, in order for a landlord to exercise the power of forfeiture, there must be an express provision in the lease that gives the landlord a right of 're-entry' or forfeiture. Such a clause will not be implied, even if the lease refers to the incorporation of the 'usual covenants'.[3]

Waiver of forfeiture

10.7   A landlord might decide, for whatever reason, that it is not in their interest to forfeit a lease and might chose to respond to a tenant's breach in a different way. Despite this freedom, the common law requires the landlord, on discovering the tenant's breach, to make

---

3   *Re Anderton and Milner's Contract* (1890) 45 Ch D 476.

a choice: they must either forfeit the lease or allow the lease to continue.[4]

10.8   If, knowing that there has been a breach of the lease which would give rise to a right to forfeit, the landlord does some act which is compatible with the lease continuing, the landlord will be deemed to have chosen not to forfeit the lease and will lose the right to do so.

10.9   This situation is usually referred to as 'waiver' of forfeiture. This is a perhaps unfortunate since the word 'waiver' is a rather over-used technical term and covers a number of quite different situations. A rather famous example of a different kind of waiver being where a landlord informs a tenant that no rent will be due during the course of a war: the landlord cannot then claim that the tenant was in breach for not paying the rent in that period.[5]

10.10   A very common situation in which waiver of forfeiture occurs is when a landlord, knowing of a tenant's breach of covenant, demands or accepts rent. Such a demand or acceptance is, of course, only consistent with the continued existence of the lease and incompatible with forfeiture. A landlord that does so is likely to lose their right to forfeit.[6]

10.11   Advisers dealing with a forfeiture situation should always assess very carefully whether a waiver of forfeiture may have arisen.

Exercising the right to forfeit

10.12   In the past a power to forfeit a lease was often expressed to be exercisable by 're-entry'. All a landlord needed to do was to re-enter the property peaceably and the lease would come to an end, though it could be brought back into existence if the tenant successfully applied to a court for relief against forfeiture.

10.13   In modern times forfeiture is almost always exercised by applying for an order for possession from a court. For tenants of a dwelling, a court order is compulsory before a lease is forfeit.[7] An attempt to evict a residential tenant unlawfully is both a tort[8] and a crime.[9]

---

4   *Mathews v Smallwood* [1910] 1 Ch 777; *Cornillie v Saha* (1996) 72 P&CR 147.
5   *Central London Property Trust Ltd v High Trees House Ltd* [1947] KB 130.
6   *Expert Clothing Service and Sales Ltd v Hillgate House Ltd* [1986] 1 Ch 340; [1985] 3 WLR 359.
7   Protection from Eviction Act 1977 s2.
8   Housing Act 1988 ss27–28.
9   Protection from Eviction Act 1977 s1.

Right to relief

10.14 Where there has been a breach of covenant a tenant will usually retain the right to ask the court to give 'relief' from forfeiture.

10.15 In general terms this permits the tenant either to pay all the arrears of rent, together with the landlord's reasonable costs, or in the case of a breach of a covenant other than one to pay the rent, to take steps to remedy the breach. In granting relief, the court will normally order that, upon the tenant taking the necessary steps that the lease continues as if it the landlord had never attempted to exercise a right to forfeit.

10.16 The specific rules on relief are convoluted since there are different statutory powers depending on whether the breach was of a covenant to pay rent or some other covenant; and whether the claim is proceeding in the High Court or county court, as well as an inherent power to give relief in all cases. In some cases a tenant will have a right to relief, while in others the court will have a discretion. Advisers should consult one of the references given at the beginning of the chapter for further details.

Breach of covenant to pay rent

10.17 The rent that is due under long leases (usually called the 'ground rent') is often of a very small amount, perhaps tens of pounds every year. Where a landlord has been inactive a tenant might well inadvertently fail to pay the rent when it falls due. Under common law this amounts to a breach of covenant and gives the landlord the right to forfeit the lease. There is anecdotal evidence that some landlords were deliberately waiting for tenants to pay late in order to threaten forfeiture as a way of extorting money from their tenants.[10]

10.18 The Commonhold and Leasehold Reform Act 2002 introduced two specific protections for tenants under long leases of dwellings: rent will not be due until the landlord has notified the tenant that it is;[11] and the landlord will not be able to forfeit for a failure to pay a small amount of rent for a small period.[12]

---

10 Hansard, 10 June 1998, col 1000, per Barry Gardner MP.

11 CLRA 2002 s166.

12 CLRA 2002 s167.

Notification that rent is due

10.19   A tenant under a long lease of a dwelling will not be liable to pay any rent until the landlord has served a notice on the tenant that rent is due.[13] The notice must be in the required form and specify:[14]

(a) the amount that is due;

(b) when it would have been due under the lease;

(c) a date for payment of the rent, which must be no earlier than when it would have been due under the lease and between 30 and 60 days (inclusive) after the service of the notice;

(d) the name of the leaseholder to whom the notice is given;

(e) the period to which the rent demanded is attributable;

(f) the name of the person to whom payment is to be made, and the address for payment;

(g) the name of the landlord by whom the notice is given and (if not specified as the address for payment given above) their address;

(h) information provided in the notes to the form set out in the Schedule to the Regulations (which gives some warning to leaseholders of their legal position).

10.20   The Welsh Regulations permit a landlord to serve a notice that is 'substantially to the same effect' as the prescribed form.[15] The English Regulations do not.

10.21   The tenant then becomes liable to pay the rent on the date specified in the notice.

10.22   For these purposes, 'rent' does not include service or administration charges[16] even if they are reserved as rent under the lease. These charges have their own, more exacting, requirements for notice.[17]

10.23   The notice must be sent to the tenant at the dwelling, unless the tenant has notified the landlord of another address (which must be in England or Wales) to which notices that rent is due should be sent, in which case the landlord must send the notice to that other address.[18]

---

13 CLRA 2002 s166.

14 Landlord and Tenant (Notice of Rent) (England) Regulations 2004 SI No 3096; Landlord and Tenant (Notice of Rent) (Wales) Regulations 2005 SI No 1355.

15 Landlord and Tenant (Notice of Rent) (Wales) Regulations 2005 SI No 1355 reg 3(2).

16 CLRA 2002 s166(7).

17 See chapter 3.

18 CLRA 2002 s166(6)·

No forfeiture for failure to pay small amounts

10.24 A landlord is also be prevented from bringing proceedings for forfeiture of a long lease of a dwelling where a 'small amount' is owed for a 'small period' for either rent, service or administration charges.[19]

10.25 Regulations have set the 'small amount' to £350, and the 'small period' to three years.[20]

10.26 The calculation of the amount owed excludes any 'default charge', that is an administration charge imposed for failure to pay rent, service or administration charges on time[21] otherwise a landlord would be able to avoid the protection given to tenants by imposing default charges that would automatically take any arrears over the specified 'small amount'.

Breach of other covenants

10.27 Where a landlord wishes to forfeit a lease because a tenant has breached a covenant, other than one to pay rent, the landlord will normally be required to serve a notice, called a 'section 146 notice', on the tenant.[22]

10.28 The notice must detail the breach of covenant that is complained of and give the tenant a reasonable time in which to remedy it. Only if the tenant fails to remedy the breach within that time, is the landlord permitted to forfeit the lease.[23]

10.29 The landlord is not required to serve a section 146 notice if the breach of covenant by the tenant is not capable of being remedied, the thinking being that since the tenant cannot put the breach right, there is no point in asking them to do so. There is a great deal of case law as to what does and does not constitute an irremediable breach of covenant which we will not discuss here.

---

19 CLRA 2002 s167.
20 The Rights of Re-entry and Forfeiture (Prescribed Sum and Period) (England) Regulations 2004 SI No 3086; Rights of Re-entry and Forfeiture (Prescribed Sum and Period) (Wales) Regulations 2005 SI No 1352.
21 CLRA 2002 s167(3).
22 Law of Property Act 1925 s146.
23 Law of Property Act 1925 s146.

Limitations on the right to forfeit: residential property

10.30 CLRA 2002 gives additional protection to long leaseholders of a dwelling. In such a case, the landlord is not be permitted to serve a section 146 notice for a breach of covenant, until 14 days after a court or post-dispute arbitral tribunal has determined that there has been a breach as alleged or the breach has been admitted by the tenant.[24]

10.31 A landlord may apply to an LVT for a determination that a breach of covenant has occurred.[25]

Breach of covenant to pay service or administration charges

10.32 Some leases are said to 'reserve' payments (which will usually be service or administration charges) as rent. Where this is the case, a failure to pay those charges will amount to a failure to pay the rent and thus permit the landlord to forfeit without serving a section 146 notice. In such a situation, where a court grants relief against forfeiture by ordering the tenant to pay all arrears of rent and the landlord's costs, the service charges owed will be treated as rent and would form part of the sum that the tenant had to pay.

10.33 Service charges are only treated as rent if they are expressly referred to as such in the lease.[26]

10.34 Whether or not service or administration charges have been reserved as rent and thus whether or not a landlord is required to serve a section 146 notice before exercising a right to forfeit, Housing Act 1996 s81 gives additional protection to residential tenants.

10.35 A landlord may not exercise a right of forfeiture for a breach of covenant to pay service or administration charges until the amount of the charge has been determined by a court, LVT or post-dispute arbitral tribunal or otherwise admitted by the tenant.[27] The service of a section 146 notice is an exercise of the right to forfeit.

10.36 Once the charge(s) have been determined, the landlord may not exercise a right of re-entry or begin proceeding for forfeiture for a further 14 days.[28]

---

24 CLRA 2002 s168.
25 CLRA 2002 s168(4)
26 *Khar v Delmounty Ltd* (1998) 75 P&CR 232; [1996] EGCS 183.
27 Housing Act 1996 s81.
28 Housing Act 1996 s81(2).

Jurisdiction of the LVT

10.37   The LVT has two distinct roles to play in the context of forfeiture. First, where there has been a breach of covenant to pay service or administration charges, in determining how much is payable.

10.38   Second, where there has been a breach of a covenant other than one to pay rent, service or administration charges, the task of the LVT is to determine whether or not there has been a breach of covenant by the tenant.[29] This is not the same as determining whether a landlord is entitled to forfeit the lease as a result or, even, whether or not the tenant should be afforded relief from forfeiture. Its competence is limited to deciding the question of whether a breach has occurred at all, not what the landlord may do about it.

10.39   A different question arises where the landlord may have behaved in such a way that there is no actionable breach at all. For example, where a lease contains a covenant prohibiting alterations without the landlord's written consent, and the landlord permits or encourages a tenant to do alterations, the landlord may be estopped from suing the tenant for the breach.

10.40   In *Swanston Grant (Luton) Management Limited v Eileen Langley-Essen*,[30] the tenant had underlet in breach of covenant. The landlord applied to the LVT for a determination that there had been a breach of covenant. Before the LVT, the tenant argued that the landlord had been well aware that she (and other tenants) had been doing so and had failed to do anything about it. This, argued the tenant, amounted to a waiver of the landlord's right to sue for breach of covenant – and therefore the landlord had no right to forfeit the lease.

10.41   The Lands Tribunal explained that there was a clear difference between (on the one hand) the waiver by a landlord of a right to forfeit and (on the other) a waiver by the landlord of a right to sue for a breach of covenant. It held that, in the latter case, the LVT did have jurisdiction to decide that the landlord had waived their right to sue for breach of covenant – in other words that the LVT's jurisdiction extends to deciding whether an actionable breach of covenant exists.

10.42   It was not necessary for the Lands Tribunal to decide whether or not the LVT could deal with questions of waiver by a landlord of the right to forfeit. However, the tone of the decision suggests that the Lands Tribunal takes the same view as the authors (ie, that the answer is 'no').

29   CLRA 2002 s168.
30   LRX/12/2007 (Lands Tribunal).

CHAPTER 11

Right to buy leases

11.1   Introduction

11.4   Advice for tenants

11.6   Service charges

11.9   Administration charges

11.10   Consultation provisions

11.11   Loans

11.14   Directions issued by the Secretary of State

Key points

- During the Right to Buy process, the landlord will serve a notice setting out the service charges expected to be payable in the first five years. Apart from increasing for inflation, the landlord will usually be forced to keep to the terms of this notice.
- There is a right to a loan from the landlord in order to pay for certain categories of service charge within the first ten years of the lease.
- There is government guidance as to when certain costs should or could be waived.

Introduction

11.1   The 'right to buy'[1] and the 'right to acquire'[2] are statutory rights for certain tenants of social landlords to purchase the leasehold or freehold of their homes. The process by which one exercises this right is beyond the scope of this work,[3] however, in the case of tenants who have purchased the leasehold of their homes, there are a number of important statutory provisions which serve to reduce the service charges payable by them or to confer upon them rights to loans in respect of their service charges.

11.2   This work does not cover the position of service charges in respect of freehold purchases, as any disputes about such charges fall outside the jurisdiction of the LVT.[4]

11.3   This chapter speaks about the position of 'right to buy' leases, rather then 'right to acquire' leases, simply because there are many more of the former. The position with right to acquire leases is, however, broadly similar.

---

1   See generally HA 1985 Pt 5.
2   See generally HA 1996 s16 and Housing (Right to Acquire) Regulations 1997 SI No 619.
3   See Arden, Partington, Hunter and Dymond, *Housing Law* (Sweet and Maxwell, looseleaf).
4   Housing Act 1985 ss45-48.

Advice for tenants

11.4   Properties which were acquired pursuant to the right to buy have a number of rights which are not given to leaseholders of other properties. The most important of these is a cap on service charges during the initial years of the lease, although other limitations on service charges also exist. Tenants need to be aware of these restrictions.

11.5   In addition, tenants should not overlook their right to a loan from the landlord in respect of service charge demands. It will usually be preferable to borrow money from the landlord than from a private company.

Service charges[5]

11.6   During the right to buy process, the landlord will serve a notice under section 125 of the Housing Act (HA) 1985. While the notice deals primarily with the proposed purchase price, it must also contain details about service charges.

11.7   The exact nature of the notice will vary from case to case. In general terms, it must provide estimates for repairs[6] and improvements[7] over a period of five years, starting no later than six months after the service of the section 125 notice.[8]

11.8   The tenant cannot be required to pay service charges in excess of those specified in the section 125 notice,[9] although an allowance is made for inflation.[10]

Administration charges[11]

11.9   Any provision of a lease granted under the right to buy which purports to allow the landlord to charge the tenant a sum for or in connection with the giving or a consent or approval is void.[12]

---

5   See chapter 2.

6   HA 1985 s125A(2).

7   HA 1985 s125B.

8   Called a 'reference period'. While the period of five years from a date no later than six months after the service of the section 125 notice is usual, other periods may be chosen: see HA 1985 s125C.

9   HA 1985 Sch 6 paras 16B and 16C.

10   Housing (Right to Buy) (Service Charges) Order 1986 SI No 2195.

11   See chapter 6.

12   HA 1985 Sch 6 para 6.

Consultation provisions[13]

11.10　For the first 30 days of a right-to-buy tenancy the consultation requirements do not apply.[14]

Loans

11.11　Where, in the first ten years after the grant of the lease,[15] service charges are levied in respect of repairs or improvements, the tenant may be able to demand a loan from the landlord. If the landlord is a housing association, then this shall take the form of an advance[16] and, in all other cases, a right to leave the whole or part of the service charge outstanding.[17]

11.12　The right to a loan only arises if:

(a) the service charge demand exceeds £1,500, with any sum which has already been demanded in a previous demand being excluded;

(b) the demand does not exceed £20,000, with any previous loans being deducted from the demand; and

(c) the amount to of the loan must exceed £500.[18]

11.13　In addition, in all other cases, the landlord has a power to make a loan on any terms that it may determine.[19] In either case, the loan is secured by way of a mortgage on the flat[20] to be repaid over three years (if less than £1,500), five years (if between £1,500 and £5,000) or ten years (if over £5,000), although the tenant may request a shorter period in each case.[21]

13　See chapter 4.

14　Service Charges (Consultation Requirements) (England) Regulations 2003 SI No 1987; Service Charges (Consultation Requirements) (Wales) Regulations 2004 SI No 684 regs 5 and 7 in each case.

15　HA 1985 s450A(2).

16　HA 1985 s450A(4)(a).

17　HA 1985 s450A(4)(b).

18　Housing (Service Charge Loans) Regulations 1992 SI No 1708 reg 3.

19　Housing (Service Charge Loans) Regulations 1992 SI No 1708 reg 5.

20　Housing (Service Charge Loans) Regulations 1992 SI No 1708 reg 6.

21　Housing (Service Charge Loans) Regulations 1992 SI No 1708 Sch 1.

Directions issued by the Secretary of State

11.14 The Secretary of State is empowered to issue directions to social land-lords[22] about service charge recovery in respect of repairs, mainten-ance or improvement works.[23] Those directions may require or permit the waiver or reduction of charges in specified circumstances.[24]

11.15 Two sets of directions have been issued.[25] Landlords have a dis-cretionary power to reduce or waive service charges for past, current and future works of repair, maintenance or improvement if (a) the total charges exceed £10,000 in a five-year period or (b) if carried out wholly or partially with the assistance of the Estate Action City Challenge, the Single Regeneration Challenge Fund or the Estates Renewal Challenge Fund, where that funding was applied for before 25 February 1997.[26]

11.16 Landlords are required to reduce service charges for repairs, maintenance or improvements carried out wholly or partially with the assistance of the Single Regeneration Challenge Fund or the Es-tates Renewal Challenge Fund, where that funding was applied for on or after 25 February 1997 and if the charges will exceed £10,000 in a five-year period.[27]

---

22 In general terms, a district council, unitary authority or registered social landlord: HA 1996 s219(4).

23 HA 1996 s219.

24 HA 1996 s219(1)(a)–(b).

25 Social Landlords Discretionary Reduction of Service Charges (England) Directions 1997; Social Landlords Mandatory Reduction of Service Charges (England) Directions 1997: see appendix A.

26 Social Landlords Discretionary Reduction of Service Charges (England) Directions 1997.

27 Social Landlords Mandatory Reduction of Service Charges (England) Directions 1997.

CHAPTER 12

Funding

12.1   **Introduction**

12.4   **Advice for tenants**

12.7   **Legal aid**

12.12   Exceptions

12.14   **Legal expenses insurance**

12.17   **Pro bono services**

Key points

• It is very unlikely that legal aid will be available for hearings before the LVT.
• Legal expenses insurance should be explored as a possible source of funding.
• In London, there are various pro bono (ie, free) groups who will provide advice, assistance and representation.

Introduction

12.1   The LVT, in common with most tribunals, is designed to be a less formal method of resolving disputes than that provided by the courts. The effect should be that parties are able to represent themselves without needing expert legal advice.

12.2   However, as the Residential Property Tribunal Service (the umbrella organisation supporting LVTs) has itself recognised,[1] some disputes involve technical and complex matters, where it may be necessary to instruct a surveyor, solicitor and/or barrister.

12.3   As a general rule, legal aid is unlikely to be available for such matters and tenants will need to be aware of other funding options.

Advice for tenants

12.4   It is too simplistic to simply say that a tenant can represent themselves before the LVT. Certain types of proceedings will require expert evidence and, in that case, it will be necessary to instruct a surveyor.

12.5   In addition, certain types of case are legally complex and, without legal assistance, tenants will find themselves at a disadvantage.

12.6   Legal aid is only available in truly exceptional circumstances. Tenants need to think innovatively when it comes to securing funding. Insurance policies are worth exploring and, in London at least, there are a number of providers of pro-bono (free) legal advice. The tenant who is unable to fund a case themselves should make full use of these resources.

---

1   www.rpts.gov.uk/faq/faq.htm: see 'Can I represent myself at a tribunal?'.

Legal aid

12.7 Legal aid is unlikely to be available for proceedings before the LVT.[2]

12.8   In addition, legal aid is subject to a strict means test. The Legal Services Commission (LSC) has an on-line calculator to provide guidance on whether or not someone is eligible for assistance.[3] In the experience of the authors, it is very unusual for leaseholders to qualify for legal aid.

12.9   The LSC has published guidance on cases which will be suitable for legal aid. That guidance only deals with service charge disputes and betrays a lack of understanding of the role of the LVT.

12.10   The LSC makes clear that a service charge dispute will not usually be eligible for legal aid unless, as a result of the leaseholder losing the dispute, it is likely that an immediate order for possession would be made.[4]

12.11   It also expresses the view that the LVT is only an appropriate forum for determining service charge disputes about 'reasonableness'[5] and that disputes about the entitlement of the freeholder to claim for an item of work are not appropriate for determination by the LVT. This is despite the fact that the Commonhold and Leasehold Reform Act 2002 expressly conferred jurisdiction on the LVT to consider such matters.[6]

Exceptions

12.12 The Lord Chancellor may, however, direct the Legal Service Commission to provide funding for proceedings before the LVT.[7]

12.13   The Lord Chancellor has issued guidance as to the types of cases in which he is likely to consider exercising this power.[8] The guidance indicates that:

(a) it would be extremely unusual for the Lord Chancellor to direct that any particular case should be funded;

(b) LVT proceedings are regarded as a low priority;

(c) tribunals (including the LVT) are intended to have procedures which are simple enough to allow people to represent themselves;

2   Access to Justice Act 1999 Sch 2 para 2.
3   www.legalservices.gov.uk/civil/guidance/eligibility_calculator.asp
4   *LSC Manual*, The Funding Code, Vol 3, para 3C-162 at 9.
5   See chapter 2.
6   See chapter 2.
7   Access to Justice Act 1999 s6(8).
8   *LSC Manual*, The Funding Code, Vol 3, para 3C-267 onwards.

(d) there must be evidence to clearly demonstrate that no alternative means of funding is available;

(e) there must be a significant wider public interest;

(f) the case must be of overwhelming importance[9] to the client;

(g) without public funding it would be practically impossible for the client to bring or defend the proceedings or the lack of public funding would lead to an obvious unfairness;

(h) the fact that an opponent is represented does not make the proceedings unfair;

(i) language difficulties alone are unlikely to justify the grant of public funding;

(j) the benchmark will be those exceptional cases where the European Court of Human Rights has indicated that the right of access to the courts has effectively been denied because of the lack of public funding.[10]

In addition, the client must also pass the usual legal aid means assessment.

Legal expenses insurance

12.14   Many people have legal expense insurance as part of their motor or home contents insurance. Some credit cards also provide insurance of this nature. While the terms of the insurance will vary from provider to provider, there are a number of common points.

12.15   First, the policy usually requires that there be a reasonable prospect of success in the claim and also that the policy holder must accept any reasonable offer of settlement. These points are usually determined in-house by the insurance company, although they may appoint an external firm of solicitors to advise them if the matter is unusual.

12.16   Second, the insurers usually have a panel of solicitors who will conduct the case on your behalf. These panels are set up by insurers to deal with cases on commercial terms that are agreed in advance. It is unusual for the insurer to appoint a solicitor not on its panel.

---

9 Defined at *LSC Manual*, The Funding Code, Vol 3, 3C-037 as meaning 'exceptional importance to the client beyond the monetary value (if any) of the claim, because the case concerns the life, liberty or physical safety of the client or his or her family, or a roof over their heads'.

10 *Steel & Morris v United Kingdom*, App No 68416/01; (2005) 41 EHRR 403, ECtHR.

Pro bono services

12.17   There are two significant pro-bono (ie, free) providers of legal advice and representation in London, although the rest of the country is less well served. Both the College of Law and BPP Law School organise schemes whereby BVC students (those who are training to be barristers) advise leaseholders and represent them in the LVT. There is, however, no guarantee that everyone who wants representation will be assisted.

12.18   The Bar Pro Bono unit has also arranged representation in some cases.

12.19   Contact details for all three organisations are found in appendix D.

CHAPTER 13

Procedure in the LVT

13.1   **Introduction**

13.4   **Advice for tenants**

13.5   **Starting a case**

13.6   Transfer

13.10   Applying to the LVT

13.11   Who may apply

13.13   Information to be included

Service charge, administration charge and estate charge applications • Estate management schemes • Right to Manage • Appointment of manager • Variation of leases • Determination of breach of covenant

13.22   Service of the application

13.25   Fees

Free applications • Application fees • Hearing fees • Multiple applicants • Waiver of fees

13.34   **Track allocation**

Paper track • Fast track • Standard track

13.41   **Interim matters**

13.42   Joinder

13.45   Consolidation and representative applications

13.50   Withdrawal

13.51   Dismissal

Inherent jurisdiction

continued

13.58   Pre-trial review

13.61   Directions

13.63   Procedure at the final hearing

13.77   Inspections

13.80   Evidence

13.85   The LVT as an expert tribunal

13.86   Adjournments

13.88   Precedent in the LVT

13.89   Costs

13.90   Power to award costs

13.92   Costs under the lease

13.95   Reimbursement of fees

13.96   Enforcement

13.99   Appeals

13.100 Permission

13.106 Review or re-hearing

13.109 Cross-appeals

13.111 Appeals from the Lands Tribunal

13.112 Judicial review

Pre-action checklist

1 Check that your complaint is one that the LVT can deal with

Commentary

The most common complaints concern the payability of a service charge or administration charge; problems with insuring the property; the variation of a lease; and problems with a manager.

An LVT cannot order a landlord to pay money back to a tenant, nor can an LVT force a landlord to carry out repairs. Only a county court has this power.

2 Contact any other tenants who might be similarly affected

Commentary

Certain applications, such as those to appoint a manager, are more likely to be successful if tenants are in agreement about the problem and the remedy.

If there is more than one applicant, fees can be shared.

3 Write a letter to the landlord, manager, etc, setting out your concerns and asking how they plan to remedy them

Commentary

It may be that your problem can be resolved without the need for an LVT to get involved. In any event, attempts to be helpful and to resolve matters without coming before the LVT are factors which may be relevant to any decision an LVT makes about costs at the end of your case.

4 If the problem cannot be resolved and you need to apply to the LVT, check whether there is any specific procedure you must follow

Commentary

This is the case with applications to appoint a manager, variation of a lease and most of the right to manage process. Failure to comply with the prescribed process may result in an LVT refusing to hear your case.

5 Complete the application form

Commentary

Not all applications have a prescribed application form. If there is no application form there is certain information that must be provided. See appendix B.

continued

> The LVT process will now start. Consider what evidence you will need in order to prove your case and begin to collect it. There is no need to show the landlord your evidence at this stage. The LVT will set a date by when all evidence must be shown to the other side and given to the LVT.

Introduction

13.1   While the LVT is designed to be an informal tribunal, it is still a judicial body and, as such, has various procedural rules with which parties need to be familiar.[1] The procedural regulations are comparatively short, particularly when compared to those used by the civil courts[2] and a great deal of guidance is to be found in the cases, as well as in the regulations. In addition, the LVT possesses a degree of inherent jurisdiction to regulate its own procedures.[3]

13.2   The LVT in Wales has its own set of procedural regulations.[4] These are referred to only where they differ from those applicable in England.

13.3   The Lands Tribunal has its own set of procedural rules[5] and a practice direction[6] which must be considered in relation to any appeal from the LVT. Copies of both are available on the Lands Tribunal website at www.landstribunals.gov.uk.

Advice for tenants

13.4   The LVT is (or should be) a more informal and accessible forum than a court. This does not mean, however, that parties can afford to be flippant or cavalier in their preparation of their cases. The LVT is

---

1   Leasehold Valuation Tribunals (Procedure) (England) Regulations 2003 SI No 2099 ('LVT Procedure Regs'); Leasehold Valuation Tribunals (Procedure) (Wales) Regulations 2004 SI No 681. The Welsh Regulations are only referred to where they differ from those applicable in England.
2   The Civil Procedure Rules 1998 SI No 3132.
3   See para 13.51 below.
4   Leasehold Valuation Tribunals (Procedure) (Wales) Regulations 2004 SI No 681.
5   Lands Tribunal Rules 1996 SI No 1022.
6   Issued on 11 May 2006.

judicial body and failure to comply with its orders and rules can lead to the case being dismissed. It is important to be realistic about the time that it will take to prepare a case, collect evidence, etc and, if a problem arises, to make an application to the LVT for more time or for other directions, rather than simply to allow matters to drift.

Starting a case

13.5   There are two ways in which a case can come before the LVT. It can be transferred from existing court proceedings or can be commenced as a free standing application.

Transfer

13.6   A case may start in the court and be transferred to the LVT.[7] If the court is faced with a question which may also be determined by the LVT, the court may order that the whole or part of the proceedings be transferred to the LVT.[8] The court retains jurisdiction over any additional or ancillary matters, including enforcement of the LVT decision.[9]

13.7   If the case is to be transferred to the LVT, the court will send notice of the transfer to all parties to the claim and send the LVT all the documents relating to the claim together with the order of transfer.[10] In practice, the LVT will often ask the applicant to complete a new application form.

13.8   In any event, the LVT will treat the case as if it were a direct application, save that any monies paid in respect of court fees shall be set off against any fees payable to the LVT.[11]

13.9   In determining whether to transfer the case, the court should have regard to the following (non-exhaustive) factors:

(a) The LVT, as an expert tribunal, which habitually inspects premises, may well be in a better position to determine service charge disputes than the county court.

---

7 CLRA 2002 Sch 12 para 3.
8 CLRA 2002 Sch 12 para 3(1)(a).
9 CLRA 2002 Sch 12 para 3(1)(b).
10 CPR Pt 56 PD 15.
11 Leasehold Valuation Tribunals (Fees) (England) Regulations 2003 SI No 2089 ('LVT Fees Regs'); Leasehold Valuation Tribunals (Fees) (Wales) Regulations 2004 SI No 683 reg 4 in each case. The Welsh Regulations are only referred to where they differ from those applicable in England.

(b) However, it may not be as well placed as a court to determine complex questions of law.

(c) Any referral to the LVT will inevitably involve delay and new directions being given.

(d) Once the county court has given directions for the management of the case, and particularly if those directions have been complied with, any transfer to the LVT will inevitably involve a delay in the dispute being determined, and a corresponding increase in costs.

(e) If the LVT is incapable of resolving all the issues in the case, this is a factor which sounds against any transfer, as it is preferable for all the matters to be resolved together at one hearing.

(f) As both the court and the LVT have the same powers to protect a tenant against claims for costs by the landlord[12] this is not a factor that points one way or the other.[13]

Applying to the LVT

13.10　The Residential Property Tribunal Service has produced application forms for a number of situations.[14] Where there is no appropriate form available, the application can properly be made by sending a letter to the LVT, containing the necessary information[15] and a statement that the applicant believes the information in the letter to be true.[16]

Who may apply

13.11　A question that is often raised by applicants and their advisers is whether a particular individual is entitled to apply to the LVT. The answer will depend on the particular jurisdiction being exercised by the LVT. In some cases there are legislative provisions which restrict who may apply. Even where there is no restriction, an LVT has the power to strike out a frivolous application.[17]

13.12　　The table below covers all the jurisdictions of the LVT covered in this book, and indicates who may apply under that jurisdiction.

12　See the discussion of LTA 1985 s20C at para 13.92 below.

13　*Aylesbond Estates Ltd v MacMillan and others* (2000) 32 HLR 1; [1999] L&TR 127.

14　Available at www.rpts.gov.uk; see also appendix B.

15　As to which, see para 13.13 below.

16　LVT Procedure Regs 2003 reg 3(1)(e).

17　LVT Procedure Regs 2003 reg 11.

Provision	Description	Applicant
Service charges		
LTA 1985 s27A	Determination of liability to pay service charge	Anyone
LTA 1985 s20ZA	Dispensation from consultation requirements	Anyone
LTA 1985 s21A	Determination that landlord has a reasonable excuse for a failure giving rise to the tenants right to withhold service charges	Landlord[18] (includes any person who has a right to enforce payment of service charges)[19]
LTA 1985 s20C	Order that costs in connection with LVT proceedings should not be regarded as relevant costs	Tenant[20]
Administration charges		
CLRA 2002 Sch 11 para 3	Variation of administration charge provision in a lease	Any party to the lease[21]
CLRA 2002 Sch 11 para 5	Liability to pay an administration charge	Anyone
Estate charges		
CLRA 2002 s159(3)	Variation of estate charge provisions in an estate management scheme	Any person on whom an obligation to pay an estate charge is imposed by the scheme
CLRA 2002 s159(6)	Determination of payability of an estate charge	Anyone

18 If an RTM company has acquired the right to manage, the RTM company has the right instead of the landlord: CLRA 2002 Sch 11 para 4(2).

19 LTA 1985 s30.

20 Includes a landlord under a lease of the whole or any part of the premises if an RTM company has acquired the right to manage: CLRA 2002 Sch 11 para 4(3).

21 Includes an RTM company, if it has acquired the right to manage: CLRA 2002 Sch 11 para 16.

Provision	Description	Applicant
Variation of leases		
LTA 1987 s35	Application to vary a long lease	A party to the lease[22]
LTA 1987 s36	Application to vary another lease in response to a section 35 application to vary a long lease	A party to the section 35 lease
LTA 1987 s37	Application to vary two or more leases	Landlord or any tenant of the leases
LTA 1987 s39(3)(b)	Application for the cancellation or modification of an order varying a lease	A person on whom a notice was required to be served under LTA 1987 s35(5)
Variation of insurance provisions		
LTA 1987 s40(1)	Variation of the insurance provisions of a dwelling	A party to the lease
Challenge to the landlord's choice of insurer		
LTA 1985 Sch para 8	Challenge to the landlord's choice of insurer	Landlord[23] or tenant[24]
Appointment of manager		
LTA 1987 s24(1)	Order appointing a manager	Tenant[25]
LTA 1987 s24(9)	Variation or discharge of order appointing a manager	Any person interested

22 Includes an RTM company, if it has acquired the right to manage: CLRA 2002 Sch 11 para 10.

23 If an RTM company has acquired the right to manage in respect of the premises, the RTM company instead of the landlord: CLRA 2002 Sch 11 para 5(2).

24 Includes a landlord under a lease of the whole or any part of the premises who is under an obligation to make payments under CLRA 2002 s103 (landlord's contribution to service charges): CLRA 2002 Sch 11 para 5(3).

25 Includes a landlord under a lease of the whole or any part of the premises, where an RTM company has acquired the right to manage: CLRA 2002 Sch 11 para 8(3).

Provision	Description	Applicant
Appointment of manager *continued*		
LTA 1987 s22(3)	Order dispensing with requirement to serve a preliminary notice before applying for appointment of a manager	Anyone
Right to Manage		
CLRA 2002 s84(3)	Determination that an RTM company was entitled to acquire the right to manage in response to a counter-notice	The RTM company
CLRA s85(2)	Order that an RTM company is to acquire the right to manage where the landlord is missing	The RTM company
CLRA 2002 s88(4)	Determination of any question arising in relation to the costs payable by an RTM company	Anyone
CLRA 2002 s94(3)	Determination of amount of payment of accrued uncommitted service charges	(1) any party, other than a tenant, of a lease of the whole or part of the premises (2) a manager appointed by the LVT (3) the RTM company
CLRA 2002 s99(1)	Determination of whether an approval is to be given under the terms of the lease	The RTM company, landlord, tenant or sub-tenant (where the approval is to be given by a tenant)
CLRA 2002 Sch 6 para 5(3)	Determination that right to manage may be exercised earlier than four years	The RTM company

Provision	Description	Applicant
Forfeiture		
CLRA 2002 s168(4)	Determination that a breach of covenant or other condition in the lease has occurred	Landlord

Information to be included

13.13   All applications must include the following information:[26]

(a) the name and address of the applicant;

(b) the name and address of the respondent;

(c) the name and address of any landlord or tenant of the property to which the application relates;

(d) the address of the premises to which the application relates;

(e) a statement that the applicant believes the facts stated in the application to be true.

13.14   In addition, each application has further specified requirements.

Service charge, administration charge and estate charge applications[27]

13.15   The following must be provided:

(a) a copy of the lease/estate management scheme;

(b) if the application is to determine the payability of service charges, the name and address of any Recognised Tenants' Association;

(c) if the application is to vary an administration charge, a draft of the proposed variation.

Estate management schemes[28]

13.16   The following must be provided:

(a) a copy of the existing estate management scheme or proposed estate management scheme;

(b) a statement that the applicant is either a natural person, a representative body or a relevant authority;

---

26 LVT Procedure Regs 2003 reg 3(1).

27 LVT Procedure Regs 2003 Sch 2 para 2.

28 LVT Procedure Regs 2003 Sch 2 para 3.

(c) any notice given under Leasehold Reform, Housing and Urban Development Act 1993 s70;

(d) any proposed variation to an estate management scheme, with a description of the proposed variation, including identification of the area by a map or plan;

(e) a copy of any consent given by the Secretary of State (in Wales, the National Assembly) under the Leasehold Reform, Housing and Urban Development Act 1993 s72.

Right to Manage[29]

13.17 The following must be provided:

(a) the name and address for service of the RTM company, the name and address of the freeholder, any intermediate landlord and manager;

(b) a copy of the memorandum and articles of association of the RTM company;

(c) where the application is by the RTM company to determine whether, following the receipt of a counter notice, it was entitled to acquire the right to manage, a copy of the claim notice and any counter notices;

(d) where the RTM company is unable to trace a landlord and applies to the LVT to determine whether it can acquire the right to manage, a statement showing that the notice inviting participation and the notice of claim were fulfilled, a copy of the notice served on all qualifying tenants, and the reasons why the landlord cannot be identified and traced;

(e) where the application relates to uncommitted service charges, an estimate of the value of the accrued but uncommitted service charges;

(f) where the RTM company wishes to grant an approval for works or the like without going through the prescribed process and applies to the LVT for dispensation, a copy of the lease;

(g) where the RTM company applies for a determination that, although the right to manage has lapsed, the RTM company should still be permitted to exercise the right to manage, the date and circumstances in which the right to manage ceased.

---

29 LVT Procedure Regs 2003 Sch 2 para 4.

Appointment of manager[30]

13.18   The following must be provided:

(a) where a preliminary notice was served, a copy of that notice;

(b) where the application is to vary an existing management order, a copy of the earlier order.

Variation of leases[31]

13.19   The following must be provided:

(a) the name and address of all persons who were served with notice of proposed variation;

(b) a draft of the proposed variation;

(c) a copy of the lease.

Determination of breach of covenant[32]

13.20   The following must be provided:

(a) a statement giving particulars of the alleged breach of covenant;

(b) a copy of the lease.

13.21   The LVT may dispense with or relax any of these requirements where no prejudice will be caused or is likely to be caused and the information which is provided is sufficient to enable the application to be determined.[33]

Service of the application

13.22   In all cases other than for the variation of a lease described in chapter 7, the LVT shall send a copy of the application to the respondent[34] and any other person that it considers appropriate[35] together with details of how to apply to be joined as a party.[36] In service charge, administration charge and estate management charge cases, the LVT shall also give notice of the application to the secretary of any recognised

---

30 LVT Procedure Regs 2003 Sch 2 para 5.
31 LVT Procedure Regs 2003 Sch 2 para 6.
32 LVT Procedure Regs 2003 Sch 2 para 7.
33 LVT Procedure Regs 2003 reg 3(8).
34 LVT Procedure Regs 2003 reg 5(1).
35 LVT Procedure Regs 2003 reg 5(3).
36 LVT Procedure Regs 2003 reg 5(4).

tenants' association and any person who is likely to be significantly affected by the application.[37]

13.23   Where an application to vary a lease is made in accordance with chapter 7, the applicant must give notice of the application to the respondent and any other person who is known or believed to be likely to be affected.[38] Failure to do so may lead to the variation being set aside and a claim for damages.[39]

13.24   The LVT may give notice by placing an advertisement in two local newspapers, at least one of which should be a freely distributed newspaper.[40] This is likely to be relevant where a very large of number of respondents are involved, for example where a council makes an application concerning all, or a large section of, its leaseholders; or where a party is missing or cannot be found.

Fees

13.25   Different fees apply to different applications. There are specific regulations dealing with the payment of fees and different regulations for England and Wales.[41] The Welsh Regulations are dealt with only to the extent that they differ from those applicable in England.

13.26   Any relevant fee must be sent with the application, save that fees incurred as a result of a transfer of proceedings from a court must be paid within 14 days of being requested.[42] The fee must be paid by cheque or postal order, drawn in favour of the Department for Communities and Local Government (in England) or the National Assembly for Wales (in Wales).[43]

Where a fee is due and not paid, the application shall not proceed until the fee is paid.[44] If the fee is still outstanding one month after it became due, the application shall be treated as withdrawn unless there are reasonable grounds for it remaining outstanding.[45]

---

37 LVT Procedure Regs 2003 reg 5(2).
38 LVT Procedure Regs 2003 reg 4.
39 LTA 1987 s39.
40 LVT Procedure Regs 2003 regs 5(5)–(6).
41 See note 11 above.
42 LVT Fees Regs 2003 reg 6.
43 LVT Fees Regs 2003 reg 6(3). The English Regulations still require payment in favour of the Office of the Deputy Prime Minister. The RPTS requires cheques, etc to be made payable to CLG.
44 LVT Procedure Regs 2003 reg 7(1).
45 LVT Procedure Regs 2003 reg 7(2).

Free applications

13.27   The following applications attract no fee:

(a) determination of the payablity of an estate management charge;
(b) variation of a lease on account of an estate management charge;
(c) variation of an estate management scheme;
(d) an RTM application;
(e) an application under Landlord and Tenant Act (LTA)1985 s20C;
(f) an application for the recognition of a tenants' association;
(g) a pre-trial review;
(h) an application to dismiss a claim as being frivolous, vexatious or otherwise an abuse of process.

Application fees

13.28   The amount payable by way of application fee varies according to the value of the application and the type of application.[46]

13.29   An application to determine the liability to pay a service charge or administration charge; a challenge to insurance premiums; variation of a lease because of an administration charge, the following fees apply.

Charge which is the subject of the application	Application fee
Not more than £500	£50
More than £500, but not more than £1,000	£70
More than £1,000, but not more than £5,000	£100
More than £5,000, but not more than 15,000	£200
More than £15,000	£350

In all cases, the fee is based on the number of dwellings which are the subject of the application.

Number of dwellings	Application fee
Five or fewer	£150
Between six and ten	£250
More than ten	£350

46 LVT Fees Regs 2003 reg 3.

Hearing fees

13.30   There is currently a hearing fee of £150.[47] It is payable within 14 days of being demanded.[48]

Multiple applicants

13.31   If there are several applicants (or cases have been consolidated[49] the fee is shared between them.[50] Joint tenants are treated as one person for these purposes.[51]

Waiver of fees

13.32   Those in receipt of the following benefits are entitled to have their fees waived:

(a) income support;
(b) housing benefit;
(c) income-based jobseeker's allowance;
(d) a working tax credit, and either
    (i) the applicant or their partner receives a tax credit with a disability or severe disability element;
    (ii) the applicant or their partner is also in receipt of a child tax credit;
(e) a guarantee credit under the State Pensions Credit Act 2002;
(f) a certificate from the Legal Services Commission (ie, legal aid) which has not been revoked or discharged and which is in respect of the proceedings before the LVT the whole or part of which have been transferred from the county court;
(g) a working tax credit where the gross annual income used to calculate the credit is £14,213 or less.[52]

13.33   An applicant's partner means either the applicant's spouse or a person of the opposite sex who is living with the applicant as their husband or wife or a person of the same sex living with the applicant in a relationship which has the characteristics of a relationship between husband and wife.[53]

---

47 LVT Fees Regs 2003 reg 5.
48 LVT Fees Regs 2003 reg 14(2).
49 As to which, see para 13.45 below.
50 LVT Fees Regs 2003 reg 7.
51 LVT Fees Regs 2003 reg 7(3).
52 LVT Fees Regs 2003 reg 8.
53 LVT Fees Regs 2003 reg 8(4).

Track allocation

13.34   The LVT has developed a practice of allocating a case to one of three tracks; the paper track; fast track or standard track. Applicants are asked to suggest a track on the application form.

Paper track

13.35   The paper track is suitable for cases which do not require an oral hearing. A case allocated to the paper track will be dealt with entirely on the basis of written representations and documents, without the need for parties to attend a hearing and make oral representations.

13.36   The LVT shall give the parties not less than 28 days' notice in writing of its intention to proceed without an oral hearing.[54] If, at any time before the determination of the case,[55] any party requests a hearing[56] then the LVT shall list the matter for an oral hearing.[57]

13.37   If the matter is dealt with on the basis of written submissions, the LVT give directions to allow this to take place, including directions for the filing and service of written submissions.[58] In practice, paper track determinations are made by a single member of the LVT.[59]

Fast track

13.38   Both the fast track and the standard track involve oral hearings, but the fast track is suited for more straightforward disputes. The LVT aims to decide fast track cases within ten weeks of the receipt of an application. The guidance from the LVT[60] is that the fast track is suitable for simple disputes about a limited number of issues, where the parties have all the relevant documents in their possession. A pre-trial review is unlikely to be held and the case should be decided within ten weeks of the receipt of the application.

Standard track

13.39   The standard track is most suitable for complex cases with a number of issues involved. It almost always involves a pre-trial review being held and detailed, case specific, directions being issued.

54   LVT Procedure Regs 2003 reg 13(1)(a).
55   LVT Procedure Regs 2003 reg 13(3).
56   LVT Procedure Regs 2003 reg 13(1)(b).
57   LVT Procedure Regs 2003 reg 13(4).
58   LVT Procedure Regs 2003 reg 13(2).
59   LVT Procedure Regs 2003 reg 13(5).
60   www.rpts.gov.uk/pubs_and_forms/html_docs/lvt-sc.htm#part4.

13.40   It is possible for a case to be re-allocated between the tracks if it becomes more (or less) complicated with the passage of time.

Interim matters

13.41　There are a number of matters which may arise before any final hearing.

Joinder

13.42　Any person may request to be joined as a party to the proceedings[61] as either an applicant or respondent.[62] The request can be made by writing a letter, explaining the reasons why the party wishes to be joined, to the LVT.

13.43   There is no need to inform the existing parties of the request[63] and it does not appear that the parties have the right to comment on the request. The parties (and the person wishing to be joined) must be sent a copy of the decision of the LVT, whether or not the LVT agrees to the request.[64]

13.44   Interestingly, there is no obvious power for a party to apply to the LVT for an order that some other party be joined to the proceedings. It may be that the power of the LVT to give 'any direction that appears to the tribunal necessary or desirable for securing the just, expeditious and economical disposal of proceedings' as part of a pre-trial review is sufficient to achieve this end.[65]

Consolidation and representative applications

13.45　A number of applications might relate to substantially the same matter(s). In those circumstances, it would be wasteful to deal with each application separately, especially if the same or similar evidence were to be called in each case. It would also give rise to the possibility of differently constituted tribunals coming to differing conclusions on similar matters.

13.46   If it appears to the LVT that a number of applications have been made in respect of the same or substantially the same matters, or

61　LVT Procedure Regs 2003 reg 6.
62　LVT Procedure Regs 2003 reg 6(2)(b).
63　LVT Procedure Regs 2003 reg 6(2)(a).
64　LVT Procedure Regs 2003 reg 6(4).
65　LVT Procedure Regs 2003 reg 12(3)(a).

include some matters which are the same or substantially the same, the LVT may propose to determine only one of the applications, as representative of all the applications.[66]

13.47   If the LVT wishes to take this course, it shall serve a notice on the parties setting out the common matters; specifying which application it proposes to determine as representative and explaining that the findings in the representative application will be binding on all the other cases. It shall invite objections to be submitted, which must be received by the LVT by a specified date.[67]

13.48   Those parties who object (for any reason) will not be treated as being part of the representative application and will continue as if their cases separately. However, the separate case may be heard at the same time as the consolidated cases.[68]

13.49   If, after the determination of the representative application, a further application is received from any person which includes any of the common matters, the LVT shall inform the parties of the findings in the representative case and, unless it receives any objections within a specified time, those previous findings will stand in the present case.[69] If an objection is received, the LVT must rule on whether or not to accept the objection or whether the findings in the representative action shall stand in the present case.[70]

Withdrawal

13.50   There is no formal procedure for withdrawing an application, although, as a matter of practice, the LVT will accept an applicant's written request to do so.

Dismissal

13.51   The LVT has the power to dismiss an application in whole or part if it appears to the tribunal that the application is 'frivolous, vexatious or otherwise an abuse of process of the tribunal.'[71] A respondent may also request that the LVT dismiss the application for the same reasons.[72]

66 LVT Procedure Regs 2003 reg 8(1).
67 LVT Procedure Regs 2003 reg 8(2).
68 LVT Procedure Regs 2003 reg 8(4).
69 LVT Procedure Regs 2003 regs 9 and 10.
70 LVT Procedure Regs 2003 regs 9(3) and 10(3).
71 CLRA 2002 Sch 12 para 7; LVT Procedure Regs 2003 reg 11(1)(a).
72 LVT Procedure Regs 2003 reg 11(1)(b).

13.52   Before exercising this power, the LVT must give not less than 21 days' notice to the applicant that it is minded to dismiss the application and grounds upon which it is so minded to act.[73]

13.53   If the applicant does not request a hearing, then the application may be dismissed.[74] If a hearing is requested, then it must be listed and the question of dismissal considered.[75]

13.54   Before dismissing any application, the LVT must:[76]

(a) remind itself of the provisions of regulation 11, ensure that proper notice has been given to the applicant and ensure that any hearing required is held;

(b) analyse the facts relating to the application under consideration and reach a conclusion as to whether the application (or some identified part of it) can properly be described as one or more of frivolous or vexatious or an abuse of the process of the tribunal;

(c) consider whether, if the application can in whole or in part properly be described as frivolous or vexatious or otherwise an abuse of process of the tribunal, the facts are such that the LVT should exercise its discretion to dismiss the application in whole or in part under regulation 11; and

(d) give clear and sufficient reasons for its conclusions.

13.55   Failure to comply with directions issued by the LVT may, in an appropriate case, justify dismissing an application under this power. The power is, however, discretionary, and the LVT will need to have regard to the reasons for any failure to comply with its directions.[77]

13.56   The Lands Tribunal has also suggested that that low value claims[78] may well also be frivolous, vexatious or otherwise an abuse of process. This does not sit easily with the decision of the Court of Appeal in *Yorkbrooke Investments v Batten*[79] that there is no de minimis rule for service charge disputes.

---

73 LVT Procedure Regs 2003 reg 11(3).

74 LVT Procedure Regs 2003 reg 11(4)(a).

75 LVT Procedure Regs 2003 reg 11(4)(b).

76 *Volosinovici v Corvan Properties Ltd* LRX/67/2006 (Lands Tribunal); see also case commentary by Joy Akah-Douglas, (2007) 11 L & T Rev 189.

77 *Volosinovici v Corvan Properties Ltd*, above, note 76; *Villatte v 38 Cleveland Square Management Ltd* [2002] EWCA Civ 1549.

78 On the facts of *Volosinovici v Corvan Properties Ltd*, above, note 76, only 50p-£1.10 of a number of items on a service charge bill appeared to be challenged.

79 (1986) 18 HLR 25; [1985] 2 EGLR 100.

Inherent jurisdiction

13.57   The LVT (and the Lands Tribunal) also possesses an inherent juris-diction to regulate its own procedures so as to prevent an abuse of process.[80] However, it will be a rare case where it is appropriate to exercise this power, given that Parliament has seen fit to confer a specific statutory power to the similar effect on the LVT.[81]

Pre-trial review

13.58   The tribunal will normally order a pre-trial review (PTR) for cases allocated to the standard track. A PTR may also be requested by the parties.[82] Unless specifically agreed otherwise, at least 14 days' notice of any such hearing must be given.[83]

13.59   If a PTR is listed it is important that the parties (or their repre-sentatives) attend. One of the key roles of a PTR is to set down dates for the service of evidence and the final hearing itself and it is im-portant for each party to have considered any dates that they wish to avoid. Although tribunals are not required to list the final hearing at the convenience of the parties, in practice many attempt to do so.

13.60   The purpose of the PTR is to:[84]

(a) give any directions that appear necessary or desirable in order to bring about the just, expeditious and economical disposal of proceedings;

(b) secure and record all agreements and admissions that can reason-ably be made in the proceedings; and

(c) record any refusal to make agreements or admissions. Any un-reasonable refusal to make an agreement or admission may have adverse costs consequences.[85]

Directions

13.61   Directions mean the steps that must be taken before the final hear-ing date. Typically they should include:

---

80 *Mean Fiddler Holdings Ltd v London Borough of Islington* ACQ/29/2001 (Lands Tribunal); *De Campomar v The Trustees of the Pettiward Estate* LRA/29&30/2004 (Lands Tribunal).

81 Although see *Trafalgar Court RTM Company Ltd v Wells and others*, CAM/ 33UF/LOA/2005/0001 (LVT) for a case where the power was exercised.

82 LVT Procedure Regs 2003 reg 12(1).

83 LVT Procedure Regs 2003 reg 12(2).

84 LVT Procedure Regs 2003 reg 12(3).

85 CLRA 2002 Sch 12 para 4.

(a) any amendments to the application;

(b) the need for any further statements of case;

(c) service of witness statements;

(d) provision for any expert evidence and the service of experts' reports;

(e) disclosure of documents;

(f) preparation of final hearing bundles; and

(g) a date for the hearing and a time estimate.

13.62 One of the major weaknesses in the procedural powers of the LVT is that it has no specific power to force parties to disclose documents as part of the litigation process. It does, however, have a power to serve a notice on any party, requiring them to provide any information that the LVT may specify.[86] Failure to comply with this request is a criminal offence, punishable by a fine.[87] It may be appropriate to exercise this power if a party is being particularly recalcitrant about providing relevant documentation.

Procedure at the final hearing

13.63 The proper approach to planning and presenting a case before the LVT is beyond the scope of this work and is well covered by general works on advocacy. This section highlights those features which are peculiar to an LVT.

13.64 The LVT is to a great extent free to organise its own procedure so that most of what is said here represents widespread practice. If in any doubt parties should ask the tribunal for guidance.

13.65 Assuming that inspection(s) (if any) have taken place in the morning,[88] it is usual for the final hearing to start in the afternoon. Parties should make sure they arrive in good time. Final hearings usually take place in public before a three-member panel.[89]

13.66 The chair, who will sit in the middle, will be legally qualified and be in charge of the conduct of proceedings. The other two members will usually not be lawyers though it is usual for at least one of them to be a surveyor. It is normal to address any remarks to the chair unless one is answering a question addressed directly by one of the other members of the tribunal. There is no need to stand when

---

86 CLRA 2002 Sch 12 para 4(1).

87 CLRA 2002 Sch 12 paras 4(3)-4(4).

88 See para 13.77 below.

89 LVT Procedure Regs 2003 reg 14(6).

making submissions. Unless otherwise stated, the tribunal members are addressed as 'Sir' or 'Madam' as appropriate.

13.67   All parties should have been given 21 days' notice of the final hearing date.[90] If one or more of the parties is not present at the final hearing, and the tribunal is satisfied that they had proper notice, then there is no objection to the final hearing continuing without their attendance.[91.]

13.68   The tribunal may want to deal with one or more preliminary matters first, in particular where there is a question of jurisdiction. It is open to the tribunal to hear argument on that point before going on to the remainder of the final hearing.

13.69   When a party is presenting their case the normal structure is very similar to that used in the county court. A party may begin their case by making a short opening speech. This should be used to explain the structure of the case the applicant intends to present, especially if it is complicated. There is no need to say very much if the case is a simple one. The party then calls their witnesses in whatever order they choose. After giving evidence there will be an opportunity for other parties to cross-examine.

13.70   Tribunals are at least partly inquisitorial and they are likely to ask detailed questions of witnesses after cross-examination, though they will frequently ask questions at other times in order to clarify answers that have been given. There is usually a seat set aside from which witnesses will give their evidence, although there is no witness box.

13.71   It is normal for witnesses to sit when giving evidence and no oath is required. It is common for a tribunal to read a witness statement rather than requiring the witness to read it aloud. The applicant and the tribunal may ask supplementary questions to expand upon any points which might be unclear.

13.72   It is normal practice for the applicant to present their case first, followed by the respondent.

13.73   After all parties have presented their cases, each is usually allowed to make a final submission to the tribunal. The purpose is to summarise the evidence and explain what one's case is in the light of the evidence heard by the tribunal. The nature of the relief sought from the tribunal should also be made clear. The party who presented their case first will usually be permitted to make their submissions last.

13.74   At the end of the hearing the question of costs should be raised.

90 LVT Procedure Regs 2003 reg 14(3).
91 LVT Procedure Regs 2003 reg 14(8).

Both parties may wish to make submissions on the reimbursement of fees and what, if any of their costs they should be awarded. Tenants should remember to make an application for protection against the landlord's costs, under LTA 1985 s20C.[92]

13.75   The decision of the tribunal may be given orally on the same day,[93] but it is more common for a written decision to be sent to the parties.[94]

13.76   If the decision contains a clerical error, omission, or other minor flaw, the tribunal should be contacted as they have the power to remedy such flaws after the decision has been handed down.[95]

Inspections

13.77   It is common practice for the LVT to inspect any property forming the subject of the application.[96] The LVT may also inspect any comparable house, premises or area to which its attention is directed although in practice is unlikely to do so unless expressly invited to by one of the parties and told the exact address.[97] This can in some cases be a very useful tactic where similar properties may be relevant. The parties must be given notice of the proposed inspection (which is usually on the morning of the final hearing).[98]

13.78   The parties are entitled to refuse consent for the LVT or the other party to enter their property,[99] although, in practice, a refusal to allow one party to enter a property will mean that the LVT declines to inspect it. There are obvious problems of fairness where one party has been excluded.

13.79   If the LVT decides to inspect a property after the hearing, it may reopen the hearing if there is any matter arising from the inspection which requires comment.[100] Additionally, if the LVT is minded to draw an adverse conclusion from what it sees at the inspection, it must inform the parties of this and invite submissions.[101]

---

92 See para 13.92 below.
93 LVT Procedure Regs 2003 reg 18(2).
94 LVT Procedure Regs 2003 reg 18(3).
95 LVT Procedure Regs 2003 reg 18(7).
96 LVT Procedure Regs 2003 reg 17(1)(a).
97 LVT Procedure Regs 2003 reg 17(1)(b).
98 LVT Procedure Regs 2003 reg 17(2).
99 LVT Procedure Regs 2003 reg 17(3).
100 LVT Procedure Regs 2003 reg 17(8).
101 *R v Paddington Rent Tribunal ex p Bell London Properties Ltd* [1949] 1 KB 666; [1949] 1 All ER 720.

Evidence

13.80   In most cases a direction for the disclosure of documents will have been made and it will usually be possible to obtain access to relevant documentation in the hands of other parties, though reasonable photocopying costs may be levied if there is a great deal of material. In cases where a party is obstructive or difficult the LVT has the authority to order the production of a document. Such an order should be requested in writing from the tribunal or at a pre-trial review.

13.81   Documentary evidence should be collected into a lever-arch file (called a 'bundle'). It is most sensible to arrange evidence in chronological order; to number each page and to put an index at the front. The tribunal will normally give a direction for the preparation of bundles and the supply of four copies to the tribunal (three for the tribunal and one for the witnesses) and one to the other parties by a certain date.

13.82   Witnesses may give their evidence orally but it is now normal for their evidence to be prepared in writing in the form of a 'witness statement'. There are no rules for the preparation of witness statements but it is good practice for them to be typed, double spaced, signed and dated by the witness and consist of numbered paragraphs for ease of reference.

13.83   If parties have additional documentation on the day of the hearing they should give it to the clerk at the earliest opportunity, with a copy also being given to all parties present. If new documents are produced during the hearing, parties have the right to have an adjournment to give them time to consider the new evidence and for advisers to take instruction on it.[102]

13.84   Such an adjournment is normally offered as a matter of course by the tribunal, though usually for a relatively brief period. Enough time should be given to allow a party sufficient opportunity to deal with the matters in the document.[103]

The LVT as an expert tribunal

13.85   The LVT is an expert tribunal and, as such, is entitled to critically evaluate the evidence in light of its own knowledge and experience. However, it must reach its decision on the evidence before it; it must

102 LVT Procedure Regs 2003 reg 16(2).
103 LVT Procedure Regs 2003 reg 16(2).

give the parties an opportunity to comment on any matters – such as its 'local knowledge' – which it intends to take into account which have not been part of the evidence (a particularly important matter where it intends to reject expert evidence) and must give reasons for its decisions.[104]

Adjournments

13.86 The LVT has the power to postpone or adjourn a hearing or a pre-final hearing review, either of its own initiative or at the request of any party.[105]

13.87 In considering whether to accede to a request for an adjournment or postponement, the LVT give reasonable notice of any postponement or adjournment to the parties[106] and then it must be convinced that it would be reasonable to adjourn, having regard to:[107]

(a) the grounds for the request;
(b) the time at which the request is made; and
(c) the convenience of the other parties.

Precedent in the LVT

13.88 The LVT is not a court and their decisions are not capable of binding each other,[108] although, in practice, the LVT is keen to promote consistency. Despite the fact that the Lands Tribunal is not a 'court of record', the LVT will generally follow the decisions of the Lands Tribunal. It is entirely proper for the Lands Tribunal to give guidance to LVTs.[109] The LVT (and Lands Tribunal) are bound by decisions of the High Court, Court of Appeal and House of Lords.

Costs

13.89 The LVT has very limited powers in respect of costs.

104 *Arrowdell Limited v Coniston Court (North) Limited* LRA/72/2005; [2007] RVR 39 (Lands Tribunal).
105 LVT Procedure Regs 2003 reg 15(1).
106 LVT Procedure Regs 2003 reg 15(3).
107 LVT Procedure Regs 2003 reg 15(2).
108 *West Midland Baptist (Trust) Association (Inc) v Birmingham Corporation* [1968] 2 QB 188.
109 *Earl Cadogan and others v Sportelli and others* [2007] EWCA Civ 1042; [2007] RVR 314.

Power to award costs

13.90   The LVT may order any person to pay costs where:[110]

(a) it has dismissed an application as frivolous, vexatious, or otherwise an abuse of process;[111] or

(b) that person has acted frivolously, vexatiously, abusively, disruptively or otherwise unreasonably in connection with the proceedings.

13.91   The LVT may order a party to pay up to £500,[112] although there is no reason why the LVT could not make multiple orders during the course of a case, where, for example, multiple adjournments have been necessitated.

Costs under the lease

13.92   Some leases will include a clause which permits the landlord to recover legal costs as a service charge. Such clauses must be clear as to their effect.[113] In particular, a clause which allows for the recovery of costs where the landlord is the applicant may not be of assistance when seeking to recover costs in proceedings where the landlord was the respondent. [114]

13.93   If the lease permits a landlord to recover his legal costs as a service charge, then a tenant may apply for an order under LTA 1985 s20C, preventing this from happening in whole or in part. This is the only relevant statutory provision.[115]

13.94   The LVT may make any order which it considers just and equitable in all the circumstances.[116] This is a broad power and exercise

---

110 CLRA 2002 Sch 12 para 10(2).

111 See para 13.51 above.

112 CLRA 2002 Sch 12 para 10(3)(a).

113 *Sella House v Mears* [1989] 1 EGLR 65; (1989) 21 HLR 147; *St Mary's Mansions v Limegate Investments Co Ltd* [2003] 1 EGLR 41; [2003] HLR 24, Matthew Marshal and Zia Bhaloo, 'Having your cake and eating it (Part 1)' (2006) 10 L & T Rev 30.

114 See, by analogy, *Morgan v Stainer* (1993) 25 HLR 467; [1993] 33 EG 87.

115 *Staghold v Takeda and another* (2005) 47 EG 146, HHJ Levy QC, Central London County Court, 8 August 2005 and *Canary Riverside Pte Ltd v Schilling* LRX/26/2005 (Lands Tribunal), rejecting a contention that CLRA 2002 Sch 12 para 10(4) represented an additional bar on the recovery of costs. See also: Timothy Fancourt QC, 'Property law update', *New Law Journal*, 14 July 2006, p1132; Sandi Murdoch, 'Financial recovery', *Estates Gazette*, 26 November 2005, p43.

116 LTA 1985 s20C; Matthew Marshal and Zia Bhaloo, 'Having your cake and eating it (Part 2)' (2006) 10 L & T Rev 65.

of which must be considered on the facts of each case. However, the following points are of general application:[117]

(a) There is no presumption either in favour of an order being made or against an order being made.

(b) The circumstances and conduct of both parties are relevant.

(c) The LVT must consider the effect of not making an order on the landlord (this will be particularly important if it is a company owned by the tenants, whose only asset is the freehold of the property).

(d) The power should be used to ensure that the effect of the primary decision is not subverted. The landlord should not recover through the backdoor what he has been denied through the front.

(e) A landlord who has behaved improperly should not expect to recover his costs of defending such conduct.

(f) An order will remove a property right from a landlord and must be seen in that light – it is not to be used as an instrument of oppression.

(g) Failure by any party to comply with directions is a relevant consideration.

(h) Even without an order, tenants are still protected by LTA 1985 s19.[118]

(i) The fact that a tenant has been successful is a very important factor.

(j) If a landlord is ordered to pay costs because he has acted frivolously, vexatiously, abusively, disruptively or otherwise unreasonably in connection with the proceedings,[119] an order under section 20C should be made.

(k) An order may properly be made in respect of only those tenants who took part in the proceedings, with other tenants being required to pay via their service charges.

(l) Offers of settlement are also relevant.[120]

---

117 *Tenants of Langford Court v Doren* LRX/37/2000; [2002] 5 JHL D8 (Lands Tribunal); *Canary Riverside Pte Ltd v Schilling* LRX/26/2005 (Lands Tribunal); *Iperion Investments v Broadwalk House Residents Ltd* [1995] 2 EGLR 47; (1994) 27 HLR 196; *Holding & Management Ltd v Property Holding and Investment Trust Plc* [1989] 1 WLR 1313; [1990] 1 All ER 938; *Volosinovici v Corvan Properties Ltd* LRX/67/2006 (Lands Tribunal).

118 As to which, see chapter 2.

119 See para 13.51 above.

120 *Loder Dyer v Cadogan Estates Ltd* [2001] EGLR 149.

Reimbursement of fees

13.95   The LVT has the power to require any party to reimburse the other party for the whole or part of any fees paid.[121] This power may not be exercised against a party who would entitled to a waiver of any application fees.[122] A successful party can expect the LVT to exercise this power in their favour.

Enforcement

13.96   Any decision of the LVT may be enforced, with the permission of the county court, in the same way as a normal county court order.[123]

13.97   The application may be made without giving notice to the other party and must (unless the court orders otherwise) be made to the court for the district where the person against whom the award was made resides or carries on business.[124]

13.98   The application must be made on form N322A and must state the name and address of the person against whom it is sought to enforce the award and how much of the award remains unpaid.[125] A copy of the LVT decision must also be filed.[126]

Appeals

13.99   An appeal from a decision of the LVT is to the Lands Tribunal.[127] In an exceptional case, it may be possible to judicially review a decision of the LVT.[128] The LVT has no power to re-open a decision.[129]

---

121 LVT Fees Regs 2003 reg 9(1).
122 LVT Fees Regs 2003 reg 9(2).
123 CLRA 2002 Sch 10 para 11; LVT Procedure Regs 2003 reg 19.
124 CPR Pt 70.4.
125 CPR Pt 70.5; CPR Pt 70 PD 4.1-4.2.
126 CPR Pt 70.6; CPR Pt 70 PD 4.3.
127 CLRA 2002 s175(1).
128 *Daejan Properties Limited v London Leasehold Valuation Tribunal* [2001] EWCA Civ 1095; [2002] HLR 23. The landlord was seeking an order that the LVT be prevented from hearing parts of the case due to a lack of jurisdiction.
129 *Penman v Upavon Enterprises Ltd* [2002] L&TR 10; [2001] 25 EG 158.

Permission

13.100 An appeal may only be made with the permission of the LVT or the Lands Tribunal.[130] The Lands Tribunal has indicated that permission to appeal should only be granted where:[131]

(a) the decision shows that the LVT wrongly interpreted or wrongly applied the relevant law;

(b) the decision shows that the LVT wrongly applied or misinterpreted or disregarded a relevant principle of valuation or other professional practice;

(c) the LVT took account of irrelevant considerations, or failed to take account of relevant considerations or evidence, or there was a substantial procedural defect;

(d) the point or points at issue is or are of potentially wide implication.

13.101 An application for permission must be made to the LVT within 21 days of the date on which the decision was sent to the parties.[132] A copy must be served on the LVT and all other parties.[133] The LVT has the power to extend this time, but any application for an extension must be made within the 21-day period.[134]

13.102 If permission is granted, the notice of appeal (together with all supporting documentation) must be filed within 28 days of the date on which the grant of permission was sent to the applicant.[135]

13.103 If the LVT refuses permission to appeal, a further application may be made to the Lands Tribunal.[136] This application must be made within 14 days of the date on which the decision refusing permission was sent to the parties.[137] The Lands Tribunal has the power to extend this time, but any application for an extension must be made within the 14-day period.[138]

13.104 The Lands Tribunal will serve the application on any other party,

---

130 CLRA 2002 s175(2).

131 Lands Tribunal Practice Direction para 5.7.

132 LVT Procedure Regs 2003 reg 20(a).

133 LVT Procedure Regs 2003 reg 20(b).

134 LVT Procedure Regs 2003 reg 24.

135 Lands Tribunal Rules 1996 r6; Lands Tribunal Practice Direction 5.2-5.5.

136 Lands Tribunal Rules 1996 r5C(1).

137 Lands Tribunal Rules 1996 r5C(2).

138 Lands Tribunal Rules 1996 r35.

but the applicant must ensure that it has given sufficient copies to the Lands Tribunal for this purpose.[139]

13.105   If the Lands Tribunal grants permission to appeal it may attach any conditions that it thinks fit[140] although it would not be appropriate to impose conditions as to costs.[141]

Review or re-hearing

13.106 Prior to the 2002 reforms, a hearing in the Lands Tribunal was a rehearing, with the effect that the whole case – evidence and submissions – was conducted afresh.[142]

13.107   However, with the introduction of the requirement to obtain permission to appeal, this is no longer the case. Now, the applicant must make clear whether or not he is seeking (a) an appeal by way of review; (b) an appeal by way of review which, if successful, will involve a consequential re-hearing or (c) an appeal by way of re-hearing. Unless the application specifies otherwise, the application is treated as an application for permission by way of review.[143]

13.108   Ultimately, the Lands Tribunal will determine the nature of the appeal, having regard to the importance of the issue and ensuring that the case is dealt with in a proportionate manner.[144]

Cross-appeals

13.109 There is no provision in the Lands Tribunal rules for a cross-appeal (ie, an appeal by one party in response to a second party having been granted permission to appeal). The time frames outlined above present significant practical problems for any party wishing to seek permission to cross-appeal.

13.110   In an effort to ameliorate the potential injustice that this may cause, the Lands Tribunal has determined[145] that it has a discretion-

---

139 Lands Tribunal Rules 1996 r5C(5).
140 Lands Tribunal Rules 1996 r5F(1).
141 Lands Tribunal Practice Direction 5.6.
142 *Re London and Winchester Properties Ltd's Appeal* (1983) 45 P&CR 429 (Lands Tribunal); *Wellcome Trust v Romines* [1999] 3 EGLR 229 (Lands Tribunal).
143 Lands Tribunal Practice Direction 5.8.
144 Lands Tribunal Practice Direction 5.9.
145 *Chelsea Properties v Earl Cadogan and Cadogan Estates* LRA/69/2006 (Lands Tribunal); *Arrowdell Limited v Coniston Court (North) Hove Limited* LRA/72/2005; [2007] RVR 39 (Lands Tribunal).

ary power[146] to entertain contentions on the part of a respondent that the result of the appeal should be more favourable to the respondent than was the original LVT decision.

Appeals from the Lands Tribunal

13.111 An appeal from the Lands Tribunal is to the Court of Appeal. The mechanics of such an appeal are outside the scope of this work, save to record that the Court of Appeal has previously noted that it will be a rare case in which it would be appropriate for a second appeal to be brought. Parliament has devised a statutory scheme whereby disputes are left to the good sense of the LVT, subject to the expert supervision of the Lands Tribunal.[147]

Judicial review

13.112 A decision of the Lands Tribunal to refuse permission to appeal is not capable of further appeal to the Court of Appeal, but can be challenged on judicial review to the High Court, although this will only be appropriate in exceptional cases. The fact that the Lands Tribunal erred in law in refusing permission will not be enough. The error must be sufficiently grave to justify the case being treated as exceptional.[148]

---

146 CLRA 2002 s175(4).
147 *Orchard Court Resident's Association v St Anthony's Homes Ltd* [2003] 2 EGLR 28, approved in *R (Sinclair Investments (Kensington) Limited v The Lands Tribunal and others* [2005] EWCA Civ 1305; [2006] 3 All ER 650; [2006] HLR 11.
148 *R (Sinclair Investments (Kensington) Limited v The Lands Tribunal and others* [2005] EWCA Civ 1305; [2006] 3 All ER 650.

CHAPTER 14

Worked examples

14.1   Appointment of a manager

14.1   Background

14.3   Pre-application process

14.13   The LVT application

14.16   The pre-trial review

14.19   Evidence

14.21   The hearing

14.25   The decision

14.29   Service charge dispute

14.29   Background

14.38   Evidence

14.40   The hearing

14.50   Decision

Appointment of a manager

Background

14.1   Anderson House is a block of six flats, all of which are owned by Ms Broome. She has given long leases of all six flats to six different tenants. The leases are all substantially similar. Anderson House is personally managed by Ms Broome.

14.2   Tenant 1 is dissatisfied with Ms Broome's management. She rarely visits Anderson House, fails to return tenant 1's phone calls and has failed to consult tenant 1 before having the common areas of Anderson House repainted. Tenant 1's lease expressly required him to be consulted about any internal improvements or repairs.

Pre-application process

14.3   Tenant 1 speaks to tenants 2, 3, 4 and 5, all of whom agree with tenant 1's complaints about Ms Broome. Tenant 6 does not wish to get involved.

14.4   Tenants 1, 2, 3, 4 and 5 write a joint letter to Ms Broome setting out their complaints. They ask her to contact them within 28 days to discuss the problem. Ms Broome never replies. See figure 1 below.

14.5   Tenants 1, 2, 3, 4 and 5 decide that Ms Broome is not someone they want to be responsible for managing the property. They visit their local Citizens Advice Bureau and discover that the LVT may have the power to order that a new manager be appointed.

14.6   They check that their property is one over which the LVT has power. Their property is one with more than two flats and does not fall within any of the exemptions set out in the Landlord and Tenant Act 1987.

14.7   Confident that the LVT could grant them the remedy that they want, they write to tenant 6, saying that they want to have a new manager appointed. Tenant 6 replies that he has no firm views and does not want to get involved.

14.8   They check to see whether there is anything they must do before applying to the LVT. They discover that there is a pre-application process set out in the Landlord and Tenant Act 1987.

14.9   First, they must send a 'preliminary notice' to the landlord and anyone else who had management duties under the lease. They check their leases and discover that only the landlord, Ms Broome, has management duties, although she has a power to appoint a managing agent if she wants.

14.10   They therefore have to send a preliminary notice to the landlord. Luckily, they have her address and send the preliminary notice by recorded delivery. They ask Ms Broome to contact them within 28 days in order to discuss their concerns. See figure 2.

14.11   Ms Broome replies that she has better things to do than answer endless letters from the tenants and that the common areas clearly needed re-painting. She cannot understand why the tenants are complaining.

14.12   The tenants decide that nothing else can be achieved without an order of the LVT.

The LVT application

14.13   There is no prescribed application form, so the tenants produce a document setting out their case. They complain that Ms Broome is in breach of her management obligations under the lease. She is given the duty to manage the property by the lease and, although she is entitled to appoint a managing agent if she wishes, that duty remains hers. By failing to consult the tenants before having the common areas re-painted, she was in breach of an obligation under the lease.

14.14   They also allege that, by failing to answer their letters and return their phone calls, she has been in breach of the code of practice of the Royal Institute of Chartered Surveyors (RICS).

14.15   The LVT receives the application, together with the relevant fee. They inform Ms Broome of the application and list a pre-trial review. The tenants and Ms Broome are each given at least 14 days' notice of the pre-trial review (PTR).

The pre-trial review

14.16   At the PTR only tenants 1, 2, 3 and 4 can attend. Tenant 5 has work commitments. Ms Broome also attends. Tenant 1 is appointed to speak on behalf of the applicants.

14.17   The PTR gives the tenants and Ms Broome dates by which they must serve any evidence, including any witness statements. The tenants are ordered to produce a short-list of three possible managers that they agree on. The case is listed for a final hearing.

14.18   The tenants have to pay a hearing fee of £150.

Evidence

14.19   The tenants send in the following evidence:

1) witness statements from tenants 1, 2, 3, 4 and 5 setting out their specific complaints against Ms Broome, together with copies of the letters that they say she did not answer;

2) copies of their leases, showing Ms Broome's duty to consult them before painting the common areas;

3) a list of three possible managers. They suggest tenant 1 as their first choice manager, and two professional management companies as second and third choices;

4) a letter from tenant 6 saying that, while he is not a part to this application, he has no objection to tenant 1 or a professional manager being appointed; and

5) letters from the two professional management companies stating that they would be willing to take over the management of the property and setting out their likely fees.

14.20   Ms Broome sends in a witness statement explaining that she has been very busy with other commitments and apologises for not answering the letters. She promises to be a better manager in the future.

The hearing

14.21   Tenant 1 speaks on behalf of the other tenants. They all confirm that their witness statements are true and that they want tenant 1 to be the manager for the property.

14.22   Ms Broome again apologises for the problems. She complains that having tenant 1 as a manager would not be fair to her as she fears that there is now bad blood between her and the tenants. She says that she wants to be a better manager of her property and promises that these problems would not occur again.

14.23   When asked by the LVT, she says that, if she could not stay as manager, she would prefer to have a professional manager appointed, rather than tenant 1.

14.24   The LVT adjourned to consider its decision.

The decision

14.25   Shortly after the hearing, the tenants and Ms Broome are sent a copy of the LVT's decision.

14.26   The LVT referred itself to Landlord and Tenant Act (LTA) 1987 s24. It found that, by not consulting the tenants before having the common area consulted, Ms Broome had been in breach of a management obligation under the lease. It also accepted that by failing to answer letters and return phone calls, Ms Broome was in breach of the RICS code of property management.

14.27   However, it noted that Ms Broome was apparently sincere in her desire to be a better property manager. It noted that tenant 1 had no experience in property management and that neither tenant 6 nor Ms Broome had any objection to a professional manager being appointed. In these circumstances, the LVT felt that it would not be 'just and convenient' to appoint tenant 1, but rather appointed one of the companies suggested by the tenants.

14.28   The company was appointed for two years and was appointed to carry out all the management duties of Ms Broome, as set out in the lease. As the tenants had been substantially successful, Ms Broome was ordered to refund their application fees.

Figure 1   Letter before action

Tenants 1, 2, 3, 4, 5
Anderson House
London
AB12 3CD

Ms Broome
Landlord Road
London
EF45 6GH

20 March 2008

Dear Ms Broome,

We are contacting you concerning the following problems arising out of your management of Anderson House.

1) We have each individually attempted to contact you in the recent past to discuss various matters, but have been unable to reach you. It appears that you are unable or unwilling to return our telephone calls or acknowledge our letters.

2) Under clause 2(a) of our leases, you are required to consult us before carrying out any internal improvements or repairs. The common areas of our property have recently been repainted without you having consulted us.

We are anxious to discuss matters with you to ensure that these problems do not occur again in the future. Please contact us within 28 days of the date of this letter in order that we might arrange a mutually convenient time to meet and discuss the situation.

Yours sincerely,

Tenants of Anderson House

Figure 2 Preliminary notice

Tenants 1, 2, 3, 4, 5
Anderson House
London
AB12 3CD

Ms Broome
Landlord Road
London
EF45 6GH

20 April 2008

Dear Ms Broome,

We last contacted you on 20 March 2008 and received no reply. For your convenience, a copy of that letter is enclosed.

This is a preliminary notice under section 22 of the Landlord and Tenant Act 1987. Please address all correspondence to 'Tenants 1, 2, 3, 4, 5, Anderson House, London, AB12 3CD.

We intend to make an application for an order that a manager be appointed for Anderson House.

You are currently exercising the management functions. It is our view you have failed to comply with clause 2(a) of our leases. By this clause you are required to consult us before carrying out any internal improvements or repairs. The common areas of our property have recently been repainted without you having consulted us. A copy of the lease is attached to this letter.

In addition, you have failed to return our numerous phone calls and letters relating to our concerns about your management of Anderson House.

We would hope that these matters can be resolved without the need for litigation. To assist in achieving this, we ask that you contact us within 28 days of the date of this letter.

If there is a mortgage secured on Anderson House, you must provide the mortgagee with a copy of this notice.

Yours sincerely,

Tenants of Anderson House

Service charge dispute

Background

14.29   Illingworth Housing Association (HA) has granted a long lease of 1 Blackacre Road to Ms Gill. Service Charges are collected each year without any difficulties and are generally in the region of £2,500–£3,000 a year.

14.30   In 2004, Ms Gill receives a service charge demand for £10,000. Three items listed on the breakdown of costs provided by Illingworth HA concern her. She has been charged £2,000 for new plants in her garden, £3,000 for cleaning services throughout the year and £1,500 for a new fence to be erected.

14.31   She feels that these charges are excessive and complains to Illingworth HA. In reply, Illingworth HA point out that, under the lease, all service charge demands are payable within 28 days. Unless the sums are paid, the HA will bring a case in the county court to recover the sums owed and may even attempt to forfeit her lease. See figure 3.

14.32   Ms Gill takes legal advice and discovers that, in her case, the LVT has a power to determine whether or not these service charges are payable by her to Illingworth HA. She writes to Illingworth HA stating that she is willing to discuss payment proposals with them, but, if the dispute cannot be resolved amicably, she will issue proceedings in the LVT.

14.33   Illingworth HA reply that, in their view, the work billed for has all been done and was all subject to competitive tender. She should therefore pay the sums demanded.

14.34   Ms Gill applies to the LVT for a determination of the payability of her 2004 service charge bill. She is aware that her lease allows Illingworth HA to recover its legal costs from her, and so asks the LVT for an order that this not be allowed to happen, as well as a determination of her service charge dispute.

14.35   Ms Gill is in receipt of jobseeker's allowance and so has her application fee waived.

14.36   The LVT contacts Illingworth HA to inform them of the application and lists a PTR.

14.37   The PTR gives Ms Gill and Illingworth HA dates by which they must serve any evidence, including any witness statements. Ms Gill, as she was in receipt of jobseeker's allowance, was also exempt from any hearing fee.

Evidence

14.38 Ms Gill submitted a copy of her lease, along with a witness statement setting out her case.

14.39 Illingworth HA submitted evidence of their tendering process, showing that the companies that provided the cleaning services and the new fence had been chosen after a competitive and open tendering process.

The hearing

14.40 Ms Gill has submitted her witness statement as requested. Her case is:

(a) £2,000 for new plants is not payable because nowhere in her lease is Illingworth HA given responsibility for tending the gardens. This has always been a tenant's own duty.

(b) £3,000 for cleaning services is excessively expensive. She could get cleaners who would do the job for £1,000.

(c) The fence only cost £1,500 because it had to be replaced. In fact it had been deteriorating for years and if it had been repaired when it first began to show signs of wear, it would have been cheaper.

14.41 Illingworth HA have submitted their witness statement. Their case is:

(a) The lease gives them a power to 'improve the general amenity of the property and recover any charges associated in so doing from the tenant'.

(b) £3,000 was a fair rate for commercial cleaners.

(c) The housing association had a policy of replacing all fences every seven years. There was no evidence that the fence should have been repaired earlier. £1,500 was a fair price for a new fence.

14.42 The LVT asked for an inspection of Ms Gill's property on the morning of the hearing. This request was accepted by Ms Gill. The LVT was particularly interested in comparing Ms Gill's fence to those of her neighbours who had not had their fences replaced.

14.43 The hearing resumed in the afternoon. The LVT decided to deal with each of the three issues in turn.

14.44 Ms Gill explained that tenants had always had responsibility for their own gardens. Illingworth HA accepted that this had been the past practice, but pointed to the clause in the lease.

14.45   When asked questions by the LVT and Illingworth HA, Ms Gill explained that she had no concerns about the quality of the cleaning but had been told by a friend who did some part-time cleaning, that £1,000 would be a fair figure. Illingworth HA relied on their tendering process, but, when questioned by Ms Gill, accepted that there had been some lower tenders.

14.46   On the fence, Ms Gill repeated her allegation that, had the fence been replaced earlier, it would have been cheaper. She accepted that she had no evidence to support this. Illingworth HA again relied on their tendering process and denied that the fence could have been replaced for less if it had been done earlier.

14.47   The LVT indicated that it would give its decision in writing later. However, it wanted to hear submissions on whether or not to allow Illingworth HA to recover its costs from Ms Gill.

14.48   Illingworth HA submitted that they had been put to expense attending and that they should be able to recover this from Ms Gill.

14.49   Ms Gill pointed to her early letters, whereby she had offered to negotiate the situation without the need for any LVT hearing. Had this been taken up, she said, no costs would have needed to be incurred.

Decision

14.50   The LVT sent a written decision to Ms Gill and Illingworth HA shortly afterwards. When dealing with the service charge application, the LVT reminded itself that it had to determine whether or not the amounts claimed were payable.

(a) On the £2,000 for new plants, the LVT found that the lease did not allow Illingworth HA to recover these costs. The clause relied on by Illingworth HA did not expressly refer to the gardens. Clauses of this nature had to be read restrictively. As such, none of the £2,000 was payable.

(b) On the £3,000 for cleaning, the LVT noted that Ms Gill had accepted that there was no concern over the quality of the work. Illingworth HA was entitled to use commercial cleaners. It did not have to rely on what independent people might charge for cleaning. In any event, Ms Gill had not provided any documentary evidence to support her figure of £1,000. However, using its own local knowledge, the LVT did feel that £3,000 was slightly expensive and substituted a figure of £2,500.

(c) On the £1,500 for the new fence, while the LVT had some sympathy for the argument that it might have been cheaper had the work been done earlier, there was no evidence at all to support this. £1,500 seemed to be a fair figure based on the evidence available to the LVT.

Accordingly, the LVT found a total of £4,000 to be payable.

14.51   The LVT decided to grant Ms Gill protection against having to pay Illingworth HA's costs. It was impressed by her early offer to discuss and negotiate the matter and the fact that Illingworth HA had declined to even explore this opportunity should be held against them.

Figure 3 Letter before action

Ms Gill
1 Blackacre Road
Manchester
IJ78 9JL

Illingworth Housing Association
College Street
Manchester
MN10 9PQ

20 March 2008

Dear Sir or Madam,

Re: Service charge demand – your ref: 00897436

I am a long leaseholder of 1 Blackacre Road. I have recently received a demand for service charges from you in respect of my property. The total bill is for £10,000. I have identified three items on the bill that I am unclear about. For your ease of reference, these are:

1) £2,000 for new plants in my garden;
2) £3,000 for cleaning services;
3) £1,500 for a new fence.

I believe the sums demanded to be excessive. I would appreciate your comments as to how each sum has been calculated. In particular, I would ask for your comments on the following:

1) Tenants have, during the whole of my time as a tenant, been responsible for their own gardens. Why have Illingworth HA now decided (a) to do work in the gardens and (b) to charge for this work?
2) £3,000 is excessively expensive. I have been told that £1,000 is a fair price for cleaning charges and I do not see why I should pay more than this.
3) Had the fence been repaired when problems first became apparent, it would not have cost £1,500 as this is the cost of a new fence.

I look forward to hearing from you at your earliest convenience and, in any event, within 28 days of the date of this letter.

Yours sincerely

Ms S Gill

APPENDICES

A   Legislation and Directions   227

B   Residential Property Tribunal Service application forms   289

C   RPTS guidance on tenants' associations   321

D   Useful addresses   327

Legislation and Directions

Landlord and Tenant Act 1985 (extracts)   228

Landlord and Tenant Act 1987 (extracts)   242

Commonhold and Leasehold Reform Act 2002 (extracts)   252

Leasehold Valuation Tribunals (Procedure) (England) Regulations 2003   270

The Social Landlords Discretionary Reduction Of Service Charges (England) Directions 1997   284

The Social Landlords Mandatory Reduction Of Service Charges (England) Directions 1997   286

LANDLORD AND TENANT ACT 1985 (EXTRACTS)

Meaning of 'service charge' and 'relevant costs'

18 (1) In the following provisions of this Act 'service charge' means an amount payable by a tenant of a dwelling as part of or in addition to the rent –

    (a) which is payable, directly or indirectly, for services, repairs, maintenance, improvements or insurance or the landlord's costs of management, and

    (b) the whole or part of which varies or may vary according to the relevant costs.

(2) The relevant costs are the costs or estimated costs incurred or to be incurred by or on behalf of the landlord, or a superior landlord, in connection with the matters for which the service charge is payable.

(3) For this purpose –

    (a) 'costs' includes overheads, and

    (b) costs are relevant costs in relation to a service charge whether they are incurred, or to be incurred, in the period for which the service charge is payable or in an earlier or later period.

Limitation of service charges: reasonableness

19 (1) Relevant costs shall be taken into account in determining the amount of a service charge payable for a period –

    (a) only to the extent that they are reasonably incurred, and

    (b) where they are incurred on the provision of services or the carrying out of works, only if the services or works are of a reasonable standard;

    and the amount payable shall be limited accordingly.

(2) Where a service charge is payable before the relevant costs are incurred, no greater amount than is reasonable is so payable, and after the relevant costs have been incurred any necessary adjustment shall be made by repayment, reduction or subsequent charges or otherwise.

(2A) . . .

(2B) . . .

(2C) . . .

(3) . . .

(4) . . .

(5) If a person takes any proceedings in the High Court in pursuance of any of the provisions of this Act relating to service charges and he could have taken those proceedings in the county court, he shall not be entitled to recover any costs.

Limitation of service charges: consultation requirements

20 (1) Where this section applies to any qualifying works or qualifying long term agreement, the relevant contributions of tenants are limited in accordance with subsection (6) or (7) (or both) unless the consulation requirements have been either –

    (a) complied with in relation to the works or agreement, or

    (b) dispensed with in relation to the works or agreement by (or on appeal from) a Leasehold Valuation Tribunal.

(2) In this section 'relevant contribution', in relation to a tenant and any works or agreement, is the amount which he may be required under the terms of

his lease to contribute (by the payment of service charges) to relevant costs incurred on carrying out the works or under the agreement.

(3) This section applies to qualifying works if relevant costs incurred on carrying out the works exceed an appropriate amount.

(4) The Secretary of State may by regulations provide that this section applies to a qualifying long term agreement –

  (a) if relevant costs incurred under the agreement exceed an appropriate amount, or

  (b) if relevant costs incurred under the agreement during a period prescribed by the regulations exceed an appropriate amount.

(5) An appropriate amount is an amount set by regulations made by the Secretary of State; and the regulations may make provision for either or both of the following to be an appropriate amount –

  (a) an amount prescribed by, or determined in accordance with, the regulations, and

  (b) an amount which results in the relevant contribution of any one or more tenants being an amount prescribed by, or determined in accordance with, the regulations.

(6) Where an appropriate amount is set by virtue of paragraph (a) of subsection (5), the amount of the relevant costs incurred on carrying out the works or under the agreement which may be taken into account in determining the relevant contributions of tenants is limited to the appropriate amount.

(7) Where an appropriate amount is set by virtue of paragraph (b) of that subsection, the amount of the relevant contribution of the tenant, or each of the tenants, whose relevant contribution would otherwise exceed the amount prescribed by, or determined in accordance with, the regulations is limited to the amount so prescribed or determined.

Consultation requirements: supplementary

20ZA(1) Where an application is made to a leasehold valuation tribunal for a determination to dispense with all or any of the consultation requirements in relation to any qualifying works or qualifying long term agreement, the tribunal may make the determination if satisfied that it is reasonable to dispense with the requirements.

(2) In section 20 and this section –

  'qualifying works' means works on a building or any other premises, and 'qualifying long term agreement' means (subject to subsection (3)) an agreement entered into, by or on behalf of the landlord or a superior landlord, for a term of more than twelve months.

(3) The Secretary of State may by regulations provide that an agreement is not a qualifying long term agreement –

  (a) if it is an agreement of a description prescribed by the regulations, or

  (b) in any circumstances so prescribed.

(4) In section 20 and this section 'the consultation requirements' means requirements prescribed by regulations made by the Secretary of State.

(5) Regulations under subsection (4) may in particular include provision requiring the landlord –

  (a) to provide details of proposed works or agreements to tenants or the recognised tenants' association representing them,

(b) to obtain estimates for proposed works or agreements,
(c) to invite tenants or the recognised tenants' association to propose the names of persons from whom the landlord should try to obtain other estimates,
(d) to have regard to observations made by tenants or the recognised tenants' association in relation to proposed works or agreements and estimates, and
(e) to give reasons in prescribed circumstances for carrying out works or entering into agreements.

(6) Regulations under section 20 or this section –
(a) may make provision generally or only in relation to specific cases, and
(b) may make different provision for different purposes.

(7) Regulations under section 20 or this section shall be made by statutory instrument which shall be subject to annulment in pursuance of a resolution of either House of Parliament.

Limitation of service charges: time limit on making demands

20B(1) If any of the relevant costs taken into account in determining the amount of any service charge were incurred more than 18 months before a demand for payment of the service charge is served on the tenant, then (subject to subsection (2)), the tenant shall not be liable to pay so much of the service charge as reflects the costs so incurred.

(2) Subsection (1) shall not apply if, within the period of 18 months beginning with the date when the relevant costs in question were incurred, the tenant was notified in writing that those costs had been incurred and that he would subsequently be required under the terms of his lease to contribute to them by the payment of a service charge.

Limitation of service charges: costs of proceedings

20C(1) A tenant may make an application for an order that all or any of the costs incurred, or to be incurred, by the landlord in connection with proceedings before a court, residential property tribunal or leasehold valuation tribunal, or the Lands Tribunal, or in connection with arbitration proceedings, are not to be regarded as relevant costs to be taken into account in determining the amount of any service charge payable by the tenant or any other person or persons specified in the application.

(2) The application shall be made –
(a) in the case of court proceedings, to the court before which the proceedings are taking place or, if the application is made after the proceedings are concluded, to a county court;
(aa) in the case of proceedings before a residential property tribunal, to a leasehold valuation tribunal;
(b) in the case of proceedings before a leasehold valuation tribunal, to the tribunal before which the proceedings are taking place or, if the application is made after the proceedings are concluded, to any leasehold valuation tribunal;
(c) in the case of proceedings before the Lands Tribunal, to the tribunal;
(d) in the case of arbitration proceedings, to the arbitral tribunal or, if the application is made after the proceedings are concluded, to a county court.

(3) The court or tribunal to which the application is made may make such order on the application as it considers just and equitable in the circumstances.

Request for summary of relevant costs (OLD)

21 (1) A tenant may require the landlord in writing to supply him with a written summary of the costs incurred –

(a) if the relevant accounts are made up for periods of twelve months, in the last such period ending not later than the date of the request, or

(b) if the accounts are not so made up, in the period of twelve months ending with the date of the request,

and which are relevant costs in relation to the service charges payable or demanded as payable in that or any other period.

(2) If the tenant is represented by a recognised tenants' association and he consents, the request may be made by the secretary of the association instead of by the tenant and may then be for the supply of the summary to the secretary.

(3) A request is duly served on the landlord if it is served on –

(a) an agent of the landlord named as such in the rent book or similar document, or

(b) the person who receives the rent on behalf of the landlord;

and a person on whom a request is so served shall forward it as soon as may be to the landlord.

(4) The landlord shall comply with the request within one month of the request or within six months of the end of the period referred to in subsection (1)(a) or (b) whichever is the later.

(5) The summary shall state whether any of the costs relate to works in respect of which a grant has been or is to be paid under section 523 of the Housing Act 1985 (assistance for provision of separate service pipe for water supply) or any provision of Part I of the Housing Grants, Construction and Regeneration Act 1996 (grants, etc for renewal of private sector housing) or any corresponding earlier enactment and set out the costs in a way showing how they have been or will be reflected in demands for service charges and, in addition, shall summarise each of the following items, namely –

(a) any of the costs in respect of which no demand for payment was received by the landlord within the period referred to in subsection (1)(a) or (b),

(b) any of the costs in respect of which –

(i) a demand for payment was so received, but

(ii) no payment was made by the landlord within that period, and

(c) any of the costs in respect of which –

(i) a demand for payment was so received, and

(ii) payment was made by the landlord within that period,

and specify the aggregate of any amounts received by the landlord down to the end of that period on account of service charges in respect of relevant dwellings and still standing to the credit of the tenants of those dwellings at the end of that period.

(5A) In subsection (5) 'relevant dwelling' means a dwelling whose tenant is either –

(a) the person by or with the consent of whom the request was made, or

(b) a person whose obligations under the terms of his lease as regards contributing to relevant costs relate to the same costs as the corresponding obligations of the person mentioned in paragraph (a) above relate to.

(5B) The summary shall state whether any of the costs relate to works which are included in the external works specified in a group repair scheme, within the meaning of Chapter II of Part I of the Housing Grants, Construction and Regeneration Act 1996 or any corresponding earlier enactment, in which the landlord participated or is participating as an assisted participant.

(6) If the service charges in relation to which the costs are relevant costs as mentioned in sub-s (1) are payable by the tenants of more than four dwellings, the summary shall be certified by a qualified accountant as –

(a) in his opinion a fair summary complying with the requirements of subsection (5), and

(b) being sufficiently supported by accounts, receipts and other documents which have been produced to him.

Written Statement of Account (NEW)

21 (1) The landlord must supply to each tenant by whom service charges are payable, in relation to each accounting period, a written statement of account dealing with –

(a) service charges of the tenant and the tenants of dwellings associated with his dwelling,

(b) relevant costs relating to those service charges,

(c) the aggregate amount standing to the credit of the tenant and the tenants of those dwellings –

(i) at the beginning of the accounting period, and

(ii) at the end of the accounting period, and

(d) related matters.

(2) The statement of account in relation to an accounting period must be supplied to each such tenant not later than six months after the end of the accounting period.

(3) Where the landlord supplies a statement of account to a tenant he must also supply to him –

(a) a certificate of a qualified accountant that, in the accountant's opinion, the statement of account deals fairly with the matters with which it is required to deal and is sufficiently supported by accounts, receipts and other documents which have been produced to him, and

(b) a summary of the rights and obligations of tenants of dwellings in relation to service charges.

(4) The Secretary of State may make regulations prescribing requirements as to the form and content of –

(a) statements of account,

(b) accountants' certificates, and

(c) summaries of rights and obligations,

required to be supplied under this section.

(5) The Secretary of State may make regulations prescribing exceptions from the requirement to supply an accountant's certificate.

(6) If the landlord has been notified by a tenant of an address in England and Wales at which he wishes to have supplied to him documents required to be so supplied under this section, the landlord must supply them to him at that address.

(7) And the landlord is to be taken to have been so notified if notification has been given to –
  (a) an agent of the landlord named as such in the rent book or similar document, or
  (b) the person who receives the rent on behalf of the landlord;
  and where notification is given to such an agent or person he must forward it as soon as may be to the landlord.

(8) For the purposes of this section a dwelling is associated with another dwelling if the obligations of the tenants of the dwellings under the terms of their leases as regards contributing to relevant costs relate to the same costs.

(9) In this section 'accounting period' means such period –
  (a) beginning with the relevant date, and
  (b) ending with such date, not later than twelve months after the relevant date,
  as the landlord determines.

(10) In the case of the first accounting period in relation to any dwellings, the relevant date is the later of –
  (a) the date on which service charges are first payable under a lease of any of them, and
  (b) the date on which section 152 of the Commonhold and Leasehold Reform Act 2002 comes into force,
  and, in the case of subsequent accounting periods, it is the date immediately following the end of the previous accounting period.

(11) Regulations under subsection (4) may make different provision for different purposes.

(12) Regulations under this section shall be made by statutory instrument which shall be subject to annulment in pursuance of a resolution of either House of Parliament.

Withholding of service charges

21A(1) A tenant may withhold payment of a service charge if –
  (a) the landlord has not supplied a document to him by the time by which he is required to supply it under section 21, or
  (b) the form or content of a document which the landlord has supplied to him under that section (at any time) does not conform exactly or substantially with the requirements prescribed by regulations under subsection (4) of that section.

(2) The maximum amount which the tenant may withhold is an amount equal to the aggregate of –
  (a) the service charges paid by him in the accounting period to which the document concerned would or does relate, and
  (b) so much of the aggregate amount required to be dealt with in the statement of account for that accounting period by section 21(1)(c)(i)
  as stood to his credit.

(3) An amount may not be withheld under this section –
  (a) in a case within paragraph (a) of subsection (1), after the document concerned has been supplied to the tenant by the landlord, or
  (b) in a case within paragraph (b) of that subsection, after a document conforming exactly or substantially with the requirements prescribed by

regulations under section 21(4) has been supplied to the tenant by the landlord by way of replacement of the one previously supplied.

(4) If, on an application made by the landlord to a leasehold valuation tribunal, the tribunal determines that the landlord has a reasonable excuse for a failure giving rise to the right of a tenant to withhold an amount under this section, the tenant may not withhold the amount after the determination is made.

(5) Where a tenant withholds a service charge under this section, any provisions of the tenancy relating to non-payment or late payment of service charges do not have effect in relation to the period for which he so withholds it.

Notice to accompany demands for service charges

21B(1) A demand for the payment of a service charge must be accompanied by a summary of the rights and obligations of tenants of dwellings in relation to service charges.

(2) The Secretary of State may make regulations prescribing requirements as to the form and content of such summaries of rights and obligations.

(3) A tenant may withhold payment of a service charge which has been demanded from him if subsection (1) is not complied with in relation to the demand.

(4) Where a tenant withholds a service charge under this section, any provisions of the lease relating to non-payment or late payment of service charges do not have effect in relation to the period for which he so withholds it.

(5) Regulations under subsection (2) may make different provision for different purposes.

(6) Regulations under subsection (2) shall be made by statutory instrument which shall be subject to annulment in pursuance of a resolution of either House of Parliament.

Request to inspect supporting accounts (OLD)

22 (1) This section applies where a tenant, or the secretary of a recognised tenants' association, has obtained such a summary as is referred to in section 21(1) (summary of relevant costs), whether in pursuance of that section or otherwise.

(2) The tenant, or the secretary with the consent of the tenant, may within six months of obtaining the summary require the landlord in writing to afford him reasonable facilities –

 (a) for inspecting the accounts, receipts and other documents supporting the summary, and

 (b) for taking copies or extracts from them.

(3) A request under this section is duly served on the landlord if it is served on –

 (a) an agent of the landlord named as such in the rent book or similar document, or

 (b) the person who receives the rent on behalf of the landlord;

 and a person on whom a request is so served shall forward it as soon as may be to the landlord.

(4) The landlord shall make such facilities available to the tenant or secretary for a period of two months beginning not later than one month after the request is made.

(5) The landlord shall –
  (a) where such facilities are for the inspection of any documents, make them so available free of charge;
  (b) where such facilities are for the taking of copies or extracts, be entitled to make them so available on payment of such reasonable charge as he may determine.
(6) The requirement imposed on the landlord by subsection (5)(a)   to   make any facilities available to a person free of charge shall not be construed as precluding the landlord from treating as part of his costs of management any costs incurred by him in connection with making those facilities so available.

Inspection etc of documents (NEW)

22 (1) A tenant may by notice in writing require the landlord –
  (a) to afford him reasonable facilities for inspecting accounts, receipts or other documents relevant to the matters which must be dealt with in a statement of account required to be supplied to him under section 21 and for taking copies of or extracts from them, or
  (b) to take copies of or extracts from any such accounts, receipts or other documents and either send them to him or afford him reasonable facilities for collecting them (as he specifies).
(2) If the tenant is represented by a recognised tenants' association and he consents, the notice may be served by the secretary of the association instead of by the tenant (and in that case any requirement imposed by it is to afford reasonable facilities, or to send copies or extracts, to the secretary).
(3) A notice under this section may not be served after the end of the period of six months beginning with the date by which the tenant is required to be supplied with the statement of account under section 21.
(4) But if –
  (a) the statement of account is not supplied to the tenant on or before that date, or
  (b) the statement of account so supplied does not conform exactly or substantially with the requirements prescribed by regulations under section 21(4),
the six month period mentioned in subsection (3) does not begin until any later date on which the statement of account (conforming exactly or substantially with those requirements) is supplied to him.
(5) A notice under this section is duly served on the landlord if it is served on –
  (a) an agent of the landlord named as such in the rent book or similar document, or
  (b) the person who receives the rent on behalf of the landlord;
and a person on whom such a notice is so served must forward it as soon as may be to the landlord.
(6) The landlord must comply with a requirement imposed by a notice under this section within the period of twenty-one days beginning with the day on which he receives the notice.
(7) To the extent that a notice under this section requires the landlord to afford facilities for inspecting documents –
  (a) he must do so free of charge, but

(b) he may treat as part of his costs of management any costs incurred by him in doing so.

(8) The landlord may make a reasonable charge for doing anything else in compliance with a requirement imposed by a notice under this section.

Request relating to information held by superior landlord (OLD)

23 (1) If a request under section 21 (request for summary of relevant costs) relates in whole or in part to relevant costs incurred by or on behalf of a superior landlord, and the landlord to whom the request is made is not in possession of the relevant information –

(a) he shall in turn make a written request for the relevant information to the person who is his landlord (and so on, if that person is not himself the superior landlord),

(b) the superior landlord shall comply with that request within a reasonable time, and

(c) the immediate landlord shall then comply with the tenant's or secretary's request, or that part of it which relates to the relevant costs incurred by or on behalf of the superior landlord, within the time allowed by section 21 or such further time, if any, as is reasonable in the circumstances.

(2) If a request under section 22 (request for facilities to inspect supporting accounts, etc) relates to a summary of costs incurred by or on behalf of a superior landlord –

(a) the landlord to whom the request is made shall forthwith inform the tenant or secretary of that fact and of the name and address of the superior landlord, and

(b) section 22 shall then apply to the superior landlord as it applies to the immediate landlord.

Information held by superior landlord

23 (1) If a statement of account which the landlord is required to supply under section 21 relates to matters concerning a superior landlord and the landlord is not in possession of the relevant information –

(a) he may by notice in writing require the person who is his landlord to give him the relevant information (and so on, if that person is not himself the superior landlord), and

(b) the superior landlord must comply with the requirement within a reasonable time.

(2) If a notice under section 22 imposes a requirement in relation to documents held by a superior landlord –

(a) the landlord shall immediately inform the tenant or secretary of that fact and of the name and address of the superior landlord, and

(b) section 22 then applies in relation to the superior landlord (as in relation to the landlord).

Liability to pay service charges: jurisdiction

27A(1) An application may be made to a leasehold valuation tribunal for a determination whether a service charge is payable and, if it is, as to –

(a) the person by whom it is payable,

(b) the person to whom it is payable,

    (c) the amount which is payable,

    (d) the date at or by which it is payable, and

    (e) the manner in which it is payable.

(2) Subsection (1) applies whether or not any payment has been made.

(3) An application may also be made to a leasehold valuation tribunal for a determination whether, if costs were incurred for services, repairs, maintenance, improvements, insurance or management of any specified description, a service charge would be payable for the costs and, if it would, as to –

    (a) the person by whom it would be payable,

    (b) the person to whom it would be payable,

    (c) the amount which would be payable,

    (d) the date at or by which it would be payable, and

    (e) the manner in which it would be payable.

(4) No application under subsection (1) or (3) may be made in respect of a matter which –

    (a) has been agreed or admitted by the tenant,

    (b) has been, or is to be, referred to arbitration pursuant to a post-dispute arbitration agreement to which the tenant is a party,

    (c) has been the subject of determination by a court, or

    (d) has been the subject of determination by an arbitral tribunal pursuant to a post-dispute arbitration agreement.

(5) But the tenant is not to be taken to have agreed or admitted any matter by reason only of having made any payment.

(6) An agreement by the tenant of a dwelling (other than a post-dispute arbitration agreement) is void in so far as it purports to provide for a determination –

    (a) in a particular manner, or

    (b) on particular evidence,

of any question which may be the subject of an application under subsection (1) or (3).

(7) The jurisdiction conferred on a leasehold valuation tribunal in respect of any matter by virtue of this section is in addition to any jurisdiction of a court in respect of the matter.

SCHEDULE: RIGHTS OF TENANTS WITH RESPECT TO INSURANCE

Construction

1   In this Schedule –

'landlord', in relation to a tenant by whom a service charge is payable which includes an amount payable directly or indirectly for insurance, includes any person who has a right to enforce payment of that service charge;

'relevant policy', in relation to a dwelling, means any policy of insurance under which the dwelling is insured (being, in the case of a flat, a policy covering the building containing it); and

'tenant' includes a statutory tenant.

Summary of insurance cover

2 (1) Where a service charge is payable by the tenant of a dwelling which consists of or includes an amount payable directly or indirectly for insurance, the tenant may by notice in writing require the landlord to supply by him with a written summary of the insurance for the time being effected in relation to the dwelling.

(2) If the tenant is represented by a recognised tenants' association and he consents, the notice may be served by the secretary of the association instead of by the tenant and may then be for the supply of the summary to the secretary.

(3) A notice under this paragraph is duly served on the landlord if it is served on –

    (a) an agent of the landlord named as such in the rent book or similar document, or

    (b) the person who receives the rent on behalf of the landlord;

and a person on whom such a notice is so served shall forward it as soon as may be to the landlord.

(4) The landlord shall, within the period of twenty-one days beginning with the day on which he receives the notice, comply with it by supplying to the tenant or the secretary of the recognised tenants' association (as the case may require) such a summary as is mentioned in sub-paragraph (1), which shall include –

    (a) the insured amount or amounts under any relevant policy, and

    (b) the name of the insurer under any such policy, and

    (c) the risks in respect of which the dwelling or (as the case may be) the building containing it is insured under any such policy.

(5) In sub-paragraph (4)(a) 'the insured amount or amounts', in relation to a relevant policy, means –

    (a) in the case of a dwelling other than a flat, the amount for which the dwelling is insured under the policy; and

    (b) in the case of a flat, the amount for which the building containing it is insured under the policy and, if specified in the policy, the amount for which the flat is insured under it.

(6) The landlord shall be taken to have complied with the notice if, within the period mentioned in sub-paragraph (4), he instead supplies to the tenant or the secretary (as the case may require) a copy of every relevant policy.

(7) In a case where two or more buildings are insured under any relevant policy, the summary or copy supplied under sub-paragraph (4) or (6) so far as relating to that policy need only be of such parts of the policy as relate –

    (a) to the dwelling, and

    (b) if the dwelling is a flat, to the building containing it.

Inspection of insurance policy etc

3 (1) Where a service charge is payable by the tenant of a dwelling which consists of or includes an amount payable directly or indirectly for insurance, the tenant may by notice in writing require the landlord –

    (a) to afford him reasonable facilities for inspecting any relevant policy or associated documents and for taking copies of or extracts from them, or

    (b) to take copies of or extracts from any such policy or documents and either send them to him or afford him reasonable facilities for collecting them (as he specifies).

(2) If the tenant is represented by a recognised tenants' association and he consents, the notice may be served by the secretary of the association instead of by the tenant (and in that case any requirement imposed by it is to afford reasonable facilities, or to send copies or extracts, to the secretary).

(3) A notice under this paragraph is duly served on the landlord if it is served on –

(a) an agent of the landlord named as such in the rent book or similar document, or

(b) the person who receives the rent on behalf of the landlord;

and a person on whom such a notice is so served shall forward it as soon as may be to the landlord.

(4) The landlord shall comply with a requirement imposed by a notice under this paragraph within the period of twenty-one days beginning with the day on which he receives the notice.

(5) To the extent that a notice under this paragraph requires the landlord to afford facilities for inspecting documents –

(a) he shall do so free of charge, but

(b) he may treat as part of his costs of management any costs incurred by him in doing so.

(6) The landlord may make a reasonable charge for doing anything else in compliance with a requirement imposed by a notice under this paragraph.

(7) In this paragraph –

'relevant policy' includes a policy of insurance under which the dwelling was insured for the period of insurance immediately preceding that current when the notice is served (being, in the case of a flat, a policy covering the building containing it), and

'associated documents' means accounts, receipts or other documents which provide evidence of payment of any premiums due under a relevant policy in respect of the period of insurance which is current when the notice is served or the period of insurance immediately preceding that period.

Insurance effected by superior landlord

4 (1) If a notice is served under paragraph 2 in a case where a superior landlord has effected, in whole or in part, the insurance of the dwelling in question and the landlord on whom the notice is served is not in possession of the relevant information –

(a) he shall in turn by notice in writing require the person who is his landlord to give him the relevant information (and so on, if that person is not himself the superior landlord),

(b) the superior landlord shall comply with the notice within a reasonable time, and

(c) the immediate landlord shall then comply with the tenant's or secretary's notice in the manner provided by sub-paragraphs (4) to (7) of paragraph 2 within the time allowed by that paragraph or such further time, if any, as is reasonable in the circumstances.

(2) If, in a case where a superior landlord has effected, in whole or in part, the insurance of the dwelling in question, a notice under paragraph 3 imposes a requirement relating to any policy of insurance effected by the superior landlord –

(a) the landlord on whom the notice is served shall forthwith inform the tenant or secretary of that fact and of the name and address of the superior landlord, and

(b) that paragraph shall then apply to the superior landlord in relation to that policy as it applies to the immediate landlord.

Effect of change of landlord

4A(1) This paragraph applies where, at a time when a duty imposed on the landlord or a superior landlord by virtue of any of paragraphs 2 to 4 remains to be discharged by him, he disposes of the whole or part of his interest as landlord or superior landlord).

(2) If the landlord or superior landlord is, despite the disposal, still in a position to discharge the duty to any extent, he remains responsible for discharging it to that extent.

(3) If the other person is in a position to discharge the duty to any extent, he is responsible for discharging it to that extent.

(4) Where the other person is responsible for discharging the duty to any extent (whether or not the landlord or superior landlord is also responsible for discharging it to that or any other extent) –

(a) references to the landlord or superior landlord in paragraphs 2 to 4 are to, or include, the other person so far as is appropriate to reflect his responsibility for discharging the duty to that extent, but

(b) in connection with its discharge by that person, paragraphs 2(4) and 3(4) apply as if the reference to the day on which the landlord receives the notice were to the date of the disposal referred to in sub-paragraph (1).

Effect of assignment

5   The assignment of a tenancy does not affect any duty imposed by virtue of any of paragraphs 2 to 4A; but a person is not required to comply with more than a reasonable number of requirements imposed by any one person.

Offence of failure to comply

6 (1) It is a summary offence for a person to fail, without reasonable excuse, to perform a duty imposed on him by or by virtue of any of paragraphs 2 to 4A.

(2) A person committing such an offence is liable on conviction to a fine not exceeding level 4 on the standard scale.

Tenant's right to notify insurers of possible claim

7 (1) This paragraph applies to any dwelling in respect of which the tenant pays to the landlord a service charge consisting of or including an amount payable directly or indirectly for insurance.

(2) Where –

(a) it appears to the tenant of any such dwelling that damage has been caused –

(i) to the dwelling, or

(ii) if the dwelling is a flat, to the dwelling or to any other part of the building containing it,

in respect of which a claim could be made under the terms of a policy of insurance, and

(b) it is a term of that policy that the person insured under the policy should give notice of any claim under it to the insurer within a specified period,

the tenant may, within that specified period, serve on the insurer a notice in writing stating that it appears to him that damage has been caused as mentioned in paragraph (a) and describing briefly the nature of the damage.

(3) Where –

(a) any such notice is served on an insurer by a tenant in relation to any such damage, and

(b) the specified period referred to in sub-paragraph (2)(b) would expire earlier than the period of six months beginning with the date on which the notice is served, the policy in question shall have effect as regards any claim subsequently made in respect of that damage by the person insured under the policy as if for the specified period there were substituted that period of six months.

(4) Where the tenancy of a dwelling to which this paragraph applies is held by joint tenants, a single notice under this paragraph may be given by any one or more of those tenants.

(5) The Secretary of State may by regulations prescribe the form of notices under this paragraph and the particulars which such notices must contain.

(6) Any such regulations –
   (a) may make different provision with respect to different cases or descriptions of case, including different provision for different areas, and
   (b) shall be made by statutory instrument.

Right to challenge landlord's choice of insurers

8 (1) This paragraph applies where a tenancy of a dwelling requires the tenant to insure the dwelling with an insurer nominated or approved by the landlord.

(2) The tenant or landlord may apply to a county court or leasehold valuation tribunal for a determination whether –
   (a) the insurance which is available from the nominated or approved insurer for insuring the tenant's dwelling is unsatisfactory in any respect, or
   (b) the premiums payable in respect of any such insurance are excessive.

(3) No such application may be made in respect of a matter which –
   (a) has been agreed or admitted by the tenant,
   (b) under an arbitration agreement to which the tenant is a party is to be referred to arbitration, or
   (c) has been the subject of determination by a court or arbitral tribunal.

(4) On an application under this paragraph the court or tribunal may make –
   (a) an order requiring the landlord to nominate or approve such other insurer as is specified in the order, or
   (b) an order requiring him to nominate or approve another insurer who satisfies such requirements in relation to the insurance of the dwelling as are specified in the order.

(5) . . .

(6) An agreement by the tenant of a dwelling (other than an arbitration agreement) is void in so far as it purports to provide for a determination in a particular manner, or on particular evidence, of any question which may be the subject of an application under this paragraph.

Exception for tenants of certain public authorities

9 (1) Paragraphs 2 to 8 do not apply to tenant of –
   a local authority,
   a National Park authority, or
   a new town corporation, ...
   unless the tenancy is a long tenancy, in which case paragraphs 2 to 5 and 7 and 8 apply but paragraph 6 does not.

(2) Subsections (2) and (3) of section 26 shall apply for the purposes of sub-paragraph (1) as they apply for the purposes of subsection (1) of that section.

LANDLORD AND TENANT ACT 1987 (EXTRACTS)

Tenant's right to apply to tribunal for appointment of manager

21 (1) The tenant of a flat contained in any premises to which this Part applies may, subject to the following provisions of this Part, apply to a leasehold valuation tribunal for an order under section 24 appointing a manager to act in relation to those premises.

(2) Subject to subsection (3), this Part applies to premises consisting of the whole or part of a building if the building or part contains two or more flats.

(3) This Part does not apply to any such premises at a time when –

    (a) the interest of the landlord in the premises is held by an exempt landlord or a resident landlord, or

    (b) the premises are included within the functional land of any charity.

(3A) But this Part is not prevented from applying to any premises because the interest of the landlord in the premises is held by a resident landlord if at least one-half of the flats contained in the premises are held on long leases which are not tenancies to which Part 2 of the Landlord and Tenant Act 1954 applies.

(4) An application for an order under section 24 may be made –

    (a) jointly by tenants of two or more flats if they are each entitled to make such an application by virtue of this section, and

    (b) in respect of two or more premises to which this Part applies;

and, in relation to any such joint application as is mentioned in paragraph (a), references in this Part to a single tenant shall be construed accordingly.

(5) Where the tenancy of a flat contained in any such premises is held by joint tenants, an application for an order under section 24 in respect of those premises may be made by any one or more of those tenants.

(6) An application to the court for it to exercise in relation to any premises any jurisdiction to appoint a receiver or manager shall not be made by a tenant (in his capacity as such) in any circumstances in which an application could be made by him for an order under section 24 appointing a manager to act in relation to those premises.

(7) References in this Part to a tenant do not include references to a tenant under a tenancy to which Part II of the Landlord and Tenant Act 1954 applies.

Preliminary notice by tenant

22 (1) Before an application for an order under section 24 is made in respect of any premises to which this Part applies by a tenant of a flat contained in those premises, a notice under this section must (subject to subsection (3)) be served by the tenant on –

    (i) the landlord, and

    (ii) any person (other than the landlord) by whom obligations relating to the management of the premises or any part of them are owed to the tenant under his tenancy.

(2) A notice under this section must –

    (a) specify the tenant's name, the address of his flat and an address in England and Wales (which may be the address of his flat) at which any person on whom the notice is served may serve notices, including notices in proceedings, on him in connection with this Part;

(b) state that the tenant intends to make an application for an order under section 24 to be made by a leasehold valuation tribunal in respect of such premises to which this Part applies as are specified in the notice, but (if paragraph (d) is applicable) that he will not do so if the requirement specified in pursuance of that paragraph is complied with;

(c) specify the grounds on which the tribunal would be asked to make such an order and the matters that would be relied on by the tenant for the purpose of establishing those grounds;

(d) where those matters are capable of being remedied by any person on whom the notice is served, require him, within such reasonable period as is specified in the notice, to take steps for the purpose of remedying them as are so specified; and

(e) contain such information (if any) as the Secretary of State may by regulations prescribe.

(3) A leasehold valuation tribunal may (whether on the hearing of an application for an order under section 24 or not) by order dispense with the requirement to serve a notice under this section on a person in a case where it is satisfied that it would not be reasonably practicable to serve such a notice on the person, but the tribunal may, when doing so, direct that such other notices are served, or such other steps are taken, as it thinks fit.

(4) In a case where –

(a) a notice under this section has been served on the landlord, and

(b) his interest in the premises specified in pursuance of subsection (2)(b) is subject to a mortgage,

the landlord shall, as soon as is reasonably practicable after receiving the notice, serve on the mortgagee a copy of the notice.

Application to tribunal for appointment of manager

23 (1) No application for an order under section 24 shall be made to a leasehold valuation tribunal unless –

(a) in a case where a notice has been served under section 22, either –

(i) the period specified in pursuance of paragraph (d) of subsection (2) of that section has expired without the person required to take steps in pursuance of that paragraph having taken them, or

(ii) that paragraph was not applicable in the circumstances of the case; or

(b) in a case where the requirement to serve such a notice has been dispensed with by an order under subsection (3) of that section, either –

(i) any notices required to be served, and any other steps required to be taken, by virtue of the order have been served or (as the case may be) taken, or

(ii) no direction was given by the tribunal when making the order.

Appointment of manager by a leasehold valuation tribunal

24 (1) A leasehold valuation tribunal may, on an application for an order under this section, by order (whether interlocutory or final) appoint a manager to carry out in relation to any premises to which this Part applies –

(a) such functions in connection with the management of the premises, or

(b) such functions of a receiver,

or both, as the tribunal thinks fit.

(2) A leasehold valuation tribunal may only make an order under this section in the following circumstances, namely –

  (a) where the tribunal is satisfied –

      (i) that any relevant person either is in breach of any obligation owed by him to the tenant under his tenancy and relating to the management of the premises in question or any part of them or (in the case of an obligation dependent on notice) would be in breach of any such obligation but for the fact that it has not been reasonably practicable for the tenant to give him the appropriate notice, and

      (ii) ...

      (iii) that it is just and convenient to make the order in all the circumstances of the case;

  (ab) where the tribunal is satisfied –

      (i) that unreasonable service charges have been made, or are proposed or likely to be made, and

      (ii) that it is just and convenient to make the order in all the circumstances of the case;

  (aba) where the tribunal is satisfied –

      (i) that unreasonable variable administration charges have been made, or are proposed or likely to be made, and

      (ii) that it is just and convenient to make the order in all the circumstances of the case;

  (abb) where the tribunal is satisfied –

      (i) that there has been a failure to comply with a duty imposed by or by virtue of section 42 or 42A of this Act, and

      (ii) that it is just and convenient to make the order in all the circumstances of the case;

  (ac) where the tribunal is satisfied –

      (i) that any relevant person has failed to comply with any relevant provision of a code of practice approved by the Secretary of State under section 87 of the Leasehold Reform, Housing and Urban Development Act 1993 (codes of management practice), and

      (ii) that it is just and convenient to make the order in all the circumstances of the case;

        or

  (b) where the tribunal is satisfied that other circumstances exist which make it just and convenient for the order to be made.

(2ZA) In this section 'relevant person' means a person –

  (a) on whom a notice has been served under section 22, or

  (b) in the case of whom the requirement to serve a notice under that section has been dispensed with by an order under subsection (3) of that section.

(2A) For the purposes of subsection (2)(ab) a service charge shall be taken to be unreasonable –

  (a) if the amount is unreasonable having regard to the items for which it is payable,

  (b) if the items for which it is payable are of an unnecessarily high standard, or

(c) if the items for which it is payable are of an insufficient standard with the result that additional service charges are or may be incurred.

In that provision and this subsection 'service charge' means a service charge within the meaning of section 18(1) of the Landlord and Tenant Act 1985, other than one excluded from that section by section 27 of that Act (rent of dwelling registered and not entered as variable).

(2B) In subsection (2)(aba) 'variable administration charge' has the meaning given by paragraph 1 of Schedule 11 to the Commonhold and Leasehold Reform Act 2002.

(3) The premises in respect of which an order is made under this section may, if the tribunal thinks fit, be either more or less extensive than the premises specified in the application on which the order is made.

(4) An order under this section may make provision with respect to –
   (a) such matters relating to the exercise by the manager of his functions under the order, and
   (b) such incidental or ancillary matters,

as the tribunal thinks fit; and, on any subsequent application made for the purpose by the manager, the tribunal may give him directions with respect to any such matters.

(5) Without prejudice to the generality of subsection (4), an order under this section may provide –
   (a) for rights and liabilities arising under contracts to which the manager is not a party to become rights and liabilities of the manager;
   (b) for the manager to be entitled to prosecute claims in respect of causes of action (whether contractual or tortious) accruing before or after the date of his appointment;
   (c) for remuneration to be paid to the manager by any relevant person, or by the tenants of the premises in respect of which the order is made or by all or any of those persons;
   (d) for the manager's functions to be exercisable by him (subject to subsection (9)) either during a specified period or without limit of time.

(6) Any such order may be granted subject to such conditions as the tribunal thinks fit, and in particular its operation may be suspended on terms fixed by the tribunal.

(7) In a case where an application for an order under this section was preceded by the service of a notice under section 22, the tribunal may, if it thinks fit, make such an order notwithstanding –
   (a) that any period specified in the notice in pursuance of subsection (2)(d) of that section was not a reasonable period, or
   (b) that the notice failed in any other respect to comply with any requirement contained in subsection (2) of that section or in any regulations applying to the notice under section 54(3).

(8) The Land Charges Act 1972 and the Land Registration Act 2002 shall apply in relation to an order made under this section as they apply in relation to an order appointing a receiver or sequestrator of land.

(9) A leasehold valuation tribunal may, on the application of any person interested, vary or discharge (whether conditionally or unconditionally) an order made under this section; and if the order has been protected by an entry registered under the Land Charges Act 1972 or the Land Registration Act 2002,

the tribunal may by order direct that the entry shall be cancelled.

(9A) The tribunal shall not vary or discharge an order under subsection (9) on the application of any relevant person unless it is satisfied –

    (a) that the variation or discharge of the order will not result in a recurrence of the circumstances which led to the order being made, and

    (b) that it is just and convenient in all the circumstances of the case to vary or discharge the order.

(10) An order made under this section shall not be discharged by a leasehold valuation tribunal by reason only that, by virtue of section 21(3), the premises in respect of which the order was made have ceased to be premises to which this Part applies.

(11) References in this Part to the management of any premises include references to the repair, maintenance, improvement or insurance of those premises.

Application by party to lease for variation of lease

35 (1) Any party to a long lease of a flat may make an application to a leasehold valuation tribunal for an order varying the lease in such manner as is specified in the application.

(2) The grounds on which any such application may be made are that the lease fails to make satisfactory provision with respect to one or more of the following matters, namely –

    (a) the repair or maintenance of –

        (i)   the flat in question, or

        (ii) the building containing the flat, or

        (iii) any land or building which is let to the tenant under the lease or in respect of which rights are conferred on him under it;

    (b) the insurance of the building containing the flat or of any such land or building as is mentioned in paragraph (a)(iii);

    (c) the repair or maintenance of any installations (whether they are in the same building as the flat or not) which are reasonably necessary to ensure that occupiers of the flat enjoy a reasonable standard of accommodation;

    (d) the provision or maintenance of any services which are reasonably necessary to ensure that occupiers of the flat enjoy a reasonable standard of accommodation (whether they are services connected with any such installations or not, and whether they are services provided for the benefit of those occupiers or services provided for the benefit of the occupiers of a number of flats including that flat);

    (e) the recovery by one party to the lease from another party to it of expenditure incurred or to be incurred by him, or on his behalf, for the benefit of that other party or of a number of persons who include that other party;

    (f) the computation of a service charge payable under the lease;

    (g) such other matters as may be prescribed by regulations made by the Secretary of State.

(3) For the purposes of subsection (2)(c) and (d) the factors for determining, in relation to the occupiers of a flat, what is a reasonable standard of accommodation may include –

    (a) factors relating to the safety and security of the flat and its occupiers and of any common parts of the building containing the flat; and

    (b) other factors relating to the condition of any such common parts.

(3A) For the purposes of subsection (2)(e) the factors for determining, in relation to a service charge payable under a lease, whether the lease makes satisfactory provision include whether it makes provision for an amount to be payable (by way of interest or otherwise) in respect of a failure to pay the service charge by the due date.

(4) For the purposes of subsection (2)(f) a lease fails to make satisfactory provision with respect to the computation of a service charge payable under it if –

(a) it provides for any such charge to be a proportion of expenditure incurred, or to be incurred, by or on behalf of the landlord or a superior landlord; and

(b) other tenants of the landlord are also liable under their leases to pay by way of service charges proportions of any such expenditure; and

(c) the aggregate of the amounts that would, in any particular case, be payable by reference to the proportions referred to in paragraphs (a) and (b) would either exceed or be less than the whole of any such expenditure.

(5) Procedure regulations under Schedule 12 to the Commonhold and Leasehold Reform Act 2002 shall make provision –

(a) for requiring notice of any application under this Part to be served by the person making the application, and by any respondent to the application, on any person who the applicant, or (as the case may be) the respondent, knows or has reason to believe is likely to be affected by any variation specified in the application, and

(b) for enabling persons served with any such notice to be joined as parties to the proceedings.

(6) For the purposes of this Part a long lease shall not be regarded as a long lease of a flat if –

(a) the demised premises consist of or include three or more flats contained in the same building; or

(b) the lease constitutes a tenancy to which Part II of the Landlord and Tenant Act 1954 applies.

(8) In this section 'service charge' has the meaning given by section 18(1) of the 1985 Act.

Application by respondent for variation of other leases

36 (1) Where an application ('the original application') is made under section 35 by any party to a lease, any other party to the lease may make an application to the tribunal asking it, in the event of its deciding to make an order effecting any variation of the lease in pursuance of the original application, to make an order which effects a corresponding variation of each of such one or more other leases as are specified in the application.

(2) Any lease so specified –

(a) must be a long lease of a flat under which the landlord is the same person as the landlord under the lease specified in the original application; but

(b) need not be a lease of a flat which is in the same building as the flat let under that lease, nor a lease drafted in terms identical to those of that lease.

(3) The grounds on which an application may be made under this section are –

(a) that each of the leases specified in the application fails to make satisfactory provision with respect to the matter or matters specified in the original application; and

(b) that, if any variation is effected in pursuance of the original application, it would be in the interests of the person making the application under this section, or in the interests of the other persons who are parties to the leases specified in that application, to have all of the leases in question (that is to say, the ones specified in that application together with the one specified in the original application) varied to the same effect.

Application by majority of parties for variation of leases

37 (1) Subject to the following provisions of this section, an application may be made to a leasehold valuation tribunal in respect of two or more leases for an order varying each of those leases in such manner as is specified in the application.

(2) Those leases must be long leases of flats under which the landlord is the same person, but they need not be leases of flats which are in the same building, nor leases which are drafted in identical terms.

(3) The grounds on which an application may be made under this section are that the object to be achieved by the variation cannot be satisfactorily achieved unless all the leases are varied to the same effect.

(4) An application under this section in respect of any leases may be made by the landlord or any of the tenants under the leases.

(5) Any such application shall only be made if –

(a) in a case where the application is in respect of less than nine leases, all, or all but one, of the parties concerned consent to it; or

(b) in a case where the application is in respect of more than eight leases, it is not opposed for any reason by more than 10 per cent of the total number of the parties concerned and at least 75 per cent of that number consent to it.

(6) For the purposes of subsection (5) –

(a) in the case of each lease in respect of which the application is made, the tenant under the lease shall constitute one of the parties concerned (so that in determining the total number of the parties concerned a person who is the tenant under a number of such leases shall be regarded as constituting a corresponding number of the parties concerned); and

(b) the landlord shall also constitute one of the parties concerned.

Orders varying leases

38 (1) If, on an application under section 35, the grounds on which the application was made are established to the satisfaction of the tribunal, the tribunal may (subject to subsection (6) and (7)) make an order varying the lease specified in the application in such manner as is specified in the order.

(2) If –

(a) an application under section 36 was made in connection with that application, and

(b) the grounds set out in subsection (3) of that section are established to the satisfaction of the tribunal with respect to the leases specified in the application under section 36, the tribunal may (subject to subsection (6) and (7)) also make an order varying each of those leases in such manner as is specified in the order.

(3) If, on an application under section 37, the grounds set out in subsection (3)

of that section are established to the satisfaction of the tribunal with respect to the leases specified in the application, the tribunal may (subject to subsections (6) and (7)) make an order varying each of those leases in such manner as is specified in the order.

(4) The variation specified in an order under subsection (1) or (2) may be either the variation specified in the relevant application under section 35 or 36 or such other variation as the tribunal thinks fit.

(5) If the grounds referred to in subsection (2) or (3) (as the case may be) are established to the satisfaction of the tribunal with respect to some but not all of the leases specified in the application, the power to make an order under that subsection shall extend to those leases only.

(6) A tribunal shall not make an order under this section effecting any variation of a lease if it appears to the tribunal –
  (a) that the variation would be likely substantially to prejudice –
    (i) any respondent to the application, or
    (ii) any person who is not a party to the application,
    and that an award under subsection (10) would not afford him adequate compensation, or
  (b) that for any other reason it would not be reasonable in the circumstances for the variation to be effected.

(7) A tribunal shall not, on an application relating to the provision to be made by a lease with respect to insurance, make an order under this section effecting any variation of the lease –
  (a) which terminates any existing right of the landlord under its terms to nominate an insurer for insurance purposes; or
  (b) which requires the landlord to nominate a number of insurers from which the tenant would be entitled to select an insurer for those purposes; or
  (c) which, in a case where the lease requires the tenant to effect insurance with a specified insurer, requires the tenant to effect insurance otherwise than with another specified insurer.

(8) A tribunal may, instead of making an order varying a lease in such manner as is specified in the order, make an order directing the parties to the lease to vary it in such manner as is so specified; and accordingly any reference in this Part (however expressed) to an order which effects any variation of a lease or to any variation effected by an order shall include a reference to an order which directs the parties to a lease to effect a variation of it or (as the case may be) a reference to any variation effected in pursuance of such an order.

(9) A tribunal may by order direct that a memorandum of any variation of a lease effected by an order under this section shall be endorsed on such documents as are specified in the order.

(10) Where a tribunal makes an order under this section varying a lease the tribunal may, if it thinks fit, make an order providing for any party to the lease to pay, to any other party to the lease or to any other person, compensation in respect of any loss or disadvantage that the tribunal considers he is likely to suffer as a result of the variation.

Effect of orders varying leases: applications by third parties

39 (1) Any variation effected by an order under section 38 shall be binding not

only on the parties to the lease for the time being but also on other persons (including any predecessors in title of those parties), whether or not they were parties to the proceedings in which the order was made or were served with a notice by virtue of section 35(5).

(2) Without prejudice to the generality of subsection (1), any variation effected by any such order shall be binding on any surety who has guaranteed the performance of any obligation varied by the order; and the surety shall accordingly be taken to have guaranteed the performance of that obligation as so varied.

(3) Where any such order has been made and a person was, by virtue of section 35(5), required to be served with a notice relating to the proceedings in which it was made, but he was not so served, he may –

(a) bring an action for damages for breach of statutory duty against the person by whom any such notice was so required to be served in respect of that person's failure to serve it;

(b) apply to a leasehold valuation tribunal for the cancellation or modification of the variation in question.

(4) A tribunal may, on an application under subsection (3)(b) with respect to any variation of a lease –

(a) by order cancel that variation or modify it in such manner as is specified in the order, or

(b) make such an order as is mentioned in section 38(10) in favour of the person making the application,

as it thinks fit.

(5) Where a variation is cancelled or modified under paragraph (a) of subsection (4) –

(a) the cancellation or modification shall take effect as from the date of the making of the order under that paragraph or as from such later date as may be specified in the order, and

(b) the tribunal may by order direct that a memorandum of the cancellation or modification shall be endorsed on such documents as are specified in the order;

and, in a case where a variation is so modified, subsections (1) and (2) above shall, as from the date when the modification takes effect, apply to the variation as modified.

Application for variation of insurance provisions of lease of dwelling other than a flat

40 (1) Any party to a long lease of a dwelling may make an application to a leasehold valuation tribunal for an order varying the lease, in such manner as is specified in the application, on the grounds that the lease fails to make satisfactory provision with respect to any matter relating to the insurance of the dwelling, including the recovery of the costs of such insurance.

(2) Sections 36 and 38 shall apply to an application under subsection (1) subject to the modifications specified in subsection (3).

(3) Those modifications are as follows –

(a) in section 36 –

(i) in section (1), the reference to section 35 shall be read as a reference to subsection (1) above, and

(ii) in subsection (2), any reference to a flat shall be read as a reference to a dwelling; and

(b) in section 38 –

(i) any reference to an application under section 35 shall be read as a reference to an application under subsection (1) above, and

(ii) any reference to an application under section 36 shall be read as a reference to an application under section 36 as applied by subsection (2) above.

(4) For the purposes of this section, a long lease shall not be regarded as a long lease of a dwelling if –

(a) the demised premises consist of three or more dwellings; or

(b) the lease constitutes a tenancy to which Part II of the Landlord and Tenant Act 1954 applies.

(4A) Without prejudice to subsection (4), an application under subsection (1) may not be made by a person who is a tenant under a long lease of a dwelling if, by virtue of that lease and one or more other long leases of dwellings, he is also a tenant from the same landlord of at least two other dwellings.

(4B) For the purposes of subsection (4A), any tenant of a dwelling who is a body corporate shall be treated as a tenant of any other dwelling held from the same landlord which is let under a long lease to an associated company, as defined in section 20(1).

(5) In this section 'dwelling' means a dwelling other than a flat.

COMMONHOLD AND LEASEHOLD REFORM ACT 2002 (EXTRACTS)

The right to manage

71 (1) This Chapter makes provision for the acquisition and exercise of rights in relation to the management of premises to which this Chapter applies by a company which, in accordance with this Chapter, may acquire and exercise those rights (referred to in this Chapter as a RTM company).

(2) The rights are to be acquired and exercised subject to and in accordance with this Chapter and are referred to in this Chapter as the right to manage.

Premises to which Chapter applies

72 (1) This Chapter applies to premises if –

(a) they consist of a self-contained building or part of a building, with or without appurtenant property,

(b) they contain two or more flats held by qualifying tenants, and

(c) the total number of flats held by such tenants is not less than two-thirds of the total number of flats contained in the premises.

(2) A building is a self-contained building if it is structurally detached.

(3) A part of a building is a self-contained part of the building if –

(a) it constitutes a vertical division of the building,

(b) the structure of the building is such that it could be redeveloped independently of the rest of the building, and

(c) subsection (4) applies in relation to it.

(4) This subsection applies in relation to a part of a building if the relevant services provided for occupiers of it –

(a) are provided independently of the relevant services provided for occupiers of the rest of the building, or

(b) could be so provided without involving the carrying out of works likely to result in a significant interruption in the provision of any relevant services for occupiers of the rest of the building.

(5) Relevant services are services provided by means of pipes, cables or other fixed installations.

(6) Schedule 6 (premises excepted from this Chapter) has effect.

RTM companies

73 (1) This section specifies what is a RTM company.

(2) A company is a RTM company in relation to premises if –

(a) it is a private company limited by guarantee, and

(b) its memorandum of association states that its object, or one of its objects, is the acquisition and exercise of the right to manage the premises.

(3) But a company is not a RTM company if it is a commonhold association (within the meaning of Part 1).

(4) And a company is not a RTM company in relation to premises if another company is already a RTM company in relation to the premises or to any premises containing or contained in the premises.

(5) If the freehold of any premises is conveyed or transferred to a company which is a RTM company in relation to the premises, or any premises containing or contained in the premises, it ceases to be a RTM company when the conveyance or transfer is executed.

RTM companies: membership and regulations

74 (1) The persons who are entitled to be members of a company which is a RTM company in relation to premises are –

   (a) qualifying tenants of flats contained in the premises, and

   (b) from the date on which it acquires the right to manage (referred to in this Chapter as the 'acquisition date'), landlords under leases of the whole or any part of the premises.

(2) The appropriate national authority shall make regulations about the content and form of the memorandum of association and articles of association of RTM companies.

(3) A RTM company may adopt provisions of the regulations for its memorandum or articles.

(4) The regulations may include provision which is to have effect for a RTM company whether or not it is adopted by the company.

(5) A provision of the memorandum or articles of a RTM company has no effect to the extent that it is inconsistent with the regulations.

(6) The regulations have effect in relation to a memorandum or articles –

   (a) irrespective of the date of the memorandum or articles, but

   (b) subject to any transitional provisions of the regulations.

(7) The following provisions of the Companies Act 1985 do not apply to a RTM company –

   (a) sections 2 (7) and 3 (memorandum), and

   (b) section 8 (articles).

Qualifying tenants

75 (1) This section specifies whether there is a qualifying tenant of a flat for the purposes of this Chapter and, if so, who it is.

(2) Subject as follows, a person is the qualifying tenant of a flat if he is tenant of the flat under a long lease.

(3) Subsection (2) does not apply where the lease is a tenancy to which Part 2 of the Landlord and Tenant Act 1954 (business tenancies) applies.

(4) Subsection (2) does not apply where –

   (a) the lease was granted by sub-demise out of a superior lease other than a long lease,

   (b) the grant was made in breach of the terms of the superior lease, and

   (c) there has been no waiver of the breach by the superior landlord.

(5) No flat has more than one qualifying tenant at any one time; and subsections (6) and (7) apply accordingly.

(6) Where a flat is being let under two or more long leases, a tenant under any of those leases which is superior to that held by another is not the qualifying tenant of the flat.

(7) Where a flat is being let to joint tenants under a long lease, the joint tenants shall (subject to subsection (6)) be regarded as jointly being the qualifying tenant of the flat.

Notice inviting participation

78 (1) Before making a claim to acquire the right to manage any premises, a RTM company must give notice to each person who at the time when the notice is given –

   (a) is the qualifying tenant of a flat contained in the premises, but

(b) neither is nor has agreed to become a member of the RTM company.

(2) A notice given under this section (referred to in this Chapter as a 'notice of invitation to participate') must –

    (a) state that the RTM company intends to acquire the right to manage the premises,

    (b) state the names of the members of the RTM company,

    (c) invite the recipients of the notice to become members of the company, and

    (d) contain such other particulars (if any) as may be required to be contained in notices of invitation to participate by regulations made by the appropriate national authority.

(3) A notice of invitation to participate must also comply with such requirements (if any) about the form of notices of invitation to participate as may be prescribed by regulations so made.

(4) A notice of invitation to participate must either –

    (a) be accompanied by a copy of the memorandum of association and articles of association of the RTM company, or

    (b) include a statement about inspection and copying of the memorandum of association and articles of association of the RTM company.

(5) A statement under subsection (4)(b) must –

    (a) specify a place (in England or Wales) at which the memorandum of association and articles of association may be inspected,

    (b) specify as the times at which they may be inspected periods of at least two hours on each of at least three days (including a Saturday or Sunday or both) within the seven days beginning with the day following that on which the notice is given,

    (c) specify a place (in England or Wales) at which, at any time within those seven days, a copy of the memorandum of association and articles of association may be ordered, and

    (d) specify a fee for the provision of an ordered copy, not exceeding the reasonable cost of providing it.

(6) Where a notice given to a person includes a statement under subsection (4)(b), the notice is to be treated as not having been given to him if he is not allowed to undertake an inspection, or is not provided with a copy, in accordance with the statement.

(7) A notice of invitation to participate is not invalidated by any inaccuracy in any of the particulars required by or by virtue of this section.

Notice of claim to acquire right

79 (1) A claim to acquire the right to manage any premises is made by giving notice of the claim (referred to in this Chapter as a 'claim notice'); and in this Chapter the 'relevant date', in relation to any claim to acquire the right to manage, means the date on which notice of the claim is given.

(2) The claim notice may not be given unless each person required to be given a notice of invitation to participate has been given such a notice at least 14 days before.

(3) The claim notice must be given by a RTM company which complies with subsection (4) or (5).

(4) If on the relevant date there are only two qualifying tenants of flats contained in the premises, both must be members of the RTM company.

(5) In any other case, the membership of the RTM company must on the relevant date include a number of qualifying tenants of flats contained in the premises which is not less than one-half of the total number of flats so contained.

(6) The claim notice must be given to each person who on the relevant date is –

(a) landlord under a lease of the whole or any part of the premises,

(b) party to such a lease otherwise than as landlord or tenant, or

(c) a manager appointed under Part 2 of the Landlord and Tenant Act 1987 (referred to in this Part as 'the 1987 Act') to act in relation to the premises, or any premises containing or contained in the premises.

(7) Subsection (6) does not require the claim notice to be given to a person who cannot be found or whose identity cannot be ascertained; but if this subsection means that the claim notice is not required to be given to anyone at all, section 85 applies.

(8) A copy of the claim notice must be given to each person who on the relevant date is the qualifying tenant of a flat contained in the premises.

(9) Where a manager has been appointed under Part 2 of the 1987 Act to act in relation to the premises, or any premises containing or contained in the premises, a copy of the claim notice must also be given to the leasehold valuation tribunal or court by which he was appointed.

Contents of claim notice

80 (1) The claim notice must comply with the following requirements.

(2) It must specify the premises and contain a statement of the grounds on which it is claimed that they are premises to which this Chapter applies.

(3) It must state the full name of each person who is both –

(a) the qualifying tenant of a flat contained in the premises, and

(b) a member of the RTM company,

and the address of his flat.

(4) And it must contain, in relation to each such person, such particulars of his lease as are sufficient to identify it, including –

(a) the date on which it was entered into,

(b) the term for which it was granted, and

(c) the date of the commencement of the term.

(5) It must state the name and registered office of the RTM company.

(6) It must specify a date, not earlier than one month after the relevant date, by which each person who was given the notice under section 79(6) may respond to it by giving a counter-notice under section 84.

(7) It must specify a date, at least three months after that specified under subsection (6), on which the RTM company intends to acquire the right to manage the premises.

(8) It must also contain such other particulars (if any) as may be required to be contained in claim notices by regulations made by the appropriate national authority.

(9) And it must comply with such requirements (if any) about the form of claim notices as may be prescribed by regulations so made.

Claim notice: supplementary

81 (1) A claim notice is not invalidated by any inaccuracy in any of the particulars required by or by virtue of section 80.

(2) Where any of the members of the RTM company whose names are stated in

the claim notice was not the qualifying tenant of a flat contained in the premises on the relevant date, the claim notice is not invalidated on that account, so long as a sufficient number of qualifying tenants of flats contained in the premises were members of the company on that date; and for this purpose a 'sufficient number' is a number (greater than one) which is not less than one-half of the total number of flats contained in the premises on that date.

(3) Where any premises have been specified in a claim notice, no subsequent claim notice which specifies –
  (a) the premises, or
  (b) any premises containing or contained in the premises,
  may be given so long as the earlier claim notice continues in force.

(4) Where a claim notice is given by a RTM company it continues in force from the relevant date until the right to manage is acquired by the company unless it has previously –
  (a) been withdrawn or deemed to be withdrawn by virtue of any provision of this Chapter, or
  (b) ceased to have effect by reason of any other provision of this Chapter.

Right to obtain information

82 (1) A company which is a RTM company in relation to any premises may give to any person a notice requiring him to provide the company with any information –
  (a) which is in his possession or control, and
  (b) which the company reasonably requires for ascertaining the particulars required by or by virtue of section 80 to be included in a claim notice for claiming to acquire the right to manage the premises.

(2) Where the information is recorded in a document in the person's possession or control, the RTM company may give him a notice requiring him –
  (a) to permit any person authorised to act on behalf of the company at any reasonable time to inspect the document (or, if the information is recorded in the document in a form in which it is not readily intelligible, to give any such person access to it in a readily intelligible form), and
  (b) to supply the company with a copy of the document containing the information in a readily intelligible form on payment of a reasonable fee.

(3) A person to whom a notice is given must comply with it within the period of 28 days beginning with the day on which it is given.

Right of access

83 (1) Where a RTM company has given a claim notice in relation to any premises, each of the persons specified in subsection (2) has a right of access to any part of the premises if that is reasonable in connection with any matter arising out of the claim to acquire the right to manage.

(2) The persons referred to in subsection (1) are –
  (a) any person authorised to act on behalf of the RTM company,
  (b) any person who is landlord under a lease of the whole or any part of the premises and any person authorised to act on behalf of any such person,
  (c) any person who is party to such a lease otherwise than as landlord or tenant and any person authorised to act on behalf of any such person, and
  (d) any manager appointed under Part 2 of the 1987 Act to act in relation to

the premises, or any premises containing or contained in the premises, and any person authorised to act on behalf of any such manager.

(3) The right conferred by this section is exercisable, at any reasonable time, on giving not less than ten days' notice –
    (a) to the occupier of any premises to which access is sought, or
    (b) if those premises are unoccupied, to the person entitled to occupy them.

Counter-notices

84 (1) A person who is given a claim notice by a RTM company under section 79(6) may give a notice (referred to in this Chapter as a 'counter-notice') to the company no later than the date specified in the claim notice under section 80(6).

(2) A counter-notice is a notice containing a statement either –
    (a) admitting that the RTM company was on the relevant date entitled to acquire the right to manage the premises specified in the claim notice, or
    (b) alleging that, by reason of a specified provision of this Chapter, the RTM company was on that date not so entitled,

and containing such other particulars (if any) as may be required to be contained in counter-notices, and complying with such requirements (if any) about the form of counter-notices, as may be prescribed by regulations made by the appropriate national authority.

(3) Where the RTM company has been given one or more counter-notices containing a statement such as is mentioned in subsection (2)(b), the company may apply to a leasehold valuation tribunal for a determination that it was on the relevant date entitled to acquire the right to manage the premises.

(4) An application under subsection (3) must be made not later than the end of the period of two months beginning with the day on which the counter-notice (or, where more than one, the last of the counter-notices) was given.

(5) Where the RTM company has been given one or more counter-notices containing a statement such as is mentioned in subsection (2)(b), the RTM company does not acquire the right to manage the premises unless –
    (a) on an application under subsection (3) it is finally determined that the company was on the relevant date entitled to acquire the right to manage the premises, or
    (b) the person by whom the counter-notice was given agrees, or the persons by whom the counter-notices were given agree, in writing that the company was so entitled.

(6) If on an application under subsection (3) it is finally determined that the company was not on the relevant date entitled to acquire the right to manage the premises, the claim notice ceases to have effect.

(7) A determination on an application under subsection (3) becomes final –
    (a) if not appealed against, at the end of the period for bringing an appeal, or
    (b) if appealed against, at the time when the appeal (or any further appeal) is disposed of.

(8) An appeal is disposed of –
    (a) if it is determined and the period for bringing any further appeal has ended, or
    (b) if it is abandoned or otherwise ceases to have effect.

Landlords etc not traceable

85 (1) This section applies where a RTM company wishing to acquire the right to manage premises –

    (a) complies with subsection (4) or (5) of section 79, and

    (b) would not have been precluded from giving a valid notice under that section with respect to the premises,

but cannot find, or ascertain the identity of, any of the persons to whom the claim notice would be required to be given by subsection (6) of that section.

  (2) The RTM company may apply to a leasehold valuation tribunal for an order that the company is to acquire the right to manage the premises.

  (3) Such an order may be made only if the company has given notice of the application to each person who is the qualifying tenant of a flat contained in the premises.

  (4) Before an order is made the company may be required to take such further steps by way of advertisement or otherwise as is determined proper for the purpose of tracing the persons who are –

    (a) landlords under leases of the whole or any part of the premises, or

    (b) parties to such leases otherwise than as landlord or tenant.

  (5) If any of those persons is traced –

    (a) after an application for an order is made, but

    (b) before the making of an order,

no further proceedings shall be taken with a view to the making of an order.

  (6) Where that happens –

    (a) the rights and obligations of all persons concerned shall be determined as if the company had, at the date of the application, duly given notice under section 79 of its claim to acquire the right to manage the premises, and

    (b) the leasehold valuation tribunal may give such directions as it thinks fit as to the steps to be taken for giving effect to their rights and obligations, including directions modifying or dispensing with any of the requirements imposed by or by virtue of this Chapter.

  (7) An application for an order may be withdrawn at any time before an order is made and, after it is withdrawn, subsection (6)(a) does not apply.

  (8) But where any step is taken for the purpose of giving effect to subsection (6)(a) in the case of any application, the application shall not afterwards be withdrawn except –

    (a) with the consent of the person or persons traced, or

    (b) by permission of the leasehold valuation tribunal.

  (9) And permission shall be given only where it appears just that it should be given by reason of matters coming to the knowledge of the RTM company in consequence of the tracing of the person or persons traced.

Withdrawal of claim notice

86 (1) A RTM company which has given a claim notice in relation to any premises may, at any time before it acquires the right to manage the premises, withdraw the claim notice by giving a notice to that effect (referred to in this Chapter as a 'notice of withdrawal').

  (2) A notice of withdrawal must be given to each person who is –

    (a) landlord under a lease of the whole or any part of the premises,

    (b) party to such a lease otherwise than as landlord or tenant,

(c) a manager appointed under Part 2 of the 1987 Act to act in relation to the premises, or any premises containing or contained in the premises, or

(d) the qualifying tenant of a flat contained in the premises.

Deemed withdrawal

87 (1) If a RTM company has been given one or more counter-notices containing a statement such as is mentioned in subsection (2)(b) of section 84 but either –

(a) no application for a determination under subsection (3) of that section is made within the period specified in subsection (4) of that section, or

(b) such an application is so made but is subsequently withdrawn,

the claim notice is deemed to be withdrawn.

(2) The withdrawal shall be taken to occur –

(a) if paragraph (a) of subsection (1) applies, at the end of the period specified in that paragraph, and

(b) if paragraph (b) of that subsection applies, on the date of the withdrawal of the application.

(3) Subsection (1) does not apply if the person by whom the counter-notice was given has, or the persons by whom the counter-notices were given have, (before the time when the withdrawal would be taken to occur) agreed in writing that the RTM company was on the relevant date entitled to acquire the right to manage the premises.

(4) The claim notice is deemed to be withdrawn if –

(a) a winding-up order ... is made, or a resolution for voluntary winding-up is passed, with respect to the RTM company, or the RTM company enters administration,

(b) a receiver or a manager of the RTM company's undertaking is duly appointed, or possession is taken, by or on behalf of the holders of any debentures secured by a floating charge, of any property of the RTM company comprised in or subject to the charge,

(c) a voluntary arrangement proposed in the case of the RTM company for the purposes of Part 1 of the Insolvency Act 1986 is approved under that Part of that Act, or

(d) the RTM company's name is struck off the register under section 652 or 652A of the Companies Act 1985.

Costs: general

88 (1) A RTM company is liable for reasonable costs incurred by a person who is –

(a) landlord under a lease of the whole or any part of any premises,

(b) party to such a lease otherwise than as landlord or tenant, or

(c) a manager appointed under Part 2 of the 1987 Act to act in relation to the premises, or any premises containing or contained in the premises,

in consequence of a claim notice given by the company in relation to the premises.

(2) Any costs incurred by such a person in respect of professional services rendered to him by another are to be regarded as reasonable only if and to the extent that costs in respect of such services might reasonably be expected to have been incurred by him if the circumstances had been such that he was personally liable for all such costs.

(3) A RTM company is liable for any costs which such a person incurs as party to any proceedings under this Chapter before a leasehold valuation tribunal only if the tribunal dismisses an application by the company for a determination that it is entitled to acquire the right to manage the premises.

(4) Any question arising in relation to the amount of any costs payable by a RTM company shall, in default of agreement, be determined by a leasehold valuation tribunal.

Costs where claim ceases

89 (1) This section applies where a claim notice given by a RTM company –
   (a) is at any time withdrawn or deemed to be withdrawn by virtue of any provision of this Chapter, or
   (b) at any time ceases to have effect by reason of any other provision of this Chapter.

(2) The liability of the RTM company under section 88 for costs incurred by any person is a liability for costs incurred by him down to that time.

(3) Each person who is or has been a member of the RTM company is also liable for those costs (jointly and severally with the RTM company and each other person who is so liable).

(4) But subsection (3) does not make a person liable if –
   (a) the lease by virtue of which he was a qualifying tenant has been assigned to another person, and
   (b) that other person has become a member of the RTM company.

(5) The reference in subsection (4) to an assignment includes –
   (a) an assent by personal representatives, and
   (b) assignment by operation of law where the assignment is to a trustee in bankruptcy or to a mortgagee under section 89(2) of the Law of Property Act 1925 (foreclosure of leasehold mortgage).

The acquisition date

90 (1) This section makes provision about the date which is the acquisition date where a RTM company acquires the right to manage any premises.

(2) Where there is no dispute about entitlement, the acquisition date is the date specified in the claim notice under section 80(7).

(3) For the purposes of this Chapter there is no dispute about entitlement if –
   (a) no counter-notice is given under section 84, or
   (b) the counter-notice given under that section, or (where more than one is so given) each of them, contains a statement such as is mentioned in subsection (2)(a) of that section.

(4) Where the right to manage the premises is acquired by the company by virtue of a determination under section 84(5)(a), the acquisition date is the date three months after the determination becomes final.

(5) Where the right to manage the premises is acquired by the company by virtue of subsection (5)(b) of section 84, the acquisition date is the date three months after the day on which the person (or the last person) by whom a counter-notice containing a statement such as is mentioned in subsection (2)(b) of that section was given agrees in writing that the company was on the relevant date entitled to acquire the right to manage the premises.

(6) Where an order is made under section 85, the acquisition date is (subject to any appeal) the date specified in the order.

Duty to pay accrued uncommitted service charges

94 (1) Where the right to manage premises is to be acquired by a RTM company, a person who is –

  (a) landlord under a lease of the whole or any part of the premises,

  (b) party to such a lease otherwise than as landlord or tenant, or

  (c) a manager appointed under Part 2 of the 1987 Act to act in relation to the premises, or any premises containing or contained in the premises,

  must make to the company a payment equal to the amount of any accrued uncommitted service charges held by him on the acquisition date.

  (2) The amount of any accrued uncommitted service charges is the aggregate of –

  (a) any sums which have been paid to the person by way of service charges in respect of the premises, and

  (b) any investments which represent such sums (and any income which has accrued on them),

  less so much (if any) of that amount as is required to meet the costs incurred before the acquisition date in connection with the matters for which the service charges were payable.

  (3) He or the RTM company may make an application to a leasehold valuation tribunal to determine the amount of any payment which falls to be made under this section.

  (4) The duty imposed by this section must be complied with on the acquisition date or as soon after that date as is reasonably practicable.

Notices

111 (1) Any notice under this Chapter –

  (a) must be in writing, and

  (b) may be sent by post.

  (2) A company which is a RTM company in relation to premises may give a notice under this Chapter to a person who is landlord under a lease of the whole or any part of the premises at the address specified in subsection (3) (but subject to subsection (4)).

  (3) That address is –

  (a) the address last furnished to a member of the RTM company as the landlord's address for service in accordance with section 48 of the 1987 Act (notification of address for service of notices on landlord), or

  (b) if no such address has been so furnished, the address last furnished to such a member as the landlord's address in accordance with section 47 of the 1987 Act (landlord's name and address to be contained in demands for rent).

  (4) But the RTM company may not give a notice under this Chapter to a person at the address specified in subsection (3) if it has been notified by him of a different address in England and Wales at which he wishes to be given any such notice.

  (5) A company which is a RTM company in relation to premises may give a notice under this Chapter to a person who is the qualifying tenant of a flat contained in the premises at the flat unless it has been notified by the qualifying tenant of a different address in England and Wales at which he wishes to be given any such notice.

Insurance otherwise than with landlord's insurer

164 (1) This section applies where a long lease of a house requires the tenant to insure the house with an insurer nominated or approved by the landlord ('the landlord's insurer').

(2) The tenant is not required to effect the insurance with the landlord's insurer if –

    (a) the house is insured under a policy of insurance issued by an authorised insurer,

    (b) the policy covers the interests of both the landlord and the tenant,

    (c) the policy covers all the risks which the lease requires be covered by insurance provided by the landlord's insurer,

    (d) the amount of the cover is not less than that which the lease requires to be provided by such insurance, and

    (e) the tenant satisfies subsection (3).

(3) To satisfy this subsection the tenant –

    (a) must have given a notice of cover to the landlord before the end of the period of fourteen days beginning with the relevant date, and

    (b) if (after that date) he has been requested to do so by a new landlord, must have given a notice of cover to him within the period of fourteen days beginning with the day on which the request was given.

(4) For the purposes of subsection (3) –

    (a) if the policy has not been renewed the relevant date is the day on which it took effect and if it has been renewed it is the day from which it was last renewed, and

    (b) a person is a new landlord on any day if he acquired the interest of the previous landlord under the lease on a disposal made by him during the period of one month ending with that day.

(5) A notice of cover is a notice specifying –

    (a) the name of the insurer,

    (b) the risks covered by the policy,

    (c) the amount and period of the cover, and

    (d) such further information as may be prescribed.

(6) A notice of cover –

    (a) must be in the prescribed form, and

    (b) may be sent by post.

(7) If a notice of cover is sent by post, it may be addressed to the landlord at the address specified in subsection (8).

(8) That address is –

    (a) the address last furnished to the tenant as the landlord's address for service in accordance with section 48 of the 1987 Act (notification of address for service of notices on landlord), or

    (b) if no such address has been so furnished, the address last furnished to the tenant as the landlord's address in accordance with section 47 of the 1987 Act (landlord's name and address to be contained in demands for rent).

(9) But the tenant may not give a notice of cover to the landlord at the address specified in subsection (8) if he has been notified by the landlord of a different address in England and Wales at which he wishes to be given any such notice.

(10) In this section –
'authorised insurer', in relation to a policy of insurance, means a person who may carry on in the United Kingdom the business of effecting or carrying out contracts of insurance of the sort provided under the policy without contravening the prohibition imposed by section 19 of the Financial Services and Markets Act 2000,
'house' has the same meaning as for the purposes of Part 1 of the 1967 Act,
'landlord' and 'tenant' have the same meanings as in Chapter 1 of this Part,
'long lease' has the meaning given by sections 76 and 77 of this Act, and
'prescribed' means prescribed by regulations made by the appropriate national authority.

Requirement to notify long leaseholders that rent is due

166 (1) A tenant under a long lease of a dwelling is not liable to make a payment of rent under the lease unless the landlord has given him a notice relating to the payment; and the date on which he is liable to make the payment is that specified in the notice.
(2) The notice must specify –
(a) the amount of the payment,
(b) the date on which the tenant is liable to make it, and
(c) if different from that date, the date on which he would have been liable to make it in accordance with the lease,
and shall contain any such further information as may be prescribed.
(3) The date on which the tenant is liable to make the payment must not be –
(a) either less than 30 days or more than 60 days after the day on which the notice is given, or
(b) before that on which he would have been liable to make it in accordance with the lease.
(4) If the date on which the tenant is liable to make the payment is after that on which he would have been liable to make it in accordance with the lease, any provisions of the lease relating to non-payment or late payment of rent have effect accordingly.
(5) The notice –
(a) must be in the prescribed form, and
(b) may be sent by post.
(6) If the notice is sent by post, it must be addressed to a tenant at the dwelling unless he has notified the landlord in writing of a different address in England and Wales at which he wishes to be given notices under this section (in which case it must be addressed to him there).
(7) In this section 'rent' does not include –
(a) a service charge (within the meaning of section 18(1) of the 1985 Act), or
(b) an administration charge (within the meaning of Part 1 of Schedule 11 to this Act).
(8) In this section 'long lease of a dwelling' does not include –
(a) a tenancy to which Part 2 of the Landlord and Tenant Act 1954 (business tenancies) applies,
(b) a tenancy of an agricultural holding within the meaning of the Agricultural Holdings Act 1986 in relation to which that Act applies, or

(c) a farm business tenancy within the meaning of the Agricultural Tenancies Act 1995 (c 8).

(9) In this section –
'dwelling' has the same meaning as in the 1985 Act,
'landlord' and 'tenant' have the same meanings as in Chapter 1 of this Part,
'long lease' has the meaning given by sections 76 and 77 of this Act, and
'prescribed' means prescribed by regulations made by the appropriate national authority.

Failure to pay small amount for short period

167 (1) A landlord under a long lease of a dwelling may not exercise a right of re-entry or forfeiture for failure by a tenant to pay an amount consisting of rent, service charges or administration charges (or a combination of them) ('the unpaid amount') unless the unpaid amount –
   (a) exceeds the prescribed sum, or
   (b) consists of or includes an amount which has been payable for more than a prescribed period.
(2) The sum prescribed under subsection (1)(a) must not exceed £500.
(3) If the unpaid amount includes a default charge, it is to be treated for the purposes of subsection (1)(a) as reduced by the amount of the charge; and for this purpose 'default charge' means an administration charge payable in respect of the tenant's failure to pay any part of the unpaid amount.
(4) In this section 'long lease of a dwelling' does not include –
   (a) a tenancy to which Part 2 of the Landlord and Tenant Act 1954 (business tenancies) applies,
   (b) a tenancy of an agricultural holding within the meaning of the Agricultural Holdings Act 1986 in relation to which that Act applies, or
   (c) a farm business tenancy within the meaning of the Agricultural Tenancies Act 1995.
(5) In this section –
'administration charge' has the same meaning as in Part 1 of Schedule 11,
'dwelling' has the same meaning as in the 1985 Act,
'landlord' and 'tenant' have the same meaning as in Chapter 1 of this Part,
'long lease' has the meaning given by sections 76 and 77 of this Act, except that a shared ownership lease is a long lease whatever the tenant's total share,
'prescribed' means prescribed by regulations made by the appropriate national authority, and
'service charge' has the meaning given by section 18(1) of the 1985 Act.

No forfeiture notice before determination of breach

168 (1) A landlord under a long lease of a dwelling may not serve a notice under section 146(1) of the Law of Property Act 1925 (restriction on forfeiture) in respect of a breach by a tenant of a covenant or condition in the lease unless subsection (2) is satisfied.
(2) This subsection is satisfied if –
   (a) it has been finally determined on an application under subsection (4) that the breach has occurred,
   (b) the tenant has admitted the breach, or
   (c) a court in any proceedings, or an arbitral tribunal in proceedings pursu-

ant to a post-dispute arbitration agreement, has finally determined that the breach has occurred.

(3) But a notice may not be served by virtue of subsection (2)(a) or (c) until after the end of the period of 14 days beginning with the day after that on which the final determination is made.

(4) A landlord under a long lease of a dwelling may make an application to a leasehold valuation tribunal for a determination that a breach of a covenant or condition in the lease has occurred.

(5) But a landlord may not make an application under subsection (4) in respect of a matter which –
  (a) has been, or is to be, referred to arbitration pursuant to a post-dispute arbitration agreement to which the tenant is a party,
  (b) has been the subject of determination by a court, or
  (c) has been the subject of determination by an arbitral tribunal pursuant to a post-dispute arbitration agreement.

SCHEDULE 6: PREMISES EXCLUDED FROM RIGHT TO MANAGE

Buildings with substantial non-residential parts

1 (1) This Chapter does not apply to premises falling within section 72(1) if the internal floor area –
  (a) of any non-residential part, or
  (b) (where there is more than one such part) of those parts (taken together), exceeds 25 per cent of the internal floor area of the premises (taken as a whole).

(2) A part of premises is a non-residential part if it is neither –
  (a) occupied, or intended to be occupied, for residential purposes, nor
  (b) comprised in any common parts of the premises.

(3) Where in the case of any such premises any part of the premises (such as, for example, a garage, parking space or storage area) is used, or intended for use, in conjunction with a particular dwelling contained in the premises (and accordingly is not comprised in any common parts of the premises), it shall be taken to be occupied, or intended to be occupied, for residential purposes.

(4) For the purpose of determining the internal floor area of a building or of any part of a building, the floor or floors of the building or part shall be taken to extend (without interruption) throughout the whole of the interior of the building or part, except that the area of any common parts of the building or part shall be disregarded.

Buildings with self-contained parts in different ownership

2 Where different persons own the freehold of different parts of premises falling within section 72(1), this Chapter does not apply to the premises if any of those parts is a self-contained part of a building.

Premises with resident landlord and no more than four units

3 (1) This Chapter does not apply to premises falling within section 72(1) if the premises –
  (a) have a resident landlord, and
  (b) do not contain more than four units.

(2) Premises have a resident landlord if –

    (a) the premises are not, and do not form part of, a purpose-built block of flats (that is, a building which, as constructed, contained two or more flats),

    (b) a relevant freeholder, or an adult member of a relevant freeholder's family, occupies a qualifying flat as his only or principal home, and

    (c) sub-paragraph (4) or (5) is satisfied.

(3) A person is a relevant freeholder, in relation to any premises, if he owns the freehold of the whole or any part of the premises.

(4) This sub-paragraph is satisfied if –

    (a) the relevant freeholder, or

    (b) the adult member of his family,

has throughout the last twelve months occupied the flat as his only or principal home.

(5) This sub-paragraph is satisfied if –

    (a) immediately before the date when the relevant freeholder acquired his interest in the premises, the premises were premises with a resident landlord, and

    (b) he, or an adult member of his family, entered into occupation of the flat during the period of 28 days beginning with that date and has occupied the flat as his only or principal home ever since.

(6) 'Qualifying flat', in relation to any premises and a relevant freeholder or an adult member of his family, means a flat or other unit used as a dwelling –

    (a) which is contained in the premises, and

    (b) the freehold of the whole of which is owned by the relevant freeholder.

(7) Where the interest of a relevant freeholder in any premises is held on trust, the references in sub-paragraphs (2), (4) and (5)(b) to a relevant freeholder are to a person having an interest under the trust (whether or not also a trustee).

(8) A person is an adult member of another's family if he is –

    (a) the other's spouse or civil partner,

    (b) a son, daughter, son-in-law or daughter-in-law of the other, or of the other's spouse or civil partner, who has attained the age of 18, or

    (c) the father or mother of the other or of the other's spouse or civil partner; and 'son' and 'daughter' include stepson and stepdaughter ('son-in-law' and 'daughter-in-law' being construed accordingly).

Premises owned by local housing authority

4 (1) This Chapter does not apply to premises falling within section 72(1) if a local housing authority is the immediate landlord of any of the qualifying tenants of flats contained in the premises.

(2) 'Local housing authority' has the meaning given by section 1 of the Housing Act 1985.

Premises in relation to which rights previously exercised

5 (1) This Chapter does not apply to premises falling within section 72(1) at any time if –

    (a) the right to manage the premises is at that time exercisable by a RTM company, or

(b) that right has been so exercisable but has ceased to be so exercisable less than four years before that time.

(2) Sub-paragraph (1)(b) does not apply where the right to manage the premises ceased to be exercisable by virtue of section 73(5).

(3) A leasehold valuation tribunal may, on an application made by a RTM company, determine that sub-paragraph (1)(b) is not to apply in any case if it considers that it would be unreasonable for it to apply in the circumstances of the case.

SCHEDULE 11: ADMINISTRATION CHARGES

Meaning of 'administration charge'

1 (1) In this Part of this Schedule 'administration charge' means an amount payable by a tenant of a dwelling as part of or in addition to the rent which is payable, directly or indirectly –

(a) for or in connection with the grant of approvals under his lease, or applications for such approvals,

(b) for or in connection with the provision of information or documents by or on behalf of the landlord or a person who is party to his lease otherwise than as landlord or tenant,

(c) in respect of a failure by the tenant to make a payment by the due date to the landlord or a person who is party to his lease otherwise than as landlord or tenant, or

(d) in connection with a breach (or alleged breach) of a covenant or condition in his lease.

(2) But an amount payable by the tenant of a dwelling the rent of which is registered under Part 4 of the Rent Act 1977 is not an administration charge, unless the amount registered is entered as a variable amount in pursuance of section 71 (4) of that Act.

(3) In this Part of this Schedule 'variable administration charge' means an administration charge payable by a tenant which is neither –

(a) specified in his lease, nor

(b) calculated in accordance with a formula specified in his lease.

(4) An order amending sub-paragraph (1) may be made by the appropriate national authority.

Reasonableness of administration charges

2 A variable administration charge is payable only to the extent that the amount of the charge is reasonable.

Variation of leases

3 (1) Any party to a lease of a dwelling may apply to a leasehold valuation tribunal for an order varying the lease in such manner as is specified in the application on the grounds that –

(a) any administration charge specified in the lease is unreasonable, or

(b) any formula specified in the lease in accordance with which any administration charge is calculated is unreasonable.

(2) If the grounds on which the application was made are established to the satisfaction of the tribunal, it may make an order varying the lease in such manner as is specified in the order.

(3) The variation specified in the order may be –
  (a) the variation specified in the application, or
  (b) such other variation as the tribunal thinks fit.
(4) The tribunal may, instead of making an order varying the lease in such manner as is specified in the order, make an order directing the parties to the lease to vary it in such manner as is so specified.
(5) The tribunal may by order direct that a memorandum of any variation of a lease effected by virtue of this paragraph be endorsed on such documents as are specified in the order.
(6) Any such variation of a lease shall be binding not only on the parties to the lease for the time being but also on other persons (including any predecessors in title), whether or not they were parties to the proceedings in which the order was made.

Notice in connection with demands for administration charges

4 (1) A demand for the payment of an administration charge must be accompanied by a summary of the rights and obligations of tenants of dwellings in relation to administration charges.
(2) The appropriate national authority may make regulations prescribing requirements as to the form and content of such summaries of rights and obligations.
(3) A tenant may withhold payment of an administration charge which has been demanded from him if sub-paragraph (1) is not complied with in relation to the demand.
(4) Where a tenant withholds an administration charge under this paragraph, any provisions of the lease relating to non-payment or late payment of administration charges do not have effect in relation to the period for which he so withholds it.

Liability to pay administration charges

5 (1) An application may be made to a leasehold valuation tribunal for a determination whether an administration charge is payable and, if it is, as to –
  (a) the person by whom it is payable,
  (b) the person to whom it is payable,
  (c) the amount which is payable,
  (d) the date at or by which it is payable, and
  (e) the manner in which it is payable.
(2) Sub-paragraph (1) applies whether or not any payment has been made.
(3) The jurisdiction conferred on a leasehold valuation tribunal in respect of any matter by virtue of sub-paragraph (1) is in addition to any jurisdiction of a court in respect of the matter.
(4) No application under sub-paragraph (1) may be made in respect of a matter which –
  (a) has been agreed or admitted by the tenant,
  (b) has been, or is to be, referred to arbitration pursuant to a post-dispute arbitration agreement to which the tenant is a party,
  (c) has been the subject of determination by a court, or
  (d) has been the subject of determination by an arbitral tribunal pursuant to a post-dispute arbitration agreement.

(5) But the tenant is not to be taken to have agreed or admitted any matter by reason only of having made any payment.

(6) An agreement by the tenant of a dwelling (other than a post-dispute arbitration agreement) is void in so far as it purports to provide for a determination –
   (a) in a particular manner, or
   (b) on particular evidence,
   of any question which may be the subject matter of an application under sub-paragraph (1).

Interpretation

6 (1) This paragraph applies for the purposes of this Part of this Schedule.

(2) 'Tenant' includes a statutory tenant.

(3) 'Dwelling' and 'statutory tenant' (and 'landlord' in relation to a statutory tenant) have the same meanings as in the 1985 Act.

(4) 'Post-dispute arbitration agreement', in relation to any matter, means an arbitration agreement made after a dispute about the matter has arisen.

(5) 'Arbitration agreement' and 'arbitral tribunal' have the same meanings as in Part 1 of the Arbitration Act 1996.

LEASEHOLD VALUATION TRIBUNALS (PROCEDURE) (ENGLAND) REGULATIONS 2003

Citation, commencement, and application

1 (1) These Regulations may be cited as the Leasehold Valuation Tribunals (Procedure) (England) Regulations 2003

(2) These Regulations shall come into force –

(a) for all purposes other than paragraph 2(a) of Schedule 1, on 30th September 2003; and

(b) for the purposes of paragraph 2(a) of Schedule 1, on 31st October 2003.

(3) These Regulations apply in relation to any application made, or proceedings transferred from a court, to a leasehold valuation tribunal in respect of premises in England on or after –

(a) in the case of an application –

(i) of the description specified in paragraph 2(a) of Schedule 1, 31st October 2003;

(ii) of the description specified in paragraph 8 of that Schedule, 28th February 2005; and

(b) in any other case, 30th September 2003.

Interpretation

2   In these Regulations –

'the 1985 Act' means the Landlord and Tenant Act 1985;

'the 1987 Act' means the Landlord and Tenant Act 1987;

'the 1993 Act' means the Leasehold Reform, Housing and Urban Development Act 1993;

'the 2002 Act' means the Commonhold and Leasehold Reform Act 2002;

'applicant' means –

(a) the person making an application to a tribunal, or

(b) the person who is the claimant or applicant in proceedings before a court which are transferred by order of the court to a tribunal;

'application' means, other than for the purposes of regulations 1, 20 and 25 –

(a) an application to a tribunal of a description specified in Schedule 1, or

(b) a transferred application;

'recognised tenants' association' has the same meaning as in section 29 of the 1985 Act;

'representative application' has the meaning given in regulation 8;

'respondent' means –

(a) the person against whom an applicant seeks an order or determination from a tribunal; or

(b) the person who is the defendant or respondent in proceedings before a court which are transferred by order of the court to a tribunal;

'transferred application' means so much of proceedings before a court as relate to a question falling within the jurisdiction of a tribunal as have been transferred to the tribunal for determination by order of the court; and

'tribunal' means a leasehold valuation tribunal.

Particulars of applications

3 (1) The particulars to be included with an application are –
  (a) the name and address of the applicant;
  (b) the name and address of the respondent;
  (c) the name and address of any landlord or tenant of the premises to which the application relates;
  (d) the address of the premises to which the application relates; and
  (e) a statement that the applicant believes that the facts stated in the application are true.

  (2) Where an application is of a description specified in paragraph 1 of Schedule 1 (enfranchisement and extended leases) the particulars and documents listed in paragraph 1 of Schedule 2 shall be included with the application.

  (3) Where an application is of a description specified in any of sub-paragraphs (b) to (f) of paragraph 2 of Schedule 1 (service charges, administration charges and estate charges) the particulars and documents listed in paragraph 2 of Schedule 2 shall be included with the application.

  (4) Where an application is of a description specified in paragraph 3 of Schedule 1 (estate management schemes) the particulars and documents listed in paragraph 3 of Schedule 2 shall be included with the application.

  (5) Where an application is of a description specified in paragraph 4 of Schedule 1 (right to manage) the particulars and documents listed in paragraph 4 of Schedule 2 shall be included with the application.

  (6) Where an application is of a description specified in paragraph 5 of Schedule 1 (appointment of manager) the particulars and documents listed in paragraph 5 of Schedule 2 shall be included with the application.

  (7) Where an application is of a description specified in paragraph 6 of Schedule 1 (variation of leases) the particulars and documents listed in paragraph 6 of Schedule 2 shall be included with the application.

  (7A) Where an application is of the description specified in paragraph 8 of Schedule 1 (determination as to breach of covenant or condition) the particulars and documents listed in paragraph 7 of Schedule 2 shall be included with the application.

  (8) Any of the requirements in the preceding paragraphs may be dispensed with or relaxed if the tribunal is satisfied that –
  (a) the particulars and documents included with an application are sufficient to enable the application to be determined; and
  (b) no prejudice will, or is likely to, be caused to any party to the application.

Notice of application under Part 4 of the 1987 Act

4 (1) The applicant shall give notice of an application under Part 4 of the 1987 Act (variation of leases) to the respondent and to any person who the applicant knows, or has reason to believe, is likely to be affected by any variation specified in the application.

  (2) On receipt of the notice under paragraph (1) the respondent shall give notice of the application to any person not already notified under that paragraph, who the respondent knows, or has reason to believe, is likely to be affected by any variation specified in the application.

Notice of application by tribunal

5 (1) On receipt of an application, other than an application made under Part 4 of the 1987 Act, the tribunal shall send a copy of the application and each of the documents accompanying it to each person named in it as a respondent.

(2) On receipt of an application of a description specified in paragraph 2 of Schedule 1 (service charges, administration charges and estate charges), the tribunal shall give notice of the application to –
   (a) the secretary of any recognised tenants' association mentioned in the particulars included in the application; and
   (b) any person, whose name and address the tribunal has, who the tribunal considers is likely to be significantly affected by the application.

(3) On receipt of an application the tribunal may give notice to any other person it considers appropriate.

(4) Any notice given under paragraph (2) or (3) shall include a statement that any person may make a request to the tribunal under regulation 6 to be joined as a party to the proceedings with details as to how such a request can be made.

(5) Any notice given under paragraph (2) or (3) may be given by local advertisement.

(6) In this regulation, 'local advertisement' means publication of the notice in two newspapers (at least one of which should be a freely distributed newspaper) circulating in the locality in which the premises to which the application relates is situated.

Request to be treated as an applicant or respondent

6 (1) Any person may make a request to the tribunal to be joined as a party to the proceedings.

(2) Any request under paragraph (1) –
   (a) may be made without notice; and
   (b) shall specify whether the person making the request wishes to be treated as –
      (i) an applicant; or
      (ii) a respondent
      to the application.

(3) The tribunal may grant or refuse a request under paragraph (1).

(4) As soon as possible after reaching its decision on a request under paragraph (1), the tribunal shall –
   (a) notify the person making the request of the decision and the reasons for it; and
   (b) send a copy of the notification to the applicant and the respondent.

(5) Any person whose request under paragraph (1) is granted shall be treated as an applicant or respondent, as the case may be, for the purposes of regulations 8 to 18, 20 and 24.

(6) In the regulations mentioned in paragraph (5) any reference to –
   (a) an applicant, or
   (b) a respondent
   shall be construed as including a person treated as such under this regula-

tion and any reference to a party shall be construed as including any such person.

Non-payment of fees

7 (1) In any case where a fee which is payable under regulation 4 or 5 of the Leasehold Valuation Tribunals (Fees) (England) Regulations 2003 is not paid in accordance with those Regulations, the tribunal shall not proceed further with the application to which the fee relates until the fee is paid.

(2) Where a fee remains unpaid for a period of one month from the date on which it becomes due, the application shall be treated as withdrawn unless the tribunal is satisfied that there are reasonable grounds not to do so.

Representative applications and other provisions for securing consistency

8 (1) Where it appears to a tribunal that numerous applications –

(a) have been made in respect of the same or substantially the same matters; or

(b) include some matters which are the same or substantially the same,

the tribunal may propose to determine only one of those applications ('the representative application') as representative of all of the applications on those matters which are the same or substantially the same ('the common matters'), and shall give notice of the proposal to the parties to all such applications.

(2) A notice under paragraph (1) shall –

(a) specify the common matters;

(b) specify the application which the tribunal proposes to determine as the representative application;

(c) explain that the tribunal's decision on the common matters in the representative application will apply to the common matters in any application made by a person to whom notice has been given under that paragraph;

(d) invite objections to the tribunal's proposal to determine the representative application; and

(e) specify the address to which objections may be sent and the date (being not less than 21 days after the date that the notice was sent) by which the objections must be received by the tribunal.

(3) Where no objection is received on or before the date specified in the notice –

(a) the tribunal shall determine the representative application in accordance with these Regulations;

(b) the tribunal need not determine the matters mentioned in paragraph (1)(a)   in any other application made by a person to whom a notice under paragraph (1) has been given; and

(c) the decision of the tribunal in respect of the representative application shall be recorded as the decision of the tribunal in respect of the common matters in any such other application.

(4) Where an objection is received on or before the date specified in the notice –

(a) sub-paragraphs (a) to (c) of paragraph (3) shall apply only to those applications in respect of which no objection was made, and

(b) the application in respect of which an objection was made may be determined together with the representative application.

Subsequent applications where notice of the representative application given

9 (1) If, after a representative application has been determined, a subsequent application is made which includes any of the common matters on which the tribunal has made a decision in its determination of the representative application, and the applicant is a person to whom a notice under regulation 8(1) was given, the tribunal shall give notice to the parties to the subsequent application of –

    (a) the matters which, in the opinion of the tribunal, are the common matters in the subsequent application and the representative application;

    (b) the decision recorded in respect of the common matters in the representative application;

    (c) the date on which notice under regulation 8(1) was given to the applicant;

    (d) the tribunal's proposal to record the tribunal's decision on the common matters in the subsequent application in identical terms to the decision in the representative application;

    (e) the address to which objections to the tribunal's proposal may be sent and the date (being not less than 21 days after the date that the notice was sent) by which such objections must be received by the tribunal; and

    (f) a statement that any objection must include the grounds on which it is made and, in particular, whether it is alleged that the notice under regulation 8(1) was not received by the person making the objection.

  (2) Where no objection is received on or before the date specified in the notice –

    (a) the tribunal need not determine the matters mentioned in paragraph 1(a); and

    (b) the decision of the tribunal in respect of the common matters in the representative application shall be recorded as the decision of the tribunal in respect of the common matters in the subsequent application.

  (3) Where an objection is received to the tribunal's proposal on or before the date specified in the notice –

    (a) the tribunal shall consider the objection when determining the subsequent application; and

    (b) if the tribunal dismisses the objection, it may record the decision mentioned in paragraph (1)(b) as the decision of the tribunal in the subsequent application.

Subsequent applications where notice of representative application not given

10 (1) If, after a representative application has been determined, a subsequent application is made which includes any of the common matters on which the tribunal has made a decision in its determination of the representative application, and the applicant is not a person to whom a notice under regulation 8(1) was given, the tribunal shall give notice to the parties to the subsequent application of –

    (a) the matters which, in the opinion of the tribunal, are the common matters in the subsequent application and the representative application;

    (b) the decision recorded in respect of those common matters in the representative application;

(c) the tribunal's proposal to record its decision on the common matters in the subsequent application in identical terms to the decision in the representative application; and

(d) the address to which objections to the tribunal's proposal may be sent and the date (being not less than 21 days after the date that the notice was sent) by which such objections must be received by the tribunal.

(2) Where no objection is received on or before the date specified in the notice –

(a) the tribunal need not determine the matters mentioned in paragraph (1)(a); and

(b) the decision of the tribunal in respect of the common matters in the representative application shall be recorded as the decision of the tribunal in respect of the common matters in the subsequent application.

(3) Where an objection is received to the tribunal's proposal on or before the date specified in the notice the tribunal shall determine the application in accordance with the following provisions of these Regulations.

Dismissal of frivolous, etc applications

11 (1) Subject to paragraph (2), where –

(a) it appears to a tribunal that an application is frivolous or vexatious or otherwise an abuse of process of the tribunal; or

(b) the respondent to an application makes a request to the tribunal to dismiss an application as frivolous or vexatious or otherwise an abuse of the process of the tribunal,

the tribunal may dismiss the application, in whole or in part.

(2) Before dismissing an application under paragraph (1) the tribunal shall give notice to the applicant in accordance with paragraph (3).

(3) Any notice under paragraph (2) shall state –

(a) that the tribunal is minded to dismiss the application;

(b) the grounds on which it is minded to dismiss the application;

(c) the date (being not less than 21 days after the date that the notice was sent) before which the applicant may request to appear before and be heard by the tribunal on the question whether the application should be dismissed.

(4) An application may not be dismissed unless –

(a) the applicant makes no request to the tribunal before the date mentioned in paragraph (3)(c); or

(b) where the applicant makes such a request, the tribunal has heard the applicant and the respondent, or such of them as attend the hearing, on the question of the dismissal of the application.

Pre-trial review

12 (1) The tribunal may, whether on its own initiative or at the request of a party, hold a pre-trial review in respect of an application.

(2) The tribunal shall give the parties not less than 14 days notice (or such shorter notice as the parties agree to) of the date, time and place of the pre-trial review.

(3) At the pre-trial review the tribunal shall –

(a) give any direction that appears to the tribunal necessary or desirable for securing the just, expeditious and economical disposal of proceedings;

(b) endeavour to secure that the parties make all such admissions and agreements as ought reasonably to be made by them in relation to the proceedings; and

(c) record in any order made at the pre-trial review any such admission or agreement or any refusal to make such admission or agreement.

(4) The functions of the tribunal in relation to, or at, a pre-trial review may be exercised by any single member of the panel provided for in Schedule 10 to the Rent Act 1977 who is qualified to exercise them.

Determination without a hearing

13 (1) A tribunal may determine an application without an oral hearing, in accordance with the following provisions of this regulation, if –

(a) it has given to both the applicant and the respondent not less than 28 days' notice in writing of its intention to proceed without an oral hearing; and

(b) neither the applicant nor the respondent has made a request to the tribunal to be heard,

but this paragraph is without prejudice to paragraph (3).

(2) The tribunal shall –

(a) notify the parties that the application is to be determined without an oral hearing;

(b) invite written representations on the application;

(c) set time limits for sending any written representations to the tribunal; and

(d) set out how the tribunal intends to determine the matter without an oral hearing.

(3) At any time before the application is determined –

(a) the applicant or the respondent may make a request to the tribunal to be heard; or

(b) the tribunal may give notice to the parties that it intends to determine the application at a hearing in accordance with regulation 14.

(4) Where a request is made or a notice given under paragraph (3) the application shall be determined in accordance with regulation 14.

(5) The functions of the tribunal in relation to an application to be determined without an oral hearing may be exercised by a single member of the panel provided for in Schedule 10 to the Rent Act 1977, if he was appointed to that panel by the Lord Chancellor.

Hearings

14 (1) Subject to regulations 8(3), 9(2) and 10(2), a hearing shall be on the date and at the time and place appointed by the tribunal.

(2) The tribunal shall give notice to the parties of the appointed date, time and place of the hearing.

(3) Subject to paragraph (4), notice under paragraph (2) shall be given not less than 21 days (or such shorter period as the parties may agree) before the appointed date.

(4) In exceptional circumstances the tribunal may, without the agreement of the parties, give less than 21 days notice of the appointed date, time and place of the hearing; but any such notice must be given as soon as possible before the appointed date and the notice must specify what the exceptional circumstances are.

(5) The tribunal may arrange that an application shall be heard together with one or more other applications.

(6) A hearing shall be in public unless, in the particular circumstances of the case, the tribunal decide that a hearing or part of a hearing shall be held in private.

(7) At the hearing –

    (a) the tribunal shall determine the procedure (subject to these Regulations) and the order in which the persons appearing before it are to be heard;

    (b) a person appearing before the tribunal may do so either in person or by a representative authorised by him, whether or not that representative is a barrister or a solicitor; and

    (c) a person appearing before the tribunal may give evidence on his own behalf, call witnesses, and cross-examine any witnesses called by any other person appearing.

(8) If a party does not appear at a hearing, the tribunal may proceed with the hearing if it is satisfied that notice has been given to that party in accordance with these Regulations.

Postponement and adjournment

15 (1) Subject to paragraph (2) the tribunal may postpone or adjourn a hearing or pre-trial review either on its own initiative or at the request of a party.

    (2) Where a postponement or adjournment has been requested the tribunal shall not postpone or adjourn the hearing except where it considers it is reasonable to do so having regard to –

    (a) the grounds for the request;

    (b) the time at which the request is made; and

    (c) the convenience of the other parties.

    (3) The tribunal shall give reasonable notice of any postponed or adjourned hearing to the parties.

Documents

16 (1) Before the date of the hearing, the tribunal shall take all reasonable steps to ensure that each of the parties is given –

    (a) a copy of any document relevant to the proceedings (or sufficient extracts from or particulars of the document) which has been received from any other party (other than a document already in his possession or one of which he has previously been supplied with a copy); and

    (b) a copy of any document which embodies the results of any relevant enquiries made by or for the tribunal for the purposes of the proceedings.

    (2) At a hearing, if a party has not previously received a relevant document or a copy of, or sufficient extracts from or particulars of, a relevant document, then unless –

    (a) that person consents to the continuation of the hearing; or

    (b) the tribunal considers that that person has a sufficient opportunity to deal with the matters to which the document relates without an adjournment of the hearing,

the tribunal shall adjourn the hearing for a period which it considers will give that person a sufficient opportunity to deal with those matters.

Inspections

17 (1) A tribunal may inspect –
  (a) the house, premises or area which is the subject of the application; or
  (b) any comparable house, premises or area to which its attention is directed.

(2) Subject to paragraph (3), the tribunal shall give the parties an opportunity to attend an inspection.

(3) The making of, and attendance at, an inspection is subject to any necessary consent being obtained.

(4) Where an inspection is to be made, the tribunal shall give notice to the parties.

(5) A notice under paragraph (4) shall –
  (a) state the date, time and place of the inspection; and
  (b) be given not less than 14 days before that date.

(8) Where an inspection is made after the close of a hearing, the tribunal may reopen the hearing on account of any matter arising from the inspection.

(9) The tribunal shall give reasonable notice of the date, time and place of the reopened hearing to the parties.

(10) Any of the requirements for notice in the preceding paragraphs may be dispensed with or relaxed –
  (a) with the consent of the parties; or
  (b) if the tribunal is satisfied that the parties have received sufficient notice.

Decisions

18 (1) This regulation applies to a decision on the determination of an application by –
  (a) a tribunal; or
  (b) a single member, as mentioned in regulation 13(5).

(2) If a hearing was held, the decision may be given orally at the end of the hearing.

(3) A decision shall, in every case, be recorded in a document as soon as possible after the decision has been made.

(4) A decision given or recorded in accordance with paragraph (2) or (3) need not record the reasons for the decision.

(5) Where the document mentioned in paragraph (3) does not record the reasons for the decision, they shall be recorded in a separate document as soon as possible after the decision has been recorded.

(6) A document recording a decision, or the reasons for a decision, shall be signed and dated by an appropriate person.

(7) An appropriate person may, by means of a certificate signed and dated by him, correct any clerical mistakes in a document or any errors arising in it from an accidental slip or omission.

(8) In this regulation, 'appropriate person' means –
  (a) where an application was determined by a single member as mentioned in regulation 13(5) –
    (i) the single member; or
    (ii) in the event of his absence or incapacity, another member of the tribunal who was appointed by the Lord Chancellor;
  (b) in any other case –

    (i) the chairman of the tribunal; or

    (ii) in the event of his absence or incapacity, another member of the tribunal.

(9) A copy of any document recording a decision, or the reasons for a decision, and a copy of any correction certified under paragraph (7) shall be sent to each party.

Enforcement

19   Any decision of the tribunal may, with the permission of the county court, be enforced in the same way as orders of such a court.

Permission to appeal

20   Where a party makes an application to a tribunal for permission to appeal to the Lands Tribunal –

  (a) the application shall be made to the tribunal within the period of 21 days starting with the date on which the document which records the reasons for the decision under regulation 18 was sent to that party; and

  (b) a copy of the application shall be served by the tribunal on every other party.

Attendance by member of Council on Tribunals

21   A member of the Council on Tribunals, who is acting in that capacity, may –

  (a) attend any hearings held, whether in public or private, in accordance with these Regulations;

  (b) attend any inspection for which any necessary consent has been obtained;

  (c) be present during, but not take part in, a tribunal's deliberations in respect of an application.

Information required by tribunal

22   Where a tribunal serves a notice requiring information to be given under paragraph 4 of Schedule 12 to the 2002 Act, the notice shall contain a statement to the effect that any person who fails without reasonable excuse to comply with the notice commits an offence and is liable on summary conviction to a fine not exceeding level 3 on the standard scale.

Notices

23 (1) Where any notice or other document is required under these Regulations to be given or sent to a person by the tribunal, it shall be sufficient compliance with the requirement if –

  (a) it is delivered or sent by pre-paid post to that person at his usual or last known address;

  (b) it is sent to that person by fax or other means of electronic communication which produces a text of the document;

  (c) where that person has appointed an agent or representative to act on his behalf –

    (i) it is delivered or sent by pre-paid post to the agent or representative at the address of the agent or representative supplied to the tribunal; or

    (ii) it is sent to the agent or representative by fax or other means of electronic communication which produces a text of the document.

(2) A notice or other document may be sent as mentioned in paragraphs (1) (b) or (c)(ii) only if that person or his agent has given his consent.

(3) A notice or other document sent as mentioned in paragraphs (1) (b) or (c)(ii) shall be regarded as sent when the text of it is received in legible form.

(4) This paragraph applies where –
   (a) an intended recipient –
      (i)   cannot be found after all diligent enquiries have been made;
      (ii) has died and has no personal representative; or
      (iii) is out of the United Kingdom; or
   (b) for any other reason a notice or other document cannot readily be given or sent in accordance with these Regulations.

(5) Where paragraph (4) applies, the tribunal may –
   (a) dispense with the giving or sending of the notice or other document; or
   (b) may give directions for substituted service in such other form (whether by advertisement in a newspaper or otherwise) or manner as the tribunal think fit.

Allowing further time

24 (1) In a particular case, the tribunal may extend any period prescribed by these Regulations, or prescribed by a notice given under these Regulations, within which anything is required or authorised to be done.

(2) A party may make a request to the tribunal to extend any such period but must do so before that period expires.

Revocation and saving

25 (1) Subject to paragraph (2) the Rent Assessment Committee (England and Wales) (Leasehold Valuation Tribunal) Regulations 1993 ('the 1993 Regulations') are hereby revoked in relation to England.

(2) The revocation in paragraph (1) shall not have effect in relation to any application made, or proceedings transferred from a court, to a tribunal before 30 September 2003.

SCHEDULE 1: DESCRIPTIONS OF APPLICATIONS

Enfranchisement and extended leases

1   Applications under –
   (a) section 21 of the Leasehold Reform Act 1967;
   (b) section 13 of the 1987 Act;
   (c) section 31 of that Act;
   (d) section 24 of the 1993 Act;
   (e) section 25 of that Act;
   (f) section 27 of that Act;
   (g) section 48 of that Act;
   (h) section 51 of that Act;
   (i) section 88 of that Act;
   (j) section 91 of that Act;
   (k) section 94 of that Act; and
   (l) paragraph 2 of Schedule 14 to that Act.

Service charges, administration charges and estate charges

2 Applications under –
   (a) section 20ZA of the 1985 Act;
   (b) section 27A of that Act;
   (c) paragraph 8 of the Schedule to that Act;
   (d) section 159 of the 2002 Act;
   (e) paragraph 3 of Schedule 11 to that Act; and
   (f) paragraph 5 of Schedule 11 to that Act.

Estate management schemes

3 Applications under Chapter 4 of Part 1 to the 1993 Act.

Right to manage

4 Applications under –
   (a) section 84 of the 2002 Act;
   (b) section 85 of that Act;
   (c) section 88 of that Act;
   (d) section 94 of that Act;
   (e) section 99 of that Act; and
   (f) paragraph 5 of Schedule 6 to that Act.

Appointment of a manager

5 Applications under –
   (a) section 22 of the Landlord and Tenant Act 1987; and
   (b) section 24 of that Act.

Variation of leases

6 Applications under Part 4 of the 1987 Act.

Cost of proceedings

7 Applications under section 20C of the 1985 Act.

Determination as to breach of covenant or condition

8 Applications under section 168(4) of the 2002 Act.

SCHEDULE 2: PARTICULARS OF APPLICATIONS

Enfranchisement and extended leases

1 (1) A copy of any notice served in relation to the enfranchisement.
   (2) The name and address of the freeholder and any intermediate landlord.
   (3) The name and address of any person having a mortgage or other charge over an interest in the premises the subject of the application held by the freeholder or other landlord.
   (4) Where an application is made under section 21(2) of the Leasehold Reform Act 1967, the name and address of the sub-tenant, and a copy of any agreement for the sub-tenancy.
   (5) Where an application is made under section 13 of the 1987 Act, the date on which the landlord acquired the property and the terms of acquisition including the sums paid.

(6) Except where an application is made under section 24, 25 or 27 of the 1993 Act, a copy of the lease.

Service charges, administration charges and estate charges

2 (1) Where an application is made under section 27A of the 1985 Act, the name and address of the secretary of any recognised tenants' association.
(2) Where an application is made under paragraph 3 of Schedule 11 to the 2002 Act, a draft of the proposed variation.
(3) A copy of the lease or, where appropriate, a copy of the estate management scheme.

Estate management charges

3 (1) A copy of any estate management agreement or the proposed estate management scheme.
(2) A statement that the applicant is either –
   (a) a natural person;
   (b) a representative body within the meaning of section 71(3) of the 1993 Act; or
   (c) a relevant authority within the meaning of section 73(5) of that Act.
(3) Where an application is made under section 70 of the 1993 Act, a copy of the notice given by the applicant under section 70(4) of that Act.
(4) Where –
   (a) approval is sought for a scheme;
   (b) approval is sought to modify the area of an existing scheme; or
   (c) approval is sought to vary an existing scheme
      a description of the area of –
      (i)   the proposed scheme;
      (ii) the proposed modification; or
      (iii) the proposed variation,
      including identification of the area by a map or plan.
(5) Where an application is made under section 70 of the 1993 Act, a copy of any consent given by the Secretary of State under section 72(1) of that Act.

Right to manage

4 (1) The name and address for service of the RTM company (within the meaning of Chapter 1 of Part 2 of the 2002 Act).
(2) The name and address of the freeholder, any intermediate landlord and any manager.
(3) A copy of the memorandum and articles of association of the RTM company.
(4) Where an application is made under section 84(3) of the 2002 Act, a copy of the claim notice and a copy of the counter notice received.
(5) Where an application is made under section 85(2) of the 2002 Act –
   (a) a statement that the requirements of sections 78 and 79 of the 2002 Act are fulfilled;
   (b) a copy of the notice given under section 85(3) of the 2002 Act together with a statement that such notice has been served on all qualifying tenants;
   (c) a statement describing the circumstances in which the landlord cannot be identified or traced.

(6) Where an application is made under section 94(3) of the 2002 Act an estimate of the amount of the accrued uncommitted service charges.

(7) Where an application is made under section 99(1) of the 2002 Act, a description of the approval sought and a copy of the relevant lease.

(8) Where an application is made under paragraph 5 of Schedule 6 to the 2002 Act, the date and circumstances in which the right to exercise the right to manage has ceased within the past four years.

Appointment of manager

5 (1) Other than where an application is made under section 22(3) of the 1987 Act, a copy of the notice served under section 22 of that Act.

(2) Where an application is made under section 24(9) of that Act, a copy of the management order.

Variation of leases

6 (1) The names and addresses of any person served with a notice in accordance with regulation 4 of these Regulations.

(2) A draft of the variation sought.

(3) A copy of the lease.

Determination of breach of covenant or condition

7 (1) A statement giving particulars of the alleged breach of covenant or condition.

(2) A copy of the lease concerned.

THE SOCIAL LANDLORDS DISCRETIONARY REDUCTION OF SERVICE CHARGES (ENGLAND) DIRECTIONS 1997

Dated February 4, 1997, the Secretary of State for the Environment in the exercise of the powers conferred upon him by sections 219 and 920 of the Housing Act 1996 and of all other powers enabling him in that behalf, hereby gives the following Directions

Citation and Commencement
These Directions may be cited as the Social Landlords Discretionary Reduction of Service Charges (England) Directions 1997 and shall come into force on 25 February 1997.

Interpretation
In these Directions –
'programme' means a programme specified in the Schedule to these Directions,
'relevant assistance' means that part of a grant or other financial assistance of any kind from any programme which is used for the costs of works of repair, maintenance or improvement.

Application
These Directions shall apply to social landlords making a service charge which is payable by a lessee in respect of a dwelling in England.

Discretion to Reduce Service Charges where Works Undertaken with Relevant Assistance
Subject to paragraph 6, where –
(a) relevant assistance is granted in respect of an application made before the date these Directions come into force, and
(b) a social landlord makes a service charge in respect of the costs of works of repair, maintenance or improvement which have been or are to be undertaken wholly or partly with such relevant assistance,
a social landlord may waive or reduce the service charge by any amount provided that the total amount of such waivers and reductions shall not exceed the total amount of relevant assistance for the costs of such works which is, in the opinion of the social landlord, attributable to the leasehold dwellings where such works have been or are to be undertaken.

Discretion to Reduce Service Charges Exceeding GBP10,000 in any Period of Five Years
Subject to paragraph 6, where service charges (whether paid or payable) exceed a total sum of GBP10,000 in respect of the same dwelling in any period of five years, a social landlord may waive or reduce such charges by any amount except that such charges shall not be waived or reduced to less than GBP10,000 in respect of the same dwelling in the same period of five years.

Criteria

The social landlord is to have regard to the following criteria in deciding whether to waive or reduce the service charge under paragraph 4 or 5 and to what extent –

(a) any estimate of the costs of the works of repair, maintenance or improvement notified to the lessee or any predecessor in title before his or their purchase of the lease of the dwelling;

(b) whether the purchase price paid by the lessee took account of the costs of the works of repair, maintenance or improvement,

(c) any benefit which a social landlord considers the lessee has received or will receive as a result of the works of repair, maintenance or improvement including an increase in the value of the lease (including a reduction in the negative value of the lease), an increase in the energy efficiency of the dwelling, an improvement in the security of the dwelling and an improvement in services or facilities,

(d) whether, upon receipt of an application by a lessee, a social landlord, having regard to the criteria set out in paragraph 7, considers that the lessee would suffer exceptional hardship in paying the service charge, and

(e) any other circumstance of the lessee which the social landlord considers relevant.

Exceptional hardship

In considering an application to reduce the service charge because of exceptional hardship a social landlord is to have regard to the following criteria –

(a) whether the dwelling is the lessee's only or principal home;

(b) the total amount of the service charges which have been paid or are payable by the lessee since the lessee's purchase of the lease of the dwelling,

(c) the amount of the service charge payable in the year in which the lessee applies for a reduction because of exceptional hardship;

(d) the financial resources available to the lessee;

(e) the ability of the lessee to raise funds to pay the service charge;

(f) the ability of the lessee to pay the service charge if the social landlord were to extend the period for payment; and

(g) any other circumstance of the lessee which the social landlord considers relevant.

Waivers and reductions

Any waiver or reduction made under any paragraph in these Directions is in addition to any other waiver or reduction which may be made.

Previous service charges

These Directions permitting the waiver or reduction of service charges shall have corresponding effect –

(a) in relation to charges already demanded so as to permit the non enforcement of the charges, and

(b) in relation to charges already paid so as to permit a refund.

THE SOCIAL LANDLORDS MANDATORY REDUCTION OF SERVICE CHARGES (ENGLAND) DIRECTIONS 1997

Dated February 4, 1997, the Secretary of State for the Environment in the exercise of the powers conferred on him by sections 219 and 220 of the Housing Act 1996 and of all other powers enabling him in that behalf, hereby gives the following Directions.

Citation, Commencement and Application
1.1 These Directions may be cited as the Social Landlords Mandatory Reduction of Service Charges (England) Directions 1997 and shall come into force on 25 February 1997.
1.2 These Directions shall apply to social landlords making a service charge which –
   (a) is payable by a lessee in respect of a dwelling in England, and
   (b) is for the costs of works of repair, maintenance or improvement undertaken wholly or partly with relevant assistance from a programme specified in paragraph 2 of these Directions,
in a case where an application for assistance from a programme is made on or after the date these Directions come into force.

Interpretation
2 In these Directions –
   'benefit' means an increase in the value of the lease (including any reduction in the negative value of the lease) which arises from the works of repair, maintenance or improvement;
   'programme' means a programme of Government assistance under section 126 of the Housing Grants, Construction and Regeneration Act 1996 which is or has been designated under the titles 'Single Regeneration Budget Challenge Fund' or 'Estates Renewal Challenge Fund';
   'relevant assistance' means that part of a grant or other financial assistance of any kind from any of the programmes which is used for the costs of works of repair, maintenance or improvement.

Mandatory Reduction of Service Charges
3.1 Subject to paragraphs 3.2 and 4 where –
   (a) a social landlord makes service charges in respect of the costs of works of repair, maintenance or improvement which have been or are to be undertaken wholly or partly with relevant assistance, and
   (b) such service charges and any service charges which the social landlord proposes subsequently to make for costs incurred in respect of such works exceed a total sum of GBP10,000 in respect of the same dwelling in any period of five years,
a social landlord shall reduce such charges to a total sum of GBP10,000 in that period of five years.
3.2 Where a social landlord considers that the works of repair, maintenance or improvement have resulted in a benefit to the same dwelling exceeding GBP10,000 in the same five year period and the social landlord has –
   (a) sent to the lessee written details of the calculation of the benefit and given

the lessee not less than 28 days from receipt of the calculation to make representations on the calculation, and

(b) considered any representations by the lessee, and

(c) sent to the lessee written notification of the decision on the lessee's representations,

subject to paragraph 4, a social landlord shall not be required to reduce charges under paragraph 3.1 provided that the social landlord shall reduce such service charges to an amount that does not exceed the benefit.

4   Where the maximum service charge to be made in respect of the same dwelling in any period of five years for the costs of works of repair, maintenance or improvement undertaken wholly or partly with relevant assistance is –

(a) specified in an application for assistance from a programme as a sum below GBP10,000, and

(b) the application is approved, and

(c) the Secretary of State agrees that the maximum service charge will be the sum specified in the application or such other sum below GBP10,000 as may be agreed by the Secretary of State;

a social landlord shall reduce any service charge so that it does not exceed the agreed sum.

Schedule: Government Assistance Programmes
Paragraph 2

Such assistance under the following statutory powers which is or has been designated under the title Estate Action (known prior to 28 November 1986 by the title of the Urban Housing Renewal Unit) –

(a) section 1 of the Local Government Grants (Social Need) Act 1969

(b) section 72 of the Local Government, Planning and Land Act 1980

(c) section 27 of the Housing and Planning Act 1986

(d) sections 54 and132 of the Local Government and Housing Act 1989

(e) section 126 of the Housing Grants, Construction and Regeneration Act 1996

Such assistance under the following statutory powers which is or has been designated under the title City Challenge–

(a) section 1 of the Local Government Grants (Social Need) Act 1969

(b) section 27 of the Housing and Planning Act 1986

(c) section 50 of the Housing Act 1988

(d) section 126 of the Housing Grants, Construction and Regeneration Act 1996

Such assistance under the following statutory powers which is or has been designated under the title Single Regeneration Budget Challenge Fund –

(a) section 11 of the Local Government Act 1966

(b) section 1 of the Local Government Grants (Social Need) Act 1969

(c) sections 2 and 3 of the Employment and Training Act 1973

(d) sections 11 and 12 of the Industrial Development Act 1982

(e) section 27 of the Housing and Planning Act 1986

(f) section 169 of the Criminal Justice and Public Order Act 1994

(g) section 126 of the Housing Grants, Construction and Regeneration Act 1996

Such assistance under the following statutory powers which is or has been designated under the title Estates Renewal Challenge Fund –
(a) section 27 of the Housing and Planning Act 1986
(b) section 126 of the Housing Grants, Construction and Regeneration Act 1996

APPENDIX B

Residential Property Tribunal Service application forms

Application for a determination of liability to pay service charges   290

Application for the determination of the liability to pay or for the variation of an administration charge   297

Application for the dispensation of all or any of the consultation requirements contained in section 20 of the Landlord and Tenant Act 1985   304

Application for the variation of a lease or leases   311

Application for a reduction or waiver of fees   318

**Residential
Property**
TRIBUNAL SERVICE

Application Form
Section 27A of the Landlord and Tenant Act 1985
Application for a determination of liability to pay service charges

This is the correct form to use if you want to ask the Leasehold Valuation Tribunal to determine the liability to pay any service charge. This includes the question of whether or not the service charge is reasonable.

Please send this application form together with the application fee and a copy of the lease to the appropriate panel office (see page 6 for panel addresses). Please do not send any other documents. If and when further evidence is needed you will be asked to send it in separately.

If you have any questions about how to fill in this form or the procedures the tribunal will use, please call us 0845 600 3178

1. DETAILS OF APPLICANT (S) (if there are multiple applicants please continue on a separate sheet)

Name:

Address (*including postcode*):

Address for correspondence (*if different*):

Telephone: *Day:*   *Evening:*   *Mobile:*

Email address: Fax:

Capacity (*e.g. landlord/tenant/managing agent*):

Representative details:

2. ADDRESS (including postcode) OF PROPERTY (if not already given)

Where details of a representative have been given, all correspondence and communications will be with them until the Tribunal is notified that they are no longer acting.

3. BRIEF DESCRIPTION OF BUILDING (e.g. *Victorian Mansion block with 12 flats*)

FORM LVT4 (5/07)

4. DETAILS OF RESPONDENT (S) (if there are multiple respondents, please continue on a separate sheet)

Name:

Address (*including postcode*):

Address for correspondence (*if different*)

Telephone: *Day:*   Evening: *Mobile:*

Email address (*if known*)   Fax:

Capacity (*e.g. landlord/manager/RTM company*):

Guidance Note

This form asks the applicant to provide the details of parties to the application. Additionally, the LVT needs to know the names and addresses of other people who may be significantly affected by the application such as other lessees in the building. Please provide a list of the names and addresses of any such person(s). If this is not possible or is impractical, then a written statement should be provided with this application.

5. DETAILS OF LANDLORD (if not already given)

Name:

Address (*including postcode*):

Telephone: *Day:*   Evening: *Mobile:*

Email address (*if known*):   Fax:

6. DETAILS OF ANY RECOGNISED TENANTS' ASSOCIATION (if known)

Name of Secretary:

Address (*including postcode*):

Telephone: *Day:*   Evening: *Mobile:*

Email address (*if known*):   Fax:

7. SERVICE CHARGES TO BE CONSIDERED BY THE TRIBUNAL

A. **Service charges for past years.**

Please list years for which a determination is sought.

1. _____   4. _____
2. _____   5. _____
3. _____   6. _____

For each service charge year, fill in one of the sheets of paper entitled **Service Charges in Question**

B. **Service charges for current or future years.**

Please list years for which a determination is sought.

1. _____   4. _____
2. _____   5. _____
3. _____   6 _____

For each service charge year, fill one of the sheets of paper entitled **Service Charges in Question**

8. OTHER APPLICATIONS

Do you know of any other cases involving either:

(a) the same or similar issues about the service charge as in this application; or

(b) the same landlord or tenant or property as in this application?

If so, please give details.

_____
_____
_____
_____
_____
_____

9. LIMITATION OF COSTS

If you are a tenant, do you wish to make a s20C application (*see Guidance Note*)   YES ☐   NO ☐

If so, why?   _____

_____
_____
_____
_____

Guidance Note

Some leases allow a landlord to recover costs incurred in connection with the proceedings before the LVT as part of the service charge. Section 20C of the Landlord and Tenant Act 1985 gives the tribunal power, on application by a tenant, to make an order preventing a landlord from taking this step. If you are a tenant you should indicate here whether you want the tribunal to consider making such an order.

10. CAN WE DEAL WITH YOUR APPLICATION WITHOUT A HEARING?

If the Tribunal thinks it is appropriate, and all the parties agree, it is possible for your application to be dealt with entirely on the basis of written representations and documents and without the need for parties to attend and make oral representations. This means you would not be liable for a hearing fee of £150 but it would also mean that you would not be able to explain your case in person.

Please let us know if you would be happy for the case to be dealt with on paper if the Tribunal thinks it appropriate.   YES ☐   NO ☐

NB: Even if you have asked for a determination on paper the Tribunal may decide that a hearing is necessary. Please go on to answer questions 11 to 13 on the assumption that a hearing will be held

11. TRACK PREFERENCES

We need to decide whether to deal with the case on the Fast Track or the Standard Track (see Guidance Note for an explanation of what a track is). Please let us know which track you think appropriate for this case.

Fast Track ☐   Standard Track ☐

Is there any special reason for urgency in this case?   YES ☐   NO ☐

If there is, please explain how urgent it is and why: _____

_____

_____

_____

Guidance Note

The Tribunal will normally deal with a case in one of three ways: on paper (see box 10 above) or "fast track",or "standard track". The fast track is designed for cases that need a hearing but are very simple and will not generate a great deal of paperwork or argument. A fast track case will usually be heard within 10 weeks of your application. You should indicate here if you think your case is very simple and can be easily dealt with. The standard track is designed for more complicated cases where there may be numerous issues to be decided or where for example, a lot of documentation is involved. A standard track case may involve the parties being invited to a Pre-Trial Review which is a meeting at which the steps that need to be taken to bring the case to a final hearing can be discussed.

12. AVAILABILITY

If there are any dates or days we must avoid during the next three months (either for your convenience or the convenience of any expert you may wish to call) please list them here.

Dates on which you will NOT be available: _____

_____

_____

13. VENUE REQUIREMENTS

Please provide details of any special requirements you or anyone who will be coming with you may have (e.g. the

use of a wheelchair and/or the presence of a translator): _____

_____

_____

_____

In London, cases are usually heard in Alfred Place which is fully wheelchair accessible. Elsewhere, hearings are held in local venues which are not all so accessible and the Clerks will find it useful to know if you or anyone you want to come to the hearing with you has any special requirements of this kind.

FORM LVT4 (5/07)

4

14. CHECKLIST

Please check that you have completed this form fully. The tribunal will not process your application until this has been done and it has both a copy of the lease and the application fee:

A copy of the lease(s) is/are enclosed. ☐

A crossed cheque or postal order for the application fee (if applicable) is enclosed. ☐

Amount of fee enclosed   £_____   Please put your name and address on the back of any cheque you send.

DO NOT send cash under any circumstances. Cash payment will not be accepted and any application accompanied by cash will be returned to the applicant.

Please ONLY send this application form, any documents listed above, the application fee and nothing else.

Guidance Note

The amount of the application fee will depend on the number of dwellings to which the application relates. To find out how much you will need to pay you should consult the following table:

Amount of Administration Charge in dipute	Application Fee
Not more than £500	*£50*
More than £500 but not more than £,1000	*£70*
More than £1,000 but not more than £5,000	*£100*
More than £5,000 but not more than £15,000	*£200*
More than £15,000	*£350*

Fees should be paid by a crossed cheque made payable to, or a postal order drawn in favour of, the Department for Communities and Local Government.

Waiver and Fees
*You will **not** be liable to pay a fee if you or your partner is in receipt of:*
* *Income Support*
* *Housing Benefit*
* *Income Based Job Seeker's Allowance*
* *A working tax credit, and either:*
    – *You or your partner receive a tax credit with a disability or severe disability element; or*
    – *You or your partner are also in receipt of a child tax credit*
* *A guarantee credit under the State Pensions Credit Act 2002*
* *A certificate issued under the Funding Code which has not been revoked or discharged and which is in respect of the proceedings before the Tribunal, the whole or part of which have been transferred from the County Court for determination by a Tribunal.*
* *A Working Tax Credit where the Gross Annual Income used to calculate the Tax Credit is £14,213 or less.*

If you wish to claim a waiver of fees you must complete another form available from the Panel office. The waiver form will not be copied to other parties in the proceedings.

If you are making several applications at the same time, even if you are using different application forms or the applications relate to different parts of the Tribunal's jurisdiction, you do not have to pay a separate fee for each application. The overall fee will be the biggest of the fees payable for each application on its own.

If you are in any doubt about the amount of fee, or have any other questions about how to fill in this form please telephone the RPTS helpline on 0845 600 3178.

15. STATEMENT OF TRUTH

I believe that the facts stated in this application are true.

Signed: Dated:

FORM LVT4 (5/07)

5

PANEL ADDRESSES

Northern Rent Assessment Panel
First Floor
26 York Street
Manchester
M1 4JB
Telephone: 0845 1002614 or 0161 237 9491
Fax: 0161 237 3656

Midland Rent Assessment Panel
Second Floor
East Wing
Ladywood House
45-46 Stephenson Street
Birmingham
B2 4DH
Telephone: 0845 1002615 or 0121 643 8336
Fax: 0121 643 7605

Eastern Rent Assessment Panel
Great Eastern House
Tenison Road
Cambridge
CB1 2TR
Telephone: 0845 1002616 or 0122 3505112
Fax: 01223 505116

London Rent Assessment Panel
10 Alfred Place
London
WC1E 7LR
Telephone: 020 7446 7700
Fax: 020 7637 1250

Southern Rent Assessment Panel
First Floor
1 Market Avenue
Chichester
Po19 1JU
Telephone: 0845 1002617 or 01243 779394
Fax: 01243 779 389

SERVICE CHARGES IN QUESTION

PLEASE USE THE SPACE BELOW TO PROVIDE INFORMATION REGARDING EACH OF THE YEARS MENTIONED IN PART 7 OF THE MAIN APPLICATION FORM.

You will be given an opportunity later to give further details of your case and to supply the Tribunal with any documents that support it. At this stage you should give a clear outline of your case so that the Tribunal understands what your application is about. **Please use one sheet per year.**

The year in question

A list of the items of service charge that are in issue (or relevant) and their value

Description of the question(s) you wish the tribunal to decide:

Any further comments you may wish to make:

Residential Property
TRIBUNAL SERVICE

Ref no. (for office use only)

Application Form

Schedule 11 to the Commonhold and Leasehold Reform Act 2002

Application for the determination of the liability to pay or for

the variation of an administration charge

This is the correct form to use if you want to ask the Leasehold Valuation Tribunal to determine liability to pay an administration charge or to vary an administration charge under paras. 5 or 3 of Schedule 11 to the Commonhold and Leasehold Reform Act 2002.

Please do not send any documents with this application form except a copy of the lease and any other documents required by section 6 of this form. If and when further evidence is needed, you will be asked to send it in separately.

If you have any questions about how to fill in this form or the procedures the Tribunal will use, please call us on 0845 600 3178.

1.   DETAILS OF APPLICANT (S) (If there are multiple applicants please continue on a separate sheet)

Name:

Address (*including postcode*):

Address for correspondence (*if different*):

Telephone: *Day:*　　　　　　　　*Evening:*　　　　　　　　*Mobile:*

Email address:　　　　　　　　　　　　　　　　*Fax:*

Capacity (*e.g. landlord/tenant/managing agent*):

Representative details:

Where the details of a representative have been given, all correspondence and communications will be with them until the Tribunal is notified that they are no longer acting.

2.   ADDRESS (including postcode) OF PROPERTY (if not already given)

3.   BRIEF DESCRIPTION OF PROPERTY (*e.g. 2 Bedroom flat in Victorian block*)

FORM LVT2 (5/07)

1

4.   DETAILS OF RESPONDENT (S) (if there are multiple Respondents please continue on a separate sheet)

Name:

Address (*including postcode*):

Address for correspondence (*if different*):

Telephone: *Day:*   *Evening:*   *Mobile:*

Email address (*if known*)

Capacity (*e.g. landlord/tenant/managing agent*):

5.   DETAILS OF LANDLORD (if not already given)

Name:

Address (*including postcode*):

Telephone: *Day:*   *Evening:*   *Mobile:*

Email address (*if known*):

6. ADMINISTRATION CHARGES TO BE CONSIDERED BY THE TRIBUNAL

This form may be used for applications for the determination of the liability to pay an administration charge or for the variation of an administration charge.

Please provide the following information on the attached sheet entitled "Administration Charge Details" (page 7) or provide the details in a separate document.

    a. The date of the lease;

    b. The clauses under which the administration charge is demanded;

    c. The grounds of the claim;

Complete a separate sheet for each administration charge challenged.

Please enclose the following documents with the application form:

    a. Copies of the relevant lease(s);

    b. Any demand(s) for the administration charge;

    c. If you wish to ask the LVT to vary the administration charge clause in the lease, a draft of the variation.

Guidance Note

An administration charge is an amount payable by a tenant of a residential property:

    a. *In connection with the grant of an approval under the lease or an application for such an approval;*

    b. *In connection with the provision of information or documents by, or on behalf of, the landlord or some other party to the lease;*

    c. *In respect of a failure to make a payment by the due date to the landlord or another party to the lease;*

    d. *In connection with a breach (or alleged breach) of a covenant or condition in the lease.*

Administration charges can be variable or fixed. A variable charge is one that is neither specified in the lease nor is calculated in accordance with a formula specified in the lease. The LVT has power only to vary fixed administration charges.

7. OTHER APPLICATIONS

Do you know of any other cases involving either: (a) the same or similar issues about an administration charge as in this application; or (b) the same landlord or tenant or property as in this application? If so please give details.

8. LIMITATION OF COSTS

If you are a tenant, do you wish to make a s20C application? (*see Guidance Note*)   YES ☐   NO ☐

If so why?

Guidance Note

Some leases allow a landlord to recover costs incurred in connection with the proceedings before the LVT as part of the service charge. Section 20C of the Landlord and Tenant Act 1985 gives the Tribunal power, on application by a tenant, to make an order preventing a landlord from taking this step. If you are a tenant you should indicate here whether you want the tribunal to consider making such an order.

FORM LVT2 (5/07)

9.   CAN WE DEAL WITH YOUR APPLICATION WITHOUT A HEARING?

If the Tribunal thinks it is appropriate, and all the parties agree, it is possible for your application to be dealt with entirely on the basis of written representations and documents and without the need for parties to attend and make oral representations. This means you would not be liable for a hearing fee of £150, but it would also mean that you would not be able to explain your case in person. Please let us know if you would be happy for your application to be dealt with in the way.

I would be happy for the case to be dealt with on paper if the Tribunal thinks it is appropriate.

YES ☐   NO ☐

NB: Even if you have asked for a determination on paper, the Tribunal may decide that a hearing is necessary. Please go on to answer questions 11 to 13 on the assumption that a hearing will be heard.

10. TRACK PREFERENCES

We need to decide whether to deal the case on the Fast Track or the Standard Track (See Guidance note for an explanation of what a track is). Please let us know which track you think appropriate for this case.

Fast Track ☐   Standard Track ☐

Is there any special reason for urgency in this case?   YES ☐   NO ☐

If there is, please explain how urgent it is and why:

_____

_____

_____

_____

Guidance Note

The Tribunal will normally deal with a case in one of three ways: on paper (see box 9 above) or "fast track", or "standard track". The fast track is designed for cases that need a hearing but are very simple and will not generate a great deal of paperwork or argument. A fast track case will usually be heard within 10 weeks of your application. You should indicate here if you think your case is very simple and can be easily dealt with. The standard track is designed for more complicated cases where there may be numerous issues to be decided or where for example, a lot of documentation is involved. A standard track case may involve the parties being invited to a Pre-Trial Review which is a meeting at which the steps that need to be taken to bring the case to a final hearing can be discussed.

11. AVAILABILITY

If there are dates or days we must avoid during the next three months (either for your convenience or the convenience of any expert you may wish to call) please list them here.

Dates on which you will NOT be available:

_____

_____

_____

12. VENUE REQUIREMENTS

Please provide details of any special requirements you or anyone who will be coming with you may have (e.g. the use of a wheelchair and/or the presence of a translator)

_____

_____

_____

In London, cases are usually heard in Alfred Place which is fully wheelchair accessible. Elsewhere, hearings are held in local venues which are not all so accessible and the Clerks will find it useful to know if you or anyone you want to come to the hearing with you has any special requirements of this kind.

FORM LVT2 (5/07)

14. CHECKLIST

Please check that you have completed this form fully. The tribunal will not process your application until this has been done. Please ensure that the following are enclosed with your application:

A copy of the lease (s) is/are enclosed. ☐

A copy of the demand (s) for the administration charge (s) is/are enclosed ☐

A draft of the variation sought (if applicable) is enclosed. ☐

A crossed cheque or postal order for the application fee (if applicable) is enclosed. ☐

Amount of fee enclosed   £ _____   Please put your name and address on the back of any cheque you send.

DO NOT send cash under any circumstances. Cash payment will not be accepted and any application accompanied by cash will be returned to the applicant.

Please ONLY send this application form, a copy of the lease, and the application fee and nothing else.

Guidance Note

The amount of the application fee will depend on the total amount of administration charge that is in dispute. To find out how much you will need to pay you should consult the following table:

Amount of Administration Charge in dispute	Application Fee
Not more than £500	£50
More than £500 but not more than £1,000	£70
More than £1,000 but not more than £5,000	£100
More than £5,000 but not more than £15,000	£200
More than £15,000	£350

Fees should be paid by a crossed cheque made payable to, or a postal order drawn in favour of, the Department for Communities and Local Government.

Waiver and Fees
*You will **not** be liable to pay a fee if you or your partner is in receipt of:*
- *Income Support*
- *Housing Benefit*
- *Income Based Job Seeker's Allowance*
- *A working tax credit, and either:*
  - *You or your partner receive a tax credit with a disability or severe disability element; or*
  - *You or your partner are also in receipt of a child tax credit*
- *A guarantee credit under the State Pensions Credit Act 2002*
- *A certificate issued under the Funding Code which has not been revoked or discharged and which is in respect of the proceedings before the Tribunal, the whole or part of which have been transferred from the County Court for determination by a Tribunal.*
- *A Working Tax Credit where the Gross Annual Income used to calculate the Tax Credit is £14,213 or less.*

If you wish to claim a waiver of fees you must complete another form available from the Panel office. The waiver form will not be copied to other parties in the proceedings.

If you are making several applications at the same time, even if you are using different application forms or the applications relate to different parts of the Tribunal's jurisdiction, you do not have to pay a separate fee for each application. The overall fee will be the biggest of the fees payable for each application on its own.

If you are in any doubt about the amount of fee, or have any other questions about how to fill in this form please telephone the RPTS helpline on 0845 600 3178.

15. STATEMENT OF TRUTH

I believe that the facts stated in this application are true.

Signed: _____   Dated: _____

FORM LVT2 (5/07)

Northern Rent Assessment Panel
1st Floor
26 York Street
Manchester
M1 4JB
Telephone: 0845 1002614 or 0161 237 9491
Fax: 0161 237 3656

Midland Rent Assessment Panel
2nd Floor
East Wing
Ladywood House
45-46 Stephenson Street
Birmingham
B2 4DH
Telephone: 0845 1002615 or 0121 643 8336
Fax: 0121 643 7605

Eastern Rent Assessment Panel
Great Eastern House
Tenison Road
Cambridge
CB1 2TR
Telephone: 0845 1002616 or 0122 3505112
Fax: 01223 505116

London Rent Assessment Panel
10 Alfred Place
London
WC1E 7LR
Telephone: 020 7446 7700
Fax: 020 7637 1250

Southern Rent Assessment Panel
1st Floor
1 Market Avenue
Chichester
Po19 1JU
Telephone: 0845 1002617 or 01243 779394
Fax: 01243 779 389

FORM LVT2 (5/07)

ADMINISTRATION CHARGE DETAILS

PLEASE USE THE SPACE BELOW TO PROVIDE INFORMATION MENTIONED IN PART 6 OF THE MAIN APPLICATION FORM.

You will be given an opportunity later to give further details of your case and to supply the Tribunal with any documents that support it. At this stage you should give a clear outline of your case so that the Tribunal understands what your application is about. Please continue on a separate sheet if necessary.

Please pick one of the following:

This is an application for the determination of the liability to pay an administration charge ☐

This is an application for the variation of an administration charge ☐

Now complete the rest of this form:

The date and term of the lease (s): _____

_____

_____

The relevant paragraphs of the lease (s): _____

_____

_____

_____

_____

_____

_____

The grounds for the application: _____

_____

_____

_____

_____

_____

_____

A draft of the variation sought (if applicable): _____

_____

_____

_____

_____

_____

FORM LVT2 (5/07)

Residential
Property
TRIBUNAL SERVICE

Ref no. (for office use only)

Application Form
Section 20ZA of the Landlord and Tenant Act 1985
Application for the dispensation of all or any of the consultation
requirements contained in section 20 of the Landlord and Tenant Act 1985

This is the correct form to use if you want to ask the Leasehold Valuation Tribunal to dispense with all or any of the consultation requirements set out in section 20 of the Landlord and Tenant Act 1985 and in the Service Charges (Consultation Requirements)(England) Regulations 2003.

Please do not send any documents with this application form other than those specified in box 14. If and when further evidence is needed you will be asked to send it in separately. **Please send this application form together with the application fee and a copy of the lease to the appropriate Panel office (see page 6 for Panel addresses).**

If you have any questions about how to fill in this form or the procedures the tribunal will use, please call us 0845 600 3178

1. DETAILS OF APPLICANT(S) (if there are multiple applicants please continue on a separate sheet)

Name:

Address (*including postcode*):

Address for correspondence (*if different*):

Telephone: *Day:*   Evening: Mobile:

Email address: Fax:

Capacity (*e.g. landlord/tenant/managing agent*):

Representative details:

Where details of a representative have been given, all correspondence and communications will be with them until the Tribunal is notified that they are no longer acting.

2. ADDRESS (including postcode) OF PROPERTY (if not already given)

3. BRIEF DESCRIPTION OF BUILDING (e.g. *Victorian Mansion block with 12 flats*)

4. DETAILS OF RESPONDENT (S) (if there are multiple respondents, please continue on a separate sheet)

Name:

Address (*including postcode*):

Address for correspondence (*if different*)

Telephone: *Day:*   *Evening:*   *Mobile:*

Email address (*if known*)   Fax:

Capacity (*e.g. landlord/manager/RTM company*):

Guidance Note

If this is an application by a landlord, then usually all tenants liable to pay a service charge for the costs in question should be joined as respondents. If tenants are not joined in this way, the landlord should provide the tribunal with a list of the names and addresses of service charge payers. If this is not possible or is impractical, then a written explanation must be provided with this application.

5. DETAILS OF LANDLORD (if not already given)

Name:

Address (*including postcode*):

Telephone: *Day:*   *Evening:*   *Mobile:*

Email address (*if known*):   Fax:

6. DETAILS OF ANY RECOGNISED TENANTS' ASSOCIATION (if known)

Name of Secretary:

Address (*including postcode*):

Telephone: *Day:*   *Evening:*   *Mobile:*

Email address (*if known*):   Fax:

306 *Leasehold disputes / appendix B*

7. DISPENSATION SOUGHT

Applicants may seek a dispensation of all or any of the consultation requirements in respect of either qualifying works or long-term agreements.

Does the application concern qualifying works?	YES ☐	NO ☐
If yes, have the works started/been carried out?	YES ☐	NO ☐
Does the application concern a qualifying long-term agreement?	YES ☐	NO ☐
If yes, has the agreement already been entered into?	YES ☐	NO ☐

For each set of qualifying works and/or qualifying long-term agreements please complete one of the sheets of paper entitled **GROUNDS FOR SEEKING DISPENSATION** (page 7)

8. OTHER APPLICATIONS

Do you know of any other cases involving either:

(a) related or similar issues about the management of this property; or

(b) the same landlord or tenant or property as in this application?

If so, please give details:

_____

_____

_____

_____

9. LIMITATION OF COSTS

If you are a tenant, do you wish to make a s20C application (*see Guidance note*)	YES ☐	NO ☐

If so, why? _____

_____

_____

Guidance Note

Some leases allow a landlord to recover costs incurred in connection with the proceedings before a LVT as part of the service charge. Section 20C of the Landlord and Tenant Act 1985 gives the Tribunal power, on application by a tenant, to make an order preventing a landlord from taking this step. If you are a tenant, you should indicate on this form whether you want the tribunal to consider making such an order.

10. CAN WE DEAL WITH YOUR APPLICATION WITHOUT A HEARING?

If the Tribunal thinks it is appropriate, and all the parties agree, it is possible for your application to be dealt with entirely on the basis of written representations and documents and without the need for parties to attend and make oral representations. This means you would not be liable for a hearing fee of £150 but it would also mean that you would not be able to explain your case in person.

Please let us know if you would be happy for the case to be dealt with on paper if the Tribunal thinks it appropriate.   YES ☐   NO ☐

NB: Even if you have asked for a determination on paper the Tribunal may decide that a hearing is necessary. Please go on to answer questions 11 to 13 on the assumption that a hearing will be held

11. TRACK PREFERENCES

We need to decide whether to deal with the case on the Fast Track or the Standard Track (see Guidance Note for an explanation of what a track is). Please let us know which track you think appropriate for this case.

Fast Track ☐   Standard Track ☐

Is there any special reason for urgency in this case?   YES ☐   NO ☐

If there is, please explain how urgent it is and why: _____

_____

_____

_____

Guidance Note

The Tribunal will normally deal with a case in one of three ways: on paper (see box 10 above) or "fast track", or "standard track". The fast track is designed for cases that need a hearing but are very simple and will not generate a great deal of paperwork or argument. A fast track case will usually be heard within 10 weeks of your application. You should indicate here if you think your case is very simple and can be easily dealt with. The standard track is designed for more complicated cases where there may be numerous issues to be decided or where for example, a lot of documentation is involved. A standard track case may involve the parties being invited to a Pre-Trial Review which is a meeting at which the steps that need to be taken to bring the case to a final hearing can be discussed.

If there are any dates or days we must avoid during the next three months (either for your convenience or the convenience of any expert you may wish to call) please list them here.

Dates on which you will NOT be available: _____

_____

_____

12. VENUE REQUIREMENTS

Please provide details of any special requirements you or anyone who will be coming with you may have (e.g. the

use of a wheelchair and/or the presence of a translator): _____

_____

_____

_____

In London, cases are usually heard in Alfred Place which is fully wheelchair accessible. Elsewhere, hearings are held in local venues which are not all so accessible and the Clerks will find it useful to know if you or anyone you want to come to the hearing with you has any special requirements of this kind.

14. CHECKLIST

Please check that you have completed this form fully. The tribunal will not process your application until this has been done. Please ensure that the following are enclosed with your application:

A copy of the lease(s) is/are enclosed. ☐

Service charge payers have been named as respondents or a list of names and addressess has been provided. ☐

A crossed cheque or postal order for the application fee (if applicable) is enclosed. ☐

Amount of fee enclosed　£_____　Please put your name and address on the back of any cheque you send.

DO NOT send cash under any circumstances. Cash payment will not be accepted and any application accompanied by cash will be returned to the applicant.

Please ONLY send this application form, any documents listed above, the application fee and nothing else.

Guidance Note

The amount of the application fee will depend on the number of dwellings to which the application relates. To find out how much you will need to pay you should consult the following table:

Number of dwellings to which application relates	Application Fee
5 or fewer dwellings	£150
Between 6 and 10 dwellings	£250
More than 10 dwellings	£350

Fees should be paid by a crossed cheque made payable to, or a postal order drawn in favour of, the Department for Communities and Local Government.

Waiver and Fees
*You will **not** be liable to pay a fee if you or your partner is in receipt of:*
- *Income Support*
- *Housing Benefit*
- *Income Based Job Seeker's Allowance*
- *A working tax credit, and either:*
  - *You or your partner receive a tax credit with a disability or severe disability element; or*
  - *You or your partner are also in receipt of a child tax credit*
- *A guarantee credit under the State Pensions Credit Act 2002*
- *A certificate issued under the Funding Code which has not been revoked or discharged and which is in respect of the proceedings before the Tribunal, the whole or part of which have been transferred from the County Court for determination by a Tribunal.*
- *A Working Tax Credit where the Gross Annual Income used to calculate the Tax Credit is £14,213 or less.*

If you wish to claim a waiver of fees you must complete another form available from the Panel office. The waiver form will not be copied to other parties in the proceedings.

If you are making several applications at the same time, even if you are using different application forms or the applications relate to different parts of the Tribunal's jurisdiction, you do not have to pay a separate fee for each application. The overall fee will be the biggest of the fees payable for each application on its own.

If you are in any doubt about the amount of fee, or have any other questions about how to fill in this form please telephone the RPTS helpline on 0845 600 3178.

15. STATEMENT OF TRUTH

I believe that the facts stated in this application are true.

Signed: _____　Dated: _____

PANEL ADDRESSES

Northern Rent Assessment Panel
First Floor
26 York Street
Manchester
M1 4JB
Telephone: 0845 1002614 or 0161 237 9491
Fax: 0161 237 3656

Midland Rent Assessment Panel
Second Floor
East Wing
Ladywood House
45-46 Stephenson Street
Birmingham
B2 4DH
Telephone: 0845 1002615 or 0121 643 8336
Fax: 0121 643 7605

Eastern Rent Assessment Panel
Great Eastern House
Tenison Road
Cambridge
CB1 2TR
Telephone: 0845 1002616 or 0122 3505112
Fax: 01223 505116

London Rent Assessment Panel
10 Alfred Place
London
WC1E 7LR
Telephone: 020 7446 7700
Fax: 020 7637 1250

Southern Rent Assessment Panel
First Floor
1 Market Avenue
Chichester
Po19 1JU
Telephone: 0845 1002617 or 01243 779394
Fax: 01243 779 389

GROUNDS FOR SEEKING DISPENSATION

PLEASE USE THE SPACE BELOW TO PROVIDE INFORMATION MENTIONED IN PART 7 OF THE MAIN APPLICATION FORM.

You will be given an opportunity later to give further details of your case and to supply the Tribunal with any documents that support it. At this stage you should give a clear outline of your case so that the Tribunal understands what your application is about. Please continue on a separate sheet if necessary.

1. Describe the qualifying works or qualifying long-term agreement concerned, stating when the works were carried out or planned to be carried out or in the case of a long-term agreement, the date that agreement was entered into or the proposed date it is to be entered into.

2. Describe the consultation that has been carried out or is proposed to be carried out.

3. Explain why you seek dispensation of all or any of the consultation requirements.

**Residential
Property**
TRIBUNAL SERVICE

Ref no. (for office use only)

Application Form

Part IV Landlord and Tenant Act 1987

Application for the variation of a lease or leases

This is the correct form to use if you want to ask the Leasehold Valuation Tribunal to vary a lease or leases under Part IV of the Landlord and Tenant Act 1987.

Please do not send any documents with this application form other than those specified in paragraph 5. If and when further evidence is needed you will be asked to send it in separately. **Please send this application form together with the application fee and a copy of the lease to the appropriate panel office (see page 6 for panel addresses).**

If you have any questions about how to fill in this form or the procedures the tribunal will use, please call us 0845 600 3178

1. DETAILS OF APPLICANT (S) (if there are multiple applicants please continue on a separate sheet)

Name:

Address (*including postcode*):

Address for correspondence (*if different*):

Telephone: *Day:*   *Evening:*   *Mobile:*

Email address: Fax:

Capacity (*e.g. landlord/tenant/managing agent*):

Representative details:

Where details of a representative have been given, all correspondence and communications will be with them until the Tribunal is notified that they are no longer acting.

2. ADDRESS (including postcode) OF PROPERTY (if not already given)

3. BRIEF DESCRIPTION OF BUILDING (e.g. *Victorian Mansion block with 12 flats*)

FORM LVT5 (6/06)

1

4. DETAILS OF RESPONDENT(S) (All other current parties to the lease(s) must be made respondents. If there are multiple respondents please continue below and on a separate sheet if required).

Name:

Address (*including postcode*):

Address for correspondence (*if different*)

Telephone: *Day:*   *Evening:*   *Mobile:*

Email address *(if known)*   *Fax:*

Capacity (*e.g. landlord/manager/RTM company*):

RESPONDENT(S) (continued)

Name:

Address (*including postcode*):

Address for correspondence (*if different*)

Telephone: *Day:*   *Evening:*   *Mobile:*

Email address *(if known)*   *Fax:*

Capacity (*e.g. landlord/manager/RTM company*):

Name:

Address (*including postcode*):

Address for correspondence (*if different*)

Telephone: *Day:*   *Evening:*   *Mobile:*

Email address *(if known)*   *Fax:*

Capacity (*e.g. landlord/manager/RTM company*):

FORM LVT5 (6/06)

5. LEASE VARIATION(S) TO BE CONSIDERED BY THE TRIBUNAL

This form may be used for applications under section 35, 36, 37 and 40 of the Landlord and Tenant Act 1987.

Please provide the following information on the attached sheet entitled "Lease Variation Details" or provide the details in a separate document.

(a) The date of the lease.

(b) The relevant terms of the lease, including any previous variation(s).

(c) A draft of the variation sought.

(d) The grounds of the claim.

Please enclose the following documents with the application form:

(a) Copies of the relevant lease(s).

(b) A list of the names and address of every person likely to be affected by the claim and a statement that each of those persons has been served with notice of the application (*see Guidance Note*).

Guidance Note

Section 35 of the Landlord and tenant Act 1987 and the LVT regulations require applicants to notify all persons known to him or her who are likely to be affected by the application that it is being made. Persons who are likely to be affected may include (but are not limited to) other lessees in the same block of flats or any mortgagee or superior landlord.

6. OTHER APPLICATIONS

Do you know of any other cases involving either:

(a) the same or similar issues about the variation of a lease or leases as in this application; or

(b) the same landlord or tenant or tenant or property as in this application?

If so, please give details.

_____

_____

_____

_____

_____

_____

7. LIMITATION OF COSTS

If you are a tenant, do you wish to make a s20C application (*see Guidance Note*)   YES ☐   NO ☐

If so, why?

_____

_____

_____

Guidance Note

Some leases allow a landlord to recover costs incurred in connection with the proceedings before the LVT as part of the service charge. Section 20C of the Landlord and Tenant Act 1985 gives the tribunal power, on application by a tenant, to make an order preventing a landlord from taking this step. If you are a tenant you should indicate here whether you want the tribunal to consider making such an order.

FORM LVT5 (6/06)

3

8. CAN WE DEAL WITH YOUR APPLICATION WITHOUT A HEARING?

If the Tribunal thinks it is appropriate, and all the parties agree, it is possible for your application to be dealt with entirely on the basis of written representations and documents and without the need for parties to attend and make oral representations. This means you would not be liable for a hearing fee of £150 but it would also mean that you would not be able to explain your case in person.

Please let us know if you would be happy for your application to be dealt with on paper if　YES ☐　　NO ☐
the Tribunal thinks it appropriate.

NB: Even if you have asked for a determination on paper the Tribunal may decide that a hearing is necessary. Please go on to answer questions 11 to 13 on the assumption that a hearing will be held

9. TRACK PREFERENCES

We need to decide whether to deal with the case on the Fast Track or the Standard Track (see Guidance Note for an explanation of what a track is). Please let us know which track you think appropriate for this case.

Fast Track　☐　　　　Standard Track　☐

Is there any special reason for urgency in this case?　　　　　　　　YES ☐　　NO ☐

If there is, please explain how urgent it is and why:　_____

_____

_____

_____

Guidance Note

The Tribunal will normally deal with a case in one of three ways: on paper (see box 8 above) or "fast track" or "standard track". The fast track is designed for cases that need a hearing but are very simple and will not generate a great deal of paperwork or argument. A fast track case will usually be heard within 10 weeks of your application. You should indicate here if you think your case is very simple and can be easily dealt with. The standard track is designed for more complicated cases where there may be numerous issues to be decided or where for example, a lot of documentation is involved. A standard track case may involve the parties being invited to a Pre-Trial Review which is a meeting at which the steps that need to be taken to bring the case to a final hearing can be discussed.

10. AVAILABILITY

If there are any dates or days we must avoid during the next three months (either for your convenience or the convenience of any expert you may wish to call) please list them here.

Dates on which you will NOT be available:　_____

_____

_____

11. VENUE REQUIREMENTS

Please provide details of any special requirements you or anyone who will be coming with you may have (e.g. the

use of a wheelchair and/or the presence of a translator):　_____

_____

_____

_____

In London, cases are usually heard in Alfred Place which is fully wheelchair accessible. Elsewhere, hearings are held in local venues which are not all so accessible and the Clerks will find it useful to know if you or anyone you want to come to the hearing with you has any special requirements of this kind.

FORM LVT5 (6/06)

12. CHECKLIST

Please check that you have completed this form fully. The tribunal will not process your application until this has been done. Please ensure that the following are enclosed with your application:

A copy of the lease(s) is/are enclosed. ☐

A list of the names and address of persons affected and served with notice of this application is enclosed. ☐

A draft of the variation(s) sought is enclosed.

Amount of fee enclosed £ _____ Please put your name and address on the back of any cheque you send.

DO NOT send cash under any circumstances. Cash payment will not be accepted and any application accompanied by cash will be returned to the applicant.

Please ONLY send this application form, any documents listed above, the application fee and nothing else.

Guidance Note

The amount of the application fee will depend on the number of dwellings to which the application relates. To find out how much you will need to pay you should consult the following table:

Number of dwellings to which application relates	Application Fee
5 or fewer dwellings	£150
Between 6 and 10 dwellings	£250
More than 10 dwellings	£350

Fees should be paid by a crossed cheque made payable to, or a postal order drawn in favour of, the Department for Communities and Local Government.

Waiver and Fees

*You will **not** be liable to pay a fee if you or your partner is in receipt of:*
- *Income Support*
- *Housing Benefit*
- *Income Based Job Seeker's Allowance*
- *A working tax credit, and either:*
  - *You or your partner receive a tax credit with a disability or severe disability element; or*
  - *You or your partner are also in receipt of a child tax credit*
- *A guarantee credit under the State Pensions Credit Act 2002*
- *A certificate issued under the Funding Code which has not been revoked or discharged and which is in respect of the proceedings before the Tribunal, the whole or part of which have been transferred from the County Court for determination by a Tribunal.*
- *A Working Tax Credit where the Gross Annual Income used to calculate the Tax Credit is £14,213 or less.*

If you wish to claim a waiver of fees you must complete another form available from the Panel office. The waiver form will not be copied to other parties in the proceedings.

If you are making several applications at the same time, even if you are using different application forms or the applications relate to different parts of the Tribunal's jurisdiction, you do not have to pay a separate fee for each application. The overall fee will be the biggest of the fees payable for each application on its own.

If you are in any doubt about the amount of fee, or have any other questions about how to fill in this form please telephone the RPTS helpline on 0845 600 3178.

13. STATEMENT OF TRUTH

I believe that the facts stated in this application are true.

Signed: _____ Dated: _____

FORM LVT5 (6/06)

Northern Rent Assessment Panel
First Floor
26 York Street
Manchester
M1 4JB
Telephone: 0845 1002614 or 0161 237 9491
Fax: 0161 237 3656

Midland Rent Assessment Panel
Second Floor
East Wing
Ladywood House
45-46 Stephenson Street
Birmingham
B2 4DH
Telephone: 0845 1002615 or 0121 643 8336
Fax: 0121 643 7605

Eastern Rent Assessment Panel
Great Eastern House
Tenison Road
Cambridge
CB1 2TR
Telephone: 0845 1002616 or 0122 3505112
Fax: 01223 505116

London Rent Assessment Panel
10 Alfred Place
London
WC1E 7LR
Telephone: 020 7446 7700
Fax: 020 7637 1250

Southern Rent Assessment Panel
First Floor
1 Market Avenue
Chichester
Po19 1JU
Telephone: 0845 1002617 or 01243 779394
Fax: 01243 779 389

FORM LVT5 (6/06)

6

LEASE VARIATION DETAILS

PLEASE USE THE SPACE BELOW TO PROVIDE INFORMATION REGARDING EACH OF THE YEARS MENTIONED IN PART 5 OF THE MAIN APPLICATION FORM.

You will be given an opportunity later to give further details of your case and to supply the Tribunal with any documents that support it. At this stage you should give a clear outline of your case so that the Tribunal understands what your application is about. Please continue on a separate sheet if neceassry.

The application is made under the Landlord and Tenant Act 1987

Section 35 ☐   Section 37 ☐

Section 36 ☐   Section 40 ☐

The grounds of the claim

The date and term of the lease(s)

The relevant terms of the lease(s)

A draft of the variation sought

FORM LVT5 (6/06)

7

Residential Property
TRIBUNAL SERVICE

Ref no. (for office use only)

Application to the Leasehold Valuation Tribunal – (LVT)

Application for reduction or waiver of fees

Regulation 8 of The Leasehold Valuation Tribunals (Fees) (England) Regulations 2003

1. DETAILS OF PROPERTY / APPLICANT

Address of property (*including postcode*):

Applicant name:

Applicant address (*including postcode*):

Date of application to LVT:

(A)

Do you, or your partner [1], have a current Public Funding (legal aid) Certificate issued in respect of the relevant proceedings which have been transferred from the County Court? If so, please send a copy to the LVT. You do not need to fill in the rest of this form.

YES ☐   NO ☐

Or

(B)

Are you, or your partner [1], in receipt of any of the following benefits?

	YOU	YOUR PARTNER
Income Support	☐	☐
Housing Benefit	☐	☐
Income-based Job Seeker's Allowance	☐	☐
Tax credit which is combined with:	☐	☐
A disability or a severe disability element (or both)	☐	☐
Child tax Credit	☐	☐
Tax Credit where the Gross Annual Income used to calculate the Tax Credit is £14,213 or less	☐	☐
Pension Credit under the State Pensions Credit Act 2002	☐	☐
(Previously referred to as the Minimum Income Guarantee)		

To allow us to assess your claim, we require confirmation from the Benefits Agency or Local Authority of your entitlement to the benefit(s) indicated above. To do this you can either take the form to your local Benefits Agency office, Jobcentre or Local Authority Office. Alternatively, return the forms to the LVT and we will send the form to the relevant Benefit or Local Authority office for confirmation.

Note [1]: *'Partner' means the applicant's spouse or a person of the opposite sex with whom he or she lives as husband and wife or a person of the same sex with whom he or she lives in a relationship which has the characteristics of the relationship between husband and wife.*

FORM LVT1 (6/06)

1

2. AGREEMENT TO PROVIDE THE LEASEHOLD VALUATION TRIBUNAL WITH DETAILS OF BENEFIT CLAIM(S)

(The person in receipt of the benefit must complete and sign this section).

I agree that the Benefits Agency/Local Authority may confirm to the Leasehold Valuation Tribunal that I was in receipt of the following benefit on the date of an application to the LVT by me or my partner. This is to verify a claim to waive fees payable for a LVT application.

Alternatively, the person in receipt of benefit can supply a current notice of entitlement to benefit. This will need to be the original that, if posted, will be returned immediately by the LVT office.

Type of Benefit received: _____

Address of Office where benefit is claimed: _____

_____

_____

_____

My name (IN CAPITALS): _____

My Signature: _____

My address (IN CAPITALS): _____

_____

_____

_____

My National Insurance Number: _____

or Local Authority reference number (for Housing Benefit): _____

3. FOR BENEFIT AGENCY / LOCAL AUTHORITY COMPLETION

I certify that the above named benefit customer was in receipt of _____

(specify benefit) on _____ (date of application to LVT), located on page 1 of this form

If benefit has ceased please give last date of entitlement : _____

Signed: _____

Section: _____   Telephone number: _____

Office Stamp

Form to be returned after completion to:

FORM LVT1 (6/06)

2

RPTS guidance on tenants' associations[1]

TENANTS' ASSOCIATIONS

What is a Tenants' Association?

A Tenants' Association is a group of tenants (lessees) who hold houses or flats on tenancies/leases from the same landlord upon similar terms which contain provisions for the payment of variable service charges. To be wholly effective an association needs to be formally recognised.

What is the role of a Recognised Tenants' Association?

The members will have come to ether to represent their common interest so that the association can with their consent and on their behalf:

- ask for a summary of costs incurred by their landlord in connection with matters for which they are being required to pay a service charge;
- inspect the relevant accounts and receipts;
- be sent a copy of estimates obtained by the landlord for intended work to their properties;
- propose names of contractors for inclusion in any tender list when the landlord wishes to carry out major works;
- ask for a written summary of the insurance cover and inspect the policy; and
- be consulted about the appointment or re-appointment of the agent managing the services.

How does an association become recognised?

There are two ways of seeking recognition. The first of these is for an association to ask the landlord for written notice of recognition. If this is given, then no further steps to establish recognition need be taken. Such recognition cannot be withdrawn by the landlord without first giving at least six months' notice to the association. If however the landlord refuses or withdraws recognition, then the association can apply for recognition to one of the five Rent Assessment Panels which constitute the Residential Property Tribunal Service (RPTS) and in whose region the properties are located. A list of the panels and their addresses is given on the contacts page [of the RPTS website].

---

1 Reproduced with the kind permission of the Residential Property Tribunal Service. See www.rpts.gov.uk/pubs_and_forms/html_docs/tenass.htm

How is application for recognition made to a panel?

An application form can be obtained from a panel office. The association will need to supply with its application:

(a) a copy of the association's constitution ('rules');
(b) a list of subscribing members 'names and their addresses;
(c) the name and address of the landlord;
(d) a description of the properties whose tenants will be eligible for membership (ie, flats/houses) and their addresses; and
(e) copies of any relevant previous correspondence with the landlord regarding recognition of the Association.

It should be noted that it is the panels' practice to pass copies of documentation received from a party to any other interested party. It follows that correspondence written 'without prejudice' or 'in confidence' cannot be accepted.

Who will deal with the matter?

In the first instance, the application will be dealt with by the clerks who comprise the administrative staff of the panel. They will deal with all correspondence and will continue to deal with the paperwork until the final decision is reached. Clerks are able to speak to you about the processes and procedures relating to the application. They cannot however give legal advice or advise you about the law relating to your application.

Consideration of the application and the decision as to whether recognition should be granted will be made by a member of the panel nominated by the panel President or by the President personally. He or she will be a qualified lawyer or valuer (a surveyor with experience of the management of housing property).

Will recognition be given automatically?

No. The panel has a discretion as to whether recognition should be granted and will need to be satisfied that the Rules of the Association are fair and democratic – also that the actual membership of the Association will represent a significant proportion of the potential membership. As a general rule, the panel would expect the membership to be not less than 60 per cent of those qualifying to join the association.

What is meant by fair and democratic?

The panel will need to be satisfied that the rules cover the following matters, among others:

• openness of membership – election of a secretary, chairman and any other officers;
• payment and the amount of the subscription – obligatory annual meetings;
• notices of meetings – voting arrangements and quorum (only one vote per flat or house will be permitted); and
• independence from the landlord.

What form should the association's rules take?

The annex to this guidance contains a set of model rules which you may find helpful in drawing up your own constitution. They may need modification to suit the particular circumstances of your association and there is no obligation to adopt them. You may prefer to draft your own rules, but you must ensure that they meet the essential criteria set out in the previous paragraph.

Who will be eligible for membership of the association?

There is no precise definition of tenants' qualifications and each case must be considered on its merits. Basically a member must be contributing to the payment of a service charge levied by a landlord and which the landlord can, under the terms of similar leases/tenancies, vary from time to time to meet expenditure incurred or to be incurred in the maintenance, repair or insurance of a block or estate of dwellings in the landlord's ownership. Tenants paying fixed rents which incorporate a non-variable service charge will not qualify for membership. Membership will not be open to landlords personally nor to persons connected with them (eg, employees of the landlord).

Tenants of shops or similar business premises (unless their tenancies incorporate residential accommodation) would not usually qualify. Membership of an association may be extended to other individuals with a common interest (for example sub tenants) but they will not have voting rights and cannot be party to the proceedings of the association in its role as a Recognised Tenants' Association.

How is recognition by a panel given and for how long will it last?

The panel member appointed to consider the application will consider all the documentation submitted including any submission made by the landlord. If that member is satisfied that recognition should be granted, he or she will issue a Certificate of Recognition. The length of validity of the certificate is at the panel's discretion but will usually be for four years. When the certificate expires, the association can apply for renewal. It is open to the panel to cancel a certificate at any time if it is considered that for some reason the association no longer merits recognition.

Can an estate have more than one recognised association?

In certain circumstances, more than one association will be recognised where there is no duplication and the interests of tenants can be seen to differ – for example separate blocks of flats (but not separate associations representing tenants in the same block).

Why form a tenants' association?

A landlord can be required to consult a recognised association regarding such matters as service charges and management which would not be so in the case of individual tenants. It should also be helpful to a landlord to consult with an association rather than to have to go to the greater trouble and expense of dealing with individual tenants.

What if there is a change of landlord?

The association with a current Certificate of Recognition should serve a notice on the new landlord if it still wishes to be consulted indicating the existence of a certificate.

If the association is unhappy with the administration of its application to the panel, to whom should it complain?

If you have a complaint about the work of the panel you should write to the panel's President. You will receive an acknowledgement within two days of receipt of your complaint. A further appeal may be made from the decision of a President to a panel constituted from the RPTS Management Board. Such appeals should be addressed to:

The Senior President
RPTS
10 Alfred Place
London WC1E 7LR

A full reply will follow within fifteen working days or you will be advised of the delay. If you remain dissatisfied, you are entitled to ask your MP to ask the Parliamentary Ombudsman to investigate your complaint.

What will it cost to make the application?

No charge is made by the panel but each party must meet their own costs.

Annex

SAMPLE DRAFT CONSTITUTION FOR AN ASSOCIATION OF TENANTS SEEKING RECOGNITION UNDER SECTION 29 OF THE LANDLORD AND TENANT ACT 1985

1   Name
The name of the Association shall be the 'The _____ Residents' Association '('the Association').

2   The property
All of the (houses and)flats, amenity areas and common areas of and at the premises known as

3   Objects of the Association
3.1 To promote and protect the common rights and interests of the members of the Association relating to the use and enjoyment of the Property.

3.2 To exercise the rights conferred upon the Association by recognition under the Landlord and Tenant Act 1985 or such other statutory rights that may be given by any subsequent enactment.

4   Membership
4.1 Membership shall be open to all persons who are lessees holding under long leases of a (house or) flat in the Property but voting shall be restricted to one vote for each (house or) flat.

4.2 Membership of the Association shall terminate:

4.2.1 upon a member giving written notice to that effect to the Honorary Secretary.

4.2.2 upon a member ceasing to be a lessee of a (house or) flat at the Property.

4.2.3 upon failure by a member to pay the annual subscription in respect of that (house or)flat for three months after the same shall become due and payable.

4.3 Membership of the Association shall be confirmed upon the payment of the first subscription and formal acceptance by the proposed member of the rules and constitution of the Association.

4.4 A copy of this constitution shall be given to each member.

4.5 The Committee may at its discretion extend associate membership to any other person or persons resident on the Property but such associate members shall not be elected as Officers or members of the Committee of the Association and shall not be entitled to any vote.

4.6 Neither the Landlord, the Landlord 's representative, any company controlled by the Landlord nor any employee of the Landlord shall be a member or associate of the Association.

5   The Officers

5.1 The Officers of the Association shall comprise a Chairman, Honorary Secretary and Honorary Treasurer who shall be members of the Association.

5.2 The Officers shall be elected annually at the Annual General Meeting and shall serve for one year but may be re-elected.

6   The Committee

6.1 The Committee of the Association shall consist of not less than (three)nor more than (five)members of the Association and the Officers of the Association.

6.2 The Committee members shall serve for three years and shall retire in rotation. Retiring Committee members may be re-elected without re-nomination.

6.3 The Committee shall be empowered to co-opt on a temporary basis other members of the Association to form sub-committees to consider such matters as the Committee or the Association shall determine and the decisions of such sub-committees shall be ratified by the Committee before implementation.

6.4 A quorum for any meeting of the Committee shall be at least ()of whom at least two must be Officers.

6.5 The Committee shall implement the objects of the Association and the resolutions of the Association.

7   Elections

7.1 The election of the Officers and Committee shall take place at the Annual General Meeting.

7.2 Nominations for the appointment of Officers and for membership of the Committee shall be proposed and seconded by two members of the Association in writing and lodged with the Honorary Secretary fourteen days prior to the Annual General Meeting and shall include the written consent of the nominee.

7.3 The Committee shall be empowered to fill any casual vacancy occurring on the Committee or among the Officers and any person so appointed shall serve until the next Annual General Meeting of the Association.

8   Finances

8.1 The financial year of the Association shall end on _____ in each year.

8.2 Accounts shall be prepared for the Association each year and these shall be audited in accordance with proper audit practice.

8.3 Auditors shall be appointed at the Annual General Meeting. Officers and Committee members shall not be eligible for appointment as auditors.

8.4 The Accounts shall be ratified by the Association at the Annual General Meeting.

8.5 The property and funds of the Association shall be held and administered by the Committee.

8.6 A resolution of the Committee shall be sufficient authority for payments or the incurring of liability for payments up to a limit not exceeding ( )hundred pounds. Beyond such limit the Committee shall seek approval of such expenditure by the Association either at the Annual General Meeting or at an Extraordinary General Meeting.

8.7 A banking account shall be opened in the name of the Association and all cheques shall be signed by an Officer and countersigned by a member of the Committee.

8.8 The annual subscription of the Association shall be decided for the ensuing year at the Annual General Meeting but shall not be altered save by a two-thirds majority of the members attending such a meeting.

9   Meetings

9.1 The Annual General Meeting of the Association shall be held not later than three months from the end of the financial year.

9.2 An Extraordinary General Meeting of the Association shall be convened at any time by the Honorary Secretary either upon the written instructions of the Committee or upon a written request signed by no fewer than (ten) members of the Association.

Useful addresses

TRIBUNAL OFFICES
Website: www.rpts.gov.uk

Corporate unit
Residential Property Tribunal Service
10 Alfred Place
London WC1E 7LR

Tel: 020 7446 7751 or 020 7446 7752
Fax: 020 7580 5684
E-mail: rptscorporateunit@communities.gsi.gov.uk

London Rent Assessment Panel
Residential Property Tribunal Service
10 Alfred Place
London WC1E 7LR

Tel: 020 7446 7700
Fax: 020 7637 1250
E-mail: london.rap@communities.gsi.gov.uk
DX: 134205 Tottenham Court Road 2

This office covers all the London boroughs.

Northern Rent Assessment Panel
Residential Property Tribunal Service
1st Floor
26 York Street
Manchester M1 4JB

Tel: 0845 100 2614 or 0161 237 9491
Fax: 0161 237 3656
E-mail: northern.rap@communities.gsi.gov.uk

This office covers the following metropolitan districts: Bolton, Bury, Manchester, Oldham, Rochdale, Salford, Stockport, Tameside, Trafford, Wigan, Knowsley, Liverpool, St Helens, Sefton, Wirral, Barnsley, Doncaster, Rotherham, Sheffield, Gateshead, Newcastle upon Tyne, North Tyneside, South Tyneside, Sunderland, Bradford, Calderdale, Kirklees, Leeds and Wakefield.

It also covers the following unitary authorities: Hartlepool, Middlesbrough, Redcar and Cleveland, Darlington, Halton, Blackburn with Darwen, Blackpool, Kingston upon Hull, East Riding of Yorkshire, North-east Lincolnshire, North Lincolnshire, Stockton-on-Tees, Warrington and York.

It also covers the following counties: Cheshire, Cumbria, Durham, Lancashire, Lincolnshire, Northumberland and North Yorkshire.

Midland Rent Assessment Panel
Residential Property Tribunal Service
2nd Floor
East Wing
Ladywood House
45–46 Stephenson Street
Birmingham B2 4DH

Tel: 0845 100 2615 or 0121 643 8336
Fax: 0121 643 7605
E-mail: midland.rap@communities.gsi.gov.uk

This office covers the following metropolitan districts: Birmingham, Coventry, Dudley, Sandwell, Solihull, Walsall and Wolverhampton.

It also covers the following unitary authorities: Derby, Leicester, Rutland, Nottingham, Herefordshire, Telford and Wrekin and Stoke on Trent.

It also covers the following counties: Derbyshire, Leicestershire, Nottinghamshire, Shropshire, Staffordshire, Warwickshire and Worcestershire.

Eastern Rent Assessment Panel
Residential Property Tribunal Service
Great Eastern House
Tenison Road
Cambridge CB1 2TR

Tel: 0845 100 2616 or 01223 505112
Fax: 01223 505116
E-mail: eastern.rap@communities.gsi.gov.uk

This office covers the following unitary authorities: Bracknell Forest, West Berkshire, Reading, Slough, Windsor and Maidenhead, Wokingham, Luton, Peterborough, Milton Keynes, Southend on Sea and Thurrock.

It also covers the following counties: Bedfordshire, Buckinghamshire, Cambridgeshire, Essex, Hertfordshire, Norfolk, Northamptonshire, Oxfordshire and Suffolk.

Southern Rent Assessment Panel
Residential Property Tribunal Service
1st Floor
1 Market Avenue
Chichester PO19 1JU

Tel: 0845 100 2617
Fax: 01243 779389
E-mail: southern.rap@communities.gsi.gov.uk

This office covers the following unitary authorities: Bath and North-east Somerset, Bristol, North Somerset, South Gloucestershire, Bournemouth, Plymouth, Torbay, Poole, Swindon, Medway, Brighton and Hove, Portsmouth, Southampton and the Isle of Wight.

It also covers the following counties: Cornwall and the Isles of Scilly, Devon, Dorset, East Sussex, Gloucestershire, Hampshire, Kent, Somerset, Surrey, West Sussex and Wiltshire.

OTHER USEFUL CONTACT DETAILS

Association of Retirement Housing Managers (ARHM)
Southbank House
Black Prince Road
London SE1 7SJ

Tel: 020 7463 0660
E-mail: enquiries@arhm.org
Website: arhm.org

BPP Legal Advice Clinics
BPP Law School
Whitehall II
Whitehall Quay
Leeds LS1 4HG

Tel: 0113 386 8267

BPP Law School
68–70 Red Lion Street
London WC1R 4NY

Tel: 020 7430 5668
Fax: 020 7831 4561
E-mail: BLAC@bppls.com

BPP Law School
2nd Floor
St James's Building
Oxford Street
Manchester M1 6FQ

Tel: 0161 235 7180
E-mail: blacm@bpplaw.co.uk

BPP Mediation Friends Project
BPP Law School
68–70 Red Lion Street
London WC1R 4NY

Tel: 020 7430 5668
Fax: 020 7831 4561
E-mail: mediation@bpplaw.co.uk

Companies House
Crown Way
Maindy
Cardiff CF14 3UZ

Tel: 0870 33 33 636
E-mail: enquiries@companies-house.gov.uk
Website: www.companieshouse.gov.uk

Lands Tribunal
Procession House
110 New Bridge Street
London EC4V 6JL

Tel: 020 7029 9780
Fax: 020 7029 9781
E-mail: lands@dca.gsi.gov.uk
Website: www.landstribunal.gov.uk

LEASE – the Leasehold Advisory Service
31 Worship Street
London EC2A 2DX
(appointment only)

Tel: 020 7374 5380
Fax: 020 7374 5373
E-mail: info@lease-advice.org
Website: www.lease-advice.org

The telephone lines are open Monday to Friday from 9.30 am to 3.30 pm.

Royal Institute of Chartered Surveyors
RICS Contact Centre
Surveyor Court
Westwood Way
Coventry CV4 8JE

Tel: 0870 333 1600
Fax: 020 7334 3811
E-mail: contactrics@rics.org
Website: www.rics.org

Tribunal Representation Service
College of Law
14 Store Street
London WC1E 7DE

Tel: 01483 216528
E-mail: ssadvice.centre@lawcol.co.uk

Index

Abuse of process
  costs, 13.90–13.91
  dismissal of applications
    generally, 13.51–13.56
    inherent jurisdiction, 13.57
Address for service
  information rights, 3.19–3.20
Adjournment
  generally, 13.86–13.87
Administration charges
  see also **Information rights; Service charges**
  advice for tenants, 6.4–6.5
  definition, 6.10–6.13
  estate management schemes, 6.43–6.46
  forfeiture for non-payment, 10.32–10.36
  formulae for calculation, 6.19–6.24
  introduction, 6.1–6.3
  LVT applications
    non-variable charges, 6.25–6.31
    variable charges, 6.32–6.42
  LVT jurisdiction, 1.13
  managers, appointment of, 8.43–8.44
  practical issues, 6.14–6.18
  purpose of regulation, 6.6–6.9
  right to buy/acquire, 11.9
  types, 6.19–6.24
Appeals
  Court of Appeal, 13.111
  Lands Tribunal
    cross-appeals, 13.109–13.110
    generally, 13.99
    judicial review of refusal of permission, 13.112
    permission, 13.100–13.105
    review/re-hearing, 13.106–13.108

Appointment of managers
  see **Managers, appointment of**
Apportionment
  service charges, 2.33–2.39
Approvals
  RTM companies, 9.95–9.100
Audits
  management audits, 3.53–3.62

Breach of covenant
  see also **Forfeiture**
  appointment of managers, 8.37–8.39
  determination by LVT, 13.20–13.21
Budgets
  RTM companies, 9.60
Bundles of documents
  LVT applications, 13.81

Chair
  generally, 1.2, 13.66
Change of landlord
  information rights, 3.14–3.16
Charities
  appointment of managers, 8.29
Compensation
  variation of leases, 7.34
Consolidated applications
  generally, 13.45–13.49
Consultation
  see also **Service charges (consultation)**
  appointment of managers, 3.69–3.75, 8.73–8.80
  right to buy/acquire, 11.10
Costs
  introduction, 13.89
  lease provisions, 13.92–13.94

Costs *continued*
power to award, 13.90–13.91
reimbursement, 13.95
Costs summaries
see **Summaries of costs**
Court of Appeal
appeals from Lands Tribunal,
13.111
Cross-appeals
generally, 13.109–13.110
Crown interests
appointment of managers, 8.30

Directions
generally, 13.61–13.62
Disclosure
generally, 13.80
Dismissal of applications
generally, 13.51–13.56
inherent jurisdiction, 13.57

Enforcement
LVT decisions, 13.96–13.98
Estate management schemes
administration charges, 6.43–6.46
Estimates
service charges
generally, 4.40–4.42
nomination of persons, 4.46–
4.58
old rules, 4.14–4.18
Evidence
bundles, 13.81
disclosure, 13.80
new evidence, 13.83–13.84
oral evidence, 13.82
witness statements, 13.82

Fast track
allocation, 13.38
Fees
application fees, 13.28–13.29
exemptions, 13.27
generally, 13.25–13.26
hearing fees, 13.30
multiple applicants, 13.31
reimbursement, 13.95
transfer fees, 13.8
waiver, 13.32–13.33
Forfeiture
advice for tenants, 10.2

breach of covenant
generally, 10.27–10.29
limitations on right to forfeit,
10.30–10.31
court orders, 10.13
definition, 10.3–10.5
exercise of right, 10.12–10.13
introduction, 10.1
LVT jurisdiction, 10.37–10.42
non-payment of administration/
service charges, 10.32–10.36
non-payment of rent
generally, 10.17–10.18
notice of rent being due, 10.19–
10.23
small amounts/periods, 10.24–
10.26
offences, 10.13
relief, 10.14–10.16
right to forfeit, 10.6
waiver, 10.7–10.11
Frivolous applications
costs, 13.90–13.91
dismissal, 13.51–13.56
Funding of applications
advice for tenants, 12.4–12.6
introduction, 1.23, 12.1–12.3
legal aid
availability, 12.7
exceptional cases, 12.12–12.13
means testing, 12.8
service charge disputes, 12.9–
12.11
legal expenses insurance, 12.14–
12.16
pro bono services, 12.17–12.19

Grant-aided works
service charges, 2.53
Guarantors
variation of leases, 7.37

Hearings
absence of parties, 13.67
adjournment, 13.86–13.87
closing speeches, 13.73
costs applications, 13.74
decisions, 13.75–13.76
evidence, 13.80–13.84
expert tribunal, 13.85
generally, 13.63–13.66

informality, 1.20–1.21
inspections, 13.77–13.79
location, 1.18–1.19
notice, 13.67
opening speeches, 13.69
order of presentation of cases,
    13.72
preliminary matters, 13.68
public funding, 1.23
representation, 1.22–1.23
rooms, 1.19
witnesses, 13.69–13.71

Identity of landlord
information rights, 3.10–3.13
Improvements
LVT jurisdiction, 1.9
service charges, 2.40–2.44
Information rights
address for service, 3.19–3.20
advice for tenants, 3.5–3.8
change of landlord, 3.14–3.16
eligible tenants, 3.3
identity of landlord, 3.10–3.13
insurance, 5.40–5.43
introduction, 3.1–3.4
management audits, 3.53–3.62
non-compliance, 3.7, 3.9
problems, 3.4
recognised tenants' associations
    appointment of surveyors,
        3.66–3.68
    consultation on managing
        agents, 3.69–3.75
    generally, 3.63
    recognition, 3.64–3.65
RTM companies, 9.48–9.51
service charge demands, 3.17–3.18
statements of account, 3.50–3.52
summaries of costs
    accounting periods, 3.31–3.34
    certification, 3.41
    contents, 3.35–3.40
    inspection of accounts, 3.46–
        3.47
    introduction, 3.30
    non-compliance, 3.48–3.49
    qualified accountants, 3.44–3.45
    RTA requests, 3.42–3.43
summaries of tenants' rights and
    obligations, 3.21–3.29

Inspections
generally, 13.77–13.79
Insurance
absence of lease provisions, 5.7–5.8
advice for tenants, 5.4–5.5
excessive premiums, 5.21–5.29
inadequate lease provisions,
    5.7–5.8
information rights, 5.40–5.43
introduction, 5.1–5.3
LVT applications
    excessive premiums, 5.21–5.29
    generally, 5.13–5.15
    remedies, 5.30–5.31
    unsatisfactory insurance,
        5.16–5.20
non-application of proceeds,
    5.32–5.35
notification of claims, 5.44–5.46
remedies, 5.30–5.31
service charges, 2.80–2.83,
    5.9–5.12
tenants required to insure
    landlord-nominated insurers,
        5.12–5.31
    tenant-selected insurers, 5.36–
        5.39
unsatisfactory insurance
    defective cover, 5.19
    generally, 5.16
    level of cover, 5.17–5.18
    non-reputable insurers, 5.20
variation of leases
    dwelling houses, 7.40–7.41
    flats, 7.12–7.13

Joinder of parties
generally, 13.42–13.44
Judicial review
refusal of permission to appeal,
    13.112

Lands Tribunal
appeals from, 13.111
appeals to
    cross-appeals, 13.109–13.110
    generally, 13.99
    judicial review of refusal of
        permission, 13.112
    permission, 13.100–13.105
    review/re-hearing, 13.106–13.108

Lands Tribunal *continued*
  procedure, 13.3
Law reports
  LVT decisions, 1.25
Leasehold Advisory Service
  (LEASE)
  generally, 1.23
Leasehold valuation tribunals
  see also **Leasehold valuation**
    tribunals (procedure)
  see also under specific subjects
  hearings
    informality, 1.20–1.21
    location, 1.18
    public funding, 1.23
    representation, 1.22–1.23
    rooms, 1.19
  history, 1.2–1.14
  jurisdiction
    administration charges, 1.13
    generally, 1.2–1.4
    improvements, 1.9
    managers, appointment of, 1.6
    problems, 1.7–1.10
    reform, 1.11–1.12
    repairs, 1.9
    right to manage, 1.12
    service charges, 1.5, 1.10–1.11,
      1.13
    variation of leases, 1.14
  members
    appointment, 1.16–1.17
    generally, 1.2, 13.65–13.66
  organisation, 1.15–1.17
  outline of book, 1.26–1.36
  precedent, 1.24
  reports of decisions, 1.25
Leasehold valuation tribunals
  (procedure)
  absence of parties, 13.67
  adjournment, 13.86–13.87
  advice for tenants, 13.4
  appeals
    Court of Appeal, 13.111
    cross-appeals, 13.109–13.110
    generally, 13.99
    judicial review of refusal of
      permission, 13.112
    permission, 13.100–13.105
    review/re-hearing, 13.106–
      13.108

  application documents
    administration charges, 13.15
    breach of covenant,
      determination of, 13.20–13.21
    contents, 13.13
    estate charges, 13.15
    estate management schemes,
      13.16
    managers, appointment of,
      13.18
    right to manage, 13.17
    service charges, 13.15
    variation of leases, 13.19
  bundles of documents, 13.81
  chair, 13.66
  consolidated applications, 13.45–
    13.49
  costs
    introduction, 13.89
    lease provisions, 13.92–13.94
    power to award, 13.90–13.91
    reimbursement, 13.95
  decisions
    enforcement, 13.96–13.98
    pronouncement, 13.75
    rectification, 13.76
  directions, 13.61–13.62
  disclosure, 13.80
  dismissal of applications
    generally, 13.51–13.56
    inherent jurisdiction, 13.57
  enforcement of decisions, 13.96–
    13.98
  entitlement to apply, 13.11–13.12
  evidence
    bundles, 13.81
    disclosure, 13.80
    new evidence, 13.83–13.84
    oral evidence, 13.82
    witness statements, 13.82
  expert tribunal, 13.85
  fees
    application fees, 13.28–13.29
    exemptions, 13.27
    generally, 13.25–13.26
    hearing fees, 13.30
    multiple applicants, 13.31
    reimbursement, 13.95
    transfer fees, 13.8
    waiver, 13.32–13.33
  forms of address, 13.66

hearings
  absence of parties, 13.67
  adjournment, 13.86–13.87
  closing speeches, 13.73
  costs applications, 13.74
  decisions, 13.75–13.76
  evidence, 13.80–13.84
  expert tribunal, 13.85
  generally, 13.63–13.66
  inspections, 13.77–13.79
  notice, 13.67
  opening speeches, 13.69
  order of presentation of cases,
    13.72
  preliminary matters, 13.68
  witnesses, 13.69–13.71
inspections, 13.77–13.79
interim matters
  consolidated applications,
    13.45–13.49
  directions, 13.61–13.62
  dismissal of applications, 13.51–
    13.57
  introduction, 13.41
  joinder of parties, 13.42–13.44
  pre-trial reviews, 13.58–13.60
  representative applications,
    13.45–13.49
  withdrawal of applications,
    13.50
introduction, 13.1–13.3
joinder of parties, 13.42–13.44
members, 13.65–13.66
notice of hearings, 13.67
precedent, 13.88
preliminary matters, 13.68
pre-trial reviews, 13.39, 13.58–
  13.60
rectification of decisions, 13.76
representative applications, 13.45–
  13.49
service
  generally, 13.22
  variation of leases, 13.23–13.24
speeches
  closing, 13.73
  opening, 13.69
starting cases
  applications, 13.10
  introduction, 13.5
  transfer, 13.6–13.9

track allocation
  fast track, 13.38
  introduction, 13.34
  paper track, 13.35–13.37
  reallocation, 13.40
  standard track, 13.39
transfer
  criteria, 13.9
  fees, 13.8
  generally, 13.6
  notices of transfer, 13.7
Wales, 13.2
withdrawal of applications, 13.50
witnesses, 13.69–13.71
Legal aid
  advice for tenants, 12.4–12.6
  availability, 12.7
  exceptional cases, 12.12–12.13
  introduction, 12.3
  means testing, 12.8
  service charge disputes, 12.9–
    12.11
Legal expenses insurance
  funding of applications, 12.14–
    12.16
Legal representation
  see also **Funding of applications**
  generally, 1.22–1.23
  pro bono services, 12.17–12.19
Limitation periods
  service charges
    applicability of Limitation Act,
      2.58–2.60, 2.66–2.67
    duration of period, 2.61–2.65
    introduction, 2.57
Loans
  service charges, 11.11–11.13
Local authority landlords
  right to manage, 9.38

Maintenance
  variation of leases
    generally, 7.10–7.11
    installations, 7.14–7.16
Management audits
  generally, 3.53–3.62
Managers, appointment of
  see also **Right to manage**
  advice for tenants, 8.5–8.6
  business tenants, 8.32
  charities, 8.29

Managers, appointment of *continued*
  conditions, 8.70
  consultation of RTAs, 3.69–3.75,
    8.73–8.80
  criteria, 8.21
  Crown interests, 8.30
  directions, 8.62
  discharge of orders, 8.63–8.67
  eligible appointees, 8.60–8.61
  eligible properties
    charities, 8.29
    Crown interests, 8.30
    exempt landlords, 8.26
    generally, 8.24–8.25
    resident landlords, 8.27–8.28
  entitlement to apply
    eligible properties, 8.24–8.30
    eligible tenants, 8.30–8.31
    introduction, 8.22–8.23
  exempt landlords, 8.26
  extent of property, 8.50–8.51
  grounds
    breach of obligations, 8.37–8.39
    entitlement to apply for
      appointment, 8.22–8.32
    generally, 8.33–8.34
    just and convenient, 8.47–8.48
    non-compliance with codes of
      practice, 8.45–8.46
    reform, 8.49
    relevant persons, 8.35–8.36
    unreasonable administration
      charges, 8.43–8.44
    unreasonable service charges,
      8.40–8.42
  interim appointments, 8.72
  introduction, 8.1–8.4
  LVT jurisdiction, 1.6, 8.71
  management functions, 8.52–
    8.55
  notices of applications
    dispensation, 8.18–8.20
    errors, 8.17
    form and content, 8.11–8.14
    reasonable period to remedy
      problems, 8.15–8.16
  remuneration, 8.56–8.59
  role of managers, 8.7–8.10
  registration of orders, 8.69
  resident landlords, 8.27–8.28
  RTM companies, 8.68

  variation of orders, 8.63–8.67
  worked example, 14.1–14.28

Paper track
  allocation, 13.35–13.37
Permission to appeal
  generally, 13.100–13.105
  judicial review of refusal, 13.112
Precedent
  LVT proceedings, 1.24, 13.88
Preliminary matters
  generally, 13.68
Pre-trial reviews
  generally, 13.39, 13.58–13.60
Pro bono **services**
  representation, 12.17–12.19
Public funding
  see **Funding of applications**

Qualifying long-term agreements
  see **Service charges (consultation)**

Reasonableness
  service charges, 2.78–2.79
Recognised tenants' associations
  appointment of surveyors, 3.66–
    3.68
  consultation on managing agents,
    3.69–3.75, 8.73–8.80
  generally, 3.63
  recognition, 3.64–3.65
  requests for summaries of costs,
    3.42–3.43
Rectification
  LVT decisions, 13.76
Re-entry
  see **Forfeiture**
Relief against forfeiture
  generally, 10.14–10.16
Rent, non-payment of
  see **Forfeiture**
Rent Assessment Committees
  generally, 1.2–1.4
Repairs
  LVT jurisdiction, 1.9
  service charges, 2.40–2.44
  variation of leases
    generally, 7.10–7.11
    installations, 7.14–7.16
Reports
  LVT decisions, 1.25

Representation
see also **Funding of applications**
generally, 1.22–1.23
pro bono services, 12.17–12.19
Representative applications
generally, 13.45–13.49
Resident landlords
appointment of managers, 8.27–8.28
right to manage, 9.36–9.37
Residential Property Tribunal Service
administration of LVTs, 1.15
Right to buy/acquire
administration charges, 11.9
advice for tenants, 11.4–11.5
consultation, 11.10
introduction, 11.1–11.3
service charges
directions by Secretary of State, 11.14–11.16
generally, 11.6–11.8
loans, 11.11–11.13
Right to manage
see also **RTM companies**
advice for tenants, 9.8–9.15
appurtenant property, 9.17
common parts, 9.32
costs of applications, 9.83–9.87
eligible properties
appurtenant property, 9.17
excluded properties, 9.31–9.39
introduction, 9.16
qualifying tenants, 9.28–9.30
self-contained buildings, 9.18
self-contained parts of buildings, 9.19–9.27
eligible tenants, 9.28–9.30
excluded properties
different ownership of self-contained parts, 9.35
existing/recent RTM companies, 9.39
introduction, 9.31
local authority landlords, 9.38
non-residential property, 9.32–9.34
resident landlords, 9.36–9.37
introduction, 9.1–9.7
local authority landlords, 9.38
LVT jurisdiction, 1.12
non-residential property, 9.32–9.34

qualifying tenants, 9.28–9.30
resident landlords, 9.36–9.37
self-contained buildings, 9.18
self-contained parts of buildings, 9.19–9.27
Rights and obligations, summaries of
generally, 3.21–3.29
RTM companies
see also **Right to manage**
acquisition of right to manage, 9.88–9.90
approvals, 9.95–9.100
articles of association, 9.46
budgets, 9.60
costs, 9.83–9.87
counternotices
effect, 9.76–9.78
form and content, 9.73–9.75
generally, 9.72
creation, 9.44–9.4
determination by LVT, 9.76–9.78
generally, 9.40–9.43
information rights, 9.48–9.51
inspection rights, 9.71
introduction, 9.2–9.7
members, 9.47
memorandum of association, 9.46
multiple companies, 9.42
nature, 9.41
notices of claim
defects, 9.68–9.69
effect, 9.70
form and content, 9.65–9.67
generally, 9.61
number of qualifying tenants, 9.62
service, 9.63–9.64
withdrawal, 9.79–9.82
notices of invitation to participate
defects, 9.57–9.58
form and content, 9.53–9.56
requirement, 9.52
response, 9.59
plans, 9.60
promoters, 9.45
pros and cons, 9.8–9.15
uncommitted service charges, 9.91–9.94
withdrawal of notices of claim, 9.79–9.82

Section 146 notices
generally, 10.27–10.29
limitations on right to serve, 10.30–10.31
Service charges
see also **Administration charges; Information rights; Service charges (consultation)**
advice for tenants, 2.3–2.6
apportionment, 2.33–2.39
burden of proof, 2.25–2.27
certificates, 2.50
comparables, 2.6
definition, 2.1, 2.7–2.11
demands
form and content, 3.17–3.18
generally, 2.51–2.52
time limits, 2.54–2.56
equitable principles
generally, 2.77
introduction, 2.68
set-off, 2.69–2.76
fixed sums, 2.11
forfeiture for non-payment, 10.32–10.36
grant-aided works, 2.53
holding by landlord
exempt landlords, 2.87
investment of trust funds, 2.88
reform, 2.92–2.95
termination of leases, 2.89–2.91
trust funds, 2.84–2.86
improvements, 2.40–2.44
insurance, 2.80–2.83, 5.9–5.12
introduction, 2.1–2.2
landlord, definition of, 2.8
lease provisions
generally, 2.28–2.30
"sweeping up" clauses, 2.31–2.3
limitation periods
applicability of Limitation Act, 2.58–2.60, 2.66–2.67
duration, 2.61–2.65
introduction, 2.57
loans, 11.11–11.13
LVT applications
appropriateness of forum, 2.21
burden and standard of proof, 2.25–2.27
eligible tenancies, 2.22–2.23
equitable principles, 2.68–2.77

in advance of works, 2.18
jurisdiction, 2.12–2.21
standing, 2.24
LVT jurisdiction
background, 1.5, 1.10–1.11, 1.13
equitable principles, 2.68–2.77
generally, 2.12–2.21
management fees, 2.48–2.49
managers, appointment of, 8.40–8.42
preconditions for recoverability
certificates, 2.50
demands, 2.51–2.52
grant-aided works, 2.53
limitation periods, 2.57–2.67
time limits, 2.54–2.56
reasonableness, 2.78–2.79
reduction, 11.14–11.16
relevant costs, 2.10
repairs, 2.40–2.44
right to buy/acquire
directions by Secretary of State, 11.14–11.16
generally, 11.6–11.8
loans, 11.11–11.13
RTM companies, 9.91–9.94
set-off
generally, 2.69–2.72
landlord's position, 2.73–2.76
stale service charges, 2.54–2.56
standard of proof, 2.25–2.27
"sweeping up" clauses, 2.31–2.3
tenant, definition of, 2.9
time limits
claims, 2.57–2.67
demands, 2.54–2.56
unfair contract terms, 2.45–2.47
variation of leases, 7.19
waiver, 11.14–11.16
worked example, 14.29–14.51
Service charges (consultation)
accounting periods, 4.26–4.32
advice for tenants, 4.6
connection to landlord, 4.36–4.39
costs threshold
generally, 4.24–4.25
old rules, 4.9–4.10
dispensation
generally, 4.62
grounds, 4.67–4.69
old rules, 4.63–4.66

estimates
  generally, 4.40–4.42
  nomination of persons, 4.46–4.58
  old rules, 4.14–4.18
inspection of information, 4.34–4.35
introduction, 4.1–4.5
observations, 4.44–4.45
old rules
  applicability, 4.7–4.8
  costs threshold, 4.9–4.10
  estimates, 4.14–4.18
  procedure, 4.11–4.18
  urgent works, 4.13
overview of procedures, 4.22–4.23
public notice, 4.43
qualifying long-term agreements
  definition, 4.60
  excluded agreements, 4.61
  generally, 4.20, 4.59
qualifying works, 4.21
relevant period, 4.33
transitional provisions, 4.70–4.72
Service
generally, 13.22
variation of leases, 13.23–13.24
Services, provision or maintenance of
variation of leases, 7.17
Set-off against service charges
generally, 2.69–2.72
landlord's position, 2.73–2.76
Speeches
closing, 13.73
opening, 13.69
Standard track
allocation, 13.39
Statements of account
generally, 3.50–3.52
Summaries of costs
accounting periods, 3.31–3.34
certification, 3.41
contents, 3.35–3.40
inspection of accounts, 3.46–3.47
introduction, 3.30
non-compliance, 3.48–3.49
qualified accountants, 3.44–3.45
RTA requests, 3.42–3.43
Summaries of tenants' rights and obligations
generally, 3.21–3.29

Sureties
variation of leases, 7.37
Surveyors
recognised tenants' associations, 3.66–3.68

Tenants' associations
see **Recognised tenants' associations**
Tenants' rights and obligations, summaries of
generally, 3.21–3.29
Third parties
variation of leases, 7.37
Time limits
see also **Limitation periods**
service charge demands, 2.54–2.56
Track allocation
fast track, 13.38
introduction, 13.34
paper track, 13.35–13.37
reallocation, 13.40
standard track, 13.39
Transfer of proceedings
criteria, 13.9
fees, 13.8
generally, 13.6
notices of transfer, 13.7
Trust funds for service charges
exempt landlords, 2.87
generally, 2.84–2.86
investment of trust funds, 2.88
reform, 2.92–2.95
termination of leases, 2.89–2.91

Unfair contract terms
service charges, 2.45–2.47

Variation of leases
advice for tenants, 7.5–7.6
compensation, 7.34
grounds
  insurance, 7.12–7.13
  introduction, 7.9
  other grounds, 7.20
  provision or maintenance of services, 7.17
  recovery of expenditure, 7.18
  repairs or maintenance of installations, 7.14–7.16
  repairs or maintenance, 7.10–7.11

Variation of leases, grounds *continued*
　service charge computations,
　　7.19
　unsatisfactory lease provisions,
　　7.21
　insurance
　　dwelling houses, 7.40–7.41
　　flats, 7.12–7.13
　introduction, 7.1–7.4
　LVT applications
　　generally, 7.7–7.8
　　making of orders, 7.30–7.38
　LVT jurisdiction, 1.14
　notification
　　failure to notify, 7.38
　　requirement, 7.39
　other leases
　　generally, 7.22–7.24

　majority of parties, 7.25–7.29
　prejudice, 7.35
　reasonableness, 7.36
　third parties, 7.37
　variation orders, 7.30–7.38
Vexatious applications
　costs, 13.90–13.91
　dismissal, 13.51–13.56

Wales
　procedural rules, 13.2
Withdrawal
　LVT applications, 13.50
　notices of RTM claims, 9.79–9.82
Witness statements
　generally, 13.82
Witnesses
　generally, 13.69–13.71

Legal Action

The only independent magazine to cover areas of interest to legal aid practitioners, advisers and local authority staff.

Each month Legal Action includes:

editorial

Legal Action's editorials are renowned and respected for their challenging and thought-provoking approach to recent events.

news and features

The news and features pages give the latest information and critical opinion on a broad range of subjects.

noticeboard

Legal Action also gives you access to information on courses, meetings, conferences, seminars, and training contracts.

law and practice

Legal Action's authoritative law and practice pages are written by a team of expert solicitors, barristers and advisers. These pages will keep you up to date with the law, practice and procedure that affect your area of work.

ISSN 0306 7963

For more information on subscription rates visit:
www.lag.org.uk/magazine

The **Adviser's Toolkit**
giving legal advice

Elaine Heslop

The Adviser's Toolkit: giving legal advice supports advisers by providing guidance on the skills and processes of advice-giving against a background of the key areas of social welfare law. It clearly illustrates each topic through the use of case studies, flow charts, examples of letters and documents. This is a highly practical resource for

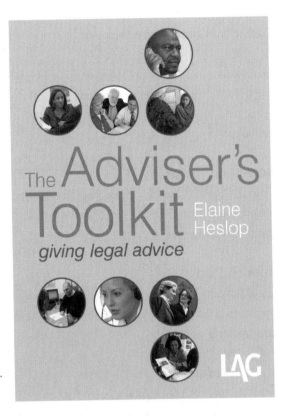

advisers working in both the voluntary and statutory sectors. It provides expert guidance from an experienced practitioner and adviser on the core advice-giving skills.

Pb 978 1 903307 49 6 c350pp October 2007 c£22

www.lag.org.uk/books

LAG

lag.org.uk

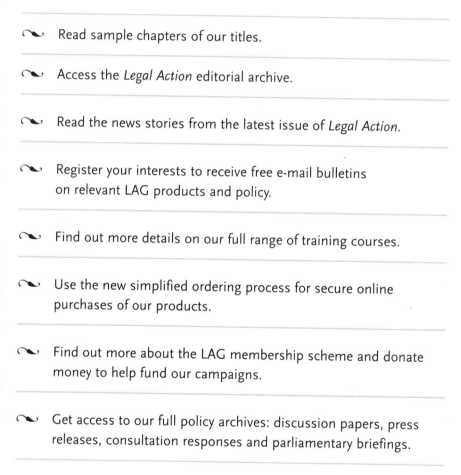

- Read sample chapters of our titles.

- Access the *Legal Action* editorial archive.

- Read the news stories from the latest issue of *Legal Action*.

- Register your interests to receive free e-mail bulletins on relevant LAG products and policy.

- Find out more details on our full range of training courses.

- Use the new simplified ordering process for secure online purchases of our products.

- Find out more about the LAG membership scheme and donate money to help fund our campaigns.

- Get access to our full policy archives: discussion papers, press releases, consultation responses and parliamentary briefings.

Legal Action Group working with lawyers and advisers to promote equal access to justice